Children's
Literature
Review

Guide to Gale Literary Criticism Series

For criticism on	Consult these Gale series
Authors now living or who died after December 31, 1959	*CONTEMPORARY LITERARY CRITICISM (CLC)*
Authors who died between 1900 and 1959	*TWENTIETH-CENTURY LITERARY CRITICISM (TCLC)*
Authors who died between 1800 and 1899	*NINETEENTH-CENTURY LITERATURE CRITICISM (NCLC)*
Authors who died between 1400 and 1799	*LITERATURE CRITICISM FROM 1400 TO 1800 (LC)* *SHAKESPEAREAN CRITICISM (SC)*
Authors who died before 1400	*CLASSICAL AND MEDIEVAL LITERATURE CRITICISM (CMLC)*
Authors of books for children and young adults	*CHILDREN'S LITERATURE REVIEW (CLR)*
Dramatists	*DRAMA CRITICISM (DC)*
Poets	*POETRY CRITICISM (PC)*
Short story writers	*SHORT STORY CRITICISM (SSC)*
Black writers of the past two hundred years	*BLACK LITERATURE CRITICISM (BLC)*
Hispanic writers of the late nineteenth and twentieth centuries	*HISPANIC LITERATURE CRITICISM (HLC)*
Native North American writers and orators of the eighteenth, nineteenth, and twentieth centuries	*NATIVE NORTH AMERICAN LITERATURE (NNAL)*
Major authors from the Renaissance to the present	*WORLD LITERATURE CRITICISM, 1500 TO THE PRESENT (WLC)*

ISSN 0362-4145

volume 63

Children's Literature Review

Excerpts from Reviews,
Criticism, and Commentary
on Books for Children
and Young People

Jennifer Baise
Editor

Thomas Ligotti
Associate Editor

Detroit
New York
San Francisco
London
Boston
Woodbridge, CT

STAFF

Jennifer Baise, *Editor*

Thomas Ligotti, *Associate Editor*

Vince Cousino, *Assistant Editor*

Maria Franklin, *Permissions Manager*
Kimberly F. Smilay, *Permissions Specialist*
Sarah Tomasek, Kelly A. Quin, *Permissions Associates*
Sandy Gore, *Permissions Assistant*

Victoria B. Cariappa, *Research Manager*
Andrew Guy Malonis, Barbara McNeil, Gary J. Oudersluys, Maureen Richards,
Cheryl L. Warnock, *Research Specialists*
Patricia T. Ballard, Tamara C. Nott, Tracie A. Richardson, *Research Associates*
Phyllis Blackman, Timothy Lehnerer, *Research Assistant*

Mary Beth Trimper, *Production Director*
Stacy Melson, *Buyer*

Michael Logusz, *Graphic Artist*
Randy Bassett, *Image Database Supervisor*
Robert Duncan, *Imaging Specialists*
Pamela Reed, *Imaging Coordinator*

Library of Congress Catalog Card Number 76-46132
ISBN 0-7876-3228-7
ISSN 0362-4145

Printed in the United States of America
10   9   8   7   6   5   4   3   2   1

Contents

Preface vii

Acknowledgments xi

Preface

Literature for children and young adults has evolved into both a respected branch of creative writing and a successful industry. Currently, books for young readers are considered among the most popular segments of publishing. Criticism of juvenile literature is instrumental in recording the literary or artistic development of the creators of children's books as well as the trends and controversies that result from changing values or attitudes about young people and their literature. Designed to provide a permanent, accessible record of this ongoing scholarship, *Children's Literature Review (CLR)* presents parents, teachers, and librarians—those responsible for bringing children and books together—with the opportunity to make informed choices when selecting reading materials for the young. In addition, *CLR* provides researchers of children's literature with easy access to a wide variety of critical information from English-language sources in the field. Users will find balanced overviews of the careers of the authors and illustrators of the books that children and young adults are reading; these entries, which contain excerpts from published criticism in books and periodicals, assist users by sparking ideas for papers and assignments and suggesting supplementary and classroom reading. Ann L. Kalkhoff, president and editor of *Children's Book Review Service Inc.*, writes that "*CLR* has filled a gap in the field of children's books, and it is one series that will never lose its validity or importance."

Scope of the Series

Each volume of *CLR* profiles the careers of a selection of authors and illustrators of books for children and young adults from preschool through high school. Author lists in each volume reflect:

- an international scope.

- representation of authors of all eras.

- the variety of genres covered by children's and/or YA literature: picture books, fiction, nonfiction, poetry, folklore, and drama.

Although the focus of the series is on authors new to *CLR*, entries will be updated as the need arises.

Organization of This Book

An entry consists of the following elements: author heading, author portrait, author introduction, excerpts of criticism (each preceded by a bibliographical citation), and illustrations, when available.

- The **Author Heading** consists of the author's name followed by birth and death dates. The portion of the name outside the parentheses denotes the form under which the author is most frequently published. If the majority of the author's works for children were written under a pseudonym, the pseudonym will be listed in the author heading and the real name given on the first line of the author introduction. Also located at the beginning of the introduction are any other pseudonyms used by the author in writing for children and any name variations, including transliterated forms for authors whose languages use nonroman alphabets. Uncertainty as to a birth or death date is indicated by question marks.

- An **Author Portrait** is included when available.

- The **Author Introduction** contains information designed to introduce an author to *CLR* users by presenting an overview of the author's themes and styles, biographical facts that relate to the author's literary career or critical responses to the author's works, and information about major awards and prizes the author has received. The introduction begins by identifying the nationality of the author and by listing the genres in which s/he has written for children and young adults. Introductions also list a group of representative titles for which the author or illustrator being profiled is best known; this section, which begins with the words "major works include," follows the genre line of the introduction. For seminal figures, a listing of major works about the author follows when appropriate, highlighting important biographies about the author or illustrator that are not excerpted in the entry. The centered heading "Introduction" announces the body of the text.

- **Criticism** is located in three sections: **Author's Commentary** (when available), **General Commentary** (when available), and **Title Commentary** (commentary on specific titles).

  - The **Author's Commentary** presents background material written by the author or by an interviewer. This commentary may cover a specific work or several works. Author's commentary on more than one work appears after the author introduction, while commentary on an individual book follows the title entry heading.

  - The **General Commentary** consists of critical excerpts that consider more than one work by the author or illustrator being profiled. General commentary is preceded by the critic's name in boldface type or, in the case of unsigned criticism, by the title of the journal. *CLR* also features entries that emphasize general criticism on the oeuvre of an author or illustrator. When appropriate, a selection of reviews is included to supplement the general commentary.

  - The **Title Commentary** begins with the title entry headings, which precede the criticism on a title and cite publication information on the work being reviewed. Title headings list the title of the work as it appeared in its first English-language edition. The first English-language publication date of each work (unless otherwise noted) is listed in parentheses following the title. Differing U.S. and British titles follow the publication date within the parentheses. When a work is written by an individual other than the one being profiled, as is the case when illustrators are featured, the parenthetical material following the title cites the author of the work before listing its publication date.

    Entries in each title commentary section consist of critical excerpts on the author's individual works, arranged chronologically by publication date. The entries generally contain two to seven reviews per title, depending on the stature of the book and the amount of criticism it has generated. The editors select titles that reflect the entire scope of the author's literary contribution, covering each genre and subject. An effort is made to reprint criticism that represents the full range of each title's reception, from the year of its initial publication to current assessments. Thus, the reader is provided with a record of the author's critical history. Publication information (such as publisher names and book prices) and parenthetical numerical references (such as footnotes or page and line references to specific editions of works) have been deleted at the discretion of the editors to provide smoother reading of the text.

- Centered headings introduce each section, in which criticism is arranged chronologically; beginning with Volume 35, each excerpt is preceded by a boldface source heading for easier access by readers. Within the text, titles by authors being profiled are also highlighted in boldface type.

- Selected excerpts are preceded by **Explanatory Annotations,** which provide information on the critic or work of criticism to enhance the reader's understanding of the excerpt.

- A complete **Bibliographical Citation** designed to facilitate the location of the original book or article precedes each piece of criticism.

- Numerous **Illustrations** are featured in *CLR*. For entries on illustrators, an effort has been made to include illustrations that reflect the characteristics discussed in the criticism. Entries on authors who do not illustrate their own works may also include photographs and other illustrative material pertinent to their careers.

Special Features: Entries on Illustrators

Entries on authors who are also illustrators will occasionally feature commentary on selected works illustrated but not written by the author being profiled. These works are strongly associated with the illustrator and have received critical acclaim for their art. By including critical comment on works of this type, the editors wish to provide a more complete representation of the artist's career. Criticism on these works has been chosen to stress artistic, rather than literary, contributions. Title entry headings for works illustrated by the author being profiled are arranged chronologically within the entry by date of publication and include notes identifying the author of the illustrated work. In order to provide easier access for users, all titles illustrated by the subject of the entry are boldfaced.

CLR also includes entries on prominent illustrators who have contributed to the field of children's literature. These entries are designed to represent the development of the illustrator as an artist rather than as a literary stylist. The illustrator's section is organized like that of an author, with two exceptions: the introduction presents an overview of the illustrator's styles and techniques rather than outlining his or her literary background, and the commentary written by the illustrator on his or her works is called "illustrator's commentary" rather than "author's commentary." All titles of books containing illustrations by the artist being profiled are highlighted in boldface type.

Other Features: Acknowledgments, Indexes

■ The **Acknowledgments** section, which immediately follows the preface, lists the sources from which material has been reprinted in the volume. It does not, however, list every book or periodical consulted for the volume.

■ The **Cumulative Index to Authors** lists all of the authors who have appeared in *CLR* with cross-references to the biographical, autobiographical, and literary criticism series published by Gale Research. A full listing of the series titles appears before the first page of the indexes of this volume.

■ The **Cumulative Index to Nationalities** lists authors alphabetically under their respective nationalities. Author names are followed by the volume number(s) in which they appear.

■ The **Cumulative Index to Titles** lists titles covered in *CLR* followed by the volume and page number where criticism begins.

A Note to the Reader

CLR is one of several critical references sources in the Literature Criticism Series published by Gale Research. When writing papers, students who quote directly from any volume in the Literature Criticism Series may use the following general forms to footnote reprinted criticism. The first example pertains to material drawn from periodicals, the second to material reprinted from books.

[1]T. S. Eliot, "John Donne," *The Nation and the Athenaeum*, 33 (9 June 1923), 321-32; excerpted and reprinted in *Literature Criticism from 1400 to 1800*, Vol. 10, ed. James E. Person, Jr. (Detroit: Gale Research, 1989), pp. 28-9.

[1]Henry Brooke, *Leslie Brooke and Johnny Crow* (Frederick Warne, 1982); excerpted and reprinted in *Children's Literature Review*, Vol. 20, ed. Gerard J. Senick (Detroit: Gale Research, 1990), p. 47.

Suggestions Are Welcome

In response to various suggestions, several features have been added to *CLR* since the beginning of the series, including author entries on retellers of traditional literature as well as those who have been the first to record oral tales and other folklore; entries on prominent illustrators featuring commentary on their styles and techniques; entries on authors whose works are considered controversial; occasional entries devoted to criticism on a single work or a series of works; sections in author introductions that list major works by and about the author or illustrator being profiled; explanatory notes that provide information on the critic or work of criticism to enhance the usefulness of the excerpt; more extensive illustrative material, such as holographs of manuscript pages and photographs of people and places pertinent to the careers of the authors and artists; a cumulative nationality index for easy access to authors by nationality; and occasional guest essays written specifically for *CLR* by prominent critics on subjects of their choice.

Readers who wish to suggest authors to appear in future volumes, or who have other suggestions, are cordially invited to contact the editor. By mail: Editor, *Children's Literature Review*, Gale Research, 835 Penobscot Bldg., 645 Griswold St., Detroit, MI 48226-4094; by telephone: (800) 347-GALE; by fax: (313) 961-6599; by E-mail: CYA@Gale.com.

Acknowledgments

The editors wish to thank the copyright holders of the criticism included in this volume and the permissions managers of many book and magazine publishing companies for assisting us in securing reproduction rights. We are also grateful to the staffs of the Detroit Public Library, the Library of Congress, the University of Detroit Mercy Library, Wayne State University Purdy/Kresge Library Complex, and the University of Michigan Libraries for making their resources available to us. Following is a list of the copyright holders who have granted us permission to reproduce material in this volume of *CLR*. Every effort has been made to trace copyright, but if omissions have been made, please let us know.

COPYRIGHTED ESSAYS IN *CLR*, VOLUME 63, WERE REPRODUCED FROM THE FOLLOWING PERIODICALS:

COPYRIGHTED ESSAYS IN *CLR*, VOLUME 63, WERE REPRODUCED FROM THE FOLLOWING BOOKS:

PHOTOGRAPHS AND ILLUSTRATIONS APPEARING IN *CLR*, VOLUME 63, WERE RECEIVED FROM THE FOLLOWING SOURCES:

Children's
Literature
Review

Robert J(oseph) Burch

1925-

American author of novels and picture books.

Major works include *Tyler, Wilkin, and Skee* (1963), *Queenie Peavey* (1966), *Simon and the Game of Chance* (1970), *The Whitman Kick* (1977), *Ida Early Comes Over the Mountain* (1980).

INTRODUCTION

Robert Burch's novels for middle graders and young adults have been noted for their honesty and realism. In his books, Burch deals with difficult life situations; some of his main characters are orphans, or their parents are mentally ill or in prison. They are sometimes troubled or difficult young people, who have to overcome their own personality conflicts before they can achieve success. However, Burch's characters are not without hope, and their circumstances are not completely dire. He commented to *Contemporary Authors* about his use of realism: "When I first started writing, more than thirty years ago, much of the realistic fiction for children was not realistic at all. Home situations were often perfect, and endings—almost always happy—were too pat. It was interesting to be one of the 'pioneers' in the so-called new realism; yet I'm not sure but what we've moved too far in the opposite direction by now. Too often *new-realism* has given way to *grim-realism*. Perhaps eventually we'll arrive at an appropriate balance."

Burch's realism expresses itself through his ability to capture a specific place and time. The author, who grew up and continues to live in rural Georgia, sets many of his novels in the rural South, or in the intermediate zones where the sprawling cities bump up against old farmlands. Critics have praised Burch's facility at capturing the feel of a place, with his accuracy of detail and ear for the language of the South. Many of Burch's novels are also set in the Depression era, which the author experienced as a boy. Burch uses the setting of the rural South in the time of the Depression not just out of nostalgia, but to form an appropriate backdrop for the serious moral problems he addresses. William H. Green wrote, "Writing from his childhood home in Fayette County, just south of Atlanta, [Burch] is a master of the regional 'problem' novel. The problems are perennial: sickness, death, poverty, disgrace, old age, and war, reflected in credible characters without morbidity, escapism, or preaching. And under Burch's hand problems evolve toward unexpected but satisfying conclusions." One of the problems Burch deftly explores in several of his novels is that of poverty; his solution is that children—and by extension, adults—do not need money to be happy. Burch's first novel, *Tyler, Wilkin, and Skee*, follows the adventures of three brothers through the course of one year during the Great Depression, when poverty touched nearly everyone in the South. Burch, as he wrote

in *Children's Literature Association Quarterly*, illustrates "one of [his] favorite themes, which is: there are so many things in life more important than money." Instead, Burch's characters know the joys of family, of church gatherings, and of simple games played with childhood friends.

Biographical Information

Burch was born in 1925 in Inman, Georgia. When he was still young, his family moved to Fayetteville, a rural county seat south of the sprawl of suburban Atlanta. Burch told *Something About the Author*, "When I was a boy, I planned to be a farmer when I grew up. Possibly this was due more to my love for farm animals, which my seven brothers and sisters and I frequently turned into pets, than a desire to earn a living from the soil." Burch's Georgia childhood ended after he graduated from high school and entered the U.S. Army. He was stationed in New Guinea and Australia, experiences which ignited his love of travel. When the war was over, Burch returned to Georgia to earn a degree in agriculture from the University of Georgia, but eventually he accepted a clerical position that allowed him to travel again, this time to Tokyo and Yokohama, Japan.

Burch returned to the United States and settled in New York City. While doing clerical work there, he began taking writing classes at Hunter College. Although he took up writing as a hobby, Burch, with the help of mentor Dr. William Lipkind, soon realized that he had a talent for writing for children. His first publication was a picture book, *The Traveling Bird*, published in 1959. After living in New York for eight years, Burch moved back to Fayetteville; he also turned to writing about the rural South of his youth.

Major Works

Tyler, Wilkin, and Skee followed three picture books; it was Burch's first novel about rural Georgia and the Depression era. The book traces the relationships and adventures of the Coley brothers: Tyler is the oldest at twelve, a responsible and quiet boy; Wilkin, aged eleven, is more outgoing and is the brother who is most comfortable dealing with other people; and little seven-year-old Skee, who has a talent for making music. The story spans one year of the boys' lives from September to August, and is filled with details of their daily chores around the farm, the boys' wonder at a neighbor's motor car, and the annual thrills of the county fair. The novel focuses on the idea that while money is tight and times are hard, families can make their own amusements and find happiness. Rural

Georgia during the Depression is also the setting for *Queenie Peavey*, Burch's popular 1966 novel about a smart, tough thirteen-year-old girl. Queenie's mother works in a factory, but her father is serving time in the penitentiary and she and her mother live in poverty. The girl's pride leads her to defend her incarcerated father against her schoolmates' jeers, convinced that when he is paroled things will improve. Queenie's rebellion makes her a troublemaker, and she allows no one but the neighbor children to see the more pleasant side of her. When Queenie faces real repercussions from her troubling behavior, she decides to play along and cooperate; in the end, she makes a genuine change to focus on her talents instead of her anger. Although Queenie's circumstances are trying—particularly as her father breaks parole and must go back to prison—she is able to overcome her many obstacles.

Simon, too, overcomes hardship in *Simon and the Game of Chance*. The novel finds the Ballard family dealing with their mother's absence; a new baby has died, and Mrs. Ballard is forced to retreat to a sanitarium to deal with the resulting depression. Simon finds himself between two sets of brothers and looking to his oldest sister Clarissa for guidance. The family also struggles with the severity of Mr. Ballard, a strict disciplinarian who shows little affection for his children. Thirteen-year-old Simon worries about losing the stability of his sister, and wishes something would happen to prevent her from marrying her fiancé Whit. When Whit is killed in an accident the day before the scheduled wedding, Simon feels immensely guilty over his fantasies, and Clarissa is dangerously consumed with grief. These misfortunes, though, seem only to bring the family closer together, and in the end they are reunited with Mrs. Ballard to face the world with both its hardships and rewards. Not all of the relationships in Burch's novels survive the obstacles they face, though. The main characters in the young adult novel *The Whitman Kick* enjoy a long friendship based on mutual love for poetry, particularly that of Walt Whitman. Alan, recently graduated and enlisted in the Army, narrates the story of his special high school relationship with Amanda. In the last years of high school, Alan and Amanda come to want different things from each other and the friendship is strained. Amanda becomes physically involved with another boy and gets pregnant; she is forced to leave school to live with relatives. Alan feels angry and betrayed by both Amanda and his mother, who has left his father to live with another man. In the end, Alan is able to realize that his anger is misdirected, and he moves toward acceptance and forgiveness of both women.

In a lighter novel, this one again for middle schoolers, Burch's character Ida Early brings joy out of sadness. The heroine of *Ida Early Comes Over the Mountain* arrives on the doorstep of the Sutton family shortly after Mrs. Sutton has died. Ida, an extraordinarily tall woman in clodhoppers and overalls, was described by Marjorie Lewis as "a mountain Mary Poppins," full of tall tales and magical housekeeping tricks. She wins the hearts of the children—Ellen, Randall, and the twins, Clay and Dewey—and helps the family recover from their loss with humor and high

adventure. But Ida, too, is human, and her feelings are hurt when Ellen and Randall's schoolmates taunt her, and the children she loves do not stand up for her. Through Ida, the two learn the importance of caring for friends.

Awards

Burch's novel *Queenie Peavy* has received many awards, including the Jane Addams Children's Book Award and the Child Study Association of America children's book award, both 1967; the Georgia Children's Book Award, 1971; and the Phoenix Award of the Children's Literature Association, in 1986. *Skinny* and *Doodle and the Go-Cart* also received the Georgia Children's Book Award. The author was awarded a fellowship in juvenile literature at the Bread Loaf Writers' Conference in 1960, and several of his books have been Weekly Reader Book Club and Junior Literary Guild selections.

AUTHOR COMMENTARY

Robert Burch

SOURCE: "The New Realism," in *Children and Literature: Views and Reviews*, by Virginia Haviland, Lothrop, Lee & Shepard Co., 1973, pp. 281-87.

I do not know what is so new about the New Realism. It would seem to me that realism dates back as far as mankind itself. And sometimes we get ourselves in trouble if we fail to take the past into consideration. Sometimes we get ourselves in trouble if we do. For instance, during 1970 Southern Baptists voted in Nashville to give sex-education courses in their churches, based on "a sound Biblical approach"; and one newspaper columnist could not resist pointing out the kind of Sunday School discussions that could possibly result from such an approach. He could visualize a poor teacher fielding questions from children about some of the stories that appear in the Bible, giving as examples: Abram lending his wife to the Pharaoh, the account of Lot and his daughters, and the way Moses and his band slew the men of Midian and many of the women, but kept thirty-two thousand virgins for themselves. The columnist added that there would be some people who would contend that such material has no place in our nation's churches, and he hoped the Baptists would not get themselves arrested.

But realism, whether new or not, is being discussed nowadays. In an article for the *New York Times*, Mr. Isaac Bashevis Singer said that "Stories for children are now being written without a beginning, middle or end." It bothered him, and it bothers me—but not much, because I agree with him that children probably will reject them. His way of putting it was that from his own experience, he knew "that a child wants a well constructed story with clear language and strict logic. . . . " I am glad that variety is offered children, but I am also glad that they do not accept everything that is offered them.

I have never found those slice-of-life stories, or whatever they are called now, very satisfactory reading experiences. And I do not care much for slice-of-life plays either. I remember the first one I saw; I was living and working in New York at the time. The playwright was gifted, with a keen ear for the speech patterns of New Yorkers; and the actors were enormously talented. During the first act I said to myself, "This is wonderful. The characters on stage are so real! Why, they sound exactly like my neighbors arguing." It continued, nothing much happening—no rising action and, as far as I could tell, no character development—but still with realistic dialogue. And by the third act I was saying, "I might as well have stayed home and listened to my neighbors." But the show was "in" at the moment, it was being talked about at parties, and I wanted to know about it, so I would have gone, even if I had known that it would bore me. We adults are like that. I am glad children are not. Mr. Singer says "it's a lot easier to hypnotize grown-ups than children. . . . easier to force . . . [us] to eat literary straw and clay than an infant in kindergarten."

Mr. Singer's article did a great deal to renew my faith in the state of children's books, for, the previous season, one of the special newspaper supplements on children's books had worried me. You will probably consider me the biggest prude you ever met when I tell you that it was a review of a picture book that bothered me. It mentioned the "New Realism," a phrase which caught my eye. The book, by a talented team and published by a fine firm, was *Bang Bang You're Dead.* In one comment on it, the reviewer said: "[S]ome parents may not relish reading to a 4-year-old such luscious lines as 'Give up, puke-face. You don't have a chance,' to which the dainty rejoinder is 'Up your nose you freak-out.'" Well, I hope there are some parents who would not relish reading it. That is how square I am. Some parents will approve, while others may not, but will accept it rather than be labeled old-fashioned.

A woman I know, an authority in the book field, defended *Bang Bang You're Dead.* She said that in using such words as puke-face in picture stories, we let the child know that we know that he knows and uses such words, helping to strengthen our lines of communication. I am not sure she is right. I do not know what a child thinks, but neither am I sure that when I was young I would have been wildly pleased that adults knew that I knew and used certain words. Would the words not have become respectable somehow, and we children have been put to the trouble of finding new ones—new till some well-meaning adult got around to making them respectable, too? I do not know that children want us to communicate with them to such an extent.

Another argument for that particular book is that our language is changing, and, of course, it is—constantly. In a *Look* magazine article on language, I read that "so much

irrational emotional baggage has been heaped on so many words that our ability to voice a gut-felt notion is stifled." Perhaps so. But I do not know that I am quite ready for gut-felt picture books. The same article also stated:

> Speech doesn't have to be linear; it can come out as a compressed overlay of facts and sensations and moods and ideas and images. Words can serve as signals, and others will understand. The way a man feels can be unashamedly expressed in sheer sound, such as a low, glottal hum, like the purring of a cat, to indicate contentment.

Are you ready for that? If not, I am ahead of you. It has already come to our house. One of my nephews, a high-school junior, often answers me with something of a grunt or a groan, and occasionally a more contented sound. I had accused him of being lazy in his speech, but I suppose he is merely advanced. He is not mumbling; he is giving me a compressed overlay of facts and sensations and images.

But I want to discuss the trend toward the so-called "New Realism." I have defended realism in children's books for a long time. You might say I have had to defend it, since I have been criticized at times for some of the grim details I have used in stories for the young. I have tried to use such details for a purpose, the purpose not being to shock but to give as accurate a picture as possible of the events taking place in a story and of the time and place in which it is set. If a story set in the Depression years tells only of church suppers or of all-day sings, what sort of picture of the times would that be? On the other hand, stories can be overloaded with details of a period. If my main purpose were to give the reader facts about the Depression, then I would write a nonfiction book.

I believe that Flannery O'Connor once said that in the South we like to write stories because we have the Bible and a little bit of history. In several books, I have used a little bit of that little bit of history, drawing background material from the Great Depression itself. However, my most recent book is a modern-day story, **Simon and the Game of Chance,** much of which is based on the premises found in Ecclesiastes. I have been accused of presenting in it a negative view of Bible-belt Christianity, but I hope that I did not. I tried to show the misuse of dogma and its effect upon the lives of those touched by it. In any event, I believe in realism in stories for the young and favor the trend toward what May Hill Arbuthnot [in *Children's Reading in the Home,* 1969] called "a frank treatment of the grave and often tragic social problems (young people) are encountering and talking about today."

Since I am primarily interested in junior novels with realistic settings, I am vitally concerned about the changes that are taking place in this kind of novel, and I find the trend toward stronger realism healthy. I do not think we should scare children, but on the other hand we should not lie to them by pretending that the world is entirely safe. C. S. Lewis [in *Of Other Worlds: Essays and Stories,* 1966] said it better than I can. He said that we need not try to keep out of a child's mind "the knowledge that he is born into a world of death, violence, wounds, adventure, heroism and cowardice, good and evil . . . ," which he says would be "to give children a false impression and feed them on escapism in the bad sense."

If we could guarantee children that the world out there would be completely safe, then fine, we could afford to give them only stories that leave that impression. But until we can, in whatever we present as being realistic, is it not cheating for it to be otherwise? No doubt, there are some books that still distort or mislead, but there are an increasing number each year that do not.

One I enjoyed recently was *Where the Lilies Bloom* by Vera and Bill Cleaver. A fourteen-year-old girl in the mountains of North Carolina struggles to keep the children in the family together in ways that are sometimes sad and sometimes hilarious, but she always does so with a fierce dignity and the rejection of charity. This book has a strong impact, an impact I think right for the children of today. If they are so far removed from poverty themselves, why should they not see that it does exist?

Another of my favorite books of recent years is Theodore Taylor's *The Cay*. It says more about loving our neighbor than any sermon I have heard in a long time, although it does not preach. Good stories never do. I suppose *The Cay* could be called an adventure story—there is a shipwreck, an attempt by two people, a man and a boy, to survive on a coral island. The boy is blind; the man is black. The man dies before there is any sign of rescue. While reading *The Cay*, I forgot that I was reading it—so to speak—as homework, finding myself thoroughly engrossed in it, and I thought of another comment by C. S. Lewis, who said that he was "almost inclined to set it up as a canon that a children's story which is enjoyed only by children is a bad children's story."

Another book I especially like is *Let the Balloon Go* by Ivan Southall. It is not perfect in every way, but what book is? It tells of a sad situation, the central character being spastic, but young people can read the book as a tale of challenge and excitement—because it is that, with a great deal of suspense—and if they get a glimpse at the same time of what it is like to be a spastic, then so much the better. I know that I felt involved in it to that extent. And no brochure from the March of Dimes campaign, or anything else, has made me feel that the cause is as urgent as I consider it since reading *Let the Balloon Go*. It is a simple story of a twelve-year-old boy and his longing to do something other boys his age take for granted: to climb a tree.

Such situations are sad, but it does not hurt the child to read about them unless his gradual development of a concern for others is considered wrong. Tragedies in literature do not depress any of us in a really harmful way. Lloyd Alexander has reminded us in the *Horn Book Magazine* of a comment attributed to De La Rochefoucauld,

which was: "We all have sufficient strength to endure the misfortunes of others." I am not sure but that we draw strength from such misfortunes. Occasionally, we all need to escape into a fantasy world, but perhaps it is good also to escape at times from our own real world into someone else's real world.

Maybe it is the same with children, and it does not matter whether a story teaches them anything or not. Mr. Singer in his article in the *New York Times* said that not everyone would agree with him, "but that we are living in a time when literature aspires more and more to be didactic and utilitarian. It doesn't seem to matter what lesson it teaches—a sociological, psychological or humanistic one—as long as it teaches." He also said that he did not know "of a single work of fiction in our time which has contributed much to psychology or sociology, or helped the cause of pacifism."

I do not know if any of the children's books of recent years will seriously contribute to these areas, but I have been interested to hear of one college that is using some of them in child and adolescent psychology courses. The students read from a list of junior novels and discuss them in class each Monday. The only drawback, it has turned out, is that they have become so interested in the experiment that book discussions run over into midweek when other ground is supposed to be covered. I think it speaks well for today's realism that the professor saw these books as a basis—or as a springboard—for discussions, and that the students were enthusiastic about them, whether or not we agree that works of fiction should teach anything.

We would all agree, however, that a story should entertain the reader, in the sense of holding his attention and making him care about it; and I feel it is more apt to do this, that the characters and the action are more likely to ring true, if the person writing the story can discuss whatever matters most to him. Maybe this is why I am excited about the New Realism. While C. S. Lewis said that "Anyone who *can* write a children's story without a moral, had better do so—that is, if he is going to write children's stories at all"; from my standpoint I cannot see how anyone could put the required amount of time and energy into a book unless he is holding it together, or trying to hold it together, with a theme of importance to himself. And I cannot imagine a theme in a children's story strong enough to hold anything together that does not, in the final analysis, turn out to be moral, or at least morally sound. Stronger stories in every sense are likely to result when the writer is free to tackle whatever is meaningful to him. And if it is to find a young audience, it must be with material meaningful to young people—no matter what the subject.

But subjects alone, no matter how important, do not make a good story. However timely and appropriate they may be, unless they are fleshed out with believable characters—I would go so far as to say with at least some characters the reader cannot only believe in but care about—

and unless something resembling a plot is provided, the finished item is not likely to be a good junior novel. John Rowe Townsend, the British author and critic, said [in *The New York Times*] that "you can't turn a bad novel into a good one by filling it with pregnancy, pot and the pill." A story should never be merely a platform from which to discuss a topic, although I admit that the themes of my stories are figurative soapboxes or platforms from which to express my own outlook on life. But a soapbox and nothing else is a rather dismal sight.

For the fun of it, I have looked back to what people were saying not so very long ago—five or ten years or there-abouts—about realistic stories for children. C. S. Lewis, who was discussing fantasy, touched on realism in an essay, saying:

> I think what profess to be realistic stories for children are far more likely to deceive them [than fantasy]. I never expected the real world to be like the fairy tales. I think that I did expect school to be like the school stories. The fantasies did not deceive me: the school stories did.

He went on to say that "All stories in which children have adventures and successes which are possible . . . , but almost infinitely improbable, are in more danger than the fairy tales of raising false expectations," and I agree with him. But today, the kind of realistic stories he had in mind are not as likely to find a publisher—or, if they do, a reader. Surely not as many of them nowadays raise false expectations about the world in which we live, and there are school stories now that are like school.

Another quote, this one by Elizabeth Enright [in *Horn Book Magazine*], whom I admired so much and whose death was a loss to all of us. She said this seven or eight years ago about realism in children's books: "It is apt to be kinder than the real thing; also neater, more just, and more exciting. Things turn out well in the end." Today, not always. Sometimes they do; sometimes they do not. She went on to say,

> But unlike life, the end of the story comes at the high point. We do not have to go on with these people through high school, college, marriage, mortgage payments, child rearing, money worries, dental problems . . . or any of the rest of it. It is our privilege to leave them in their happiness forever. . . .

I am glad that there are still books that end happily. I hope there will never be a brand of realism that rules out happy endings. But I somehow get the feeling that realism to some people has come to mean only the harsher side of life. Surely, in life there are as many happy endings as sad ones, so to be truly realistic, should books not average out accordingly?

For all children, whether they face the world as gradually as we would have them, or have to face it earlier, I think that when it comes to realism in their stories, honesty is what we owe them. Is it too much to ask that anything we present as being realistic be realistic?

Robert Burch

SOURCE: "Stories From the Front Porch," in *Children's Literature Association Quarterly,* Vol. 9, No. 4, Winter, 1984-85, pp. 164-67.

I'm glad to be with you. I've looked forward to this visit for a long time. For me, one of the real joys of writing children's books is in getting to know people who take children and their books seriously. You inspire me to take greater pride in what I do.

I only wish I had been with you twenty years ago when I was an authority on many subjects. I could have told you professors how to teach children's literature and the ones of you who work with children how to interest them in reading. I could have told my fellow writers how to produce books, and I could have given the ones of you who are parents a few pointers on bringing up your children.

But I've come to realize that anyone who has ever taken a children's lit course—to say nothing of anyone who has taught one—knows more about books than I do, and any writer who recognizes a plot when he or she sees one knows more about writing. Being an old bachelor, howev-er, I'm still pretty much an expert on raising children; but I'll spare you my views on that topic.

One of my favorite subjects for a long time has been realism in children's books, and in the past I've made talks in defense of stronger realism in stories for the young. But maybe that's been discussed enough. I have a niece who teaches seventh grade, and occasionally she lends me books that have been of special interest to her students. One day she said that she'd thought of bringing me a copy of Judy Blume's *Forever,* but that she had decided I was not really sophisticated enough to handle it! It was about that time that I put away my soapbox for promoting the so-called new realism.

What I'd like to talk about tonight could be summed up in the theme for your conference, *The Pride of Place: Wellspring of Story,* as it has to do with my own back-ground—or rather, my home territory, the rural South—and what there is about it that inspires and stimulates me as a writer—and at times frustrates me—along with some of my objectives in writing stories of a specific locale that I hope may say something to children of whatever region they're in.

I grew up in Fayetteville, a small town in Georgia. (The one in North Carolina, by the way; is probably the one you've heard of. Ft. Bragg is situated there, and it's the biggest of the eleven Fayettevilles in the United States.)

As an adult I worked at jobs in various parts of the coun-try and various parts of the world, until I began freelanc-ing in the early sixties and moved back home—and more or less stayed put for a long time. Then I took to the road again in the late seventies, and in '81 I wound up three years of combining travel, or gypsy-wandering, with writing. But as of now, I've settled back home again—possibly forever. It could be that I'm travel-weary, but more likely it's that I'm too old, too tired, and too broke to move around any more!

Regions, like people, are never all good or all bad, and I have moved about so much that I'm confused at times as to whether I fit in anywhere. But I keep setting stories in the rural South, and I've been thinking on what there is about it that always draws me back.

If anyone asked *how* I came to use the area as background for stories, however, I could answer in one word: reluctantly. At first, I was not inspired to write about the South, I was browbeaten into it. In New York I took a course from Dr. William Lipkind, the Will of the Will and Nicholas picture book team, and he kept asking why I didn't write about the years of my own youth. I argued that I grew up in a little country town during the Depression, and stories about those years would be depressing. He insisted that wasn't necessarily so, until finally I started a story of three brothers on a Georgia farm just to show him how wrong he was. Instead, it showed me how wrong I'd been, and I've set stories in familiar home territory ever since—not always during the Depression; sometimes in the changing South of today—and also during the years of the Second World War—which marked the end of an era for the country and the end of boyhood for me. One day I was a child and the next day I was grown, or thought I was, and a soldier in the South Pacific.

Because of Dr. Lipkind's insistence, when I finally looked back at the early nineteen-thirties, I discovered that the Depression provided a convenient backdrop on which to hang one of my favorite themes, which is: there are so many things in life more important than money.

If I have a soapbox nowadays, that's it. I was saddened not long ago to read that in a survey of 250,000 college freshmen, more than sixty percent rated "being very well-off financially" as their top goal in life. There's nothing wrong in wanting to get ahead, but is it healthy for financial gain to be anyone's top goal in life?

Maybe together we can help get across the idea to children that values are misplaced when materialism comes first—which is something I earnestly believe, whether in the old days of nowadays—and in any part of the country.

In the rural South perhaps we've had more experience at being poor than anyone else. By the time the rest of the nation felt that Depression, in our part of the country we were already down because of the devastation wrought by the boll weevil and a disastrous drop in the price of cotton.

Reynolds Price once said that his father lost the only house he ever built because he couldn't borrow fifty dollars to make the next payment. He was discussing the effect of the Depression on Southern writers at a festival in Tennessee some years ago. He said, "And the sort of people who are likely to write, it seems to me, are not having the

sorts of problems now that I had as a boy—not seeing their parents humiliated, say, in the way that I did or that, sixty years before, a generation of Southern writers saw their parents humiliated by Reconstruction."

In several stories, I've written about children from families who are about as poor as they can be and still survive, but nevertheless are not bowed down in poverty. It's the spirit of people like them in real life that has inspired me to want to help spread the word that the things money can buy are not what really matter. This was the central idea in that first realistic book that Dr. Lipkind coaxed out of me, *Tyler, Wilkin, and Skee.* You know, I was never able to convince Northern friends that it was not purely autobiographical. If it had been, for instance, there would have been eight children in the family instead of only three. I was asked so often, "Were you Wilkin or were you Skee?" that one day I asked why no one mistook me for Tyler. I was told that nobody mistook me for Tyler because he was the sober, level-headed one.

One of the things that those three boys have going for them is an understanding family, and I don't know if secure family relationships are valued more highly in the rural South than elsewhere, but it is one of the things that I think is good about us: the strength of the family. I've been told that we stuck together in the old days because we couldn't afford to stick anywhere else, but that isn't so. Even in these more affluent times, members of the families I know are concerned about each other—not just parents and brothers and sisters, but aunts, uncles—even cousins down the line till they're so distant that we forget them, or such soreheads that we try to forget them.

A while back I was reading a speech that Norma Klein had made, and I especially liked her views on family life in children's books. Let me read you one of her comments: "Sometimes it seems we have gone in one leap from the idealized perfect parents of Beverly Cleary—whose books, incidentally, I love—to the parent monsters in Paul Zindel. What I've always disliked in Zindel's books—and I take him as typical of a genre—is the simplisticness of the portrayal of the parents. They usually have no redeeming features. Communication with them is impossible. I see in this a kind of pandering to what some adolescents might like to think of the world—namely, that their generation alone is sensitive and idealistic, that anyone of their parents' generation is a phony and a cheat."

After family, comes church. Certainly religion is a major element of life in the South. Country churches were, and often still are, not only houses of worship but centers for community life. In some of my stories set in the thirties, the church services and the church-related programs are almost the only times the people see each other. There were school activities then too, but often even the youngest children rode long distances to school. Families did not always have cars—and even for those who did, there were few paved roads—when I was a child there wasn't *a* paved road in my country—and there was always work to be done at home. Therefore, many parents didn't turn out for anything less auspicious than a high school graduation. But there was usually a church at the nearest crossroads, which might be several miles away but was still near enough to go for a box supper or a Sunday all-day singing. I've included some of these activities in several books, building the plot around a Christmas pageant in one instance, with a party afterward where a selfish boy learns that it *is* more blessed to give than to receive. More recently, in **Christmas with Ida Early,** I also used a pageant—or tableau—of a church in a small community.

Rural churches have changed to some extent in recent years: The pump organ has been replaced by an electric one, and the sanctuary has probably been renovated. Many have added a fellowship hall because the church, even though it no longer provides the only outings for the families who live nearby, is still an important part of the social life of the community.

Best of all, they still have church suppers—sometimes as fundraisers and sometimes as neighborly get-togethers. When I'm home, I attend two or three a year. Pit barbecue is the specialty of one church near me, and an annual purlieu supper is the main attraction at another. I wouldn't miss the purlieu one for anything! The dish, in the event you're not familiar with it, is made with whatever can be grown, caught, or shot close to home. I swore off it for a while as a child when my older brothers told me that the smallest pieces of meat in it came from chipmunks. I'm sure that wasn't true, although even now I don't inquire about the recipe.

In addition to the social aspect, rural churches, of course, provide religious training. In my youth, they tried hard to sharpen our views of right and wrong, and I suppose they still do.

In one book, I used as the father a religious fanatic and a tyrant. One adult accused me of presenting in it a negative view of Christianity in the rural South—but I hope that I didn't. I tried to show the misuse of dogma and its effect upon the lives of those touched by it. I'm sure I didn't convince the man, because he was a near-fanatic himself. He had argued with me earlier about an incident in **Tyler, Wilkin, and Skee,** in which the boys play an old game with hymn books, asking and answering questions with song titles. In one part of it, Tyler, quoting the title of a hymn, asks, "What Shall I Do to be Saved?" and his younger brothers, Wilkin and Skee, answer: "Rescue the Perishing."

Well, the pious old gentleman scolded me. He said that the Bible clearly states that man is saved by faith alone. I personally have always put a lot of stock in people who rescue the perishing, but I explained to the man that I didn't present the answer as anything more than one of the boys thought appropriate. He said, well, in that case he guessed it was all right—if my purpose was to show the Wilkin and Skee were weak in theology!

So much for religion in this part of the country, which has alternately inspired and exasperated me.

Another thing that inspires me about the rural South is the beauty of the actual countryside. I've emphasized it a bit in some books. In one, for instance, there's an old sailor, coming back for a glimpse of home, and he remarks so often on the soft Georgia hills that at least the children in the story begin to take their surroundings less for granted.

I don't think it's necessary for me to go into great detail in describing countryside—after all, a junior novel is not a travelogue—but young readers should get some notion of rural settings if stories take place in them, whether swamps, peach orchards, woods, pastures, or whatever. Of the settings I've used, my favorite from a scenic standpoint, would have to be the gristmill area in **Two That Were Tough.** Millponds always make me wish I were a painter.

A few years ago, I spent the fall in Virginia, near the Shenandoah Valley, and the mountains were so beautiful that I almost wished I could live there forever. The following winter, in Arizona, I felt the same way about the desert. That was followed by a sojourn in Saratoga, California, and I was certain that *it* was the prettiest spot I'd ever seen! So I am fickle, or maybe it's that I like variety. At the risk of sounding like a Department of Tourism, I must say that the many varieties of natural beauty found in Georgia are enough to inspire anyone. With our mountains at one end of the state and flat land and a wilderness area, the Okefenokee Swamp, at the other, and my favorite countryside, the red-clay hills in between, we're really blessed—to say nothing of having the seacoast or Guale, including the Golden Isles.

But more important than the looks of an area are its people, and one of the things about rural Georgia that stimulates me as a writer is that its people are as varied as its landscape.

When children read stories that are set in the South, they should get an inkling of what some southerners are like. They should meet characters who are decent, good people—and maybe a few who are not. It's not the purpose of a realistic story to show only the good.

Maybe children, in reading for pleasure, begin to get a notion of what other people are like. At least, they don't have closed minds about them the way we adults sometimes do. In our reading we may on occasion accept only what reinforces our own prejudices. And certainly there are enough southern novels for anyone to take his pick and believe what he wants to.

I had the pleasure of meeting Elizabeth Janeway some years ago, and she said that the South, as it existed in the minds of most people in other parts of the country was covered by a deep layer of clichés. She felt that all too often they were the Nasty-South clichés, at that, and that they had taken the place of people. To many outsiders, she felt, the South had become the haunt of Captain Hook and the alligator and the pirates. That was true at the time, but it has changed somewhat in recent years.

I don't read as widely as I should and have not made a study of southern novels, but occasionally in the ones I've read I've come across small things that maybe help perpetuate clichés—not necessarily nasty ones. For instance, in one there's a young man who goes courting and takes his girlfriend a silver ring and a bag of chitterlings. I complained one evening at home, "That writer's telling others what they already believe about us! Whoever heard of a young man taking his girlfriend a silver ring and a bag of chitterlings?" One of my brothers said, Yeah, I was right. According to him, it should have been a gold ring.

An Atlanta journalist once said that we Georgians are a composite of three of our state's fictional characters: Jeeter Lester of *Tobacco Road,* Scarlett O'Hara, and Brer Rabbit. I forget what he said we do and don't have in common with Jeeter and Scarlett, but as for Brer Rabbit, well, it seems that while some southerners may on occasion be as cunning and wily as he was, Brer Rabbit went lickety-split. And no southerner ever goes lickety-split!

New Yorkers do! I lived in New York eight years and when I first moved there I was certain that everyone I saw rushing down the street was on the way to a concert or a play, a museum, an art gallery, or a major sports event—so many exciting things are there to do in the big city. After getting to know people, however, I discovered that some of them were hurrying because they were doing special things, but a good many others were on the way home to put their feet up and watch television, or bowl with the neighborhood team, or have a couple of beers at the corner tavern. For such endeavors, they still went lickety-split.

I personally am inspired by our pace in the South, and if we don't always appear industrious it may not be that we're lazy, but only that we've stopped to think a moment. At least, that's my excuse! To borrow from Walt Whitman, "I loaf and invite my soul!" I borrowed extensively from Walt Whitman for my only young adult novel, *The Whitman Kick.* In it, the hero and heroine are turned onto poetry to the extent that they sometimes communicate through the lines of a poet—especially when they're avoiding direct confrontations that might hurt. Walt Whitman came to my rescue whenever I needed him. He had also been dead long enough for his work to be in the public domain! I used some modern poets too, and ran into stumbling blocks and one stone wall in connection with permission to quote even a few lines from them.

The central character in the story, like me, was a senior in high school when the bombs fell on Pearl Harbor, but the war was only background for his problems in growing up and learning to forgive and accept. As any of you know who have worked with children, every generation of young people think they're the first to have these problems. My central characters *and I* were amazed

that a poet had summed up our feelings a hundred years before we had them.

When I mentioned to a couple of friends that I was preparing this talk, both of them asked if I wasn't inspired by the natural courtesy and helpfulness of southerners. I hadn't thought about it, but I suppose I am. Yet people in other parts of the country have these qualities too. During my years in New York I knew firsthand not only northern helpfulness but northern hospitality. But maybe some southerners—*not all of us*—do take helpfulness to unbelievable lengths—trusting the stranger, certain that his motives are honorable.

An old family friend of mine lives six miles out in the country, and her family worries about her not being cautious in befriending motorists when they have trouble nearby. In earlier years the road was so rough that nobody ventured onto it who wasn't a neighbor, but that's no longer true. Yet she still is inclined to help stranded travelers by telling them to take her car and go back into town for whatever help they're needing. If there are passengers along, they can rest in her home, and if there are children, she has been known to babysit till the adults return. One of these days she may wind up with a carload of rotten children that nobody wants bad enough to come back for! Meanwhile, she will be both helpful and hospitable; times can change but she will not.

Once, soon after Atlanta had discovered one-way streets, this same lady was driving into the city on a seasonal shopping trip. Most of us then knew only one way to get in and out of town, so the one-way streets caused us real headaches. On her first introduction to them, she had started to make a lefthand turn to go half-a-block to where she had been parking for at least thirty years. A policeman directing traffic yelled at her, "Hey, Lady, you can't turn in here!" She stuck her head out the window and called back to him, "Yes, I think I can make it if you'll just step back a little." She motioned him aside and made her turn.

To what southern characteristic can I tie in that illustration? Resistance to change. We're sometimes accused of being against change of any sort, but resistant or not, the rural South is changing drastically. For many years my hometown, as small as it was, was the only incorporated town in the county, but in the past twenty-five years a new, planned city has gone up ten miles away, and although we've pretty much adjusted to each other by now, there have naturally been some problems between the old and the new. One of my friends says that the time will come when the citizens of the new Peachtree City will drive over to Fayetteville on a Saturday night to see us natives. Perhaps we can turn out in costume for their benefit. I've been thinking I'd get a stand and sell postcards and ashtrays and the like, but the trouble is that in Fayetteville we're not as "native" as we once were ourselves. We have several shopping centers now, and on the main road in from Atlanta, which has been four-laned, there are various drive-in businesses—one-hour cleaners, photomats—and of course, a McDonald's! At a program I attended a while back over at East Carolina one of the participants, Janice Faulkner, said that she would remind us that Tobacco Road has now been paved. And last month on a television program, Tom Wicker of the *New York Times* said that Tobacco Road is now an interstate. I would add to those descriptions of it and say that in many places it has become a strip.

But I wanted to talk mainly about what I like in the South, and I have definitely been inspired by the novelists of the region. Many of us in the writing field are indebted to them.

Eudora Welty is quoted as saying we're inclined to write in the South because we have front porches upon which we sit and hear and tell stories by the hour. Other people have given other reasons that southerners write. Incidentally, I'm tired of the critics with their big joke that more southerners can write books than can read them.

The reasons for our being writers vary. Some say that writing grows naturally out of conditions of conflict. Flannery O'Connor said that we write because we have the Bible and a little history.

I like Miss Welty's front porch theory best. Air-conditioning has changed things now, but I grew up on porches. In summer the house was often too hot to be really comfortable anywhere else till later in the evening, so the family gathered on the front porch after supper. Children, when they tired of catching lightning bugs or scrapping with each other, sat on the steps and listened to the grown-ups. At our house we heard stories from two porches—ours and the one across the road, where an elderly lawyer lived who was also our representative in the state legislature. The reason we heard stories from his porch was that he was partially deaf and spoke as if everyone else were. He and his son-in-law, also a lawyer and also interested in politics, talked on their porch in the cool of the evening, and we didn't really pay much attention to what they were saying, except when we'd hear the old man preface a remark with, "Now, confidentially . . . " Then we listened very carefully. The son-in-law lived there until last year, when he died at almost-ninety, and until a few years ago I lived in our old homeplace across the road. But for years neither of us sat on our front porch.

One final story to illustrate the varied individuality of my southern neighbors, who have been a constant inspiration to me. When I was a child a man up the street went into Atlanta with some of his friends one night and had such a good time that he wasn't ready to come back when they were. The next day, still drunk but knowing he'd better get home, he hired a taxi to bring him—an unheard of extravagance then or now. Maybe he got lucky in a poker game. In any event, when he arrived home, the nice old lady who lived next door was weeding flowers in her front yard, and the man decided that she probably had never ridden in a taxi. So he paid the cab driver to take her on a short ride about town.

All of us children in the neighborhood were impressed, and afterward we asked the old lady, "How was it? What was it like, riding in a taxi?" She thought for a moment and said, "Well, to tell us the truth, it rode a lot like an automobile."

So I would hope that children—or adults—whether meeting southerners in books or in real life, will decide that, "Well, we're a lot like human beings."

Robert Burch

SOURCE: "Acceptance of Phoenix Award," in *Proceedings of the Thirteenth Annual Conference of the Children's Literature Association,* May 16-18, 1986, pp. 32-3.

The following is Robert Burch's acceptance speech for the Phoenix Award, which he delivered at the annual conference of the Children's Literature Association in Kansas City in May, 1986.

Thank you very much. I'm grateful to all of you for this award and am deeply honored. In our age of disposable wares, including books that are timely one day and old-hat the next, anyone writing in the children's field is fortunate to have a book that "hangs in there," as it were, for any real length of time, but to have it win an award from so distinguished a group as yours is very special indeed.

And I'm delighted to have this opportunity to be with you again. After the Charlotte conference, I felt that I had a number of new friends. By now, I consider you *old friends*. And, for giving me this splendid award, you are certainly my *good friends*.

Did you know that the Phoenix is the symbol of Atlanta—which is home territory for me? I live in a country town just south of it. Of course, it wasn't until after Sherman burned down Atlanta that we needed this appropriate symbol! But the Phoenix has served as a reminder to all Georgians over the years that it is possible to rebuild from ashes. The Phoenix that you've given me will serve as a reminder that it's possible to produce work that lasts—twenty years, at least. Of course, a true phoenix, according to most of the Greek writers, lasted five hundred years or longer, but I'm glad you settled on *twenty* for the award. Incidentally, when I bragged to friends that I was to receive it, several of them said, in effect, "Isn't that a neat award?" The idea of recognizing something nowadays that isn't brand new seemed somehow revolutionary, and they felt that the members of the Children's Literature Association must be very astute and highly discerning people to have created the award. I explained to them that you were very astute and highly discerning in giving it to *Queenie Peavy*!

That isn't really the way I feel. There are many other books deserving of this year's award, which makes me especially pleased that *Queenie Peavy* was chosen. I have to admit that I started writing the book for the wrong reason. After I'd written several of my earlier stories, a writer friend in New York dismissed them as *un*creative efforts: "They're purely autobiographical," she insisted. "All those yarns about ragged-ass boys growing up during the Great Depression."

I asked what I needed to do to prove that I was what she called a *real writer,* and she said, "Use a girl for a central character. Then I'll know it isn't your life story."

I don't know now why it seemed important to convince her of anything—probably the motivation was less than honorable—but I started the story just to show her that I could write it. Of course, somewhere along the line I became genuinely concerned about Queenie.

When I visited with you in '84, your conference theme was Pride of Place: Wellspring for Story, which I like very much as it summed up thoughts I'd been trying to put together about the rural South as inspiration for writing. This year's theme, From Hannibal to Oz: Journeys in Children's Literature, appeals to me, also, as journeys of any sort have always interested me.

Queenie Peavy's "journey" was, without her realizing it— perhaps without my realizing it—an inward quest of the mind and spirit. At first, she's in a blind alley because of the fierce loyalty to her father and her need to believe that he cares about her. When she faces the truth as it is instead of as she wishes it to be, she heads in the right direction. In a final scene, when she deliberately tosses away the stone instead of aiming it, I hope that young readers are convinced that she has chosen the positive route and will stay on it.

Incidentally, my working title for the book had been *A Stone's Throw* as Queenie was literally a crack shot with a stone. Also, she was within a stone's throw of leading a decent life if she'd learn to behave herself. Annis Duff, my editor at the time, suggested giving the book a different name.

To some extent, I've overdone character names in titles, although in that instance I'm glad it was used. But I almost always have title trouble. That's one reason I'm so impressed by the ones of you who not only plan your conferences but come up with themes for them that are interesting and provocative.

I've never started a story without first giving it a title. The problem has been that frequently the story I write bears little resemblance to the story I'd planned. I have a new book that's scheduled for publication in October, and my working title for it was *The Poet Laureate of The Sixth Grade at Stokes Elementary School in Flag City, Georgia.* In addition to sounding as if E. L. Konigsburg had helped me with it, it was, of course, much too long. So I shortened it to *The Poet Laureate of the Sixth Grade,* but later changed that—for two reasons: 1) Elementary students probably don't know what a poet laureate is, and 2) They may not *want to know* what a poet laureate is! So the title—already on the dust jacket and too late change again—

is *King Kong and Other Poets.* King Kong is the pseudonym of one of the students in a poetry-writing contest.

I thought of bringing a couple of pages of manuscript to read while I have a captive audience, but instead, I'll read one of the children's poems. It's written by a kid who chose as his pen name, Alexander the Great, Military Conqueror and King of Macedonia. His pseudonym indicates that at least he's been paying attention in social studies. The poem goes like this:

> Once I took a river ride
>   With my brother and his bride.
> It was just before their wedding day
>   Which is over now, and they're home
>   to stay.
>
> When they got back from their honeymoon
>   They moved in with us and took over
>   my room.
> If we go on the river for another ride
>   I wish that I could drown the bride.

No doubt, you'll be relieved to know that he doesn't win the contest. There's a girl in the class, however—a mousy-looking new kid—who exhibits, if not special talent, at least enthusiasm for writing poetry.

Because all the other children have written about their own lives, they assume that her poems are from firsthand experience, also, and are envious when she writes of her privileged life, her loving family, and a collection of exotic pets and expensive toys. They don't understand poetic license, and she's able to use her poetry as a vehicle for acceptance, even though acceptance at first is based on misconception. Later, when she realizes that the friendship is real, her life begins to change.

I wanted to write a story about someone who doesn't fit in, and I enjoyed working with themes of special meaning to me: reality and dreams, indirect and intentional deception, poverty and wealth, and the age-old questions of "Who am I?" and "On what basis will I be accepted?"

In a sense, her story is a journey. It's a journey toward the discovery of the power of friendship, which, to me, is one of the most pleasant and meaningful journeys any of us take in life. And that brings me back to where I started— our being friends, you and me, and the pleasure it is to be with you.

Thank you again for the Phoenix Award.

GENERAL COMMENTARY

William H. Green

SOURCE: "A Harvest of Southern Realism," in *Children's Literature: Annual of The Modern Language Association*

Group on Children's Literature and The Children's Literature Association, Vol. 7, 1978, pp. 256-57.

Writing from his childhood home in Fayette County, just south of Atlanta, [Robert Burch] is a master of the regional "problem" novel. The problems are perennial: sickness, death, poverty, disgrace, old age, and war, reflected in credible characters without morbidity, escapism, or preaching. And under Burch's hand problems evolve toward unexpected but satisfying conclusions. In *Doodle and the Go-Cart,* the son of a marginal farmer dreams of buying a go-cart. With and without his mule's help, Doodle undertakes money-making projects and, despite pneumonia and bad timing, saves nearly enough money. In the end we expect Doodle either to give up or to buy the machine, but Burch is shrewder. Offered a chance to sell the mule, Doodle postpones the go-cart another year. Delicately and unexpectedly, we are left with the moral that material dreams are good but friends (even mule-friends) take precedence. Similarly, in *Hut School and the Wartime Home-Front Heroes,* set during World War II, expectation is oddly fulfilled. A popular young teacher seems marked for departure almost from the beginning. Not only do her methods cause trouble, but she is mysteriously absent for a medical examination, and the book is pervaded with a sense that good and bad times both pass. But neither teaching nor illness dispatches Miss Jordan; she joins the WAVES and the young protagonist's father is suddenly drafted. So *Hut School* ends in suspension, appreciation for the past and apprehension for the future. *Two That Were Tough,* Burch's most recent book, explores old age, a heavy subject for a children's book. It tells of a stubborn old grist-mill owner and a wild chicken, both faced with obsolescence. Dwindling business, influenza, an ice storm, and a daughter in Atlanta gradually force Mr. Hilton to abandon his mill. Fearing the chicken will perish without him, he traps it to take to Atlanta. Then suddenly he releases it, and the bird returns to the woods, a living symbol of the old man's unsubdued spirit. Even strong men must retire, but wild birds die free. Like *Queenie Peavy* and Burch's other novels, these three unfold in clear, almost faultless style with close attention to regional and historical detail. He has deep and solid roots.

TITLE COMMENTARY

THE TRAVELING BIRD (1959)

Mary Ake

SOURCE: "Remarks of Mary Ake," in *Proceedings of the Thirteenth Annual Conference of the Children's Literature Association,* May 16-18, 1986, p. 24.

[Robert Burch's] first work, *The Traveling Bird* (1959), reminds me of the later Shel Silverstein book, *The Giving Tree.* Or rather the reverse, I suppose. In this case, it is not a tree but a bird—a very special, wise bird that sets out to help a young boy realize his heart's desire. The parakeet is given to the boy, who really wants a puppy. The bird tries to help the child by locating a puppy lost in a storm and guiding the boy through the somewhat dangerous rescue. Then, alas, the true owner of the dog comes to claim it. During the first part of the story, the boy does not really care much for the bird. In fact, he resents the creature, because he still wants a puppy. Despite the bird's best efforts to win the boy's friendship, it simply doesn't work out. One day the bird takes the child to a pet store and tells him to choose any dog in the shop. Ecstatic, the boy returns home with a new puppy, so joyful he forgets even to thank the bird. When the next morning the boy returns to the pet store for the bird, he finds it gone. The pet store owner explains that the bird had arranged to be exchanged for a puppy, sacrificing himself that the boy might find joy. In tears, the boy runs away leaving behind the puppy that had followed him to the shop. Then, realizing the generosity of the bird and his own responsibility to both bird and dog, he goes back and gets the puppy, intending to care properly for it.

The writing is uneven, and the story is preachy. However, Burch's skill at touching the emotions is evident already in this first book, and, in retrospect, his present narrative style is recognizable in its beginnings.

TYLER, WILKIN, AND SKEE (1963)

Margery Fisher

SOURCE: A review of *Tyler, Wilkin, and Skee,* in *Who's Who in Children's Books: A Treasury of the Familiar Characters of Childhood,* Holt, Rinehart and Winston, 1975, p. 309.

Tyler, Wilkin, and Skee, the three Coley boys, live in a country district in Georgia. Their father works in a sawmill and they share between them much of the care of the hens, Vivian the surly cow and the routine household chores. It is the time of the Depression and money is short. Fortunately these lively boys are well able to make their own amusements—especially Skee, who has inherited a gift for music from his mother and can find a song for any occasion. His older brothers sometimes find it necessary to put seven-year-old Skee in his place, but the resilient youngster can usually hold his own. Wilkin is spokesman for the trio; he is 'better at talking to people outside the family'. When he wins a prize in his grade at school he refuses to go forward in his worn dungarees and boldly commandeers a pair of trousers from Mr Grayson's scarecrow for the occasion.

Robert Burch spent his own childhood in just such a country community as the one he uses as a setting for his three cheerful young characters and their exploits. Their loyalty to one another, their self-sufficiency and their gift for taking life as it comes, are all clearly shown to be the product of their environment and of their upbringing in a house full of affection and cheerfully accepted discipline. As Robert Burch shows, in spite of the Depression (or perhaps partly because of it) the characters he has created make the most of their circumstances.

D. A. Young

SOURCE: A review of *Tyler, Wilkin, and Skee,* in *The Junior Bookshelf,* Vol. 54, No. 5, October, 1990, pp. 238-39.

The University of Georgia Press has decided to enter the world of children's publishing with a rather sumptuous re-issue of one of the most popular works of this well-established author. First published in 1963 it harks back to the hard-hit Depression-era South of the Mid-Twenties. Money was scarce. The highlight of the lives of the three brothers was the visit to the local store to trade in three or four dozen eggs for domestic supplies. If they were lucky there might just be enough for a can of Pepsi to be shared between them. The main road was a dirt road and the most prized possession a home made catapult. The very simplicity of their life enhanced their enjoyment. They became part of the American dream of frugal happiness won by hard, self-reliant work in an unfriendly environment—a dream to be drowned in the sprawl of industrial growth but one for which the nostalgic longing will never die.

We spend a year with the Coley family. Each month has its chapter of simple joys and triumphs. May shows Wilkin receiving his school award kitted out in pants from a scarecrow. July is the time that no one will buy their figs. Every month chronicles a making of virtue out of necessity. Every hardship enriches the character.

They don't write books like this nowadays which is a very good reason Robert Burch's works should be kept in print.

Mary Weichsel Ake

SOURCE: "Robert Burch's Forte: Books Laid in Rural Georgia," in *The Phoenix Award of The Children's Literature Association, 1985-1989,* edited by Alethea Helbig and Agnes Perkins, The Scarecrow Press, 1993, pp. 48-9.

The episodic *Tyler, Wilkin, and Skee* introduces us to the setting of Burch's best works: rural Georgia. It concerns three close brothers during the Depression and deals with the farm life Burch knows well through his own experiences. Its events rise out of memories of his youth, and its force from his ability to recreate them clearly and memorably for us and link them to our own lives at the same time. Malcom Usrey puts it well: "Although Robert Burch has used a regional setting, he universalizes the action, characters, and themes of his

fiction. His novels speak elemental truths: wealth does not necessarily create happiness; material progress does not change the basic needs of people; rural life and the land are important to any nation; poverty is not always degrading; and family and community, good or bad, are usually what people make them."

Each chapter in *Tyler, Wilkin, and Skee* tells a separate story about a year's mostly everyday happenings. But some episodes relate special occurrences. The brothers enjoy riding in the neighbor's automobile, a rare treat. When they are promised a ride to the county fair in September, they are elated and look forward to the occasion with eager anticipation. But when the car comes by, it is filled with relatives of the neighbor and there is room for only one of the Coley boys. Though sadly, they decline the ride, sticking together then—as in all things important. The next August, however, all win a trip with their 4-H project. The book exudes gentle humor, the warmth of a loving family, simple living (the not-rich-but-never-got-poor feeling is strong), and of neighbor helping neighbor. This book stands as a worthy forerunner of Burch's later highly successful novels like *Skinny* and *Queenie Peavy.*

SKINNY (1964; British edition, 1965)

Priscilla L. Moulton

SOURCE: A review of *Skinny,* in *The Horn Book Magazine,* Vol. XL, No. 3, June, 1964, pp. 285-86.

Skinny is the recently orphaned and illiterate son of a Southern sharecropper. These are the happy hours and the poignant longings of his eleventh summer. While waiting for a place in an orphanage, Skinny helps Miss Bessie run her hotel and endears himself to everyone with his amusing innocence. Miss Bessie would adopt him if she were a married lady, and Skinny would like to stay with her. For a time the attentions of a guest set both Miss Bessie and Skinny dreaming; but the guest goes away, and dreams go with him. The ending is undeniably sad. Its reality is hard to accept until surprise and disbelief give way to the recognition that a boy of Skinny's mettle can cope with whatever life offers. Regional dialogue, the warmth of Southern hospitality, and genuine humor heighten the pleasure of knowing this memorable boy. There is nothing complex about Skinny; his wishes are out for all to see. And he is drawn with affectionate insight.

The Junior Bookshelf

SOURCE: A review of *Skinny,* in *The Junior Bookshelf,* Vol. 29, No. 5, October, 1965, pp. 286-87.

Skinny is introduced to us, welcoming guests to the hotel where he is employed as a houseboy. There is nothing special about either the boy or the hotel, yet as the story progresses they both become very special.

Skinny is an orphan and the novel covers the weeks while he is waiting to be taken into an orphanage. Nothing very exciting happens, it is simply an episode in his life and the life of the town; the circus comes and Skinny makes friends with one of the boys there, a highway bridge nearby is finished . . . As the boy can neither read nor write, he is torn between the desire for freedom, that is not to go to the orphanage but to run away and earn his own living, and the desire for the education he will get if he goes there.

The story is set in the southern United States and the heavy atmosphere of the hot summer days is well brought out. There is nothing deep in the plot and yet this is a most moving book. The little boy is a very real character and so are Miss Bessie, who owns the hotel, and the other servants.

This is a book that can be read at many levels by both boys and girls, therefore it will be a valuable asset to any school library.

Margery Fisher

SOURCE: A review of *Skinny,* in *Growing Point,* Vol. 4, No. 6, December, 1965, p. 625.

Skinny lives with Miss Bessie in her small-town hotel, in Georgia in the 1930's. His friends the coloured cook and the odd job man are the recipients of his youthful confidences, and as he battles through chores and encounters we get a most vivid picture of the South and of a boy whose orphan state is mitigated by his lively curiosity and by the devotion of his scruffy mongrel pup. A story warm-hearted and with a strong atmosphere of place and time.

D. J.'S WORST ENEMY (1965)

Virginia Kirkus' Service

SOURCE: A *review of D. J.'s Worst Enemy,* in *Virginia Kirkus' Service,* Vol. XXXIII, No. 1, January 1, 1965, p. 9.

This is another of Robert Burch's plumb friendly, slight sketches of life on a deep southern farm a generation or more ago. Once again the actual story is frail and hinges on a continuity of minor but indigenous episodes; the chores (shucking and loading corn, or picking peaches) or the occasional pleasures (frog-gigging or a picnic at the millpond). Most of this story which is told in the initialed first person as well as the local idiom concerns D. J.'s relationship with his worst enemy, his much younger (5½ to his own 12 years) brother Skinny

Little Renfrew who tags along all the time until he gets sick, very sick. "Where you been at?" they say around here. Readers of the earlier books will know just where—it's a likable if minimal regional portrait with a message about growing up and growing together.

Virginia Haviland

SOURCE: A review of *D. J.'s Worst Enemy,* in *The Horn Book Magazine,* Vol. XLI, No. 2, April, 1965, pp. 169-70.

D. J., a seventh-grader, recounts incidents of work and play with family and friends in a story set in the Georgia peach country. His friend Nutty supports him in exploits against the enemy neighbor boys and sympathizes with him in resenting both his eighth-grade sister's superiority and the tagging-along of his small brother, whose extraordinary gift for imitating any kind of sound enables him to play wonderful tricks. There is nothing bland about the regional picture of farming and peach-picking or about the portrayal of family relationships; rather, there is a striking vitality, due to D. J.'s keen perception and humor and his growth in appreciation of his family.

D. A. Young

SOURCE: A review of *D. J.'s Worst Enemy,* in *The Junior Bookshelf,* Vol. 58, No. 2, April, 1994, pp. 63-4.

Twelve year old D. J. Madison could be a transatlantic cousin of the star of the *Just William* stories. They share the same impregnable confidence in their own superiority and are both equally blind to their own misjudgements. The irony of D. J.'s situation is heightened by the fact that he is the narrator of this saga of American family life in the rural South during the Thirties Depression. It was the time the true American character was forged with its emphasis on self-reliance, its concern for family life, its sense of justice and honest simplicity.

D. J.'s Worst Enemy was first published in 1965 and the present re-issue is a recognition of its status as a classic story of that golden age of childhood which some enjoyed and others would have liked to have had.

QUEENIE PEAVY (1966)

Virginia Kirkus' Service

SOURCE: A review of *Queenie Peavy,* in *Virginia Kirkus' Service,* Vol. XXXIV, No. 8, April 15, 1966, p. 428.

Queenie Peavy is the sort of girl you can welcome on the printed page and rather dread in the library—an oversized, bright thirteen year old, self-assured, argumentative; a girl tall enough to look you in the eye and chip-on-the-shoulder proud enough to insist on it. The author has captured an obsessive, stubborn pride that can drive the Queenie type to rebellious behavior in school and quarrelsome exchanges with her agemates. She's convinced that she is the only person who knows she's nice and reveals her good qualities only before her hardworking mother, two neighboring small children and her flock of hens. (Her lonely conversations with the idiotic birds are some of the best passages in the book.) The setting is Depression-ridden Georgia and the Peavys live on the next farm to what seems a prosperous Negro family who live and eat much better than Queenie and some of her friends. The difference is a hardworking man around the farm. Queenie's father is in the penitentiary and the years of typical small town, child-chanted cruelties have rasped Queenie into the personification of a Bad Attitude who is fast enough with a stone to kill a bird on the wing. Loyalty and instant retaliation for all slights are Queenie's offerings to an absent father who is paroled at just the point where Queenie is in hot water with the school and the town. Queenie adjusts too quickly and with uncharacteristic calm to the potentially shattering realization that her swiftly re-jugged father really hadn't been worth fighting for. This won't bother readers and thirteen is sometimes capable of abrupt shifts through personal insight. The dialogue, characterizations and plot are excellent, the atmosphere, time, and place come over with strength, it's the author's best book so far and Queenie, as a book and a girl, is preeminently likable.

Zena Sutherland

SOURCE: A review of *Queenie Peavy*, in *Bulletin of the Center for Children's Books*, Vol. 19, No. 10, June, 1966, p. 159.

A story of the depression era in rural Georgia. Queenie is big and tough, a troublemaker in school and a scrapping, rock-throwing hoyden out of school; she has home responsibilities because her mother works in a canning plant. Her father is in jail. Every time Queenie is taunted about this, she fights back; finally she gets into real trouble when she causes a boy to break his leg. After some talks with the principal and with a friendly judge, Queenie decides she ought to curb her temper and to be more cooperative; the first reactions are so rewarding that she turns over a new leaf. The writing has just a little of the dated Penrod-and-Sam flavor, but the book gives a convincing picture of the impact of hard times on a rural community. Queenie's father is paroled; bitter, he violates his parole by carrying a gun and is sent back to jail. This realistically brings home to Queenie the acid fact that her father's leaving jail won't solve her problems, but that she must solve them by herself. One pleasant aspect of the story is in Queenie's relationship with the children next door. Dover Corry is eight and his little sister five; they are Negro neighbors who are better off than Queenie's family, and the two children depend on Queenie for the peculiar kind of affection that is partly shown in child-like imaginative play and partly the protection of a girl who can take an adult role.

Publishers Weekly

SOURCE: A review of *Queenie Peavy*, in *Publishers Weekly*, Vol. 189, No. 24, June 13, 1966, p. 128.

Robert Burch has already written three stories of small-town life in Georgia that have won him respectful admiration. The small-town emphasis kept me, a confirmed city woman, from going overboard in *my* admiration. But Queenie Peavy's got me: she is a remarkable girl—she is a rebel with character—and Robert Burch's funny and compassionate account of her good and bad times during the depression years makes for a story of character—which makes it a rare book in these days of safe subjects and safe reissues.

Booklist

SOURCE: A review of *Queenie Peavy*, in *Booklist*, Vol. 62, No. 20, June 15, 1966, p. 998.

Unable to cope with the unhappiness caused by her idolized father's imprisonment and goaded by the taunts of her schoolmates, thirteen-year-old Queenie vents her angry resentment against the world with an air of defiant indifference and well-aimed rocks. Only at home is Queenie relaxed and cheerful. When circumstances force the spirited, intelligent girl to recognize the probable consequences of her recalcitrant behavior and the truth about her father, she has the courage to accept reality and the responsibility of determining her own course of action. Queenie's emotional conflicts are well portrayed, and the story has vitality and significance which extend beyond its immediate background of Georgia during the Depression years.

Ruth Hill Viguers

SOURCE: A review of Queenie Peavy, in *The Horn Book Magazine*, Vol. XLII, No. 4, August, 1966, pp. 433-34.

The author of **Skinny**, one of the most appealing young illiterates of fiction, has created in Queenie a girl who will be even harder to forget. Her vulnerability to teasing because she is so unfortunate as to have a father in prison is covered by an I-don't-care attitude and a braggadocio that prompts her to excel at a number of things, "most of them unworthy of her attention." There is no straining here to formulate a story about a problem child. On the surface the account is as dispassionate as a case study, but considerably more convincing, and Queenie is so real that the reader becomes deeply involved in everything that concerns her. As in many such actual situations, there is no riddance from the obstacle that makes life difficult and often disheartening for Queenie. When she finally learns how to face her particular problem and discovers the satisfaction of excelling in things that are worthy of her attention, the reader feels not merely satisfied but triumphant. Queenie's story will do far more than meet "needs"; it will add another friend to the marvelously varied assembly waiting for all children who read good books.

RENFROE'S CHRISTMAS (1968)

Rebecca Lukens

SOURCE: "Remarks of Rebecca Lukens," in *Proceedings of the Thirteenth Annual Conference of the Children's Literature Association,* May 16-18, 1986, p. 25.

. . . *Queenie Peavy,* stands as an example of what we hoped to see in the run of problem novels of the 1960's and early 70's. But, as book after book appeared, we were often disappointed, for little of the fiction that followed measured up to *Queenie,* for a variety of reasons. First of all, few had Burch's skill in characterization, not only of protagonist but also of minor characters, followed by his development of significant themes relevant not only to childhood but to all human beings. In addition, he successfully evokes setting, gives the flavor of southern dialogue, and all with subtle humor.

Looking quickly at the novel, we meet Queenie on page one, chapter one, called "Deadly Aim":

> Queenie Peavy was the only girl in Cotton Junction who could chew tobacco. She could also spit it—and with deadly aim. She could do a number of things with a considerable degree of accuracy, most of them unworthy of her attention.

Immediately Queenie is not only interesting, but surely atypical, clearly defiant, no doubt troublesome, perhaps even delinquent. We follow her as she chews and spits tobacco, throws rocks with absolute accuracy, challenges the boys in her class at almost anything, arranges the downed sapling so that nasty taunting Cravey Mason falls into the creek—and is simultaneously the best student in the class. She does what we would have liked to do: Queenie is the perfect combination of personal achievement and the universal wish to rebel against conforming and to be oneself, to jump out of the bushes and scare smaller children and yet be beloved by them. Most certainly, she represents a universal wish to retaliate against those who taunt us, sneer at our families, or denigrate us in any way. She has the courage to go alone to see the judge, even though she is afraid he will send her off to the reformatory. She holds her head up when she hears cries of "Queenie's daddy's in the chain gang!" and eagerly awaits her father's return on parole. Queenie is proud, competent, and loyal—traits we admire and wish for ourselves.

Involved in Queenie's struggles, we root for her and fear for her; what's more, we explain her to her teachers, apologize for her to the principal, advise her about her defiant behavior, and earnestly hope she will be strong enough to

control her actions. We know long before Queenie does what the themes of the novel are. She tells Ol' Domnick the rooster, deceiver of his hens, "They don't know when you're lying and when you're not!" and we mutter, "Queenie, listen to yourself." Queenie, thinking about how her father is violating his parole, admits to herself that she had known "all the time, and refused to face up to it, that he had brought on his own troubles." Again we mutter, "Queenie, you're talking about yourself." As she faces the one remaining window in the church tower and raises her throwing arm, she says to herself, "But who are you hurting in the long run?" this time we mutter, "Right, Queenie. You must know whom you're hurting."

Robert Burch has created a believable, memorable character, made us care and kept us in suspense about her, and brought the internal conflict to a most satisfactory close. While we have anxiously cheered the recalcitrant Queenie, we know she has made some essential discoveries. We applaud her for her strength to change.

Publishers Weekly

SOURCE: A review of *Renfroe's Christmas,* in *Publishers Weekly,* Vol. 194, No. 12, September 23, 1968, p. 96.

Christmas comes to a farm in Georgia. It brings to a young boy there a wished-for plow-line (that he can use as a lasso), a yo-yo, and a Mickey Mouse watch. But the real gift it brings him is a sense of compassion, a gift that will enrich the rest of his life. Robert Burch, who conveys his own compassion in his earlier story *Queenie Peavy,* conveys it again in *Renfroe's Christmas.*

Margaret A. Dorsey

SOURCE: A review of *Renfroe's Christmas,* in *School Library Journal,* Vol. 15, No. 2, October, 1968, p. 177.

A real plum is *Renfroe's Christmas* by Robert Burch, a gracefully written story of Christmas in rural northern Georgia. Eight-year-old Renfroe is uncomfortably aware that he is selfish. After half-hearted, self-conscious attempts to remedy that situation, he suddenly and spontaneously gives away "the finest thing I've ever owned"—his new Mickey Mouse watch—to a retarded boy because it has made him smile. This understated story with its excellent characterizations has year-round as well as holiday appeal.

Kirkus Service

SOURCE: A review of *Renfroe's Christmas,* in *Kirkus Service,* Vol. XXXVI, No. 19, October 1, 1968, p. 1111.

The Madison kids are at it again, confronting the hard to handle with a fairly sturdy grip but in a much briefer compass. Renfroe's at the age when he'll divide a 75¢

store credit into a 25¢ knife for brother D. J. and a 50¢ knife for himself. Told he's getting selfish, he counters with "I believe I like getting presents best, no matter what's more blessed." He is honest, and he honestly looks into—and at first shelves a decision about—what's right and wrong. Should he have given his lasso to three neighbors with only an apple, an orange and a candy bar for Christmas? Should he have given friend Nutty use—or possession—of his yo-yo after a Christmas of needed clothes? Each time he talks himself out of it and each time the angel he put on the smokehouse door seems a little less friendly. The author doesn't say what impels him to approach retarded Nathan Godfrey but the boy's apparent interest in Renfroe's new watch, so different from his usual blank stares, starts the wheels turning and Renfroe gives up this most prized present. The point is clear, the use of the angel as conscience and object of wind movement can stand up, and some of the exchanges are fast and funny, but ending with his first white Christmas is a bit flaky.

Christian Science Monitor

SOURCE: A review of *Renfroe's Christmas,* in *The Christian Science Monitor,* November 29, 1968, p. B3.

A little sentiment, a little realism sugared by test, a little quiet aching of a child's desire, a little selfishness, a large unselfishness—and Christmas in Alabama—make *Renfroe's Christmas.* It is a tale with a moral, but the children are real. Rocco Negri's gentle, unsentimental black and white pictures prove it.

JOEY'S CAT (1969)

Kirkus Reviews

SOURCE: A review of *Joey's Cat,* in *Kirkus Reviews,* Vol. XXXVII, No. 5, March 15, 1969, p. 299.

The best thing about *Joey's Cat* is that several times the key word is on the next . . . page and there's some fun in getting to it. Otherwise it's a case of how to maneuver the cat's kittens into the house when mother thinks they belong in the garage, infused with some of the warmth that permeates the author's other books. The light blue and black illustrations [by Don Freeman] could be more sprightly but this is one of the few racially untroubled picture books featuring a black boy.

Pamela Marsh

SOURCE: A review of *Joey's Cat,* in *The Christian Science Monitor,* May 1, 1969, p. B3.

Without benefit of color—beyond a pale blue wash—Don Freeman's drawings are nevertheless full of liveliness and atmosphere helping Robert Burch tell a more than usually full story about how a small boy's cat had kittens and how his mother wanted them kept out of the house. Incidentally, the family in *Joey's Cat* is black.

Booklist

SOURCE: A review of *Joey's Cat,* in *Booklist,* Vol. 65, No. 18, May 15, 1969, pp. 1071, 1074.

A warm and pleasurable picture-book story about a little black boy and his cat. When danger in the form of a lurking possum threatens her kittens in the garage, Joey's cat, backed by Joey, convinces Joey's reluctant mother that the place for tiny kittens is in the house. The text is simple, the two-color illustrations undistinguished but engaging.

Zena Sutherland

SOURCE: A review of *Joey's Cat,* in *Bulletin of the Center for Children's Books,* Vol. 22, No. 10, June, 1969, pp. 154-55.

A quiet, pleasant, and realistic story about a small Negro boy and his pet. Joey's cat had put her newborn kittens in the garage where nobody could reach them; when she started carrying them out one day, Joey told his father that there was something the cat seemed to be afraid of, and sure enough, there was a big 'possum. Father (a policeman) trapped the animal, but Joey carried the box of kittens into the house. Mother, who said, "Don't get any ideas about bringing those kittens inside this house!" changed her mind when she saw them, and Joey's cat and her babies were firmly ensconced in the kitchen. Although it is low-keyed, this has all the ingredients of read-aloud popularity: a happy family, small animals, a mild crisis happily ended, and a basic wish granted.

SIMON AND THE GAME OF CHANCE (1970)

Kirkus Reviews

SOURCE: A review of *Simon and the Game of Chance,* in *Kirkus Reviews,* Vol. XXXVIII, No. 19, October 1, 1970, p. 1094.

Against a contemporary small-town Georgia backdrop, Simon Ballard lives—life is the Game of the title—and learns, through both private and shared family problems posed with deliberacy but handled with quiet grace. They seem to be around just for the solving, however, and while it's good to see Mrs. Ballard restored to her children and thirteen-year-old Simon no longer uncomfortable as the anomalous middle-child among six, the resolutions are never fully developed. Mr. Ballard's orthodoxy, complete with Scriptural citations, proves later to stem from overreaction to his Depression youth; now it unites the rest of the Ballards as, evidently, only trouble can. First the death of a new baby precipitates Mrs. Ballard's "withdrawal" (not without nebulous precedent) and subsequent hospitalization; Clarissa, nineteen, postpones college to run the household and becomes engaged to Whit, which Simon finds personally threatening. When Whit dies on the day before the wedding in a much-foreshadowed furnace explosion, Clarissa's melancholy rings terrible echoes and then impends another departure (to school) with more ambivalence for Simon who hopes something will stay her again . . . and feels guilty. Mr. Bradley begins to loosen up, presumably on the advice of his wife's doctors, and Simon slowly 'discovers' him and thereafter himself; indeed the whole family acquires perspective and tempering humor—but it's hard to see why, and harder to see how. Saturated with tragedy, bearing down on the psychology button, the story yields to a "way of rejoicing" that comforts without convincing.

Booklist

SOURCE: A review of *Simon and the Game of Chance,* in *Booklist,* Vol. 67, No. 9, January 1, 1971, p. 370.

It is a difficult year for thirteen-year-old Simon Bradley, too big to be a child but not quite grown up. His mother is taken to a sanitarium to recover from extreme depression after the death of the baby, and his father, a stern, Bible-quoting man, evinces little understanding of Simon's needs. Simon's feelings of guilt over wishing for something to happen to keep his beloved sister Clarissa home are intensified when her fiance is killed. While the story is somewhat cheerless and slow moving, it has a quiet strength derived from the sympathetic portrayal of the family interrelationships.

Virginia Haviland

SOURCE: A review of *Simon and the Game of Chance,* in *The Horn Book Magazine,* Vol. XLVII, No. 1, February, 1971, p. 53.

Again, the author uses Georgia as a background in this story of a large family composed of highly individual personalities. Much of the characterization and the problem handling will demand maturity of the reader. The story is told from the point of view of thirteen-year-old Simon, the third of five boys, whose development owes much to his sister, Clarissa, the oldest child in the family. Simon experiences family tragedy in the death of a new little sister, in Mamma's withdrawal (requiring sanitarium treatment), and in the death of Clarissa's fiancé, and rejoices with the family in Mamma's final return home and in Dad's relaxation of his narrow authoritarian views (*his* father had drunk himself to death and his mother had become a religious fanatic). Episodes sharpen with details of the basically loving, though often prickly, relationships. One sees Simon learning when to stay silent in order not to ruin a bit of progress; understanding that "'Life is a game

of chance'"; acknowledging that his father has come a long way in permitting him to play basketball and the family to play a "game of chance"—Monopoly. Simon exhibits the courage, honesty, imagination, and selfless love that are credible in a real, anxious, sensitive child.

Zena Sutherland

SOURCE: A review of *Simon and the Game of Chance,* in *Bulletin of the Center for Children's Books,* Vol. 24, No. 11, July-August, 1971, p. 167.

Simon is one of six children in a family ruled by a stern, tyrannical father who is against any kind of fun, and who is given to long lectures punctuated with Biblical quotations. When the mother of the family becomes mentally ill after the death of a child, it is Clarissa, the only girl, who runs the family. Simon is resentful when Clarissa becomes engaged and is filled with guilt when his wish that something would happen to prevent the marriage coincides with the death of his sister's fiance. The story, written with depth and perception, ends on an encouraging note: mother is home, Clarissa has recovered to an extent from her bereavement and has assured Simon that she understands how he felt, and father has made a few conciliatory gestures. The characterization and style of writing are polished, and if there is little development, it is perhaps the more realistic in a story that focuses on relationships within a family with problems rather than on action.

THE HUNTING TRIP (1971)

June Goodwin

SOURCE: A review of *The Hunting Trip,* in *The Christian Science Monitor,* November 11, 1971, p. B3.

The only things worth slightly more than a shrug in **The Hunting Trip** are the watercolor drawings [by Susanne Suba] of a balding, pillow-shaped man, his incongruously young wife, and lots of dogs with brown, oval spots. But the vapid story provokes no curiosity and moralizes too much about not killing animals for food.

Sidney D. Long

SOURCE: A review of *The Hunting Trip,* in *The Horn Book Magazine,* Vol. XLVIII, No. 1, February, 1972, pp. 39-40.

An eager hunter takes his "very young wife" on a hunting trip, but each time he raises his gun, she voices a sweetly reasonable objection. The grass finches are too small, doves would be a waste of bullets, and "'[i]nstead of two squirrels, wait and shoot one duck. I could roast it for our supper.'" As a result of her delaying tactics, they spend a fine day out-of-doors but shoot nothing; so the husband trades his bullets for cherry jam and peanut butter, and they have a delicious—vegetarian—supper. The illustrations are witty and beautiful. On predominantly white pages, deft sketches accented by watercolor depict the paunchy hunter and his cheerful companion and suggest the exhilaration of a crisp November day. But although appreciation of nature and reverence for life are evident in both text and illustrations, the naïveté of the wife and the determination of the husband leave the reader with the uneasy feeling that the next hunting trip might have a far different ending.

Booklist

SOURCE: A review of *The Hunting Trip,* in *Booklist,* Vol. 68, No. 11, February 1, 1972, p. 465.

Charming watercolor illustrations add to the gentle humor of a picture-book story about a man who takes his young wife along when he goes hunting. Every time the man raises his gun and takes aim his wife, who cannot bear to have the birds and animals killed, cleverly talks him out of shooting. When at the end of the day they return empty handed and the man exchanges his bullets for peanut butter and jam his wife keeps repeating cheerily that hunting is such fun.

DOODLE AND THE GO-CART (1972)

Kirkus Reviews

SOURCE: A review of *Doodle and the Go-Cart,* in *Kirkus Reviews,* Vol. XL, No. 8, April 15, 1972, p. 476.

As soon as Doodle sees his first go-cart he knows he has to have one, but the $200.00 price is not easy for a Georgia farm boy to raise. A succession of money-making schemes is tried and abandoned—selling scarecrows, running errands on muleback, guiding fishermen—until a neighbor introduces him to beaver trapping, which supplemented by some pay and gifts from his supportive father earns him $153.00 before he's put to bed for weeks with bronchitis complications and forbidden even after his recovery to resume trapping. So far both Doodle and the story have been preoccupied with raising money for the go-cart, but when he's offered $70.00 for Addie Flowers, his mule and companion, he rejects the idea and instead makes plans to sell bird houses and wild strawberries come summer. The banality and ultimate sentimentality of the plot are only partly redeemed by the homely particulars of "dirt farm" living and the good-natured but corny banter of Doodle's family and neighbors.

Virginia Haviland

SOURCE: A review of *Doodle and the Go-Cart,* in *The Horn Book Magazine,* Vol. XLVIII, No. 4, August, 1972, p. 368.

Doodle Rounds, an inventive, eager, sixth-grade Georgia farm boy, wants to earn two-hundred dollars for a go-cart. Without allowing an easy success, the author provides a realistic blend of failures and accomplishments. He treats with quiet humor Doodle's fruitless attempts at moneymaking—a fishing-guide service, the making of scarecrows, and "Doodle's Mule Transportation"—and balances these with the profitable trapping of beaver and muskrat. Since Doodle is interrupted in his ventures before earning enough money, Mr. Rounds decides to let Doodle sell the mule, Addie Flowers. (Mr. Rounds had kept the old creature because "there's nothing like plowing a mule to keep you in tune with nature.") The solid characterization—as if the characters were all neighbors of the author—gives the story the fidelity of the author's other writings about his own region. The ink-line sketches [by Alan Tiegreen] are substantial; they catch mood, humor, and action admirably.

Rae Marshall

SOURCE: A review of Doodle and the Go-Cart, in *School Library Journal,* Vol. 19, No. 1, September, 1972, p. 74.

Set in rural Georgia, this above-average contemporary story will be appreciated by kids interested in raising money to get things they want. Doodle tries out a go-cart at a party and thereafter longs to own one. Since his father is a dirt farmer, Doodle tries to acquire the money by selling rides on his mule, Addie Flowers, and by fashioning and selling scarecrows. These ploys fail, but Doodle does earn some money (not enough) from the sale of beavers he traps. Doodle's father finally offers him an opportunity to sell the mule, but Doodle decides he'd rather hawk birdcages next than obtain a go-cart without his mule there to watch him race around the pasture. Plot development is plausible, and the good relationship between the imaginative Doodle and his father is well handled.

Zena Sutherland

SOURCE: A review of *Doodle and the Go-Cart,* in *Bulletin of the Center for Children's Books,* Vol. 26, No. 7, March, 1973, p. 103.

Instantly smitten by the go-cart he had seen at a party, Doodle was determined to get one despite the fact that a go-cart cost $200. He could have one, his father said, if he earned the money—but how could a farm boy earn that much? Doodle tries various projects, accumulates over $150, and has to stop his most lucrative project, trapping, when he becomes ill. When he is offered the profit to be gained if the family's mule is sold, Doodle decides he can't give up a loved animal—and sets about planning another project, spurning the chance to get his go-cart then and there. Written in a pleasant, light style but slow-moving and fragmented, a story that stresses a boy's perseverance and resourcefulness.

HUT SCHOOL AND THE WARTIME HOME-FRONT HEROES (1974; also as *Home-Front Heroes,* 1992)

Kirkus Reviews

SOURCE: A review of *Hut School and the Wartime Home-Front Heroes,* in *Kirkus Reviews,* Vol. XLII, No. 8, April 15, 1974, p. 423.

Rationing, radio drama and victory gardens are now prime material for revival, so its easy to get in the spirit with Kate Coleman when she discovers that the War is bringing adventure to her corner of rural Georgia. Even school becomes exciting when her sixth grade class must move into a farmer's hut across the field because of overcrowding, and led by Kate, all the town kids pitch in to help labor-short Farmer Poe harvest his cotton crop so that Zach and Tootie Poe can come back to school. Only once, when Ivy Holbrook's brother is killed in action, does the war strike closer than sugar shortages and cabbage hoeing, but harder times ahead are foreshadowed as the beloved teacher Miss Jordan enlists in the Waves and Dad reveals that he has been drafted. References to Ish Kabibble, Fibber McGee and Veronica Lake fly fast and furious in and around the episodic plot, and one can't help recalling Zibby O'Neal's *War Work* which captured the spirit of homefront humor and patriotism without relying so obviously on mass-media memory props. Though this is seldom more than an agreeable nostalgia piece, the author of **Queenie Peavy** injects small-town schooldays with a spark or two of distinguishing vitality.

Booklist

SOURCE: A review of *Hut School and the Wartime Home-Front Heroes,* in *Booklist,* Vol. 70, No. 17, May 1, 1974, p. 998.

The Americans have been fighting the second World War for two years by the time Kate Coleman enters sixth grade; she and her parents are nearly used to living with gas rationing and a host of other inconveniences. This year, on account of the war, Kate has some new experiences: attending school in a primitive cabin to accommodate temporary overcrowding, learning of the death of a classmate's brother, and working the Georgia cotton fields to help fill a labor shortage. Along with all this comes Miss Jordan, Kate's teacher, who dares to show her class that learning can be fun. Scenes from this book, unpretentiously filled with details of everyday life, provide an entertaining look at a time which may at first seem light years away but which, ironically, has numerous parallels to our time.

Virginia Haviland

SOURCE: A review of *Hut School and the Wartime Home-Front Heroes,* in *The Horn Book Magazine,* Vol. L, No. 4, August, 1974, p. 374.

The story of several months in small-town Georgia during World War II seems less a piece of historical fiction than accounts about the period usually do; such matters as gasoline rationing appear quite contemporary. Kate and her sixth-grade class move temporarily into a garden storage cabin because their school suddenly must accommodate seventy new children. Miss Jordan, Kate's teacher, and the pupils undertake projects based on generosity and patriotism. The classmates, led by Kate, volunteer for cottonpicking, to enable two farm children to shorten their seasonal absence from school; sorrowfully but bravely, they face the news of soldiers' deaths and of their beloved teacher's enlistment. The story displays affection for and empathy with children; the clear glimpse of the period is comparable to that in the Moffat stories set in war-time Connecticut.

Zena Sutherland

SOURCE: A review of *Hut School and the Wartime Home-Front Heroes,* in *Bulletin of the Center for Children's Books,* Vol. 28, No. 1, September, 1974, p. 2.

Kate and her sixth grade classmates accept with grace the fact that they must move into a hut; their school is short of space since the Ordance Depot children have been sent there. There is a plot thread in this World War II story, but the appeal of the book is in the authenticity of the period detail and the growing understanding of the children of what war means. There are plenty of lively incidents, a few characters who seem overdrawn (a harsh schoolteacher and a surly farmer) while most of the children are convincing, and some local (Georgia) color. The book is weakened by the inclusion of too many current titles of movies, songs, et cetera; good research, but at times intrusively incorporated.

THE JOLLY WITCH (1975)

Barbara Elleman

SOURCE: A review of *The Jolly Witch,* in *Booklist,* Vol. 72, No. 7, December 1, 1975, p. 512.

What is a jolly witch to do when deposited with a cross old woman, her unsmiling son, their whining cat, and a canary that never sings? Cluny, who can't be anything but jolly, resolves to make the best of the situation. With her broom, Ol' Blue, Cluny attempts to teach the woman to fly, and the resulting incidents should make children chuckle. In return the woman teaches Cluny to cook—without spiders! In the predictable conclusion Ol' Blue swishes the woman away while a smiling son, a purring cat, and a singing canary cavort happily below with the jolly witch.

Ruth B. Stoffer

SOURCE: A review of *The Jolly Witch,* in *School Library Journal,* Vol. 22, No. 5, January, 1976, p. 35.

Cluny is deported from the witch colony because, like many a primary-grade witch before her, she is too young, pretty, and jolly. Left by a peddler on the doorstep of a most unjolly old housewife and her handsome son, she soon switches roles with the old crone through a bit of witchy trickery. The plot is developed with impudent dialogue and amusing details, and the format, 6" x 8" pages with a fair amount of print and black-and-white ink sketches [by Leigh Grant], may qualify this as younger fiction.

Zena Sutherland

SOURCE: A review of *The Jolly Witch,* in *Bulletin of the Center for Children's Books,* Vol. 29, No. 6, February, 1976, p. 92.

Traded to a peddler because she was too merry a witch, little Cluny was deposited on the doorstep of a cross old woman with a handsome, dour son and two morose pets. The old woman didn't like Cluny's cheerfulness but let her stay so that the jolly witch could teach her to fly; little by little, Cluny improved the atmosphere and made its inhabitants happy. She even put the old woman on her own broomstick, which flew back to its home, leaving a smiling son, a purring cat, a singing canary, and a happy Cluny. The illustrations are adequate; the story, simply and smoothly told, has a bit of humor echoed in the illustrations, but the story line is slight.

TWO THAT WERE TOUGH (1976)

Kirkus Reviews

SOURCE: A review of *Two That Were Tough,* in *Kirkus Reviews,* Vol. XLIV, No. 20, October 15, 1976, p. 1136.

. . . [T]his ruminative friendship, between old Mr. Hilton, owner of a decaying grist mill, and Wild Wings, a feral chicken that roosts in the millyard, is sheer unmodulated melancholy. In the course of an 80 page vignette Mr. Hilton comes to accept the necessity of leaving his home to live with a daughter in Atlanta, and gives up a plan to capture Wild Wings and take him along. . . . That's all, but Burch's habit of echoing and explicating the old man's most obvious thoughts (" . . . if he were drawing up a list today, he would be especially thankful that he had not broken any bones when he fell from the ladder") robs the tough old companions of their dignity and gives us a tale that's not so much poignant as anemic.

Gale K. Shonkwiler

SOURCE: A review of *Two That Were Tough,* in *School Library Journal,* Vol. 23, No. 5, January, 1977, pp. 87-88.

Mr. Hilton, a gristmill owner living in rural Georgia, is reluctant to give in to his daughter Mildred's insistent requests that he move to her home in Atlanta so she can take care of him. During his last year in the country he becomes increasingly fond of a spunky chicken named Wild Wings who symbolizes his youthful spirit and independence. However, a few mishaps (he falls off a ladder trying to capture the bird) and a bout with the flu convince him that the move to his daughter's place is inevitable. Conveniently, some new neighbors arrive who agree to see the Wild Wings through the winters. Although children will undoubtedly enjoy the antics of the rambunctious chicken, the problems of aging are not made at all compelling and readers will not readily take an interest in the old man's plight.

Denise M. Wilms

SOURCE: A review of *Two That Were Tough,* in *Booklist,* Vol. 73, No. 11, February 1, 1977, p. 805.

Mr. Hilton has held at bay the compromises old age inflicts for a long time, but now he knows that his physical unsteadiness will force him to accede to his daughter's wishes that he leave his gristmill and come to live in Atlanta. The elderly man's decline is paralleled in the fortunes of a tough old rooster named "Wild Wings" that makes its home around the mill. The rooster's concessions to old age—a too narrow escape from a fox, roosting in the shelter of Mr. Hilton's porch earlier in the year—are what give impetus to Mr. Hilton's appraisal of his own situation. The regretful resignation he feels at his impending loss of independence is mitigated when friendly new neighbors make it possible for him to leave the old bird free but assured of a helping handout in the winter. The similarities between Mr. Hilton and Wild Wings are too deliberately defined, but this obviousness is tempered by the reality of incidents bearing on both their lives. Personality comes to dominate, and the strong sentiment underlying the story isn't really maudlin. Bittersweet, with some staying power.

Zena Sutherland

SOURCE: A review of *Two That Were Tough,* in *Bulletin of the Center for Children's Books,* Vol. 30, No. 8, April, 1977, p. 118.

Old Mr. Hilton lives alone in the Georgia countryside, his once-busy gristmill idle most of the time; his married daughter urges him to come to Atlanta and live with her, but he resists adamantly until he is ill. Then he promises that he will move next winter. All alone, Mr. Hilton has been talking to a scrappy rooster that has gone feral since his owners, next door, moved away; "Wild Wings," the old man calls him, and compares himself to the chicken: proud, solitary, and self-sufficient. He wants to take this bit of his old life with him, but when the time to move comes, Mr. Hilton decides that Wild Wings should have his freedom while he can. This has a poignant message about old age and dependency, but it may not appeal to some young readers, and there is a static quality to the text that is not compensated for by a device like the interaction between animals in De Jong's *Along Came a Dog* or by any plot line; this is a series of episodes and, while the writing is smooth, the wistful inevitability of the situation is depressing.

THE WHITMAN KICK (1977)

Booklist

SOURCE: A review of *The Whitman Kick,* in *Booklist,* Vol. 74, No. 5, November 1, 1977, p. 467.

Alan Ponder, a newly enlisted 17-year-old soldier at the start of World War II, reminisces about his last two high school years, when his longtime special friendship with Amanda Moore crumbled as she turned away from Alan's immaturity to go steady with another boy who made her pregnant. Alan also recalls close relationships with his father, two sisters, and his mother, who left the family to live with her husband's brother—a scandal the small Georgia town did not let go unnoticed. As Alan struggled with his feelings—at first hating both his mother and Amanda—he gradually came around to realizing that he could forgive and accept others as they are. Believable characterizations and natural dialog enhance a bittersweet teenage story.

Kirkus Reviews

SOURCE: A review of *The Whitman Kick,* in *Kirkus Reviews,* Vol. XLVI, No. 1, January 1, 1978, p. 7.

It's 1942 and Alan Ponder, at "barely seventeen" the youngest man in his army barracks, remembers the days before Pearl Harbor—especially his junior year with Amanda, his special friend since sixth grade. But just as their relationship is verging on something more, Amanda is forbidden to see Alan because his mother has run off to Alabama, causing a scandal in their small Georgia town. Before long Amanda is going with Alan's sister's boyfriend, and though Irene gets Hap back for keeps, Amanda meanwhile gets pregnant. And Alan, deserted by both his mother and Amanda, is unyielding in his resentment. The bittersweet coating on all of this is a bit thick but nevertheless effective, blending as it does the ambience of time and place with the changing personal relationships that Alan finds hard to accept.

Zena Sutherland

SOURCE: A review of *The Whitman Kick,* in *Bulletin of the Center for Children's Books,* Vol. 31, No. 7, March, 1978, pp. 107-08.

Writing for older readers than he usually does, and doing it very well indeed, Burch tells the story of Alan's last two

years of high school through Alan. Newly inducted into the army, Alan remembers . . . he and Amanda had been friends since sixth grade, sharing a love of poetry, and they were just beginning to become physically aware of each other in their junior year. Amanda's socially ambitious mother ruled that her daughter must stop seeing Alan; in part she considered him personally undesirable, in part she disdained him because—as the whole town knew—his mother had gone off and had been living with another man. When trying to outwit Amanda's mother by setting up an arranged double date, Alan loses his love, for she briefly falls for the other boy. The affair is soon over, but Amanda is pregnant. When she comes to Alan for a friend's comfort, he rejects her. Bitterly she points out that his weakness is in never being able to forgive, and he remembers this when his mother returns; at first hostile, he relents in time to save the relationship. And in time, he thinks of Amanda with love. Forgiving, he stops en route to the induction center to send her a fine copy of *Leaves of Grass* in memory of their shared love of Whitman's poetry. The love story is nicely balanced with family relationships, the characterization and dialogue are excellent, and the book gives a poignant, credible picture of adolescence and of a small Georgia community in the 1940's.

Ann A. Flowers

SOURCE: A review of *The Whitman Kick,* in *The Horn Book Magazine,* Vol. LIV, No. 2, April, 1978, p. 168.

The small southern town of Ellenville, Georgia, at the beginning of World War II is the setting for a novel of young love cast in a pensive mood. Alan Ponder's best friend and constant companion was Amanda Moore, who at sixteen was a year older than he. Their long friendship was based on many common intellectual interests, especially poetry; but Alan, unfortunately, was not sufficiently mature to be aware of Amanda's growing emotional needs. As a result, the girl began to go out with another young man and became pregnant. She went away to stay with relatives, and Alan—hurt and furious—finished school and joined the army. Creating a small-town atmosphere is one of the author's special strengths; many of the ancillary characters, such as Alan's weak father and Amanda's snobbish mother, are well done. The first-person, present-tense narrative, however, is flat and the motivation is sometimes unconvincing. Yet the unhappy ending of a relationship that could have been strong and enduring, were it not betrayed by chronological mismatching, has a bittersweet authenticity.

WILKIN'S GHOST (1978)

Linda Silver

SOURCE: A review of *Wilkin's Ghost,* in *School Library Journal,* Vol. 25, No. 1, September, 1978, p. 131.

Rural Georgia during the Depression is once again the scene of Burch's novel. The middle brother of *Tyler, Wilkin, and Skee* tells the story, evoking almost drowsy visions of a time which seems, in retrospect, very simple, very basic, very innocent. Interwoven with the events of everyday life and the up and down though loving relationship of the brothers with one another and with their parents, is the story of Wilkin's friendship with Alex—a runaway boy whom Wilkin first sees under the supposedly haunted hanging tree. This ghostly image symbolizes Alex who remains throughout the story a likable, exciting but elusive figure—one whose apparent desire to become a solid part of the community is always dubious. On the verge of hopping a freight with his friend, who entices him with stories of the world "out there," Wilkin learns the truth about Alex and realizes that he has been taken in. A modest story in design and execution, this portrays believable characters and events, and places them in a setting that is totally real. *Wilkin's Ghost* is less episodic and more serious than Burch's previous book but it offers the same down-to-earth, good-natured picture of boyhood past.

Paul Heins

SOURCE: A review of *Wilkin's Ghost*, in *The Horn Book Magazine*, Vol. LV, No. 5, October, 1978, p. 514.

When thirteen-year-old Wilkin Coley, the rural Georgia boy whose life was filled with chores, heard the train whistle at night, he thought, "Someday I'd go somewhere too; I'd see a lot of places." Wilkin was somewhat superstitious and believed a local legend that the tree from which a man had been hanged was haunted. To his relief he discovered that the white object he saw during a thunderstorm was only the shirt of Alex Folsom, a boy of about fifteen, who had just returned from Atlanta after an absence of two years. Alex had been accused of stealing but denied his guilt. Wilkin generously befriended the older boy, helped him when he was sick, and found work for him. Tired of his humdrum life, the farm boy, who was actually on the best of terms with his parents and brothers, decided to run away to Atlanta with Alex but was deterred at the last moment when Alex proved after all to be a liar and a thief. Brief, telling strokes present the activities of local farm life; and as in *Tyler, Wilkin, and Skee,* the characterization of the Coley family and their neighbors excels in its perceptiveness and humor. The first-person presentation of Wilkin's experiences and errors of judgment, however, is somewhat low-keyed, and Alex's inconsistent actions leave the reader with unanswered questions.

Denise M. Wilms

SOURCE: A review of *Wilkin's Ghost,* in *Booklist,* Vol. 75, No. 7, December 1, 1978, p. 615.

While housesitting for the Todd sisters, Wilkin Coley crosses paths with Alex Folsom, a boy slightly older than himself whom he remembers as having been accused of robbing the local general store two years ago. As Alex explains his plight—he's left home in Atlanta because of a hostile new stepfather and isn't up to facing his disreputable local relatives just yet—Wilkin begins to figure ways to ease Alex' predicament. Most importantly, he arranges for Alex to stay with the Todd sisters on their return and to work for Mr. Larson, the man whose store Alex allegedly robbed. Alex does right by all concerned, vindicating his reputation and fitting in well all around, until the darker side of his personality surfaces in a confrontation with Wilkin the night the two are set to run off by freight train to Atlanta. Set in the rural Georgia of the 1930s, the story is jolting and thought-provoking yet brightened by the family solidarity of the Coleys and the inherent sensibility of a stunned but emotionally intact Wilkin.

Zena Sutherland

SOURCE: A review of *Wilkin's Ghost,* in *Bulletin of the Center for Children's Books,* Vol. 32, No. 6, February, 1979, p. 96.

After a long absence, the three brothers of *Tyler, Wilkin, and Skee* are back; it is thirteen-year-old Wilkin who tells the story, set in rural Georgia in 1935. The "ghost" who frightens Wilkin when he's alone in the woods proves to be Alex Folsom, an older boy who has come back to the area although he left under suspicion of being a thief. Wilkin is convinced that Alex has changed, talks a storekeeper into giving him a job, and helps him find lodging. One of his bonds with Alex is their common dream of riding the railroad and seeing the world. Wilkin's family situation is depicted with warmth and affection, and Burch gives an excellent view—flavored by details of locale and period—of both the local community and the farm family. Wanderlust impels Wilkin, nevertheless, to agree to Alex's plans of running away—but just as they are about to go off, Wilkin discovers that his friend had indeed been a thief in the past and has, even more recently, done some shoplifting and has committed another theft and let another boy stand accused. And so the train goes off into the night and Wilkin sadly turns back. The plot is not a strongly dramatic one, despite the ending, but the writing style, setting, characterization, and dialogue more than compensate.

IDA EARLY COMES OVER THE MOUNTAIN (1980)

Marjorie Lewis

SOURCE: A review of *Ida Early Comes Over the Mountain,* in *School Library Journal,* Vol. 27, No. 2, October, 1980, p. 142.

A beautifully wrought story of a mountain Mary Poppins, Ida Early, who shows up in the Sutton's doorway one day during the Depression, looking for a place to stop awhile.

Initially wary of this strange woman who looks a lot like a towering scarecrow in overalls and clodhoppers, the family succumbs to her charm when she whirls her sweater about her head and flings it neatly onto the coatrack across the room. Besides, since Mrs. Sutton's death, a woman is needed to take care of the four children: Randall, who narrates the book, Ellen, and the young twins Dewey and Clay, who adore Ida at first sight. The book works on two levels—the hilarious account of Ida Early's exotic housekeeping in which real cleverness and skill is as effective and amazing as any fantasy magic, and the gentle, touching story of an ungainly woman's longing for beauty and femininity. That both levels meet, resolve themselves satisfactorily, and leave the characters deeply changed is the true success of this fine book.

Zena Sutherland

SOURCE: A review of *Ida Early Comes Over the Mountain,* in *Bulletin of the Center for Children's Books,* Vol. 34, No. 4, December, 1980, pp. 66-67.

The place is rural Georgia, the time is the Depression Era, and the protagonist is a tall, awkward, merry woman who shows up at the Sutton home looking for a job. Since the mother of the four Sutton children has died recently, Mr. Sutton takes Ida Early on as a housekeeper. Ida Early is casual about chores and tells tall tales about her past, but her humor and understanding endear her to the children. Burch has created a memorable character, but she's more than entertaining: through their embarrassment when Ida Early appears at school, is jeered at for her appearance (haystack hair, overalls, and clodhoppers) and not defended by the two older Sutton children, the latter learn the shame of denying a friend. The lesson is gently taught, with a poignant tenderness, and Ida Early's sudden departure (and subsequent return) gives structure to an otherwise episodic story, written with a light, sure touch.

Paul Heins

SOURCE: A review of *Ida Early Comes Over the Mountain,* in *The Horn Book Magazine,* Vol. LVI, No. 6, December, 1980, p. 639.

The motherless Sutton children—Randall, aged eleven; Ellen, aged twelve; and the five-year-old twins Clay and Dewey—were glad when their father hired Ida Early as a housekeeper. After the departure of Aunt Ernestine, whom Randall thought of "as a battleship" always ready for war, the children thoroughly enjoyed the games and antics of the plain tall woman scarcely out of her teens, who was dressed in overalls and clodhopper shoes and had "hair that looked like a frazzled hearthbroom." One day in the schoolyard, however, some children made fun of her, and Ida Early tried to change her appearance and subdue her manner, thus creating a crisis in the lives of the Sutton children. The story set in Georgia during the Depression is at first episodic, but halfway through it

is given a stronger focus when the genial but rustic Mary Poppins-like character is temporarily rebuffed. Much of the humor is derived from the tall-tale elements, and a spirit of good-natured fun is predominant in the storytelling.

Judith Goldberger

SOURCE: A review of *Ida Early Comes Over the Mountain,* in *Booklist,* Vol. 77, No. 8, December 15, 1980, p. 571.

When Ida Early arrives unannounced at the Sutton doorstep, Randall's father hires her to care for the family. Disapproving Aunt Earnestine notes Ida's deficiencies: she has peculiar habits that children should not learn (such as tossing clothes onto hat racks across the room) and has a way of getting others to do her work. But Ida supplies the essential ingredient for a motherless family—loving attention—and the Suttons, after dispensing with Aunt Earnestine's self-righteous presence, soon find Ida's bizarre appearance, autobiographical tall tales, and excellent biscuits comfortable. Her portrait, together with the family interactions, form the mainstay of a story set in rural Georgia toward the end of the Depression; both plot and viewpoint wander in a relaxed, mildly frustrating way. But there is enough substance to hold the book together and make it memorable.

Kirkus Reviews

SOURCE: A review of *Ida Early Comes Over the Mountain,* in *Kirkus Reviews,* Vol. XLIX, No. 1, January 1, 1981, p. 6.

A Depression-era, Blue Ridge Mary Poppins, Ida Early turns up grinning on the Suttons' doorstep just when they need her. Their mother has died some months earlier and their Aunt Earnestine, who has been "taking care of" them, is critical and stern. The Suttons happily replace her with Ida, a six-foot scarecrow in overalls and brogans, with a tossing, roping, and shooting aim to beat the traveling carnival's crack shot, and a memory so good "she can recall things that never even happened." Most of her recollections concern her past exploits as world champion of just about every activity you can mention. Her stories, her goofy grin, and her unorthodox housekeeping and good cooking win the hearts of the five-year-old Sutton twins, their father, and the older children Ellen (twelve) and Randall (eleven). Still, Ellen and Randall fail to come to Ida's defense when their schoolyard friends make fun of her looks, and as a result Ida is hurt and withdrawn and the two children are filled with remorse. After that you can never forget the wistful side of Ida—but you can trust her to rise to the occasion when she finds herself on the school stage with a rope in her hand, an angry bear loose in the audience, and her former tormentors cheering her on. Ida never disappoints but she won't hesitate to teach a hard lesson when it's called for. And she's a real, zesty original.

CHRISTMAS WITH IDA EARLY (1983)

Kirkus Reviews

SOURCE: A review of *Christmas with Ida Early,* in *Kirkus Reviews,* Vol. LI, No. 17, September 1, 1983, p. 160.

A falloff from **Ida Early Comes Over the Mountain**—full of plaudits for the Suttons' earthy Mary Poppins, but short on fresh ways for her to shine. Dour, disapproving Aunt Earnestine comes for a visit and comes down with the flu; saved by Ida's nursing, she's almost unrecognizable—playing five-card-draw with the twins on Christmas Eve, presenting Ida herself with "decadent" lounging pajamas on Christmas. (Earnestine might have been different, Mr. Sutton has reminded the children, had there been an Ida Early to brighten up *her* motherless childhood.) Ida's chief antagonist, though, is the new young minister—as much of a stick-in-the-mud, it quickly appears, as his older predecessor. Their running battle climaxes at the Christmas Eve manager-"tableau"—when Ida, a Wise Man, has the donkey yodel at the end of each stanza of "Silent Night." (Earlier and better, she uses her knack for ventriloquism to have the Thanksgiving turkey save his neck.) Not surprisingly, Brother Preston asks her not to come back for the evening performance—but only she, of course, can get the donkey into the manger (or handle the wild dog who disrupts the performance). Randall and Ellen, the two older Sutton children, speak up to Brother Preston about the true religious spirit; hen Frizzy demonstrates it—with much cackling—by laying an egg on stage; and Ida, unresentful and uncowed, hikes over to the next county to get illegal Christmas firecrackers . . . inviting Brother Preston for the show. (En route, with the frost turning everything silver: "The splendor of the greatest cathedral in the world couldn't compare with it.") Sadly: sentimental farce.

Jean Hammond Zimmerman

SOURCE: A review of *Christmas with Ida Early,* in *School Library Journal,* Vol. 30, No. 2, October, 1983, p. 178.

Burch has written another well-crafted novel about life in the rural South. A sequel to **Ida Early Comes Over the Mountain,** it continues the story of Ida Early, a tall, fun-filled character who arrived one day without warning and became the housekeeper and friend of the Sutton family. Here, the Sutton children try to encourage a romance between Ida and a preacher straight from the seminary. They never succeed but the conflicts between serious Brother Preston and free-spirit Ida provide the tension needed to keep the plot moving. The books about Ida Early are successful because they are based on the realization that life is sometimes hard and that is is better met with humor, courage and good spirit. As a result, despite the fun of the situations and characterizations, the books never degenerate into mere silliness. Ida Early is a heroine worth knowing.

Barbara Elleman

SOURCE: A review of *Christmas with Ida Early,* in *Booklist,* Vol. 80, No. 3, October 1, 1983, p. 236.

Life for the Suttons has never been the same since the zesty Ida Early came to be their cook, housekeeper, and friend. Her eccentric antics and tall tales ramble through one family escapade after another, all recounted with good humor from 12-year-old Randall's point of view. When the new preacher decides to put on a living Christmas tableau that involves some real animals—and Ida—readers can be sure that the festivities will be far from normal. A captivating story with lots of heart, and a recommended December read-aloud that will elicit lots of laughs and a few thoughtful moments as well.

Mary M. Burns

SOURCE: A review of *Christmas with Ida Early,* in *The Horn Book Magazine,* Vol. LIX, No. 6, December, 1983, pp. 693-94.

Ida Early is a genuine original—a memorable character in children's literature. She and Mary Poppins have much in common: Both nurture a family of children, bring order out of chaos, and utter pronouncements notable for their common sense. But there the resemblance ends, for Ida Early's adventures are in the tall-tale tradition of American humor. The story of her latest escapades, which follows **Ida Early Comes Over the Mountain** but can also stand alone, focuses on Thanksgiving and Christmas celebrations into which she interjects her own inventive touches. To save the turkey, which has become a pet, she reveals her talents as a ventriloquist and, with the aplomb of a master chef, substitutes tuna casserole. In contrast, the Christmas festivities have more poignant overtones, for her good intentions bring her into confrontation with a conservative young minister. Much to the disappointment of the matchmaking Sutton children, who think her well suited to be a clergyman's wife, she is summarily dismissed from the cast of the Nativity tableau. But with the savoir faire born of experience she assures them that the minister will undoubtedly join the family for Christmas dinner: "He and I may not agree on everything, but at least we can talk about it. . . . And he likes my cooking." Ida is colorful, charitable, and long suffering—but hardly mild. Her flights of fancy temper truth with kindness, making hard times bearable without minimizing difficulties. A fine choice for reading aloud, the book evokes a specific time and place—the Depression in the rural South—and suggests a universal, timely theme.

KING KONG AND OTHER POETS (1986)

Betsy Hearne

SOURCE: A review of *King Kong and Other Poets,* in *Bulletin of the Center for Children's Books,* Vol. 40, No. 2, October, 1986, p. 22.

Mousy-looking newcomer Marilyn seems a misfit in Andy's sixth-grade class until she wins a newspaper contest for one of her poems and is elected "poet laureate" by her schoolmates. Still, she remains a puzzle to most of them. Living in a ritzy resort, she seems to get everything she wants, yet often appears sad and resistant to overtures of friendship. What Andy finds out when he gets past her whimsically humorous verses is a lonely person whose mother has died and whose father has had a nervous breakdown. Although the characters and group dynamics are realistic, there's no action in the book outside of Marilyn's emerging happiness as her father improves. Ultimately, this is a vignette—the passage of two children through a brief friendship—that will hold readers with a tug of sympathy for the protagonist.

Kirkus Reviews

SOURCE: A review of *King Kong and Other Poets,* in *Kirkus Reviews,* Vol. LIV, No. 19, October 1, 1986, p. 1508.

Marilyn, the new girl in Andy's class, is hard to get to know. She's mousy-looking and doesn't say much. But when she wins first prize in a city-wide poetry contest, she earns the respect of her sixth-grade classmates, who elect her their poet laureate. Through the poems she writes that year, Marilyn is able to communicate with the other children. But is what she writes the truth? She claims to live in exclusive Garden Hills and to come from a wealthy and impressive family. However, as the year progresses, the students learn that some of what Marilyn writes is the truth—and some is what she wishes were the truth. Several children are disappointed and accuse her of lying; others are curious; still others, like Andy, are simply forgiving and want to know the "real" Marilyn.

For the thoughtful reader, a gentle story of acceptance and adjustment: Andy and his classmates struggle to understand Marilyn, who is grappling with her own problems as she and her father try to adjust to her mother's death. The story is evenly told with interesting, real, and likeable characters, but the telling is quiet and the mystery about Marilyn so light that some young readers may give up on the story, and those who stay with it may feel disappointed. Marilyn's "mystery" is touching but not extraordinary; the unraveling is sketchy.

Publishers Weekly

SOURCE: A review of *King Kong and Other Poets,* in *Publishers Weekly,* Vol. 230, No. 18, October 31, 1986, p. 69.

A quiet loner named Marilyn stymies her new sixth grade class in a small Georgiatown, who lives in Garden Hills, an exclusive resort. Then one of her poems wins a contest and she becomes the class "poet laureate," portraying herself as a pampered rich girl. But Marilyn's poems reflect her imaginings of a happier time; her father is a sullen handyman at Garden Hill, recovering from a nervous breakdown. When he recovers, they leave town, with Marilyn having affected the lives of those who knew her. Burch describes Marilyn both through her poetry and through the eyes of Andy, a classmate, a technique that reveals both her flaws and her heroism. The author of *Queenie Peavey* and other notable books provides another tale about a poignant but never pathetic heroine, whose outwardly simple story reveals important underlying themes.

Rita Auerbach

SOURCE: A review of *King Kong and Other Poets,* in *School Library Journal,* Vol. 33, No. 6, February, 1987, pp. 76, 78.

Marilyn, the enigmatic, reclusive new student in Andy's sixth-grade class, lives in the elegant resort Garden Hills, which is off-limits to her classmates. She begins to reveal herself, however, when she wins a local writing contest and is named the class poet laureate. But the family and menagerie of pets she claims in her poems seem only to be wishful fantasies, and Andy finds their friendship alternatively encouraging, frustrating, and hurtful. Is her father a caretaker at the resort or a grieving former electronics executive? Did Marilyn deceive her classmates or merely exercise legitimate "poetic license"? (It is surprising in a book by Burch to find a character's value measured by her father's financial situation. This is undoubtedly one of the issues the author wants his readers to ponder, but children may not question the equation of professional status with personal worth.) As Marilyn returns to live in California, readers are almost certain that they know the truth, but enough doubt remains to leave them thinking about her for some time. Marilyn is not nearly so memorable a character as Burch's *Queenie Peavy* or Ida Early (all Viking), but young readers should enjoy puzzling over the questions of truth and deception raised here.

Additional coverage of Burch's life and career is contained in the following sources published by The Gale Group: *Contemporary Authors,* Vols. 5-8R; *Contemporary Authors New Revision Series,* Vols. 2, 17, 71; *Dictionary of Literary Biography,* Vol. 52; *Junior DISCovering Authors;* *Major Authors and Illustrators for Children and Young Adults;* **and** *Something about the Author,* Vols. 1, 74.

George Cruikshank
1792-1878

English illustrator, author/illustrator, and reteller.

Major works include *German Popular Stories* (by Jacob Ludwig and Carl Wilhelm Grimm, 1823), *Oliver Twist; or, The Parish Boy's Progress* (by Charles Dickens, 1838), *Jack Sheppard* (by W. Harrison Ainsworth, 1839), *George Cruikshank's Fairy Library* (three volumes, 1853-54), *The Bottle* (1847).

Major works about the illustrator include *The Life of George Cruikshank: In Two Epochs* (by Blanchard Jerrold, 1882), *George Cruikshank: A Catalogue Raisonne of the Work Executed During the Years 1806-1877* (by A. M. Cohn, 1924), *George Cruikshank: His Life and Work as a Book Illustrator* (by Ruari McLean, 1948), *George Cruikshank: A Revaluation* (edited by Robert L. Patten, 1974), *The Caricatures of George Cruikshank* (by John Wardroper, 1977), *The Man Who Drew the Drunkard's Daughter: The Life and Art of George Cruikshank* (by Hilary and Mary Evans, 1978).

INTRODUCTION

An illustrator, political cartoonist, and painter who was also a writer, Cruikshank is considered the preeminent graphic artist of his day. Acknowledged as the first important English artist to make his living as a book illustrator, he worked for seventy-five years and was extremely popular for more than fifty years. Cruikshank illustrated great eighteenth-century English novels as well as the melodramas and costume dramas of the nineteenth century; in addition, he provided the pictures for several works that drew from other traditions, such as continental literature and folklore. Both humorist and moralist, Cruikshank is generally regarded as an artistic genius whose published works—over 200 illustrated volumes as well as chapbooks, almanacs, and illustrations for periodicals—provide an accurate, perceptive reflection of three eras of English society. He is also considered a master caricaturist and graphic innovator as well as a major proponent of the narrative tradition in visual art. Recognized as a particularly versatile artist with a wide range of both subject and emotion, Cruikshank is praised for his imagination, ingenuity, and humor as well as for his technical skill. He is ultimately regarded as an artist whose works emphasize his profound concern for humanity while depicting the essential drollery of life.

Cruikshank wrote and illustrated socially-minded pamphlets and retold classic folk and fairy tales with a decidedly moralistic slant. However, he is best known as an artist. Cruikshank provided the illustrations for works by such authors as Tobias Smollett, Henry Fielding, Robert

Southey, Washington Irving, Victor Hugo, Harriet Beecher Stowe, and Sir Walter Scott. He is considered the definitive illustrator of several books, most notably *Oliver Twist* by Charles Dickens and the works of W. Harrison Ainsworth, a popular English writer of historical fiction. Especially well known as an illustrator for children, Cruikshank provided the pictures for volumes of fairy stories and folktales, most notably those collected by the Brothers Grimm; two books by Juliana Horatia Ewing; and several works with strong child appeal such as John Bunyan's *Pilgrim's Progress*, Daniel Defoe's *Robinson Crusoe*, Miguel de Cervantes's *Don Quixote*, and *The Adventures of Baron Munchausen*. As with his adult works, Cruikshank is often considered the best illustrator of several of these books, especially the two volumes of Grimm's fairy tales—*German Popular Stories* and *Grimm's Goblins* (1867)—that include his art. Cruikshank often depicts the supernatural in his books. He filled his works with fairies, sprites, brownies, and gnomes as well as witches, ogres, and devils, placing them in realistic contexts. Although he had an affinity for the grotesque and the macabre, Cruikshank underscored many of his books with humor and often employed visual puns and parodies in his art.

A self-taught artist, Cruikshank worked exclusively in black and white; later in his life, he became a oil painter and watercolorist of some note. Considered the heir to such artists as William Hogarth, James Gillray, and Thomas Rowlandson, Cruikshank drew subjects that were designed to elicit laughter, stimulate the imagination, and spur action on serious social and moral issues. Cruikshank characteristically favored woodcuts and etchings; the latter are often lauded for their delicate lines and subtle shadings. His art also reflects Cruikshank's distinctive style. Using squiggled lines, somewhat skewed perspectives, and wild exaggeration, he drew figures that are acknowledged for their realistic facial expressions as well as their expressive postures and gestures. He is also credited for his use of detail—his crowd scenes are thought to be especially well drawn—as well as for the accuracy of his architectural settings and period costumes. The novelist and poet G. K. Chesterton, writing about *Oliver Twist,* claimed that Cruikshank's art had "a kind of cramped energy," and the movement and vitality of his pictures, as well as their dramatic, theatrical quality, are often noted. Setting many of his pictures in and around his home of London, Cruikshank depicted the full range of English society—dandies and aristocrats as well as those from the middle and lower classes. Meant to be "read" by the viewer, his illustrations are often praised for their ability to represent, and even improve on, the narratives that they accompany.

Biographical Information

Born in London, Cruikshank was the son of Isaac Cruikshank, a Scottish caricaturist and watercolorist who moved to England and became a designer and etcher, and Mary McNaughton, who was born in Perth, Scotland, and is described by biographer Ruari McLean as "hot-tempered, but . . . an excellent mother." Cruikshank had a sister, Eliza, who died as a child and an older brother, Isaac Robert, who became the painter and caricaturist Robert Cruikshank. As a boy, Cruikshank received little schooling and no art training. He learned to make illustrations and caricatures while working in his father's studio, providing assistance on lithographs, engravings, designs for valentines, and other art work. When Cruikshank was seven, one of his illustrations was used in an edition of *The Adventures of Baron Munchausen* that his father had designed. At twelve, Cruikshank earned his first commission with an etching for a lottery ticket. Cruikshank worked during his teenage years as a designer, as an illustrator of songs, and as the delineator of current events that received public attention. Although he thought seriously about entering the theater or the military, Cruikshank decided to focus on illustration, caricature, and engraving as more lucrative pursuits. Since his father had died in 1811, the artist needed enough income to take care of his mother and sister as well as himself. Cruikshank began his professional career as a caricaturist for *The Scourge,* a satirical magazine. He then began to submit political and satirical cartoons to other popular periodicals. In 1819, Cruikshank illustrated his first book, James Caulfield's *Portraits, Memoirs, and Characters of Remarkable Persons,* a

work published in four volumes. At around the same time, Cruikshank created what he would later consider his most important design: sketches for the Bank Restriction Barometer. The result of the publicity for these sketches was the passage of a bill by Parliament regarding the resumption of cash payments and the repeal of the death penalty for passing forged one-pound notes. In 1824, Cruikshank married his first wife, Mary Ann. In 1827, he created his first original book, *Illustrations of Time,* a collection of his drawings; Cruikshank later produced several other collections of his art.

Cruikshank often worked with the authors whose books he illustrated, giving them visual ideas to verbalize. His final illustrations were often based on verbal or written hints given to him by the author rather than on written text. Although usually successful, this process led Cruikshank into personal difficulties with Charles Dickens. Cruikshank claimed that he was responsible for suggesting the idea for *Oliver Twist* to Dickens—the subject, the plot, and the characters. He claimed that he had followed a London thief for weeks, sketching him. A talented actor, Cruikshank stated that he had acted out the man's character for Dickens, who turned the rascal into Fagin. The author countered that he had seen a series of Cruikshank's illustrations for the life of a London thief and that he decided to set Oliver's adventures in London; the rest, he said, was his own invention. Most contemporary critics believe that Cruikshank was strictly the illustrator of *Oliver Twist.* Whatever its genesis, the novel was a great success, both for its text and its pictures. The latter were so popular that a doggerel verse that began "The dreadful Jew / that Cruikshank drew" was widely circulated; in addition, Henry James claimed that he was frightened as a boy by the "vividly terrible images" in Cruikshank's drawings for *Oliver Twist.* Cruikshank also claimed that he came up with the idea for *The Miser's Daughter* (1842), a novel by W. Harrison Ainsworth.

Dickens and Cruikshank were later to disagree publicly regarding the latter's decision to retell "Cinderella," "Jack and the Beanstalk," "Hop o' My Thumb," and "Puss in Boots" in *The Cruikshank Fairy Book* as didactic messages about the evils of alcohol. Although he enjoyed drinking and smoking earlier in his life, Cruikshank had became a temperance crusader in his mid-fifties and even served as the vice-president of the London Temperance League. He had also published two popular wordless books, *The Bottle* and its sequel *The Drunkard's Children* (1848), that outlined the destruction of a family due to the influence of alcohol; after drinking gin, the father becomes a raving lunatic, the son a robber, and the daughter a prostitute. Dickens was abhorred by the way in which Cruikshank used the beloved traditional tales in *The Cruikshank Fairy Book* for his own purpose, and wrote a scathing essay, "Fairies and Frauds," in his magazine *Household Words;* Cruikshank responded in kind with "A Letter from Hop o' My Thumb to Charles Dickens Esq.," an essay in *George Cruikshank's Magazine.* Unfortunately for Cruikshank, Dickens's influence on the public was stronger. The plan to continue to publish additional volumes of the fairy books was aborted, and the incident began to affect Cruikshank's popularity, a situation amplified by the artist's insistence on writing and illustrating temperance tracts.

In 1847, Cruikshank's wife contracted tuberculosis and was confined to a sanitarium; she died in 1849. The next year, Cruikshank married Eliza Widdison. The artist regretted that he lacked formal training and that he had not become an oil painter, since painters received more respect than illustrators and political cartoonists. After receiving brief instruction at the Royal Academy of Art, he began painting in oils and watercolors and exhibiting at the National Gallery of Art in London. His best known work from this period is the oil painting "The Worship of Bacchus; or, The Drinking Customs of Society," a huge canvas that he completed at the age of seventy. Biographer John Wardroper claimed that the painting depicts "the evils of drink in a dozen easy lessons"; it is currently on display at the National Gallery. In 1863, Cruikshank exhibited over a thousand of his drawings, etchings, and engravings. The exhibition was criticized because of the artist's self-censorship: he insisted on excluding pieces from his earlier life that he felt were too liberal or radical. Cruikshank died in 1878 and was buried at St. Paul's Cathedral. After his death, the artist was recognized as a great and influential illustrator, an adept judge of human nature, and a sincere social reformer; his works have also become extremely popular with collectors. Biographers Hilary and Mary Ann Evans said of Cruikshank that "the strange ways in which we behave is vivid in every picture he drew—we are his single and lifelong preoccupation. . . . And so, all his life, George put his talents to work to change the world."

Critical Reception

Cruikshank is considered a born illustrator, a natural talent whose works provide incisive commentary on the Victorian Age while giving delight to children. Considered an artist of extraordinary range, power, and technical command who used his illustrations for both entertainment and social reform, he is credited with evoking the comic, tragic, dramatic, and magical equally well. He is also praised as a delineator of children and childhood; biographer Blanchard Jerrold wrote, "This is Cruikshank's own kingdom, by a right of genius which no one can dispute." Cruikshank is often considered the counterpart of Dickens in portraying the lower end of the spectrum of British society. Believing that artists have a social responsibility, he attacked sham and injustice in works that, although pointedly satiric, are generally thought to provide the desired effect with subtlety and taste. Although many of his creations are whimsical, Cruikshank is credited with responding with particular strength to adversity, fear, and loneliness. He is consistently praised for his evocation of human emotion as well for his depiction of villains; for example, Cruikshank's drawing "Fagin in the Condemned Cell" in *Oliver Twist* is considered a masterpiece. As an illustrator for children, Cruikshank is celebrated for creating pictures that blend action, character, humor, and sensitivity to match the spirit of his sources.

Dickens is quoted as saying, "He is the only designer fairyland has had." Writing in the *Westminster Review,* William Makepeace Thackery noted, "He is a friend to the young especially. . . . He loves children in his heart. . . . His drawings abound in feeling for these little ones. . . ." Thackery concluded, "Of all the artists that ever drew, from Michael Angelo upwards and downwards, Cruikshank was the man to illustrate the [German nursery tales] and give them their proper admixture of the grotesque, the wonderful, and the graceful." In his introduction to *German Popular Stories,* John Ruskin stated that Cruikshank's illustrations "were unrivalled in masterfulness of touch since Rembrandt (in some qualities of delineation unrivalled even by him)."

Although reviewers consistently acclaim Cruikshank's artistic gifts and perceptive observations of humanity, they also acknowledge that his output was uneven in quality and that both his early and later works are ephemeral. Cruikshank is also criticized for turning fairy tales into cautionary tales in his books for children as well as for creating art that was, perhaps due to his lack of formal training, less sophisticated than that of the fine artists of his day. However, most commentators view Cruikshank as an artist who created works that are remarkable for depicting the natural and the supernatural with particular authenticity and zest. Dickens called him "the Great George," while Thackery called him "a fine rough English diamond." In his essay "Some Foreign Caricaturists," poet Charles Baudelaire stated, "The special merit of George Cruikshank is his inexhaustible abundance of grotesque. A verve such as his is unimaginable. The grotesque flows inevitably and incessantly from Cruikshank's knitting needle, like pluperfect rhymes from the pen of a natural poet." John Fowles, who used a drawing by Cruikshank and author Frederick Marrayat as the basis for his novel *The French Lieutenant's Woman,* wrote in his essay "Introduction: Remembering Cruikshank" that the artist is "by far the greatest of the Victorian illustrators and cartoonists." Fowles added, "Humor ought to be a religion; and Cruikshank, an honored saint of that church." Writing in the *New Statesman & Republic,* Roy Porter said that Cruikshank "was master of them all," while Blanchard Jerrold stated that "no hand could have produced such works as those of George Cruikshank. . . ." Ruari McLean claimed, "Probably no other illustrator has ever made so many pictures that haunt the memory for their own sakes. . . ." Writing in *The Graphic Works of George Cruikshank,* Richard A. Vogler concluded that the artist's characters "will live forever in his graphic art because they awaken in us, his viewers, a liberating sense of his own identity."

COMMENTARY

William Makepeace Thackeray

SOURCE: "George Cruikshank," in *The Westminster Review,* Vol. XXXIV, No. LXVI, June, 1840, pp. 1-20.

[W]e are moved by the sight of some of Mr. Cruikshank's works—the "busen füblt sich jügendlich erschüttert," the "schwankende gestalten" of youth flit before one again,— Cruikshank's thrush begins to pipe and carol, as in the days of boyhood; hence misty moralities, reflections, and sad and pleasant remembrances arise. He is the friend of the young especially. Have we not read all the story-books that his wonderful pencil has illustrated? Did we not forego tarts, in order to buy his 'Breaking-up,' or his 'Fashionable Monstrosities' of the year eighteen hundred and something? Have we not before us, at this very moment, a print—one of the admirable *Illustrations of Phrenology*—which entire work was purchased by a joint-stock company of boys, each drawing lots afterwards for the separate prints, and taking his choice in rotation? The writer of this, too, had the honour of drawing the first lot, and seized immediately upon "Philoprogenitiveness"—a marvellous print (our copy is not at all improved by being coloured, which operation we performed on it ourselves)—a marvellous print, indeed,—full of ingenuity and fine jovial humour. A father, possessor of an enormous nose and family, is surrounded by the latter, who are, some of them, embracing the former. . . . It is full of grotesque beauty. The artist has at the back of his own skull, we are certain, a huge bump of philoprogenitiveness. He loves children in his heart; every one of those he has drawn is perfectly happy, and jovial, and affectionate, and innocent as possible. He makes them with large noses, but he loves them, and you always find something kind in the midst of his humour, and the ugliness redeemed by a sly touch of beauty. The smiling mother reconciles one with all the hideous family: they have all something of the mother in them—something kind, and generous, and tender.

Knight's in Sweeting's alley; Fairburn's in a court off Ludgate hill; Hone's in Fleet street—bright, enchanted palaces, which George Cruikshank used to people with grinning, fantastical imps, and merry, harmless sprites,— where are they? Fairburn's shop knows him no more; not only has Knight disappeared from Sweeting's alley, but, as we are given to understand, Sweeting's alley has disappeared from the face of the globe—Slop, the atrocious Castlereagh, the sainted Caroline (in a tight pelisse, with feathers in her head,) the "Dandy of sixty," who used to glance at us from Hone's friendly windows—where are they? Mr. Cruikshank may have drawn a thousand better things, since the days when these were; but they are to us a thousand times more pleasing than anything else he has done. How we used to believe in them! to stray miles out of the way on holidays, in order to ponder for an hour before that delightful window in Sweeting's alley! in walks through Fleet street, to vanish abruptly down Fairburn's passage, and there make one at his "charming gratis" exhibition. There used to be a crowd round the window in those days of grinning, good-natured mechanics, who spelt the songs, and spoke them out for the benefit of the company, and who received the points of humour with a general sympathizing roar. Where are these people now? You never hear any laughing at HB.; his pictures are a great deal too genteel for that—polite points of wit, which strike one as exceedingly clever and pretty, and cause one to smile in a quiet, gentleman-like kind of way.

There must be no smiling with Cruikshank. A man who does not laugh out right is a dullard, and has no heart; even the old Dandy of sixty must have laughed at his own wondrous grotesque image, as they say Louis Philippe did, who saw all the caricatures that were made of himself. And there are some of Cruikshank's designs, which have the blessed faculty of creating laughter as often as you see them. As Diggory says in the play, who is bidden by his master not to laugh while waiting at table—"Don't tell the story of Grouse in the Gun-room, master, or I can't help laughing." Repeat that history ever so often, and at the proper moment, honest Diggory is sure to explode. Every man, no doubt, who loves Cruikshank, has his Grouse in the Gun-room. There is a fellow in the 'Points of Humour' who is offering to eat up a certain little general, that has made us happy any time these sixteen years; his huge mouth is a perpetual well of laughter—buckets-full of fun can be drawn from it. We have formed no such friendships as that boyish one of the man with the mouth. But though, in our eyes, Mr. Cruikshank reached his *apogée* some eighteen years since, it must not be imagined that such is really the case. Eighteen sets of children have since then learned to love and admire him, and may many more of their successors be brought up in the same delightful faith. It is not the artist who fails, but the men who grow cold—the men, from who the illusions (why illusions? realities) of youth disappear one by one; who have no leisure to be happy, no blessed holidays. . . .

We know not if Mr. Cruikshank will be very well pleased at finding his name in such company as that of Clown and Harlequin; but he, like them, is certainly the children's friend. His drawings abound in feeling for these little ones, and hideous, as in the course of his duty, he is from time to time compelled to design them, he never sketches one without a certain pity for it, and imparting to the figure a certain grotesque grace. In happy school-boys he revels; plumb-pudding and holidays his needle has engraved over and over again;—there is a design in one of the comic almanacs of some young gentlemen who are employed in administering to a schoolfellow the correction of the pump, which is as graceful and elegant as a drawing of Stothard. Dull books about children George Cruikshank makes bright with illustrations—there is one published by the ingenious and opulent Mr. Tegg, of Cheapside—from which we should have been charmed to steal a few wood-cuts. It is entitled *Mirth and Morality,* the mirth being, for most part, on the side of the designer—the morality, unexceptionable certainly, the author's capital. Here are then, to these moralities, a smiling train of mirths supplied by George Cruikshank—see yonder little fellows butterfly-hunting across a common! Such a light, brisk, airy, gentleman-like drawing was never made upon such a theme. Who, cries the author

> Who has not chased the butterfly,
> And crushed its slender legs and wings,
> And heaved a moralizing sigh;
> Alas! how frail are human things?

A very unexceptionable morality truly, but it would have puzzled another than George Cruikshank to make mirth out of it as he has done. Away, surely not on the wings of these verses, Cruikshank's imagination begins to soar; and he makes us three darling little men on a green common, backed by old farm-houses, somewhere about May. A great mixture of blue and clouds in the air, a strong fresh breeze stirring, Tom's jacket flapping in the same, in order to bring down the insect queen or king of spring that is fluttering above him,—he renders all this with a few strokes on a little block of wood not two inches square, upon which one may gaze for hours, so merry and lifelike a scene does it present. What a charming creative power is this, what a privilege—to be a god, and create little worlds upon paper, and whole generations of smiling jovial men, women, and children half inch high, whose portraits are carried abroad, and have the faculty of making us monsters of six feet curious and happy in our turn. Now, who would imagine that an artist could make anything of such a subject as this? The writer begins by stating,—

> I love to go back to the days of my youth,
> And to reckon my joys to the letter,
> And to count o'er the friends that I have in the world,
> *Ay, and those who are gone to a better.*

This brings him to the consideration of his uncle. 'Of all the men I have ever known,' says he, 'my uncle united the greatest degree of cheerfulness with the sobriety of manhood. Though a man when I was a boy, he was yet one of the most agreeable companions I ever possessed. . . .

George Cruikshank has produced a charming design, in which the uncles and nephews are so prettily portrayed that one is reconciled to their existence, with all their moralities. Many more of the mirths in this little book are excellent, especially a great figure of a parson entering church on horseback,—an enormous parson truly, calm, unconscious, unwieldy. . . .

Being on the subject of children's books, how shall we enough praise the delightful. German nursery tales, and Cruikshank's illustrations of them? We coupled his name with pantomime a while since, and sure never pantomimes were more charming than these. Of all the artists that ever drew, from Michael Angelo upwards and downwards, Cruikshank was the man to illustrate these tales, and give them just the proper admixture of the grotesque, the wonderful, and the graceful. May all Mother Bunch's collection be similarly indebted to him; may *Jack the Giant Killer* may *Tom Thumb,* may *Puss in Boots,* be one day revivified by his pencil. Is not Whittington sitting yet on Highgate Hill, and poor Cinderella (in that sweetest of all fairy stories) still pining in her lonely chimney nook? A man who has a true affection for these delightful companions of his youth is bound to be grateful to them if he can, and we pray Mr. Cruikshank to remember them.

It is folly to say that this or that kind of humour is too good for the public, that only a chosen few can relish it. The best humour that we know of has been as eagerly received by the public as by the most delicate connoisseur. There is hardly a man in England who can read but will laugh at Falstaff and the humour of Joseph Andrews; and honest Mr. Pickwick's story can be felt and loved by

Frontispiece to "Puss in Boots."

any person above the age of six. Some may have a keener enjoyment of it than others, but all the world can be merry over it, and is always ready to welcome it. The best criterion of good humour is success, and what a share of this has Mr. Cruikshank had! how many millions of mortals has he made happy! We have heard very profound persons talk philosophically of the marvellous and mysterious manner in which he has suited himself to the time . . .

The famous classical dinners and duel in *Peregrine Pickle* are also excellent in their way. The distant view of the city in the duel, and of a market-place in *The Quack Doctor,* are delightful specimens of the artist's skill in depicting buildings and back-grounds. They are touched with a grace, truth, and dexterity of workmanship that leave nothing to desire. . . .

For Jews, sailors, Irishmen, Hessian boots, little boys, beadles, policemen, tall Life Guardsmen, charity children, pumps, dustmen, very short pantaloons, dandies in spectacles, and ladies with aquiline noses, remarkably taper waists, and wonderfully long ringlets, Mr. Cruikshank has a special predilection. The tribe of Israelites he has studied with amazing gusto; witness the Jew in Mr. Ainsworth's

Jack Sheppard, and the immortal Fagin of *Oliver Twist.* Whereabouts lies the comic *vís* in these persons and things? Why should a beadle be comic, and his opposite a charity boy? Why should a tall Life Guardsman have something in him essentially absurd? Why are short breeches more ridiculous than long? What is there particularly jocose about a pump, and wherefore does a long nose always provoke the beholder to laughter? These points may be metaphysically elucidated by those who list. It is probable that Mr. Cruikshank could not give an accurate definition of that which is ridiculous in these objects, but his instinct has told him that fun lurks in them, and cold must be the heart that can pass by the pantaloons of his charity boys, the Hessian boots of his dandies, and the fan-tail hats of his dustmen, without respectful wonder.

We can submit to public notice a complete little gallery of dustmen. There is, in the first place, the professional dustman, who, having in the enthusiastic exercise of his delightful trade, laid hands upon property not strictly his own, is pursued, we presume, by the right owner, from whom he flies as fast as his crooked shanks will carry him.

What a curious picture it is—the horrid rickety houses in some dingy suburb of London, the grinning cobbler, the smothered butcher, the very trees which are covered with dust—it is fine to look at the different expressions of the two interesting fugitives. The fiery charioteer who belabours yonder poor donkey has still a glance for his brother on foot, on whom punishment is about to descend. And not a little curious is it to think of the creative power of the man who has arranged this little tale of low life. How logically it is conducted, how cleverly each one of the accessories is made to contribute to the effect of the whole. What a deal of thought and humour has the artist expended on this little block of wood; a large picture might have been painted out of the very same materials, which Mr. Cruikshank, out of his wondrous fund of merriment and observation, can afford to throw away upon a drawing not two inches long. . . .

Mr. Cruikshank has a fine eye for homely landscapes, and renders them with great delicacy and taste. Old villages, farm-yards, groups of stacks, queer chimneys, churches, gable-ended cottages, Elizabethan mansion-houses, and other old English scenes, he depicts with evident enthusiasm.

Famous books in their day were Cruikshank's *John Gilpin* and *Epping Hunt;* for though our artist does not draw horses very scientifically,—to use a phrase of the *atelier,*—he *feels* them very keenly; and his queer animals, after one is used to them, answer quite as well as better. Neither is he very happy in trees, and such rustical produce; or rather, we should say, he is very original, his trees being decidedly of his own make and composition, not imitated from any master.

The horses of *John Gilpin* are more of the equestrian order than those in the other, and, as here the artist has only his favourite suburban buildings to draw, not a word is to be said against his design. The inn and old buildings are charmingly designed, and nothing can be more prettily or playfully touched. . . .

The rush, and shouting, and clatter are excellently depicted by the artist; and we, who have been scoffing at his manner of designing animals, must here make a special exception in favour of the hens and chickens: each has a different action and is curiously natural.

Happy are children of all ages who have such a ballad and such pictures as this in store for them! It is a comfort to think that wood-cuts never wear out, and that the book still may be had at Mr. Tilt's for a shilling, for those who can command that sum of money. . . .

Besides these, we must mention, in the line of our duty, the notable tragedies of *Tom Thumb,* and *Bombastes Furioso,* both of which have appeared with many illustrations by Mr. Cruikshank. The 'brave army' of Bombastes exhibits a terrific display of brutal force, which must shock the sensibilities of an English radical. And we can well understand the caution of the general, who bids this *soldatesque effrénée* to begone, and not to kick up such a row. Such a troop of lawless ruffians let loose upon a populous city would play sad havoc in it; and we fancy the massacres of Birmingham renewed, or at least of Badajoz, which, though not quite so dreadful, if we may believe his Grace the Duke of Wellington, as the former scenes of slaughter, were nevertheless severe enough; but we must not venture upon any ill-timed pleasantries in presence of the disturbed King Arthur, and the awful ghost of Gaffer Thumb.

In the supernatural we find Cruikshank reigning supreme. He has invented in his time a little comic pandemonium, peopled with the most droll good-natured fiends possible. We have before us Chamisso's 'Peter Schlemihl,' with Cruikshank's designs translated into German, and gaining nothing by the change. The 'Kinder und Haus-Maerchen' of Grimm are likewise ornamented with a frontispiece, copied from that one which appeared to the amusing version of the English work. The books on Phrenology and Time have been imitated by the same nation; and even in France, whither reputation travels slower than to any country except China, we have seen copies of the works of George Cruikshank. . . .

The German tales we have mentioned before. **'The Prince Riding on the Fox,' 'Hans in Luck,' 'The Fiddler and His Goose,' 'Heads off,'** are all drawings which, albeit not before us now, nor seen for ten years, remain indelibly fixed on the memory—*"heisst du etwa Rumpelstilzchen?"* There sits the queen on her throne, surrounded by grinning beef-eaters, and little Rumpelstiltskin stamps his foot through the floor in the excess of his tremendous despair. In one of these German tales, if we remember rightly, there is an account of a little orphan who is carried away by a pitying fairy for a term of seven years, and passing that period of sweet apprenticeship among the imps and sprites of fairy-land. Has our artist been among the same company, and brought back their portraits in his sketch-book? He is the only designer fairy-land has had. Callot's imps, for all their strangeness, are only of the earth, earthy. Fuseli's fairies belong to the infernal regions; they are monstrous, lurid, and hideously melancholy. Mr. Cruikshank alone has had a true insight into the character of the 'little people.' They are something like men and women, and yet not flesh and blood; they are laughing and mischievous, but why we know not. Mr. Cruikshank, however, has had some dream or other, or else a natural mysterious instinct (as the Seherinn of Prevorst had for beholding ghosts), or else some preternatural fairy revelation, which has made him acquainted with the looks and ways of the fantastical subjects of Oberon and Titania. . . .

We must not forget to mention *Oliver Twist,* and Mr. Cruikshank's famous designs to that work. The sausage scene at Fagin's; Nancy seizing the boy; that capital piece of humour, Mr. Bumble's courtship, which is even better in Cruikshank's version than in Boz's exquisite account of the interview; Sykes's farewell to the dog; and the Jew,—the dreadful Jew—that Cruikshank drew! What a fine touching picture of melancholy desolation is that of Sykes and the dog! The poor cur is not too well drawn; the landscape is stiff and formal; but in this case the faults, if faults they be, of execution rather add to than diminish the effect of the picture: it has a strange, wild, dreary, broken-hearted look; we fancy we see the landscape as it must have appeared to Sykes, when ghastly and with bloodshot eyes he looked at it. As for the Jew in the dungeon, let us say nothing of it—what can we say to describe it! What a fine homely poet is the man who can produce this little world of mirth or woe for us! Does he elaborate his effects by slow process of thoughts, or do they come to him by instinct? Does the painter ever arrange in his brain an image so complete, that he afterwards can copy it exactly on the canvass, or does the hand work in spite of him? . , .

Whether it be ill-paid or well, what labour has Mr. Cruikshank's been! Week by week, for thirty years, to produce something new; some smiling offspring of painful labour, quite independent and distinct from its ten thousand jovial brethren; in what hours of sorrow and ill health to be told by the world, 'Make us laugh or you starve—Give us fresh fun; we have eaten up the old and are hungry.' And all this has he been obliged to do—to wring laughter day by day, sometimes, perhaps, out of want, often certainly from ill-health or depression—to keep the fire of his brain perpetually alight, for the greedy public will give it no leisure to cool. This he has done and done well. He has told a thousand truths in as many strange and fascinating ways; he has given a thousand new and pleasant thoughts to millions of people; he has never used his wit dishonestly; he has never in all the exuberance of his frolicsome humour, caused a single painful or guilty blush; how little do we think of the extraordinary power of this man, and how ungrateful we are to him!

Here, as we are come round to the charge of ingratitude, the starting post from which we set out, perhaps we had better conclude. The reader will perhaps wonder at the high-flown tone in which we speak of the services and merits of an individual, whom he considers a humble

scraper on steel, that is wonderfully popular already. But none of us remember all the benefits we owe him; they have come one by one, one driving out the memory of the other; it is only when we come to examine them all together as the writer has done, who has a pile of books on the table before him—a heap of personal kindnesses from George Cruikshank (not presents, if you please, for we bought, borrowed, or stole every one of them), that we feel what we owe him. Look at one of Mr. Cruikshank's works, and we pronounce him an excellent humourist. Look at all, his reputation is increased by a kind of geometrical progression; as a whole diamond is a hundred times more valuable than the hundred splinters into which it might be broken would be. A fine rough English diamond is this about which we have been writing.

German Popular Stories

SOURCE: An advertisement to *German Popular Stories,* William Clowes and Sons, Limited, 1907, pp. iii-iv.

[*The following advertisement for* German Popular Stories *first appeared in 1868.*]

More than forty years ago (in 1823) Mr. Edgar Taylor presented to English readers the first selection which had been made from the famous "Hausmärchen," or *German Popular Stories* of the Brothers Grimm. The first volume, which had been selected and translated by Mr. Taylor and a circle of relatives, appeared with twelve wonderful etchings by George Cruikshank, and was received with so much favour that, three years after, a *second* series was prepared by Mr. Taylor alone, to which the same artist contributed ten more illustrations. Both series passed through two or three editions soon after publication; and when Messrs. Robins the publishers retired from business, the work became very scarce. At the present day, when the collectors of the works of Cruikshank are greatly increasing in number, the two volumes, originally sold for 12*s.*, are worth at least £5 or £6! They are the most prized of all the fine works of the great master. On the continent, too, these etchings quickly attracted attention. Copies were made in Germany; and one Ambrose Tardieu, a Frenchman, took such a special fancy to them that he copied the first series to the best of his ability, and then issued them in a small volume *as his own production.*

The present volume is a faithful reprint of *both series.* The etchings, most carefully following the originals, are considered masterpieces of reproduction. What is thought of these designs by artists in this country Mr. John Ruskin very eloquently told us many years ago in his "Elements of Drawing;" and, only recently, Mr. Hamerton, in his new work, "Etching and Etchers," speaks of the favourite of all these etchings, the well-known **"Two Elves and the Shoemaker,"** in these words:—"This pleasant tale was so well adapted to the genius of Cruikshank, that it has suggested one of the very best of all his etchings. The two Elves, especially the nearer one, who is putting on his breeches, are drawn with a point at once so precise and vivacious, so full of keen fun and inimitably happy invention, that I have not found their equal in comic etching anywhere. It is said that these elves are regarded with peculiar affection by the great master who created them, which is only natural, for he has a right to be proud of them. The picturesque details of the room are etched with the same felicitous intelligence; but the marvel of the work is in the expression of the strange little faces, and the energy of the comical wee limbs."

John Ruskin

SOURCE: An introduction to *German Popular Stories,* William Clowes and Sons, Limited, 1907, pp. v-xiv.

[*Ruskin's introduction was printed in the 1868 edition of* German Popular Stories.]

[The illustrations in this volume] are of quite sterling and admirable art, in a class precisely parallel in elevation to the character of the tales which they illustrate; and the original etchings, as I have before said in the Appendix to my 'Elements of Drawing,' were unrivalled in masterfulness of touch since Rembrandt; (in some qualities of delineation unrivalled even by him). These copies have been so carefully executed that at first I was deceived by them, and supposed them to be late impressions from the plates (and what is more, I believe the master himself was deceived by them, and supposed them to be his own); and although, on careful comparison with the first proofs, they will be found no exception to the terrible law that literal repetition of entirely fine work shall be, even to the hand that produced it,—much more to any other,—for ever impossible, they still represent, with sufficient fidelity to be in the highest degree instructive, the harmonious light and shade, the manly simplicity of execution, and the easy, unencumbered fancy, of designs which belonged to the best period of Cruikshank's genius. To make somewhat enlarged copies of them, looking at them through a magnifying-glass, and never putting two lines where Cruikshank has put only one, would be an exercise in decision and severe drawing which would leave afterwards little to be learnt in schools. I would gladly also say much in their praise as imaginative designs; but the power of genuine imaginative work, and its difference from that which is compounded and patched together from borrowed sources, is of all qualities of art the most difficult to explain; and I must be content with the simple assertion of it.

And so I trust the good old book, and the honest work that adorns it, to such favour as they may find with children of open hearts and lowly lives.

Blanchard Jerrold

SOURCE: in *The Life of George Cruikshank: In Two Epochs,* Chatto and Windus, 1883, 392 p.

[William Makepeace] Thackeray dwells lovingly on Cruikshank's success as a delineator of children and the humours of childhood; and particularly on his inimitable illustrations to children's books. This is Cruikshank's own kingdom, by a right of genius which none can dispute. . . .

When his **"Life in London and Paris," "Phrenological Illustrations," "Humourist," "Points of Humour,"** and many series of book illustrations—comprehending a notable quantity of his best creations—are estimated, in conjunction with his hand-to-mouth work for the caricature shops, and the whole has been surveyed at once, the connoisseur stands literally amazed at the fecundity of the artist. Within the range of this decade of feverish activity is amassed such wealth of fancy, of invention, of jocund spirit, of sympathy for suffering, of rage over wrong, of minute observation of men and things, and withal such conscientious, ever-improving execution with pencil and needle, and lithographic ink and tinting-brush, upon wood and stone, and steel and copper; as not all the caricaturists or comic artists who have swarmed in Fleet Street since the Queen's coronation day could equal, if they made a joint show of their best. Cruikshank was lavish with his fancy, and his humour lives upon the smallest subject. He never made one poor little idea stand alone, as the practice is in the comic or satirical cartoons of the present day. It was his wont to support his dominant conception with a score of helpful accessories. He laid every detail under contribution towards the elucidation of the story to be told. His caricatures, as well as his serious pictures, abound in admirable by-play. His power of concentrating interest is unmatched. His chairs and tables speak. There is life in every accessory. *Nature morte* did not exit for him. "Dead as a door-nail" he could not understand; for under the magnetism of his etching-needle the nail would laugh and speak. He was so full of life himself—a hornpipe dancer in his eighty-fourth year—that, in spite of him, he infused it into anything he touched. No artist ever threw such movement and infused such vital breath into his pictures, as this untaught man of genius spontaneously breathed into his etchings and woodcuts. A scrimmage by him inclines the beholder to lift his arm to protect himself. When he leads off a dance upon copper, you involuntarily hum a jig. When his characters are merry, you laugh outright with them.

On the other hand, is his mood solemn, he can make your heart beat quick, and send you shuddering away, with his images in your brain—presences you will find it hard to banish. "The awful Jew that Cruikshank drew" lingered for years in Thackeray's mind; and the profound impression which it made on the public, when it appeared, has not faded even now.

More searching observation than that of Cruikshank in his prime was never possessed by an artist. His range did not stretch beyond the suburbs of London, except perhaps to Margate in the hoy, but all that came within it he made his own. Out of the suburban landscapes he conjured fairy scenes; and Highgate and Hampstead supplied him with distant horizons which his imagination widened at his will. Thackeray declared that Cruikshank had a fine eye for homely landscapes, and yet his trees are as bad as his horses. "Old villages, farm-yards, groups of stacks, queer chimneys, churches, gable-end cottages, Elizabethan mansion-houses, and other old English scenes, he depicts with evident enthusiasm." His scenes to Brough's **"Life of Falstaff"** are exquisitely drawn. Where Falstaff is arrested at the suit of Mrs. Quickly, and again when he persuades her to lend him more money, the old houses are fine picturesque studies.

But London, and London streets and suburbs, constituted Cruikshank's world in his heyday; and he caught all the phases of this his universe, save and except its upper classes. He lived in the midst of the people; he was of them. His humble fortunes cast his lot, in his early time, among the poorer classes of professional men. He was passionately fond of the stage, and was familiar with the popular comedians of the minor theatres, and the landlords of the houses which they and he frequented. He lived at Islington, and belonged to a club called "The Crib," which had a room at the Sir Hugh Myddelton public-house, of which Joseph Grimaldi, the clown, was president. Mr. C. L. Gruneisen, who made Cruikshank's acquaintance at "The Crib," related how on one occasion, when a member bantered George rather savagely, and he—contrary to his custom—had borne the "chaff" without replying, he presently turned to him, and holding up his hand, showed a caricature of his assailant executed upon his thumb-nail, and said, "Look here! See how I have booked him!"

It was in this and kindred scenes with which Cruikshank was familiar in his prime, and out of the excesses which, as we have seen, Professor Wilson—himself no fastidious liver—tried to tempt him by promises of a higher and wider fame, that Cruikshank drew the matchless gallery of contemporary life, in which the humours, passions, whims, and absurdities of our fathers and grandfathers are snatched from oblivion, and left to inform and brighten the page of the future historian.

"We can submit to public notice," says Mr. Thackeray, "a complete little gallery of dustmen. Here is, in the first place, the professional dustman, who, having in the enthusiastic exercise of his delightful trade, laid hands upon property not strictly his own, is pursued, we presume, by the right owner, from whom he flies as fast as his crooked shanks will carry him. What a curious picture it is—the horrid rickety houses in some dingy suburb of London, the grinning cobbler, the smothered butcher, the very trees which are covered with dust—it is fine to look at the different expressions of the two interesting fugitives. The fiery charioteer who belabours yonder poor donkey has still a glance for his brother on foot, on whom punishment is about to descend. And not a little curious is it to think of the creative power of the man who has arranged this little tale of low life. How logically it is conducted! how cleverly each one of the accessories is made to contribute to the effect of the whole! What a deal of thought and humour has the artist expended on this little block of wood! a large picture might have been painted out of the very same materials which Mr.

Cruikshank, out of his wondrous fund of merriment and observation, can afford to throw away upon a drawing not two inches long. From the practical dustmen we pass to those purely poetical. Here are three of them, who rise on clouds of their own raising, the very genii of the sack and shovel. Is there no one to write a sonnet to these? and yet a whole poem was written about Peter Bell the waggoner, a character by no means so poetic. And, lastly, we have the dustman in love. The honest fellow is on the spectator's right hand; and having seen a young beauty stepping out of a gin-shop on a Sunday morning, is pressing eagerly his suit." His arms are round the young beauty's neck, her face is hidden behind the dustman's fantail hat.

That society of dustmen, which Cruikshank used to observe, when he lived in Dorset Street, Salisbury Square, sank deep into his mind. In the **"Triumph of Cupid,"** many years later, we shall still find the dustman. He is lying in the foreground, "compelled to bite the dust"— while the artist smokes his long pipe, and Cupid, astride his slippers, toasts a heart at the fire. That long pipe (only it was honest clay, and not the magnificent meerschaum to which George has treated himself in his vision) was his companion for many a year. "Yes, I remember Mr. Cruikshank very well when I was a little girl," writes an old friend of his. "When he came, a long clay pipe was sent for. He would sit smoking it after dinner, and we were greatly amused by the energetic gesticulation with which he accompanied his conversation." His was a handsome face, with steely blue eyes that struck through you. They flashed as brightly as the eyes of Mr. Dickens, but they had no merriment—only keenness, and a certain fierceness in them. Those eyes penetrated all the mysteries of London life, and peered through clouds of tobacco-smoke, and over foaming tankards in all kinds of strange and queer places.

"For Jews, sailors, Irishmen, Hessian boots, little boys, beadles, policemen, tall life-guardsmen, charity children, pumps, dustmen, very short pantaloons, dandies in spectacles, and ladies with aquiline noses, remarkably taper waists, and wonderfully long ringlets," says Thackeray, "Mr. Cruikshank has a special predilection. The tribe of Israelites he has studied with amazing gusto: witness the Jew in Mr. Ainsworth's ***Jack Sheppard,*** and the immortal Fagin of ***Oliver Twist.*** Whereabouts lies the comic *vis* in these persons and things? Why should a beadle be comic, and his opposite a charity boy? Why should a tall life-guardsman have something in him essentially absurd? Why are short breeches more ridiculous than long? What is there particularly jocose about a pump? and wherefore does a long nose always provoke the beholder to laughter? These points may be metaphysically elucidated by those who list. It is probable that Mr. Cruikshank could not give an accurate definition of that which is ridiculous in these objects, but his instinct has told him that fun lurks in them, and cold must be the heart that can pass by the pantaloons of his charity boys, the Hessian boots of his dandies, and the fantail hats of his dustmen, without respectful wonder."

George Cruikshank also created the ladies of the Sairy Gamp order. We find one in a set of his Lottery Puffs, published in January 1818—a midwife with a prodigious bonnet. And does she not appear as Mrs. Toddles, the ancestress of Mrs. Brown of our day, in the *Omnibus*? The debt of the humorists and public caricaturists who have lived and flourished (ay, flourished as poor George never did) on the crumbs of his Rabelaisian banquet of humour, is immeasurable. Many of the comic London characters of to-day are only his figures re-dressed. They are seen through the spectacles which he invented. Only, the fine fancy, the rollicking gaiety, the cumulation of fun in some four inches square of box-wood, are thinly spread over square feet. Think of Cruikshank's Irishmen! Thackeray says of them,—

"We have said that our artist has a great love for the drolleries of the Green Island. . . . We know not if Mr. Cruikshank has ever had any such good luck as to see the Irish in Ireland itself, but he certainly has obtained a knowledge of their looks, as if the country had been all his life familiar to him. Could Mr. O'Connell himself desire anything more national than the following scene? or would Father Mathew have a better text to preach upon? There is not a broken nose in the room that is not thoroughly Irish."

The observer of all the humours of London life, the member of Mr. Joseph Grimaldi's Club at the Sir Hugh Myddelton, and of many other very free-and-easy theatrical, artistic, and literary clubs of the hour, nursed very serious and ambitious designs, even while he threw out his pictorial squibs for his daily bread. It is sad to think that even the mighty quantity of work which he got through, and of work that filled publishers' pockets, and set up laughing faces from the Highlands to Portsmouth, was never well paid enough to give him ease to do justice to his genius. . . .

It has been said that Cruikshank knew more of London than the author of the [*Sketches by Boz*] which he illustrated. He may have had a longer experience of London streets and mysteries; but Dickens, in his London Sketches, written before he came in contact with the artist, had proved how deeply his young eyes had penetrated the mysteries of the great city, and how thoroughly his fresh heart had been stirred.

The first paper is on "Our Parish." In this lies the germ of *Oliver Twist*. Simmons is the father of Bumble. But scattered through the Sketches may be found all the experience of which Oliver Twist was the riper and more artistic and dramatic expression. The career of the Parish Boy was exactly the romance the author of these wonderful pictures of London would write. Had Cruikshank suggested these, and led the young author from scene to scene, we might have understood part of his claim to the conception of the romance; but he was called in by the publisher, Macrone, to illustrate the magazine papers which he had bought for republication from the young author for a trifle. . . .

I will now set before the reader impartially the story of Cruikshank's contention as to his share in *Oliver Twist*. In his letter to the *Times*, Cruikshank said:—

"When *Bentley's Miscellany* was first started, it was arranged that Mr. Charles Dickens should write a serial in it, and which was to be illustrated by me; and in a conversation with him as to what the subject should be for the first serial, I suggested to Mr. Dickens that he should write the life of a London boy, and strongly advised him to do this, assuring him that I would furnish him with the subject, and supply him with all the characters, which my large experience of London life would enable me to do.

"My idea was to raise a boy from a most humble position up to a high and respectable one—in fact, to illustrate one of those cases of common occurrence where men of humble origin, by natural ability, industry, honest and honourable conduct, raise themselves to first-class positions in society. As I wished particularly to bring the habits and manners of the thieves of London before the public (and this for a most important purpose, which I shall explain one of these days), I suggested that the poor boy should fall among thieves, but that his honesty and natural good disposition should enable him to pass through this ordeal without contamination; and after I had fully described the full-grown thieves (the *Bill Sykeses*) and their female companions, also the young thieves (the *Artful Dodgers*) and the receivers of stolen goods, Mr. Dickens agreed to act on my suggestion, and the work was commenced, but we differed as to what sort of boy the hero should be. Mr. Dickens wanted rather a queer kind of chap; and, although this was contrary to my original idea, I complied with his request, feeling that it would not be right to dictate too much to the writer of the story, and then appeared 'Oliver Asking for More'; but it so happened just about this time that an inquiry was being made in the parish of St. James's, Westminster, as to the cause of the death of some of the workhouse children who had been 'farmed out.' I called the attention of Mr. Dickens to this inquiry, and said that if he took up this matter, his doing so might help to save many a poor child from injury and death; and I earnestly begged of him to let me make Oliver a nice pretty little boy; and if we so represented him, the public—and particularly the ladies—would be sure to take a greater interest in him, and the work would then be a certain success. Mr. Dickens agreed to that request, and I need not add here that my prophecy was fulfilled; and if any one will take the trouble to look at my representations of 'Oliver,' they will see that the appearance of the boy is altered after the two first illustrations, and, by a reference to the records of St. James's parish, and to the date of the publication of the *Miscellany*, they will see that both the dates tally, and therefore support my statement.

"I had, a long time previously to this, directed Mr. Dickens's attention to Field Lane, Holborn Hill, wherein resided many thieves and receivers of stolen goods, and it was suggested that one of these receivers, a Jew, should be introduced into the story; and upon one occasion Mr. Dickens and Mr. Harrison Ainsworth called upon me, and in course of conversation I described and performed the character of one of these Jew receivers,—and this was the origin of Fagin."

Cruikshank maintained that his designs were all the result of consultations with Dickens—in which he was as much the creator as the author; and that he never saw any of the MS. of the novel until it was nearly finished. No; he saw the proofs of the early sheets. The family tradition was to the effect that Dickens, calling one day in Amwell Street, saw a series of illustrations which Cruikshank had prepared for a story he had in his mind of the life of a thief. Dickens was so struck with them, and with the artist's account of his plan, that he determined to make London the scene of Oliver Twist's adventures. Cruikshank's intimate knowledge of low life in every part of London made him the most efficient and penetrating illustrator of Dickens's book: this, and nothing more.

And now let me quote Mr. Forster's summary dismissal of the charge—for it is nothing less—that Dickens was indebted to Cruikshank for the idea, and for many of the incidents and characters, of **Oliver Twist.**

"The publication had been announced for October, but the third volume illustrations interrupted it a little. This part of the story, as we have seen, had been written in anticipation of the magazine, and the designs for it having to be executed 'in a lump,' were necessarily done somewhat hastily. The matter supplied in advance of the monthly portions in the magazine formed the bulk of the last volume as published in the book; and for this the plates had to be prepared by Cruikshank, also in advance of the Magazine, to furnish them in time for the separate publications; Sykes and his Dog, Fagin in the Cell, and Rose Maylie and Oliver, being the three last. None of these Dickens had seen until he saw them in the book on the eve of publication, when he so strongly objected to one of them, that it had to be cancelled. 'I returned suddenly to town yesterday afternoon,' he wrote to the artist at the end of October, 'to look at the latter pages of **Oliver Twist** before it was delivered to the booksellers, when I saw the majority of the plates in the last volume for the first time. With reference to the last one—Rose Maylie and Oliver—without entering into the question of great haste, or any other cause, which may have led to its being what it is, I am quite sure there can be little difference of opinion between us with respect to the result. May I ask you whether you will object to designing this plate afresh, and doing so *at once,* in order that as few impressions as possible of the present one may go forth? I feel confident you know me too well to feel hurt by this inquiry, and with equal confidence in you I have lost no time in preferring it.' This letter, printed from a copy in Dickens's handwriting, fortunately committed to my keeping, entirely disposes of a wonderful story, originally promulgated in America, with a minute conscientiousness and particularity of detail that might have raised the reputation of Sir Benjamin Backbite himself. Whether all Sir Benjamin's laurels, however, should fall to the original teller of the tale, or whether any part of them is the property of the alleged authority from which he says he received it, is unfortunately not quite clear. There would hardly have been a doubt, if the fable had been confined to the other side of the Atlantic, but it has been reproduced

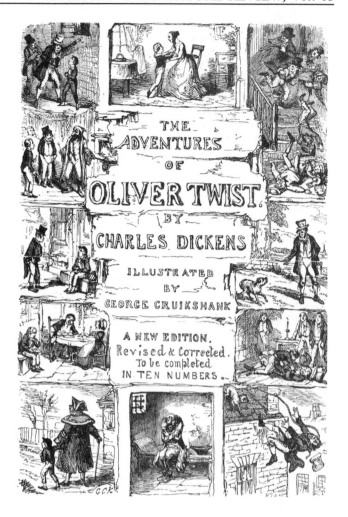

Frontispiece to Oliver Twist.

and widely circulated on this side also, and the distinguished artist whom it calumniates by fathering its invention upon him, either not conscious of it, or not caring to defend himself, has been left undefended from the slander. By my ability to produce Dickens's letter, I am spared the necessity of characterizing the tale, myself, by the one unpolite word (in three letters) which alone would have been applicable to it."

Cruikshank was alive, and living within half an hour's drive of Mr. Forster's library, when he put the case in this roundabout, and, I must say, unwarrantably uncivil way. But let us see what this story was that came from across the Atlantic in the columns of the *Round Table.* It is Dr. Shelton Mackenzie who speaks. "In London I was intimate with the brothers Cruikshank, Robert and George, but more particularly the latter. Having called upon him one day at his house (it was then in Myddelton Terrace, Pentonville), I had to wait while he was finishing an etching, for which a printer's boy was waiting. To while away the time, I gladly complied with his suggestion that I should look over a portfolio crowded with etchings, proofs, and drawings, which lay upon the sofa. Among these, carelessly tied together in a wrap of brown paper, was a series of some twenty-five or thirty drawings, very carefully finished, through most of which were carried the well-known portraits of Fagin, Bill Sykes and his Dog, Nancy, the Artful Dodger, and Master Charles Bates—all well known to the readers of *Oliver Twist.* There was no mistake about it; and when Cruikshank turned round, his work finished, I said as much. He told me that it had long been in his mind to show the life of a London thief by a series of drawings engraved by himself, in which, without a single line of letterpress, the story would be strikingly and clearly told. 'Dickens,' he continued, 'dropped in here one day, just as you have done, and, whilst waiting until I could speak with him, took up that identical portfolio, and ferreted out that bundle of drawings. When he came to that one which represents Fagin in the condemned cell, he studied it for half an hour, and told me that he was tempted to change the whole plot of his story; not to carry Oliver Twist through adventures in the country, but to take him up into the thieves' den in London, show what their life was, and bring Oliver through it without sin or shame. I consented to let him write up to as many of the designs as he thought would suit his purpose, and that was the way in which Fagin, Sykes, and Nancy were created. My drawings suggested them, rather than individuality suggesting (*sic*) my drawings.'" Mr. Forster adds, "Since this was in type I have seen the Life of Dickens published in America by Dr. Shelton Mackenzie, in which I regret to find this story literally repeated. The only differences from it as here quoted are that 1847 is given as the date of the visit; that besides the 'portraits' named, there are said to have been 'many others who were not introduced;' and that the final words run thus: 'My drawings suggested them, rather than his strong individuality my drawings.'"

In 1872, George Cruikshank published his "Statement of Facts" on this subject, and on his subsequent controversy with Mr. Harrison Ainsworth. This is his final reply to Mr. Forster. I give it that the reader may draw his own conclusions.

"A question has been asked *publicly*," says the artist, "and which, I grant, is rather an important one in this case, and that is, *Why have I not until lately claimed to be the originator of Oliver Twist?* To this I reply, that ever since these works were published, and even when they were in progress, I have in private society, when conversing upon such matters, always explained that the *original ideas and characters* of these works *emanated from me;* and the reason why I *publicly* claimed to be the originator of *Oliver Twist* was to defend Dr. R. Shelton Mackenzie, who was charged by Mr. John Forster, in his *Life of Mr. Charles Dickens,* with publishing a *falsehood* (or a word of 'three letters,' as he describes it), whereas the Doctor was only repeating what I had told him at the time *Oliver Twist* was in progress. Mr. Forster designates Dr. Mackenzie's statement as 'a wonderful story,' or 'a marvellous fable;' and in a letter from the Doctor in the *Philadelphia Press,* December 19th, 1871, he says, *'My wonderful story was printed in an American periodical years before Mr. Dickens died;'* and then asks, 'Why did not Mr.

Forster inquire into this matter at the time? for surely he must have known it.' And I presume Mr. Dickens must have heard of this 'wonderful story,' the truth of which he *did not deny—for this reason, because he could not.* And with respect to Mr. Ainsworth's insinuation as to my 'labouring under a delusion' upon this point, as all my literary friends at that time knew that I was the originator of *Oliver Twist,* and as Mr. Ainsworth and I were at that time upon such intimate terms, and both working together on *Bentley's Miscellany,* is it at all likely that I should have concealed such a fact from him? No, no! he knew this as well as I did, and therefore, in this matter at any rate, it is *he* who is 'labouring under a delusion.' And I will here refer to a part of my letter, which was published in the *Times,* December 30th, 1871, upon the origin of *Oliver Twist,* wherein I state that Mr. Ainsworth and Mr. Dickens came together one day to my house, upon which occasion it so happened that I then and there *described* and *performed* the character of 'Fagin,' for Mr. Dickens to introduce into the work as a 'receiver of stolen goods,' and that some time after this, upon seeing Mr. Ainsworth again, he said to me, 'I was so much struck with your description of that Jew to Mr. Dickens, that I think you and I could do something together.' Now I do not know whether Mr. Ainsworth has ever made any allusion to this,—perhaps he *disdains* to do so,—but perhaps he may give this also a 'positive contradiction,' and if he does, then all I have to say is, that his memory is gone."

This controversy, and a subsequent one, arose from Cruikshank's habit of exaggeration in all things. . . .

Never has a single figure enacted by mortal artist been so talked and written about as Fagin. How and when he was conceived, where the artist found his model, what share Dickens had, and what part belonged to Cruikshank of "the awful Jew," are points of controversy which have been kept alive in society as much by Cruikshank's own acting of his idea, and his many accounts of his conception, as by the deep impression made by that dreadful wretch glaring in the condemned cell. The writer of the obituary notice of Cruikshank in the *Daily News* himself heard Cruikshank relate that Fagin was sketched from a rascally old Jew whom he observed in the neighbourhood of Saffron Hill; "and," he added, "I watched him for weeks, studying him." Fagin possessed Cruikshank's mind to the end of his life. He was always ready to talk about him, and to act him. . . .

On Cruikshank's illustrations to *Oliver Twist,* how many critics have dwelt; and by them, how many writers have pointed their moral! Ruskin, in his chapter on Vulgarity, [in *Modern Painters*] turns for his illustration to Landseer and Cruikshank.

"Cunning," he remarks, "signifies especially a habit or gift of over-reaching, accompanied with enjoyment and a sense of superiority. It is associated with small and dull conceit, and with an absolute want of sympathy or affection. Its essential connection with vulgarity may be at once exemplified by the expression of the butcher's dog in Landseer's 'Low Life.' Cruikshank's Noah Claypole, in the illustrations to *Oliver Twist,* in the interview with the Jew, is, however, still more characteristic. It is the intensest rendering of vulgarity absolute and utter with which I am acquainted."

Mr. Paget, in his admirable article on Cruikshank's genius, already quoted, becomes eloquent on the prodigious effect on his time which the pictorial moralist achieved, especially by his illustrations to *Oliver Twist:*—

"More than forty years have passed since the appearance of these works; and if we were asked who, through that period, has been the most faithful chronicler of the ways, customs, and habits of the middle and lower classes of England, we should answer, George Cruikshank. In his pictures of society there is no depth which he has not sounded. From the murderer's cell to the pauper's death-bed there is no phase of crime and misery which has not served him to point a moral. But his sympathies are never perverted, or his sense of right and wrong dimmed by the atmosphere in which he moves. He is a stern though kindly moralist. In his hands vice is vice—a foe with whom no terms are to be kept. Yet, with what true feeling, what consummate skill, does he discriminate the shades of character, the ranks and degrees of crime, the extent and limits of moral corruption! In none of his works is this so apparent as in what we are inclined to rank as the most refined and complete of all, namely, the illustrations to *Oliver Twist.* Charles Dickens and George Cruikshank worked cordially hand in hand in the production of this admirable work, and neither will grudge to the other his share in the fame which has justly attended their joint labours. The characters are not more skilfully developed, as the story unfolds itself, by the pen of Dickens, than by the pencil of his colleague. Every time we turn over this wonderful series, we are more and more impressed with the genius that created, and the close observation of human nature which developed, the characteristics of Oliver through every varying phase of his career, from the memorable day when he 'asked for more.' . . .

We say this in no spirit of exaggeration, but with a profound conviction that no hand could have produced such works as those of George Cruikshank, which was not the index and the organ of a heart deeply imbued with the finest sympathies of humanity, and an intellect highly endowed with power of the keenest perception and the subtlest analysis." . . .

[H]e was never more at home than in his illustrations to the life of his old Islington friend and boon companion, Joe Grimaldi, which Dickens unwillingly consented to edit for Mr. Bentley. Dickens put the manuscript in order, and strung it together—dictating connecting bits to his father, whom Mr. Forster describes as revelling in the work. John Dickens revelled in work as well as play; in a bowl of gin punch, which it was his delight to mix at the Rainbow, in Fleet Street, and over which I have heard him tell many a capital story, not more than in his work as first manager of the Parliamentary staff of the *Daily News.*

Dickens described the manuscript of the life of the celebrated clown as twaddle, and was astonished at its success.

"Seventeen hundred Grimaldis have been already sold," he wrote to Forster, "and the demand increases daily!" Perhaps he did not rate at their full value George Cruikshank's etchings, which had a habit, in those days, of making "twaddle" palatable to the public very often. Over Grimaldi, Dickens and Cruikshank parted as author and artist; but they continued fast friends for many years after. . . .

Poor Samuel Phillips, who was hearty in spirit, albeit he lived for many years at death's door, says of him: "George is popular among his associates. His face is an index of his mind. There is nothing anomalous about him and his doings. His appearance, his illustrations, his speeches, are all alike—all picturesque, artistic, full of fun, feeling, geniality, and quaintness. His seriousness is grotesque, and his drollery is profound. He is the prince of caricaturists, and one of the best of men."

In a whimsical account of an amateur strolling excursion, in which Cruikshank was one of the company (1847), supposed to be written by Mrs. Gamp, Dickens has vividly described the illustrator of *Oliver Twist:*—

"I do assure you, Mrs. Harris, when I stood in the railways office that morning, with my bundle on my arm, and one patten in my hand, you might have knocked me down with a feather, far less porkmangers which was a lumping against me, continual and sewere all round. I was drove about like a brute animal and almost worritted into fits, when a gentleman with a large shirt-collar, and a hook nose, and a eye like one of Mr. Sweedlepipes's hawks, and long locks of hair, and wiskers that I wouldn't have no lady as I was engaged to meet suddenly a turning round a corner, for any sum of money you could offer me, says, laughing, 'Halloa, Mrs. Gamp, what are *you* up to?' I didn't know him from a man (except by his clothes); but I says faintly, 'If you're a christian man, show me where to get a second-cladge ticket for Manjester, and have me put in a carriage, or I shall drop.' Which he kindly did, in a cheerful kind of a way, skipping about in the strangest manner as ever I see, making all kinds of actions, and looking and vinking at me from under the brim of his hat (which was a good deal turned up) to that extent, that I should have thought he meant something, but for being so flurried as not to have no thoughts at all until I was put in a carriage along with an individgle—the politest as ever I see—in a shepherd's plaid suit with a long gold watch-guard hanging round his neck, and his hand a trembling through nervousness worse than a aspian leaf." Presently they fell into conversation.

"'P'raps,' he says, 'if you're not of the party, you don't know who it was that assisted you into this carriage!'

"'No, sir,' I says, 'I don't indeed.'

"'Why, ma'am,' he says, a-wisperin, 'that was George, ma'am.'

"'What George, sir? I don't know no George,' says I.

"'The great George, ma'am,' says he. 'The Crookshanks.'

An illustration for "Clement Lorimer," by Angus Reach.

"'If you'll believe me, Mrs. Harris, I turns my head, and see the wery man a-making picters of me on his thumb nail, at the winder! While another of 'em—a tall, slim, melancolly gent, with dark hair, and a bage vice—looks over his shoulder, with his head o' one side as if he understood the subject, and cooly says, 'I've draw'd her several times—in *Punch*,' he says too! The owdacious wretch!'" . . .

[W. H. Wills wrote:] "The force of George Cruikshank's character lay in the single-minded earnestness with which he carried out his objects. These throughout his life were numerous and always good. Zeal and energy glowed out of him upon whatever he undertook, whether saving a family from starvation (and there are instances in which he could only have done this at the risk of stinting himself), or rehearsing the character assigned to him in a private play, or commanding a regiment of volunteers, or advocating and advancing the temperance cause at every conceivable sacrifice of time and money. It was not until after his second marriage that he took to temperance. In his first wife's lifetime he sacrificed to the jolly god rather oftener than occasionally; and surely no man drank with more fervour and enjoyment, nor carried his liquor so kindly, so merrily. Then was the time to hear him sing 'Lord Bateman' in character, and costume improvised from

table-covers, table-napkins, and antimacassars—anything he could lay hands on—with the laughing help of his host. He was what Albert Smith called 'great fun' in this song at any time.

"Even when dependent upon his pencil and etching-needle for means of existence, if any good was to be done for a decayed brother artist or literary friend, George was only too ready (for his own prosperity) to throw down his tools, and stroll about the country with a theatrical company, or go anywhere to solicit subscriptions and make speeches, or to settle to his work-table again to make gratuitous sketches for bazaars and charities. When acting in Edinburgh, for Leigh Hunt's benefit, with Charles Dickens and his brilliant *dramatis personæ*, news came to him that a country editor, with a large family, whom he had often previously helped, was on the edge of ruin for the want of fifty pounds. 'I *must* send it to the poor fellow,' he said to Dickens, 'immediately.' 'That would be very kind to him,' answered Dickens, 'but very unkind to yourself. By-the-bye, have you got fifty pounds in your pocket?' 'Oh dear, no,' was Cruikshank's reply, 'but I want you to lend me the money to send to him—now—at once.' Dickens's rejoinder was not resort to his cheque book, but the remark that he knew George's incapable friend would be as badly off as ever after the execution had been paid out of his house, even if the money was sent. 'Then,' he added, 'you would deny yourself all sorts of things and be miserable till you paid me back. That I can't stand, so I must decline.'" . . .

[B]etween 1849 and 1853] Cruikshank illustrated two Christmas stories by Mrs. Gore, **"The Snowstorm"** and **"The Inundation,"** in Angus B. Reach's *Clement Lorimer*, the *Songs of the late Charles Dibdin*, Frank Smedley's *Frank Fairlegh*, and *Uncle Tom's Cabin*—representing some seventy etchings, and as many wood-blocks. The Frank Fairlegh etchings introduced Cruikshank to Frank Smedley, and led to a final venture in the magazine form, with which David Bogue, the publisher, had resolved to test finally the hold the artist still had on the public.

Bogue had long been Cruikshank's fast friend and admirer, and was loth to believe that his name had ceased to be an attraction to the British public upon a title-page. Moreover, he had had some recent successes with the "inimitable" George. In two years the *Sandboys*, in which was his amazingly minute **"All the World Going to See the Exhibition"** and his drawing of the transept, packed with myriads of people at the opening ceremony . . . [H]is recent Fairy Library had been a failure. Dickens (in *Household Words*), among others, had protested against teetotalism being introduced into fairyland; and had, two years previously, even ridiculed what was called Cruikshank's temperance fanaticism, in a paper called "Whole Hogs." These attacks, no doubt, helped to put an end to *George Cruikshank's Fairy Library*, after he had illustrated with some exquisitely dainty scenes **"Puss in Boots," "Hop o' my Thumb," "Jack and the Beanstalk,"** and **"Cinderella."** Cuthbert Bede, in a "Reminiscence of Cruikshank" in *Notes and Queries*, remarks: "It was very evident from that article, 'Frauds on the Fairies,' and also from a previous one from the same pen, called 'Whole Hogs,' that Dickens considered Cruikshank to be occasionally given over to the culture of crotchets, and to the furious riding of favourite hobbies. But in all these things it is indisputable that the great moral artist was firmly persuaded that he was acting in the cause of suffering humanity, and engaged upon some work for the amelioration of his fellow-creatures. And whatever was the act, and however small and trivial it might appear in the sight of the majority, Cruikshank threw himself into it heart and soul, and, like everything else he put his hand to, he did it with all his might."

To be driven from fairyland, which was the realm of his happiest dreams, was a bitter disappointment, and he felt deeply the blow of the friend who drove him forth from it.

Dickens had said of him and his fairies,—

"He is the only designer fairyland has had. Callot's imps, for all their strangeness, are only of the earth, earthy. Fuseli's fairies belong to the infernal regions; they are monstrous, lurid, and hideously melancholy. Mr. Cruikshank alone has a true insight into the 'little people.' They are something like men and women, and yet not flesh and blood; they are laughing and mischievous, but why we know not. Mr. Cruikshank, however, has had some dream or the other, or else a natural mysterious instinct, or else some preternatural fairy revelation, which has made him acquainted with the looks and ways of the fantastical subjects of Oberon and Titania."

When this wizard of the etching-needle, some fifteen years after he had drawn "the awful Jew," pretended to put forth a whole Fairy Library of his own, the author of the Jew sat himself down and wrote:—

"We have lately observed, with pain, the intrusion of a Whole Hog of unwieldy dimensions into the fairy flower-garden. The rooting of the animal among the roses would in itself have awakened in us nothing but indignation; our pain arises from his being violently driven in by a man of genius, our own beloved friend, Mr. George Cruikshank. That incomparable artist is, of all men, the last who should lay his exquisite hand on fairy text. In his own art he understands it so perfectly, and illustrates it so beautifully, so humorously, so wisely, that he should never lay down his etching-needle to 'edit' the Ogre, to whom with that little instrument he can render such extraordinary justice. But, to 'editing' Ogres, and Hop-o'-my-Thumbs, and their families, our dear moralist has in a rash moment taken, as a means of propagating the doctrines of Total Abstinence, Prohibition of the Sale of Spirituous Liquors, Free Trade, and Popular Education. For the introduction of these topics, he has altered the text of a fairy story; and against his right to do any such thing we protest with all our might and main. Of his likewise altering it to advertise that excellent series of plates, **'The Bottle,'** we say nothing more than that we foresee a new and improved edition of 'Goody Two Shoes,' edited by E. Moses

and Son; of the 'Dervish' with the box of ointment, edited by Professor Holloway; and of 'Jack and the Beanstalk,' edited by Mary Wedlake, the popular authoress of 'Do you Bruise your Oats yet?'"

Dickens goes on to point out what would become of our great books if such a precedent were to be followed. "Imagine a total abstinence edition of **Robinson Crusoe,** with the rum left out. Imagine a peace edition, with the gunpowder left out, and the rum left in. Imagine a vegetarian edition, with the goat's flesh left out. Imagine a Kentucky edition, to introduce a flogging of that 'tarnal old nigger Friday, twice a week. Imagine an Aborigines Protection Society edition, to deny the cannibalism and make Robinson embrace the amiable savages whenever they landed. Robinson Crusoe would be 'edited' out of his island in a hundred years, and the island would be swallowed up in the editorial ocean." Then follows a most humorous story of "Cinderella," edited by a stump orator on Temperance, Ocean Penny Postage, Sanitary Science; ending with this pleasant moral: "Frauds on the Fairies once permitted, we see little reason why they may not come to this, and great reason why they may. The Vicar of Wakefield was wisest when he was tired of being always wise. The world is too much with us, early and late."

Poor George Cruikshank dropped his pencil, and Cuthbert Bede has told us how he found the artist, on an October day in 1853, still smarting from the effects of Dickens's article. Cruikshank, however, was not the man to feel a blow and sit down under it. . . .

Cruikshank had no sooner an organ of his own, than he buckled on his armour, and prepared for a lively assault upon the author of the two *Household Words* articles. In the second (and last) number of "George Cruikshank's Magazine" (to which I have already referred) is a letter from Hop-o'-my-Thumb to Charles Dickens, Esq., upon "Frauds on the Fairies," "Whole Hogs," etc. It is in Cruikshank's homely style, but the reader will see that it is not without several good home-thrusts. He begins:—

"Right trusty, well-beloved, much-read, and admired Sir,— My attention has lately been called to an article in *Household Words,* entitled 'Frauds on the Fairies,' in which I fancy I recognise your master hand as the author—and in which article, as it appears to me, you have gone a *leetle* out of your way to find fault with our mutual friend George Cruikshank, for the way in which he has edited **'Hop-o'-my-Thumb and the Seven League Boots.'** You may, perhaps, be surprised at receiving a letter from so small an individual as myself; but, independently of the deep debt of gratitude which I feel that I owe to that gentleman, for the way in which he has edited my history, my anxiety to maintain the honour and credit of the noble family to which I belong impels me to take up my pen (made from the quill of a humming-bird), to endeavour to justify the course adopted by my editor, and also to take the liberty of setting you right upon one or two points in which you are entirely mistaken.

"These may seem bold words, from such a mite as I am, to such a literary giant as you are; but I have had to deal with giants in my time, and I am not afraid of them, and I shall therefore take leave to tell you, that although you may have held in your memory some of the remarkable facts in my interesting history, yet that you were ignorant of the general character of the whole; and the only way in which I can account for a man of your remarkable acuteness having made such a great mistake is, that you have suffered that extraordinary seven-league boot imagination of yours to run away with you into your *own* Fairy Land,—and thus have given your *own* colour to this history; and, consequently, a credit and a character to the old editions which do not belong to them."

Cruikshank then quotes passages from Dickens's article, and continues: "Now this, which you call 'Frauds on the Fairies,' in my humble opinion, might as well have been called 'Much Ado about Nothing'; for, had my editor been altering the text of any standard literary work, the writing of any man of mark—one of your own glorious books, for example—then indeed, you might have raised a hue and cry; but to insist upon preserving the entire integrity of a fairy tale, which has been and is constantly altering in the recitals, and in the printing of various editions in different countries, and even counties, appears to my little mind like shearing one of your own 'whole hogs,' where there is 'great cry and little wool.'"

Then Cruikshank asks where is tenderness or mercy in Tom Thumb's father, when he induces his wife to take their seven children into the forest to perish miserably of hunger, or to be devoured by wild beasts? "My editor," Hop-o'-my-Thumb proceeds, "seeing that such a statement was not only disgusting, but against nature, and consequently unfit for the pure and parent-loving minds of children, felt certain that any father acting in such a manner must either be *mad* or *under the influence of intoxicating liquor,* which is much the same thing, and therefore, wishing to avoid any allusion to such an awful affliction as insanity, has accounted for my father's unnatural conduct by attributing it to that cause which marks its progress, daily and hourly, by acts of unnatural brutality." Farther on, Hop-o'-my-Thumb, referring to the little peculiarity of the young ogres "biting little children on purpose to suck their blood," asks if that be one of the good things to be nourished in a child's heart. "And I should also like to know," he adds, "what there is so enchanting and captivating to '*young fancies*' in this description of a father (ogre though he be) cutting the throats of his own seven children? Is this the sort of stuff that helps to '*keep us ever young,*' or give us that innocent delight which we may share with children?" Having thanked Mr. Cruikshank for rescuing his moral character from the gross imputations former biographers had cast upon it, representing him to be, in the transaction of the seven-league boots and the mother of the slaughtered children, "an *unfeeling, artful liar, and a thief,*" and his parents "*receivers of stolen goods,*'," he turns upon Mr. Dickens for his attempt to throw ridicule upon the Temperance question, and also his "evident contempt, and even hatred,

against that cause,' as shown in his "Whole Hogs." Hop-o'-my-Thumb hereupon valiantly and defiantly remarks: "This is not the place, nor is it my purpose, now to discuss the Temperance question, but I take the liberty of telling you that it is a question which you evidently do not understand, for if you did, your good heart and sanguine disposition would make you, if possible, a more enthusiastic advocate than my editor."

About the good intentions of both artist and critic there cannot be any doubt in any honest mind.

Cruikshank had his parting thrust at his assailant; he could not help that:—

"You are generally," he says to his friend Dickens, "most happy in your titles; but, in this instance, the application seems singularly inappropriate. The 'whole hog' should, by rights, belong to those parties who patronise pork butchers; and the term as applied to the peace people would be better used in regard to the Great Bear, or any other war party; and surely, as to any allusion to the 'unclean animal,' in connection with total abstinence, the term would more properly attach to those who wallow in the mire, and destroy their intellects by the use of intoxicating liquors, until they debase themselves to the level of the porcine quadruped! And, as far as my editor is concerned, I consider it a great act of injustice to mix him up with other questions, and with which, *you know,* he has nothing whatever to do. I have therefore to beg that in future you will not drive your 'whole hogs' against us, but take them to some other market, or keep them to yourself, if you like; but we'll none of 'em, and therefore I take this opportunity of driving them back."

The controversy is closed with a capital cut of Hop-o'-my-Thumb driving some prodigious porkers back to *Household Words.* . . .

Cruikshank gives his views on popular education in his homely simple way:—

"One of the great social questions of the day is the necessity and importance of a general or national system of education for the humble classes, upon such a comprehensive plan as shall give every child born in the United Kingdom a certain amount of book knowledge, and also of moral and religious training, as they are, or *ought* to be, entitled to as juvenile members of a civilized community—such training as may prepare them to fill useful and honest positions in life, or, perhaps, be the first step to those high stations so often filled by honest, hardworking, mercantile men, or ingenious mechanics. Now, every thinking and right-minded person will agree that this object is a most desirable one, and that no innocent child should be so neglected as to be allowed to grow up in a state of savage ignorance; and at the first blush nothing seems more easily to be accomplished, in a wealthy and intelligent country like ours, than to arrange such a general system as is here alluded to, and to provide the ways and means. Well! all this *would be* simple and easily accomplished, but for one obstacle—namely, the differences in the religious opinions of a portion of the adult population. Yes, strange as it may appear,—nay, monstrous as it is,—nevertheless these religious differences have been, and are now, the only bar to the adoption of any wide and general system of secular education."

"It is of course impossible to please all parties; but few persons, I imagine, could surely object to a national system of education upon the following plan:—In the first place, an Act of Parliament should be passed, making it *imperative* that every child should receive some education, and where the parents are destitute or depraved, then that the State shall take the position of the parents, and educate and train up all the neglected and helpless children. In the second place:—In the schools, let reading, writing, and arithmetic be taught (with other branches of education, if possible, or required), and such moral training as will teach a child the difference between RIGHT and WRONG—and here let the schoolmaster's duty cease, and that of the ministers of religion begin. And in the third place:—Let it be the duty of the clergyman, and ministers of all denominations, to instruct all those children who belong to their particular church, chapel, or sect, in the religious belief of their parents; but when the parents do not attend any place of worship, or profess any particular creed—then, that the clergy of the Established Church be allowed to instruct all such children in the religion of the State. By such an arrangement as this, it appears to me that if all the poor helpless children of the land were schooled in the common elements of reading, writing, etc., for five days in the week, and the clergy and ministers of all denominations were to instruct these children one day in the six in the religion of the class to which they belong (independent of the Sunday), that then all parties might be satisfied, and a great objection done away with as to the great general system which I here propose for secular instruction and moral and religious training."

He goes on to remark that a reformatory may be wanted in any country, under any circumstances, "but why should we have *Ragged* Schools in RICH ENGLAND?" He proceeds to argue that there would be no need for either Ragged Schools or Reformatories if the use of "strong drink" were abolished; and he calls upon "the grown-up people not to allow innocent children to starve and fall into evil ways, because they cannot agree upon the mode of cutting a SLICE OF BREAD AND BUTTER." He adds: "But as prevention *is* better than cure, I call upon all those who delight in good works to aid the Temperance cause, which is, in truth, the only radical cure for the evils complained of."

The tail-piece to this characteristic pamphlet—as charming as it is characteristic—is a brightly-executed drawing on wood of Britannia seated upon the British lion, couchant, with her arms about "her ragged and reformatory pets."

George Somes Layard

SOURCE: "George Cruikshank: A Defence," in *Temple Bar,* Vol. 99, No. 397, December, 1893, pp. 560-67.

"By the way, did you ever see anything like Lady Godiva Trotter's dress last night? People *will* go on chattering, although *we* hold our tongues; and after all, my good soul, what will their scandal matter a hundred years hence?"

So wrote Thackeray in one of his delightful *Roundabouts,* but he wrote it, we must remember, of the nobodies, the Browns, Joneses and Robinsons (and of Mesdames Brown, Jones and Robinson), and not of the men and women whose names are, and ever will be, household words with us, so long as Art endures and is inseparable from our existence. If we want to see how these ought to be regarded by us, and with what jealousy we should treat their reputations, just let us glance for a moment at another of these secular sermons, and see how the master treats of two men, famous, admired, beloved, the Goldsmith and the Gibbon of our time, Washington Irving and Macaulay, dead just within a month of each other, and keeps on saying:—"But we are not talking about faults—we want to say *Nil nisi bonum.*"

Something, I know, it may be possible to say and write against George Cruikshank, and such will have to be written some day, with all deliberation, when a full and authentic account of his life is considered advisable, but the time for that has not yet come in the opinion of those who have special sources of information to draw upon; and surely we can wait until that moment arrives, when it will be possible to see how the lights will predominate over the shadows (as they assuredly will do), and confine ourselves, in our fragmentary discourses on this great artist, to *Nil nisi bonum.*

Some time ago it was my privilege to point out in the pages of *Temple Bar* how, by a strange and undesigned coincidence, it was provable to demonstration that certain impressions taken from etched plates, and declared by George Cruikshank solemnly to be early "proofs," but which on the surface were very suspicious, and were consequently declared by the *cognoscenti* to be "spurious," were, in fact, in the state that the artist affirmed them to be. Nor did I pretend at the time that, by proving him to be in the right in this particular instance, it must therefore be concluded that everything that has been said against "the man that drew the awful Jew" is false and unsustainable. On the contrary, I said in so many words, that doubtless many of the hard things that have been said of him had a foundation in fact, but what I did think made it worth while to take up the cudgels in his defence was the opportunity that was here afforded of showing that, although he had his failings, he was not so degraded as to have deserved to be put in the dock and charged with false and fraudulent pretences like any common criminal. For, let us not mince matters, this is what the question at issue really was. And, at least as regards those plates to **"The Miser's Daughter,"** with which I was dealing, I defy any one to say that the answer was not complete and conclusive. I had found something new and good to say of George Cruikshank, and I thought it was worth

An illustration for "Jack and the Beanstalk."

while saying it, and I maintain that, if some laudable action were to be discovered in the life of the arch-traitor of the human race, and some reviewer thought it worth while to show that he was not quite as black as he was painted, that would be no excuse for raking up again, by way of contrast, matters distasteful and un-savoury and to his discredit. Surely, as I said in the article to which I refer, surely we are not so in love with the sediment that lies at the bottom of every life that we must be constantly prodding down to the bot-tom, and befouling the nice purity which has come uppermost. And it is not only because I protest against the modern tendency to say *Nil nisi malum* about George Cruikshank that I take up my pen to answer Mr. Spiel-mann's remarks upon my article in the pages of the *Graphic,* but also because I think that due care should be taken by a gentleman who speaks with the authority that his acknowledged position in the artistic world gives his utterances, to make quite sure that the state-ments that he makes are not likely to be misunderstood by the general reader.

The Dial

SOURCE: A review of *The Cruikshank Fairy Book,* in *The Dial,* Vol. XXIII, No. 276, December 16, 1897, p. 398.

The Cruikshank Fairy-Book ought to be one of the most popular of the year, for it contains four of the good old stories told in the good old way. **"Puss in Boots," "Jack and the Beanstalk," "Hop-o'-my-Thumb,"** and **"Cinder-ella"** are always new; and when the fine old Cruikshank illustrations are printed with them, they become irresistible. The drawings have a delightful amount of action and char-acter, and yet they are adroitly kept in harmony with the tales. This is much the most important of the year's reprints.

Robert Allerton Parker

SOURCE: "The Great George," in *The Arts,* Vol. VI, No. 4, October, 1924, pp. 210-24.

The casual visitor who chances upon the Cruikshank col-lection in the Widener Memorial Library at Harvard, or who even glances at A. S. W. Rosenbach's catalogue, gains a fresh appreciation of Thackeray's exclamation: "What amazing energetic fecundity do we find in him!" These words were published in 1840; and the prolific activ-ity of the "great George" was to continue at least thirty years longer. Copies of all of Cruikshank's drawings and plates, it was said, would fill a "couple of wagons"; and one early addict boasted that he had collected eight large "elephant" volumes of them. Nearly every one, in the heyday of Cruikshank's fame, collected his drawings.

In this age, when eyes are incessantly assailed by pic-tures, photographs, "comic" strips, "rotogravure" sections, posters and motion pictures, it is hard to imagine the psychology of an age deprived of them. And, therefore, we misinterpret the amazing popularity enjoyed for more than half a century by such an illustrator as George Cruik-shank. His intrinsic merits—they are real and solid and tangible—had little to do with the imposing structure of his popularity. All the personality of anecdote and senti-mental logrolling which gathered about his pictures, and which led people to the belief that artists of this type were as great—if indeed not greater—than the authors whose works they interpreted, was the result of other forces. Investigation would probably reveal that this ep-och, which did not enjoy the advantages of the photo-engraving process, the camera, or the motion-picture, actually hungered for the pictorial representation of its own immediate life—a new form of picture-writing. Men like Cruikshank worked incessantly to satisfy this demand, and the popularity he so rapidly achieved attests not only to the reality of this deeply-rooted craving for pictures that told a story, but to the enthusiastic gratitude enjoyed by the public when this appetite was satisfied.

What surprises us today is not so much the triumphant popularity of the great George, as the high quality of his engraving and draughtsmanship. One of George Cruikshank's earliest passions was for the theatre. All of his engravings are alive with a powerful theatrical sense, sometimes not too effectively controlled. His set-tings, whether interior or exterior, are rich in evocative architectural detail. Effective "properties" and accessories abound. If it be a street scene, he makes us read the signs over the shops and interests us in the style of lettering in which they are painted. He can suggest the glamorous effulgence of the interior of a candlelit theatre with the most skillful economy of means. At first sight some of the engravings might seem overcrowded. But we must remember that in a sense these illustrations were to be *read,* to be studied, for in their crowded boundaries Cruikshank sought to concentrate a maximum of suggestion and evocation, to stimulate to utmost the aroused imagination of the reader. It is easy enough today to object, as Gleeson White has done, to the excessive and puerile caricature that finds its way into the works of this school, to the trite and ineffective bits of melodrama; but to do so is to criticize an individual for the idiosyncrasies of his period. . . .

Cruikshank carried over into the nineteenth century the ebullient health, the gusto, the spirited vitality of the eighteenth. He inherited something of the raciness, the rich indigenous power of Hogarth, the animal vigor of Rowlandson, the crudity of Gillray. In contrast to his successors of the sixties, or more refined contemporaries like Leech, his satire was, as a French commentator pointed out, like a series of rough invectives compared to the pointed epigrams of a gentleman in evening clothes.

Cruikshank's popularity was based on the firmest of foundations. Cockney to the core, a doughty and magnificent Philistine, perfervid in his patriotism and prejudices, he expressed in his prints and plates all that was dear to hearts of oak in that period. When in 1811 the dreadful night of imbecility descended upon the savage genius of Gillray, this boy of nineteen was acclaimed his logical successor. His fame increased steadily during the Regency.

A century ago the British public was completely and heartily Francophobe; and Cruikshank's twenty-one color plates made in 1822 to illustrate David Carey's **"Life in Paris"** added enormously to his prestige. The book comprises "the Rambles, Sprees and Amours of Dick Wildfire of Corinthian celebrity, and his Bang-up Companions, Squire Jenkins and Captain O'Shuffleton, with the Whimsical Adventures of the Halibut Family, &c. . . . " Looking for the first time at these engravings of Cruikshank, we are amazed at all the realistic touches which give them such an air of verisimilitude and authenticity. His Parisians are indefatigable in their gayety, deceitful, immoral and shoulder-shrugging, and never quite a match for the superior intelligence and skillful tactics of the English visitors. We praise Cruikshank's skill in observing the Parisian scene, his suggestive evocation of the atmosphere by architectural background and Gallic customs. And even when we learn that in the whole eighty-six years of his active life "good old George" never got any nearer to Paris than the amphibious and semi-British Boulogne (where he disgustedly spent one rainy day), our admiration is by no means shattered. Whether he evolved those authentic touches from the hidden recesses of his inner consciousness or, whether, resorting to a practice that has in our own day become so popular and profitable, he used "scrap," we cannot deny him an extraordinary power of vivid reconstruction.

By the time the youthful Queen had ascended the throne and the Victorian spirit in arts and letters had begun to crystallize, Cruikshank was almost a national institution. But this idolatry had brought with it no corrupting prosperity. George saw far less talented men—fashionable painters of the day—achieve fame and fortune, the commendations of, and even membership in, the Royal Academy—while his own powers were superciliously looked down upon as slightly inferior, and even somewhat vulgar. Had he only known it, the Academy had likewise looked down in his time upon Hogarth, preferring the amiable and anemic productions of the now forgotten Mr. Penny to those of the self-taught Hogarth.

Cruikshank was a great popular idol when the youthful Charles Dickens was called in to write "letterpress" about a series of his engravings. *Sketches by Boz* was the result. A subtle conflict, at first barely perceptible, began to take root in Cruikshank's mind. The illustrations for *Oliver Twist* aroused scarcely less enthusiasm than the novel itself; and Cruikshank was temperamentally ready to agree with those admirers who acclaimed him as greater than the young novelist. The public was especially impressed with the illustration of **"Fagin in the Condemned Cell"** and doggerel was printed about

> "The dreadful Jew
> That Cruikshank drew . . . "

In his tribute to Cruikshank, Thackery expressed the contemporary enthusiasm: "What a fine touching picture of melancholy desolation is that of Sykes and the dog! The poor cur is not too well drawn, the landscape is stiff and formal; but in this case the faults, if faults they be, of execution rather add to than diminish the effect of the picture: it has a strange, wild, dreary broken-hearted look; we fancy we see the landscape as it must have appeared to Sykes, when, ghastly and with bloodshot eyes he looked at it." . . .

Reputed himself to have been in earlier years of a most convivial disposition, with a penchant for low life and the beery atmosphere of London pubs and clubs, the etcher who had vitalized the racy pages of Smollett with his illustrations of Humphrey Clinker and Peregrine Pickle, as well as free-and-easy society depicted in Fielding's *Tom Jones,* fell under the spell of the temperance agitation, a movement of which the excesses furnish one of the most colorful chapters of Victorian culture. Drink, according to these agitators, was responsible not only for poverty but all the social evils. Inspired perhaps by unconscious memories of Hogarth's "Gin Lane," and with all the fiery enthusiasm of the sinner who has returned to the straight and narrow path, with the rigid rectitude of a reformed Magdalen, Cruikshank created his pictorial tale of **"The Bottle"**—although it should be noted in passing that he had attained the mature age of 56 before he himself gave up the consolation of alcohol. The popularity of **"The Bottle"** spread like wildfire. Dickens was deeply impressed by it; and the general public "ate it up." It was even dramatized and played to crowded houses. Into his engravings of the public houses and the gin palaces, the beer-shops and other such disreputable resorts, there creeps—at least so it seems to our unsympathetic eyes—a note of regretful reminiscence, an unconscious caressing by the artist of his remembrance of those things so irretrievably past. But not even to himself does he admit it, nor deviate from the stern logic of his tale. His graphic fable is that of a decent, self-respecting working man and his worthy wife, the parents of two handsome children, a boy and a girl. The man and his wife attain a comfortable and respectable middle age. Then one day, there being a roast goose for dinner, the husband, in a jocular mood, makes the fatal mistake of sending out for a bottle of gin, and persuades his good wife to take a drop after the stuffing. Thereupon with the inevitability of a tragedy of Sophocles, the whole family promptly drinks itself to destruction. So great was the success of **"The Bottle"** that the great George immediately prepared a sequel, tracing the life of the ill-fated son and daughter, who go through gin palace and beer-shop and dancing resort, until they are brought up for robbery.

The young man is convicted and dies aboard the hulks; while the daughter, shamed and desolate and driven mad by the disgrace, throws herself from London bridge and perishes in the dark and chilly waters below. Mr. Dickens confessed himself profoundly impressed with this final scene of the tragedy, though he did not share Cruikshank's ardor for temperance agitation.

Cruikshank never ceased regretting that he had not taken up painting. Painters were honored by the Royal Academy and even elected to that august body, while pictorial satirists and illustrators, who conferred life upon the characters of literature of history, by the mere fact that they had chosen a humbler—though at that time a more difficult medium—must perforce content themselves with the plaudits of the multitude. Some such reasoning as this must have impelled Mr. Cruikshank in his declining years to paint a huge canvas dealing with the un-Victorian revels of Bacchus. His admirers bought it and presented it to the National Gallery, where, if I am not mistaken, it may still edify the avowed enemies of drink.

But despite the indignation of Messrs. Forster and Ainsworth, who flatly contradicted the old gentleman's claims of co-authorship when he made them in 1872, the great George was by no means without honor in his own country. And when finally, in his eighty-sixth year, he passed away *The Times* in a leading article acclaimed him in one respect, and perhaps the most important, from the point of view of Victorian esthetics, the superior of Hogarth. "It is something remarkable," proclaimed *The Times,* "that a satirist who chastised fashionable and popular vice for more than sixty years almost without intermission should not have left one drawing behind him that might not be handed around the family circle of any English household. In this respect, at least, Cruikshank might claim to be superior to Hogarth." And it may have been this success of Cruikshank in finally obliterating from his plates the more offensive features of his artistic ancestry—the coarse animal vigor of Rowlandson, the

bounding but not always respectable vitality of Hogarth, or the savage, slashing satire of Gillray, rather than any noteworthy originality, that won for him a final resting place in St. Paul's.

John Fowles

SOURCE: "Introduction: Remembering Cruikshank," in *George Cruikshank: A Revaluation,* edited by Robert L. Patten, Princeton University Press, 1974, pp. xxv-xxviii.

Captain Frederick Marryat, the nautical novelist, visited Lyme Regis in the fall of 1819 and did some sketches that he passed on for "improvement" to a friend. The friend's name was George Cruikshank. One of the results was a print that I shamelessly adapted for my novel *The French Lieutenant's Woman.* It shows a happy gentleman *voyeur* ensconced over a beach, telescope glued to his eye, and deeply absorbed in bird-watching—the birds in this case consisting of a charming batch of plumply naked Regency ladies tumbling and disporting themselves in the sea. *Hydromania!* reads the legend, *or a Touch of the Sub-Lyme and Beautiful* (1819)—a horrid pun on Edmund Burke's noble and unreadable *Philosophical Enquiry into . . . the Sublime and Beautiful* (1756). It shocked the worthy citizens of Lyme at the time and has gone on shocking them a little ever since; our definitive local history (published in 1927) feels obliged to pronounce the thing a tasteless lampoon without any historical basis at all. Yet it is curious: Lyme likes to boast of its artistic connections. All the guidebooks proudly parade Henry Fielding, Jane Austen, Tennyson, Whistler, and a host of obscurer figures; but never Cruikshank. I mention all this because the rancor of Lyme somehow reflects what has happened to the poor man in the history of British art. It is as if he made too much fun of too many things; and we've been making him pay for it ever since.

Of course "illustrations by Cruikshank" still raises the price in every second-hand bookseller's catalogue, but fashion and taste seem adamantly to refuse him serious consideration. . . . In this green-and-gold context of English pastoral mysticism Cruikshank may seem to cut rather a shabby urban figure; and then at the other extreme we have become an age of violent satire, and find Gillray's excesses and savageries more "significant" than Cruikshank's toleration. Current taste in England has also leapt ahead and fallen heavily, a lot too heavily in my opinion, for the camp fancies of Kate Greenaway and Walter Crane. Doré and Gavarni have their claques. There is a new vogue for the artists of the great period of *Punch;* over the last ten years I have watched the prices of drawings by Tenniel, Leech, Keene and du Maurier rise like rockets. Even to Cruikshank's own most immediate rival in the field of book illustration, Hablot K. Browne ("Phiz"), history seems to have dealt a much kinder hand. . . .

Indeed, I think what is possibly Cruikshank's finest series of book illustrations, those for Maxwell's *History of the Irish Rebellion in 1798* (1845), can be compared only to

Goya. Of course they contain unfair propaganda against the Irish and lack the universality of the great Spaniard's rage against human injustice and cruelty. For all that, they still strike savagely off the page. Look at the brilliantly differentiated faces of the two Irish rebels impaling the Loyal Little Drummer in the illustration of that title: the one is an active sadist, the other is a mindless doer of his job. And then see the child dancing with joy in the background, the blandly watching face of the soldier behind, and the officer seemingly oblivious of what is going on. Ireland 1798—or a certain village in Vietnam a year or two ago?

In his illustrations for another indifferent text—Ainsworth's **Jack Sheppard** (1840)—we see a further side of Cruikshank's mastery: his ability to create an indelible image. I never run across Sheppard's name without immediately evoking that white-faced young demon with his bizarrely ferocious eyebrows and jet-black Joan-of-Arc crewcut. Think of Fagin, Bill Sikes, the Artful Dodger: it is Cruikshank who has proved as inimitable as his author.

Needless to say, there were other Cruikshanks: the forerunner of du Maurier, critic of middle-class foibles; the humorous vignettist; the temperance fanatic. All those aspects of his work bring him down to a lower level and perhaps define his essential weakness: too much humor, not enough anger—a very English combination. Chronologically, my genial little joke against Lyme must have been done between work on the cuts for the Hone pamphlets; and something I did not reveal at the beginning—the print copies to the point of plagiarism a previous jibe by Rowlandson against hydromania at Margate. To our authenticity-obsessed modern minds all this may seem a grave criticism of Cruikshank, indeed dangerously near make him guilty of the fault I have already laid at Phiz's door: a soft center. But I don't think so: it simply shows his humanity and his breadth—if you like, the Augustan eighteenth century still triumphing over the narrower nineteenth.

We can see that breadth—of technique as well as of spirit—right down among the trivia: in the distinctly hasty yet vivid little drawings for **Sunday in London,** in the much more elaborate "strip cartoon" series, **The Progress of Mr. Lambkin** (*The Bachelor's Own Book,* 1844). In both there is a richness of observed detail and open honesty about the life portrayed. No Dr. Bowdler here, no Victorian prudery; but a full ration of the human heart.

I detect two great figures behind Cruikshank. The first is Hogarth, of course. Cruikshank never mastered oil, and given the age-old European award of primacy to that medium, I suppose he has to be placed on a lower pinnacle. But I suspect that if he and Hogarth had been Japanese, it might well have been the latter who now stood in the shade. Lists of artistic merit are strictly for fools, however, and the important thing is that these two English graphic masters did share, behind their personal neuroses, their particular exaggerations, an identity of spirit. They both attacked hypocrisy and anything that smelt of the complacent Establishment; more interested

in man himself than in nature, they had the city in their blood; and for all their ruthless attacks on the stupidity and bestiality of *Homo sapiens,* they never lost faith in his essential humanity.

Behind them again, a greater figure still, and not an artist—that arch-destroyer of the puritanical and the illiberal, that founding father of the open society, that presiding spirit of both the Renaissance and our own century, François Rabelais. To be sure, he and Cruikshank would hardly have seen eye to eye over the divinity of the bottle. But I go back to my little print of Lyme, to the naked girls in the gentle September sea, to the delighted face of the watching man. The basic design may be stolen from Rowlandson, but it is far more than a mere copy. I still see in it the quintessence of Rabelais' smiling humanism, the *substantifique moëlle,* the real marrow of his gigantic comic bone.

Humor ought to be a religion; and Cruikshank, an honored saint of that church.

E. D. H. Johnson

SOURCE: "The George Cruikshank Collection at Princeton," in *George Cruikshank: A Revaluation,* edited by Robert L. Patten, Princeton University Press, 1974, pp. 1-33.

Cruikshank's turn to book illustration in 1823 liberated inherent faculties both for the purely comic and for the fantastic which lay at the heart of his vision, but which had hitherto been suppressed in the service of political satire. His first excursions in the vein of whimsical drollery which he was to make so peculiarly his own occurred in the forty etchings which appeared in the four volumes of an exceedingly rare publication, **The Humourist: A Collection of Entertaining Tales, Anecdotes, Repartees, Witty Sayings, Epigrams, Bon Mots, Jeu d'Esprits, etc.** (1819-20). In addition to the first issue in boards, Princeton has a complete set of undivided proofs in color of Cruikshank's enchanting plates. The shift from political to social commentary is further marked in the illustrations to Pierce Egan's **Life in London** (1821); but this famous work, a collaborative undertaking of the Cruikshank brothers, is less significant in George's career than John Fairburn's publication in the following year of David Carey's **Life in Paris,** for the illustrations of which he was solely responsible. Although there is no evidence that the artist ever visited Paris, the twenty-one colored plates and twenty-two engravings on wood present an admirably spirited account of high and low life in the French capital, as experienced by those Regency bloods, Dick Wildfire, Squire Jenkins, and Captain O'Shuffleton. In addition to the first issue of the first edition and two sheets of preliminary sketches in pencil, Princeton possesses an unique set of these cuts on large paper, made expressly for George IV. . . .

Cruikshank cherished a particular fondness for nautical subject-matter in which he found an inexhaustible well of mirth. Has anyone ever evoked the ludicrous miseries of seasickness so hilariously? Among his most brilliantly comic treatments of naval life are the twelve colored etchings and sixteen woodcuts which he made in 1826 for *Greenwich Hospital: A Series of Naval Sketches, descriptive of the Life of a Man-of-War's Man. By an Old Sailor.* In such scenes as **"Sailors Carousing," "Sailors on a Cruise"** (in a stage coach), and **"Crossing the Line,"** the artist captured with incomparable vivacity the frolics of tars ashore and at sea. The "Old Sailor," who supplied the text, was Captain M. H. Barker, for whom Cruikshank illustrated seven works in all. One of these was *Nights at Sea: or, Sketches of Naval Life during the War,* serialized in *Bentley's Miscellany* in 1837-38. Three of Cruikshank's seven etchings exist in admirable watercolor versions at Princeton. One of these, **"The Battle of the Nile,"** depicts a cyclorama of the famous naval engagement as presented at "Bart'lemy Fair." A drunken onlooker is hurling oranges at the spectacle, thus endangering the indignant showman whose head rears up from the middle of the sea. A rough preliminary sketch in pen-and-ink of the scene, identified in Cruikshank's hand as by Captain Barker, suggests the closeness of collaboration between author and illustrator.

As Cruikshank's fame grew, he formed the habit of issuing sets of his illustrations in large proofs on india paper for separate sale. This was the case with the wood engravings for both William Cowper's *The Diverting History of John Gilpin* and Thomas Hood's *The Epping Hunt,* published by Charles Tilt in 1828 and 1829 respectively. The increasingly benign and tolerant humor reflected in the works which he selected for illustration during the 1820s, expressive of the more genial temper of the times which he was helping to define, led in 1830 to one of his most satisfying performances, the fifty-one woodcuts for William Clarke's light-hearted *Three Courses and a Dessert.* Thackeray recognized the happy wedding of cut and text in this unjustly neglected work: " . . . some of the best designs of our artist and some of the most amusing tales in our language"; but the author, more modest, stated simply that the *plates* were sure to please even if the *dishes* failed to do so. No artist subsequent to Callot and della Bella had succeeded in making the engraving accommodate so great a wealth of narrative implication within so little space—as witness **"The Deaf Postillion"** or the minute vignette depicting the alternate courses of action confronting the man precariously perched on a fence-post with iron spikes before and behind, a ramping bull on one hand and equally savage watchdogs on the other. In this volume, as well, the illustrator gave free rein to his penchant for endowing inanimate objects with human characteristics, in anticipation of a similar practice in Dickens's early fiction. "Cruikshank never tired of making still life into quick life," Jerrold acutely observed; and no one who has sympathetically studied the colloquy of three sapient lemons or the portrait of a pontifical mushroom in *Three Courses and a Dessert* is ever again likely to take those homely kitchen staples quite so much for granted.

Meanwhile, in that *annus mirabilis* 1823, Cruikshank staked his claim to an even more original and unexplored province of humor. The new departure was announced in the twelve etched designs which he created for a selection of *German Popular Stories. Translated from the "Kinder und Haus Märchen," collected by M. M. Grimm from Oral Tradition.* This was the first appearance of Grimm's fairy tales in English, translated by John Edward Taylor and "a circle of relatives"; and it was followed in 1826 by a second volume of which Taylor was the sole translator and to which Cruikshank contributed another ten etchings. It is probably not excessive to state that Cruikshank's version once and for all fixed the way that English-speaking peoples think of fairyland. Indeed, the artist's drawings achieved matching popularity in Germany, and so took hold in France that an illustrator, Ambroise Tardieu, in 1830 brazenly passed off lame copies as his own work. "Mr. Cruikshank," wrote Thackeray, "alone has had a true insight into the character of the 'little people.' They are something like men and women, and yet not flesh and blood; they are laughing and mischievous, but why we know not. Mr. Cruikshank, however, has had some dream or the other, or else a natural mysterious instinct . . . , or else some preternatural fairy revelation, which has made him acquainted with the looks and ways of the fantastical subjects of Oberon and Titania." No volumes in the Cruikshank canon are more eagerly sought after by collectors than *German Popular Stories.* . . .

In the same year (1868) Grimm's tales were re-issued in a single volume with copies of the plates and an introduction by Ruskin, who, it will be remembered, had claimed that the quality of Cruikshank's etchings for this work in some respects rivalled and even excelled Rembrandt. . . .

During this period Cruikshank further indulged his fancy in the sixteen full-page woodcuts designed for *Italian Tales. Tales of Humour, Gallantry, and Romance* (1824). . . .

Akin to the renewed interest in folklore as yet another literary strain emanating from Germany to nourish the Romantic sensibility in England was a fascination with the supernatural. To this influence Cruikshank also showed himself alertly sensitive in the eight etched illustrations which he conceived for a translation of A. von Chamisso's tale of the man who bartered away his shadow to the devil, *Peter Schlemihl,* published in 1823 (1824). The English version was by a Dr. Bowring; but, like Taylor the translator of Grimm, his name was absent from the title page—mute evidence of the fact that Cruikshank's designs were expected to recommend these works to the public. In addition to copies of the first and second issues of the first edition of *Peter Schlemihl,* there exists at Princeton a proof of the front plate, worked on by the illustrator and with three marginal pencil sketches. In 1825 the illustrator further explored this macabre vein in four etched illustrations for Victor Hugo's *Hans of Iceland* in an anonymous translation (even the author's name was not given). . . . The Foreword offers the following apology by the translator: "This single pretension to a favorable consideration [the fact that Hugo's text had been greatly condensed] he feels is considerably strengthened

Title page and illustration from Sketches by Boz.

by the four very ingenious and spirited etchings, by Mr. George Cruikshank which his labours have been the occasion of introducing, and which give this volume an attraction wholly unknown to the original."

J. Robins, the publisher of *Hans of Iceland,* also issued in 1830 Cruikshank's *Twelve Sketches illustrative of Sir Walter Scott's Demonology and Witchcraft.* The artist's greatness as a book illustrator resulted in part from the unerring tact with which he chose scenes congenial to his temperament and skills; and such plates as **"The Corps de Ballet"** with its use of animistic detail, and **"Fairy Revenge,"** in which there is an element of malice approaching cruelty, present a felicitous blending of humor and uncanniness. . . .

On all lovers of Punch and Judy, Cruikshank conferred a priceless boon in perpetuating that ancient spectacle through the twenty-four etchings and four woodcuts commissioned by Septimus Prowett for publication in 1828. These appeared in a volume with accompanying dialogue and a pioneering account of the origin of puppet plays and their history in England by the drama critic and notorious forger, John Payne Collier. In the interests of

fidelity to the source material, Cruikshank and his collaborator during the autumn of 1827 arranged for private performances by an old Italian street entertainer, Piccini, who not only adhered to the traditional mode of presentation, but who owned a set of glove puppets immeasurably superior to any of English make. Piccini moved his portable stage indoors, and stopped the performance on demand to enable the artist to catch the figures in characteristic poses, while Collier made a transcript of the dialogue. . . . This masterpiece was followed in 1830 by the publication of two burlesques with woodcut illustrations by Cruikshank: Kane O'Hara's adaptation of Fielding's *Tom Thumb,* and W. B. Rhodes's *Bombastes Furioso.* The Foreword of the former has these words of praise for Cruikshank: "The pencil of the Artist has in these times the power which in days of yore was ascribed to the wand of the Enchanter Merlin—by it Tom Thumb is again called into an existence, which promises to be lasting as the well-earned fame of his facetious historian, George Cruikshank."

Shakespeare, predictably, inspired a number of Cruikshank's theatrical scenes. At Princeton there are three finished sepia drawings, signed and dated 1833, which take outrageous liberties with famous episodes in the great tragedies: "Macbeth and the Witches," "Othello and Desdemona," and "Hamlet and the Ghost." These drawings were presumably designed for burlesque songheads; but the great nineteenth-century collector of Cruikshank, Edwin Truman, who originally owned them, thought that only the last was ever published. The artist had a particular fondness for *A Midsummer-Night's Dream.* Two of the oil sketches at Princeton show Bottom adorned with the ass's head, and there is, as well, a finished watercolor of the same subject. During the 1860s Cruikshank paid eloquent tribute to Shakespeare's dramatic imagination in an elaborately conceived painting of the playwright as a babe in the cradle surrounded by the creations he was to bring into being. The print is entitled **"All the World's a Stage: The First Appearance of William Shakespeare, on the Stage of 'The Globe'"** . . .

In mid-career, from about 1830 to 1845, Cruikshank devoted a major portion of his energies to book illustration. Since many of the contemporary novels which he illustrated first appeared in serial form, this was the period of his association with two of the leading periodicals of the day as their favored artist. To *Bentley's Miscellany,* principally under the successive editorships of Dickens and Ainsworth, he contributed 131 etchings and four woodcuts between 1837 and 1843, deliberately producing poor work towards the end in order to provoke a break with Bentley. Thereafter from 1842 to 1846 he worked for *Ainsworth's Magazine,* in the pages of which appeared sixty-three etchings and twenty-two woodcuts of his designing. Ainsworth's handsome tribute announcing Cruikshank as the illustrator of his magazine in its first number says a great deal about the foundations on which his reputation rested at this time:

> In securing the co-operation of this admirable artist, the strongest assurance is given, not only of unequalled excellence in tragic and humorous illustration, but of an anxious and thoughtful principle of responsibility in the exercise of that power. No work can need a surer guarantee than that which is conveyed in the association of an artist, who has passed an important portion of his life in satirizing and ridiculing human follies, without giving one moment's pain to a fellow-creature; who has faithfully delineated almost every diversity of character, without creating a single enemy. . . .

The Preface to the first series of *Sketches by Boz* (1836), later discarded, indicated how eagerly the budding novelist welcomed the support of the established illustrator when Macrone undertook to publish a collection of his journalistic accounts of **"Every-Day Life and Every-Day People"**:

> Entertaining no inconsiderable feeling of trepidation at the idea of making so perilous a voyage in so frail a machine, alone and unaccompanied, the author was naturally desirous to secure the assistance and companionship of some well-known individual, who had frequently contributed to the success, though his well-earned reputation rendered it impossible for him ever to have shared the hazard of similar undertakings. To whom, as possessing this requisite in an eminent degree could he apply but to GEORGE CRUIKSHANK?

For the First Series of the *Sketches* in two volumes Cruikshank produced sixteen etchings; for the Second Series in one volume (1837) an additional ten, increased to twelve in the second edition. This number grew to forty when the *Sketches* were issued in twenty parts (November 1837-June 1839), of which twenty-seven were rather coarsely re-etched in larger form. . . .

Meanwhile, Dickens as editor had inaugurated the monthly numbers of *Bentley's Miscellany* in January 1837 with *Oliver Twist,* which continued to appear with interruptions through the first five volumes, adorned by what are probably Cruikshank's most famous illustrations. Before the magazine run was completed, the novel was published in three volumes in 1838. A new edition, revised and corrected, came out in ten parts, as well as in a single volume, in 1846. For this the majority of the original plates were re-etched and considerably altered. . . .

Concurrent with the last installments of *Oliver Twist,* there began to appear in *Bentley's Miscellany* William Harrison Ainsworth's *Jack Sheppard: A Romance.* Although Cruikshank was to illustrate entirely or in part seven novels by Ainsworth, whose popularity at this time rivalled Dickens's, the relationship between the artist and the lesser novelist still awaits the kind of intensive investigation that Cruikshank's partnership with Dickens has received. If it is reasonable to say that the story of *Oliver Twist* is inseparably linked for the majority of readers with the illustrator's rendering of such episodes as Oliver asking for more gruel or Sikes about to leap to his death or Fagin in the cell awaiting execution, how much more justifiable is Thackeray's statement that Ainsworth's story of his unprincipled young scoundrel would be wholly forgotten without the life imparted to it by the illustrator's art: "With regard to the modern romance of *Jack Sheppard,*" Thackeray wrote, "it seems to us that Mr. Cruikshank really created the tale, and that Mr. Ainsworth, as it were, only put words to it. Let any reader of the novel think over it for a while, now that it is some months since he has perused and laid it down—let him think and tell us what he remembers of the tale? George Cruikshank's pictures—always George Cruikshank's pictures." Indeed, perused separately, these plates not only carry the story-line, but do so with immeasurably greater economy and dramatic force than Ainsworth's wooden narrative. Both in the choice of incidents and in the accumulation of detail within each scene to amplify its significance, Cruikshank shows his debt to Hogarth's "moral progresses." Indeed, Hogarth and his father-in-law, Sir James Thornhill, are pictured among the artists taking a likeness of the condemned protagonist in his cell in the cut entitled **"The Portrait."** The etcher's change of medium from copper to steel plates at about this time allowed for important technical developments, notably in the treatment of facial expression and in the creation of atmospheric effects through the finer handling of light and shade. . . .

For the survival of Cruikshank as a comic artist, . . . one must turn back to the early publications which were largely planned as well as executed by him.

Because of its duration, the *Comic Almanack* offers an unusually rich ground for surveying Cruikshank's mirroring of early Victorian England. Quite as much as Dickens, the artist's depiction of **"Every-Day Life and Every-Day People"** qualifies him to be regarded as the historian of his society throughout its middle and lower reaches. Like the *Sketches* and *Pickwick Papers,* the early numbers of the *Almanack* record traditional ways of life that were rapidly being superseded. These are inimitably reflected in the introductory etchings to the issues in the opening years of the periodical's career, each of which celebrates some festive occasion appropriate to the month, whether feast-days religious in origin, Twelfth Night, Valentine's Day, St. Patrick's Day, Michaelmas Day, St. Crispin's Day, St. Cecilia's Day, Christmas; or such secular holidays as Lord Mayor's Day, Boxing Day, Guy Fawkes' Day. In their superb vitality and inventiveness these plates rank among Cruikshank's most masterly achievements, even above the similar illustrations for *Sketches by Boz.* The settings, often street scenes, are scrupulously localized to bring out the frolic mood of the occasions. And no stage director ever more carefully disposed his throng of actors to achieve a totality of impression. The artist's skill in discriminating facial expression has often been remarked; but to this should be added his pantomimic sense of the revealing posture or gesture. Note, for example, the varied antics of his urchins and dogs, as they are swept into the whirling vortices of activity. . . .

Not even fairyland was immune to Cruikshank's censorial fervor. The artist's love of whimsy had found recurrent expression throughout his long career. In 1848, for example, he produced an enchanting series of twelve etchings on six plates for an expurgated version of Giambattista Basile's **Pentamerone,** adapted by J. E. Taylor, whose translation of Grimm he had illustrated twenty-four years earlier. There followed the seven woodcuts, engraved by J. Thompson, for E. G. Flight's **The True Legend of St. Dunstan and the Devil,** (1852), again in the illustrator's best diabolic manner. During the ensuing decade Cruikshank illustrated four children's tales, gathered under the title of the **Fairy Library: "Hop o' my Thumb and the Seven League Boots"** (1853), **"The History of Jack and the Bean-Stalk"** (1854), **"Cinderella and the Glass Slipper"** (1854), and **"Puss in Boots"** (1864). There were in all thirty-nine designs on twenty-four plates, and four wrapper designs. In furnishing the text for these stories, the artist took occasion to modify them and to insert cautionary lessons of his own, including warnings against drink. Such liberties with the traditional fairy-lore which he so loved moved Dickens to a good-humored protest, entitled "Frauds on the Fairies," published in *Household Words,* October 1853. Cruikshank's rather lame and unconvincing defence of his action, **"A Letter from Hop o' my Thumb to Charles Dickens, Esq.,"** first appeared in *George Cruikshank's Magazine,* and was incorporated in subsequent addresses to his public in both **"Cinderella"** and **"Puss in Boots."** Happily the fanciful charm of the illustrations is in no way spoiled by the didactic bias of Cruikshank's textual commentary.

Ronald Paulson

SOURCE: "The Tradition of Comic Illustration from Hogarth to Cruikshank," in *George Cruikshank: A Revaluation,* edited by Robert L. Patten, Princeton University Press, 1974, pp. 56-7, 60.

Cruikshank began and, with some of his authors at least, continued, giving them visual ideas to verbalize. He was the last of a series of very special cases of artists who pursued a career of independent emblematic art parallel with one of illustration. Coupled with Cruikshank's compatible versatilities was the popularity in the 1830s of travel books or sporting scenes in which illustration may have priority over text, and in which both text and illustration contribute different perspectives.

[W]ith the advent of the serial publication of the *Pickwick Papers* and **Oliver Twist,** which launched the remarkable Dickens combination of text and illustration, the two became chronologically co-present for the first time. The illustration was usually not based on a written text but either on a few verbal or written hints or on some sort of common agreement between artist and author. The mixed-media effect of monthly serial publication involved the physical priority of the visual image. The reader ordinarily saw first the illustrations, sewn in at the front of the monthly part, and then read the text and related the two versions of the story. The earlier procedure of illustrating a subsequent edition, with "illustration" meaning representation of something in a known text, has now been replaced by a writer-artist collaboration for a visual-verbal effect with more the structure of emblem than illustration. *Punch* was founded in 1841, and the cartoon that was developed in its pages worked in a similar way: one looked at the picture, wondering what it meant, interested and puzzled; then read the caption, which was sometimes quite long; and then returned to the picture, which now meshed with the caption to make a joke.

Thus two independent views were brought together—Dickens and Cruikshank, Dickens and Seymour, Dickens and Phiz—and a kind of marriage was effected between an emblematic writing and an impressionistic, pointed, selective, moment in the illustration. The writer could be as interpretative as he liked, in fact creative in the emblem-reader's sense; the illustration singled out one crucial moment, though the artist might employ in it emblems of his own. In this sort of collaboration the illustrator has access of his own to the emblem tradition and can introduce pigs and donkeys as emblems of sloth and stubbornness that do not appear in the text, as Dickens introduces emblems of his own that do not appear in the illustration. One of the elements of the Dickensian comedy is the incongruity of the isolated, frozen moment of fleeting action and expression versus the duration suggested by the pictures on the walls, and even lower levels of transient action by the parallel cavorting of animals. And this is reflected in the style of the text set against that of the illustration, the rhetorical flourish of Dickens' prose style against the austerity, the "meanness," of Cruikshank's line.

For it is not, as Chesterton said, as if Fagin drew his own picture, but rather that Cruikshank develops one aspect of the Dickensian whole, which Dickens can fit into the larger formulation of his prose. Even if we include the memories of anti-semitic cartoons in his depiction, a minimalist Fagin appears in Cruikshank's drawings; Dickens' Fagin only begins its onion-like growth from this meager figure.

In *Sketches by Boz,* Miller has noticed, "London was for the young Dickens, in his disguise as Boz, . . . a set of signs, a text to interpret." This is precisely as if Dickens moved from a Hogarth print to the London around him and read it in the same way; both are images of a hidden text, and the writer's task is to interpret it. "What he sees at first are things, human artifacts, streets, buildings, vehicles, objects in a pawnbroker's shop, old clothes in Monmouth Street. These objects are signs, present evidence of something absent. Boz sets himself the task of inferring from these things the life that is lived among them." . . .

Dickens himself represents the verbal equivalent of the beginning of the comic tradition in Hogarth's *Hudibras* and *A Harlot's Progress,* while Cruikshank represents the end of it, the artist returning from emblem to illustration and putting himself back in the hands of his author. . . .

Anthony Burton

SOURCE: "Cruikshank as an Illustrator of Fiction," in *George Cruikshank: A Revaluation,* edited by Robert L. Patten, Princeton University Press, 1974, pp. 93-128.

Much of Cruikshank's work fell fairly quickly into obscurity. His early political caricatures were ephemeral, and so were most of his early illustrative works, while the books he illustrated in the last thirty years of his life were few, and were seldom reprinted. It was his illustrations for the novels of Dickens and Ainsworth—novels which remained popular and were often reprinted—that kept him in the public eye; and these illustrations have usually been made to stand as representative of his work as a whole. Now that we have an opportunity to reassess his entire output, we may profitably isolate his illustrations of fiction as one distinct part of it, and consider how far they have a special character.

Book illustration in its widest sense is the provision of pictures that relate to the text of a book. The pictures may be purely decorative, simply filling the space on the page which the text does not extend to cover; or, at the other extreme, they may be purely informative. The highest order of illustration is that which attempts to give an imaginative response to a work of imagination: interpretative illustration.

"Successful interpretation," as Philip James says [in *English Book Illustration 1800-1900*], "implies the need for a reflection of the author's style." Cruikshank's success in matching the style and mood of the novelists whose books he illustrated was often remarkable, and much of

this essay is devoted to demonstrating it. Since the demonstration is, after all, a matter of critical judgment, no theoretical advance notice of it is needed here. But one point should be stressed.

It is obvious that, when an artist is illustrating a long and complicated narrative, he is faced, in choosing his subjects, with various problems of selection and emphasis. Usually he comes to the written narrative after the author has finished it, and has the advantage that he sees it whole. Many of the stories that Cruikshank illustrated, however, appeared in monthly installments. This meant that in producing an illustration the artist could not refer to his memory of the story as a whole, for generally it was still being written; he worked with his knowledge of the story as it had developed up to the point at which his illustration was called for. We might expect that an artist working in such conditions would be more sensitive to changes and developments in the tone and mood of a story, and would feel the movement of a narrative more keenly, than an artist working with a whole book in mind. Furthermore, illustrations to monthly installments occurred frequently and regularly and might well reflect the recurrent emphases which an author would introduce into his monthly parts; hence, the illustrations themselves might well take on a sequential or narrative force.

If Cruikshank's illustrations to fiction prove to have a special character, this is not only the result of his extraordinary sympathy with many of the authors he worked for, but also partly the result of the method of monthly publication, which forced him into a much closer and longer collaboration with his authors than usually exists between a writer and an illustrator. . . .

Certainly Cruikshank's work shows that he can be counted among those artists whom Edward Ardizzone ranks as born illustrators, for Cruikshank has the two characteristics necessary for such beings: "The first is that their creative imagination is fired by the written word rather than the thing seen; the second is that when it comes to their illustrations, they would rather make them up than have recourse to life." For such illustrators, Ardizzone recommends copying as a source of inspiration, so it may be as well to consider at this point whether, in his illustrations to fiction, Cruikshank copied, and what there was to copy from.

Many of his earliest illustrations for fiction—mere bread and butter work—were done in the second and third decades of the nineteenth century for children's books and cheap chapbooks. Often enough he contributed only a crudely etched frontispiece which would later be blotched with color by hand; there is seldom much to be learned from a frontispiece about an artist's comprehension of a work. Or, sometimes, he would provide designs for a set of woodcuts, as in the case of Wallis's *Juvenile Tales* (1822-23) or in the series of story books by William Gardiner. His illustrations for Gardiner's oeuvre were re-used from one little volume to another, for each volume consisted of a number of separate stories, and the possibilities of permutation were endless. If these illustrations really are, as the title-pages claim, by Cruikshank, they are quite uninspired. Indeed, there is little in Gardiner's tales to inspire. Although they are dressed up in Oriental trappings, so as to fascinate the juvenile mind, and although they are granted the additional allurement of illustrations, their clear aim is to convince the child that he must suppress his imagination. In tale after tale, this subversive force (symbolized in "The History of Prince Iris" as a Purple Horse) drives unfortunate youths into wild and visionary courses which only lead to disillusion, or perhaps to the depressing appearance of "an old man with a long white beard, leaning on a staff." "'My name is Experience,' said the aged Sire; 'Rise, and follow me, for thou art now cured of thy folly . . . '" It is hard to imagine Cruikshank responding enthusiastically to this kind of thing, and it is no surprise that his illustrations are untouched by his peculiar genius and are no better than run-of-the-mill chapbook cuts.

A much more interesting case is **Robinson Crusoe.** By the beginning of the nineteenth century this work was firmly established in chapbook literature (where it rubbed shoulders with such tales as *The History of Tom Thumb* and *The Life of Jack Sprat*), and many sets of crude illustrations to it were in circulation. One set of seven woodcuts is, indeed, attributed to "Cruikshank." They are livelier than some, but not noticeably better than, for instance, the set of six in William Davison of Alnwick's *New Specimen of cast-metal ornaments* (c. 1815). These are worth noting: the fact that a printer's supplier included cuts for **Robinson Crusoe** among the ships, royal arms, blocks for tea-packet labels, and other miscellaneous illustrations that he offered for sale in his specimen, tells us something of the great popularity of **Robinson Crusoe** in cheap illustrated editions. . . .

Cruikshank, whether or not it was he who made the series of chapbook cuts attributed to him, must have been well acquainted with such popular illustrations to *Robinson Crusoe;* and I think that they must have been in his mind when he designed the wood-engraved illustrations for Major's 1831 edition of Defoe's story. Although Cruikshank withholds none of his skill and understanding from these, they relate in scale and composition (and, of course, technique) to the chapbook cuts.

To judge from his Preface, the publisher John Major hoped, so far as possible, to reach both a popular and a cultivated audience with this edition. He seems to think of the book preeminently as a children's story, but emphasizes in a footnote that "it has also been pronounced to deserve a place in the library of every scholar and man of taste": therefore, he claims, "the TEXT . . . is restored in this edition by a careful collation with the early copies." Furthermore, the book, although modest in format, is excellently printed by William Nichol; and Major, when he compares its illustrations with "the celebrated Series by the admirable Stothard," implies that his book will hold its own against the ample Cadell and Davies edition of 1820 in which Stothard's illustrations made their second appearance. The comparison of Stothard's and Cruikshank's illustrations will help us to perceive the special virtues of the latter.

They are, above all, more spirited than Stothard's, which are like most of his work in taking refinement to the edge of enfeeblement. In Stothard's plates, Crusoe looks listless, even when he comes upon the footprint: he looks askance at it, morosely, not at all "like one thunderstruck." Cruikshank's Crusoe, more like a chapbook mannikin, recoils melodramatically, with tense limbs. But besides this somewhat naive vigor, there is in Cruikshank's illustration a characteristic touch of psychological penetration, which distinguishes his treatment of this incident from Stothard's and from the chapbook tradition. Crusoe is accompanied by his dog. In many illustrations the dog, like Crusoe, looks anxiously at the footprint. In Stothard's plate the dog is not taking notice at all, and seems to be looking through Crusoe's legs at the sea. But in Cruikshank's illustration, the dog, recoiling, looks anxiously at Crusoe as Crusoe looks anxiously at the footprint: and this, surely, is right and natural. . . .

After **Robinson Crusoe** Cruikshank did not further draw on or develop the popular tradition of illustration by small wood-engravings. For by 1831 he had found his own style of illustrating fiction: by full-page etchings. His adoption of this style can be dated to 1823, when he produced his etchings for **Points of Humour.** "It is remarkable," Cornelis Veth observes [in *Comic Art in England* (1930)], "that in these he almost suddenly found his own style, a style wholly different from that shown in his political prints. . . . His own manner manifests itself not only in a more sober form of caricature, but in the handling of the lights and shadows, in which he at once attained excellence." Added force is given to this remark if one recalls that 1823 also saw the appearance of Cruikshank's eight etched illustrations to Chamisso's **Peter Schlemihl.** These are outstanding among his book illustrations, although they are among the earliest. Peter Schlemihl, it will be remembered, sells his shadow to a grey gentleman in return for a magical purse which provides an inexhaustible supply of money. Riches do not, however, protect him from the horrified rebuffs of his fellow men when they discover his lack of a shadow; and the grey gentleman dogs him in pursuit of his soul. Shadows and lights, then, play an important part in the story, and in his etchings Cruikshank renders them both brilliantly and subtly, achieving effects which would be impossible with wood-engraving. Outstanding is his illustration to chapter iv, showing Peter awaiting the return of the grey gentleman after a year and a day. Peter sits eyeing his clock (as midnight approaches) in front of a flaring lamp; all the furniture casts deep shadows but Peter sits shadowless in the full glare; arms folded and one hand raised to his mouth in a gesture of fear. The upper half of his body is in an attitude not unlike that of Fagin in the condemned cell; that later etching is a much grimmer study of terror, but the comparison is permissible, perhaps, in order to emphasize how well Cruikshank has caught the uncanny, frightening, sometimes desperate tone of the German tale. . . .

Peter Schlemihl was an exceptional achievement; *Points of Humour* established a style that was to be typical of Cruikshank. It appeared in two parts in 1823 and 1824. Of the ten "Points" in the first part, four illustrate Burns's "Jolly Beggars" and three of those are no more than caricatures. The rest of the etchings illustrate short anecdotes and are subtler, fuller productions. The Preface remarks upon the difficulty of selecting subjects for illustration. "No artist can embody a point of wit," the writer observes. We have seen that this is not true of Cruikshank, but still, it is reasonable to argue that "those ludicrous subjects only which are rich in the humour of *situation* are calculated for graphic illustration," and it is to situations that Cruikshank accordingly applies himself. He proves to be very good at conveying the differing feelings that activate the various persons brought together in a situation, and at indicating how the persons are interacting with each other. Any artist could draw a procession of priests falling downstairs (Point IX), but Cruikshank's special skill is revealed in, for example, Point X in his depiction of the baffled resentment of Cardinal Bernis, the sarcastic courtesy of Prince B, and the surprise, glee, and expectation of the watching attendants. . . .

Cruikshank illustrated a wide range of fiction. He produced exceptionally good illustrations of the great eighteenth-century English novels. And the literature of his own day offered him a variety of subjects: sensation and melodrama, costume drama, high life, low life, middle-class life, commercial life, nautical life. For several of the works he illustrated, his etchings are much more than occasional embellishments: by virtue sometimes of his choice of subjects and sometimes of his manner of composition, they link up with each other so as to form a sequence alongside the written narrative. Cruikshank seems to have responded with special intensity to descriptions of certain situations, themes and states of mind: extremes of adversity, imprisonment, escape, moments of encounter, and opposing passions whether in a group or an individual, inspire some of his best designs. All these qualities are most vividly seen in his illustrations to *Oliver Twist.*

If any single illustration has secured immortality for Cruikshank, it is his etching of **"Fagin in the Condemned Cell."** It is an extremely simple image: a single seated figure against a background which is hardly more than two areas of dark tone, one being covered with cross-hatching and the other with a stippled effect. As we have seen in *Peter Schlemihl, Robinson Crusoe,* and *Jack Sheppard,* Cruikshank provided some of his most powerful designs when he was given the opportunity to illustrate loneliness, and the fears and struggles that accompany extreme adversity. The intensity of his feeling for such subjects suggests that he readily identified himself with fictional characters in such circumstances. We know that he identified himself with Fagin. There is no need here to repeat the anecdotes collected in Blanchard Jerrold's biography; they fall into two classes, some telling how Cruikshank, for years after the appearance of *Oliver Twist,* liked to act the part of Fagin, others telling how he settled

on Fagin's pose in the condemned cell by himself assuming it before a mirror. On this evidence we may venture to conclude that some of Cruikshank's illustrations were the result of a kind of dramatic re-enactment by the artist of the incident he was illustrating, and that they are, therefore, in a specially intimate way, disclosures of aspects of his personality. Chesterton [in *Charles Dickens (1906)*] put this point in rather overblown terms: in his eyes, Cruikshank's drawings

> have a dark strength: yet he does not only draw morbidly, he draws meanly. In the doubled-up figure and frightful eyes of Fagin in the condemned cell there is not only a baseness of subject; there is a kind of baseness in the very technique of it. It is not drawn with the free lines of a free man; it has the half-witted secrecies of a hunted thief. It does not look merely like a picture of Fagin; it looks like a picture by Fagin.

This certainly testifies to Chesterton's sense of Cruikshank's close identification with his subject. It was Chesterton also who produced a phrase which seems to me to be quite the most suggestive description of Cruikshank's peculiar talent, and which hints at the qualities in his personality that shaped his talent and that are disclosed in his work. "There was about Cruikshank's art," said Chesterton, "a kind of cramped energy. . . . "

This is indeed to be found in "Fagin in the condemned Cell." Fagin had made his last previous appearance in the *Oliver Twist* illustrations in the nineteenth plate, "The Jew & Morris Bolter begin to understand each other," where he was to be seen grinning hugely and stretching his crooked legs wide apart in luxurious enjoyment of his cunning. In the condemned cell he has snatched himself together and crouches abjectly on his bed. His knees are bent and his body bends over them in that foetus-like posture to which a man will sometimes revert in acute terror. His shackled legs are held close together and his arms are clutched tight to his body. All his muscular power seems to be exerted in holding himself rigidly still, in cramping himself. And yet energy glares from his face; in his piercing eyes and bared teeth an animal fierceness seems to spring out to the attack. There is nothing to attack save his own raised hand, so his fierceness is turned on himself. . . .

[Cruikshank] has extremely well conveyed the dominant mood of *Oliver Twist,* the mood of anxious expectation that is generated by a story of subjection and liberation, of oppression and compassion, of exclusion and inclusion. It is such themes as these that have inspired Cruikshank to his most compelling illustrations for other works. In *Jack Sheppard* there is the frank thrill of physical confinement and escape. In *Peter Schlemihl* there is Peter's spiritual enthrallment to the grey gentleman, his consequent repudiation by his fellow men, and the strange deliverance offered by the seven-league boots. In *Robinson Crusoe* there are the psychological constraints and exertions of the hero's struggle for survival. If there is a single phrase that will cover this complex of feelings which Cruikshank represents and evokes so powerfully, it is Chesterton's phrase, "cramped energy."

Surely also, Cruikshank's line—so delicately precise, so forcefully restless—is aptly described by this phrase. And may it not be applied to his personality as well as his works? Since no good biography of him has yet been written, it would be rash to develop this notion; but the man who shines through the anecdotes of his contemporaries is characterized by an effervescent good nature strangely curbed by eccentricity and obsession. The phrase "cramped energy," then, evokes the personality; and more particularly denotes the special, distinguishing quality of his best illustrations of fiction.

Harry Stone

SOURCE: "Dickens, Cruikshank, and Fairy Tales," in *George Cruikshank: A Revaluation,* edited by Robert L. Patten, Princeton University Press, 1974, pp. 213-47.

In the *Examiner* for 23 July 1853, Forster had reviewed George Cruikshank's latest production, an edition of *Hop-o'-my-Thumb* rewritten and illustrated by the "illustrious George." *Hop-o'-my-Thumb* was to be the first pamphlet in a series of similar redactions by Cruikshank, the entire series to bear the title, *George Cruikshank's Fairy Library.* In his review of *Hop-o'-my-Thumb,* Forster lauded Cruikshank's designs, pointed out that he had interpolated social doctrines into the story, concluded that this was perhaps good, and urged readers to support the series. Dickens read Forster's review in Boulogne, and it gave him an idea for *Household Words.* "I have . . . thought," he wrote Wills on 27 July 1853, of an article "to be called Frauds upon the Fairies—*apropos* of George Cruikshank's editing." Then he went on:

> Half playfully and half seriously, I mean to protest most strongly against alteration—for any purpose—of the beautiful little stories which are so tenderly and humanly useful to us in these times when the world is too much with us, early and late; and then to re-write Cinderella according to Total-abstinence, Peace Society, and Bloomer principles, and expressly for their propagation.

> I shall want his book of *Hop o' My Thumb* (Forster noticed it in the last Examiner) and the most simple and popular version of Cinderella you can get me. I shall not be able to do it until after finishing Bleak House, but I shall do it the more easily for having the books by me. So send them, if convenient, in your next parcel.

Dickens' idea and the consequences that flowed from it not only put an end to his long friendship with Cruikshank—already seriously strained—but served to epitomize (and in part to generate) some of his most deeply held beliefs concerning art and life. . . .

All unwittingly, Cruikshank had challenged some of Dickens' formative childhood experiences, some of his fundamental concerns and credos. Dickens was convinced that the literature he read as a child had been crucial to his imagination. He was equally certain that the literature he

read as a youth had prevented him from perishing. The literature of childhood was the source of all his "early imaginations"; the literature of youth "kept alive my fancy, and my hope of something beyond that place and time." At the center of the latter period was the blacking warehouse, and Dickens literally believed that reading, and the imagination nurtured by that reading, allowed him—but only barely allowed him—to survive. Dickens came to these conclusions much later as he looked back on his early years. His books reflect this judgment and his commitment. His writings are rich with nostalgic allusions to the childhood literature that soothed and sustained him. By the time of the autobiographical *David Copperfield* (1849-50) he was so certain of the benign influence of that early reading, that he made his own reading experiences a central feature of young David's survival and development. About this time too he turned his own experiences into articles of faith. In a period of early desolation (so his syllogism ran), literature, especially childhood literature, had saved him; in an iron time, literature could help save others. He came increasingly to enunciate this principle. In March 1850, in the manifesto which inaugurated *Household Words,* he reaffirmed this childhood-engendered belief. In that manifesto he asserted his faith in literature as salvation. *Household Words* would "teach the hardest workers at this whirling wheel of toil, that their lot is not necessarily a moody, brutal

An illustration for "Hop O' My Thumb."

fact, excluded from the sympathies and graces of imagination." And Dickens ended his declaration by alluding to an "old fairy story" and promising that he would "Go on!"

By 1850, then, Dickens strongly and consciously associated the literature of childhood with the greatest of public ends. The literature of childhood nursed the imagination, ministered to an iron time, and softened dehumanizing toil. What Dickens most valued in that literature was its ability to nurture the imagination. Without imagination (or "fancy," as Dickens often called it) human beings could not be truly human. He therefore set his face against any attempt to make literature serve narrow, anti-imaginative ends. Here again he remembered the lessons of his childhood. For there was a deadly as well as a saving literature of childhood. The deadly literature of childhood was a dreary counterbalance to the childhood literature that had helped save him. His writings are sprinkled with disparaging references to this "other" literature, the off-putting literature of his early years. . . .

On the other hand he surrounded the pictures in his childhood geography book with fanciful imaginings, revelled in the wit and ingenuity of *Aesop's Fables,* and associated all that was unforgettable or marvellous in *The Arabian Nights, The Tales of the Genii, Robinson Crusoe,* and similar works, with the comings and goings and responses of his everyday life. The test in all such matters was very simple. He attacked all childhood literature that was given over to dour prosing; he exalted all childhood literature that was wild or fanciful or free.

The literary quintessence of that wild freedom was the fairy tale. More and more through the 1840s and the early 1850s Dickens was coming to regard the fairy tale as a paradigm of imaginative art. The fairy tale was an emblem, at once rudimentary and pure, of what contemporary society needed and what it increasingly lacked. The fairy tale was also inextricably associated with childhood; it shaped the very character of future generations. In Dickens' lexicon the fairy tale was becoming a shorthand way of emphasizing a contemporary danger and suggesting an essential solution. The lesson, Dickens felt, was clear. In an age when men were becoming machines, art—and that quintessential childhood version of art, the fairy tale—must be cherished and must be allowed to do its beneficent work of nurturing man's birthright of feeling and fancy.

So Dickens had come to believe when, in July 1853, in his rose-begirt villa high above Boulogne, he leafed through the pages of the *Examiner* and lighted upon Forster's review of Cruikshank's *Hop-o'-my-Thumb.* Given Dickens' attitude toward childhood literature, his response was predictable. The review evoked a powerful array of active and slumbering feelings. His childhood memories of fairy tales, his conviction that he had been succored by early imaginative reading, his hatred of didactic children's literature, his sense of the importance and sanctity of fairy tales—all these elements contributed to his response. But there were other factors as well. Dickens had been Cruikshank's friend

and companion for almost twenty years, and the tangled history of their personal relationship added a powerful point to what Dickens soon after did.

Dickens and Cruikshank first met on 17 November 1835, shortly after John Macrone, Dickens' publisher, arranged to have Cruikshank illustrate the forthcoming *Sketches by Boz,* Dickens' first book. At the time Dickens was twenty-three and virtually unknown; Cruikshank was forty-three and the pre-eminent graphic artist of the day. In the circumstances one might have expected the younger man to defer, in artistic matters at least, to his famous illustrator. But Dickens soon made clear that his view of their relationship—a view later duplicated in all his subsequent dealings with illustrators—was that Cruikshank should illustrate what he had written. In the case of *Sketches by Boz* First Series (1836), virtually everything that Cruikshank was to illustrate had already been published before Cruikshank set to work—so precluding any possibility of interference—but in later works that was not the case, and Dickens, as we shall see, had to establish his ascendancy. Yet even though Cruikshank had to follow rather than lead, he had considerable freedom. Within limits he could choose which of Dickens' sketches and which episodes within those sketches he would illustrate. More important, he could render Dickens' scenes (so long as he did not subvert what Dickens had written) through his own vision of their reality. This allowed him to be creative in his own right, and since Dickens' vignettes were congenial to Cruikshank's imagination, his illustrations for *Sketches by Boz* are among his best. As a consequence Cruikshank was chosen to illustrate *Sketches by Boz* Second Series (1836), and to provide additional etchings for the first one-volume collected edition of *Sketches by Boz* (1839). Cruikshank also illustrated or contributed to five minor works written, edited, or otherwise touched by Dickens: **"Public Life of Mr. Tulrumble"** (in *Bentley's Miscellany* 1837), ***Memoirs of Joseph Grimaldi*** (1838), **"Full Report of the Second Meeting of the Mudfog Association"** (in *Bentley's Miscellany,* 1838), ***The Loving Ballad of Lord Bateman*** (1839), and ***The Pic Nic Papers*** (1841). There was one other joint effort, and this the best known. In terms of wide circulation and of capturing the public consciousness, the great success in the Dickens-Cruikshank canon was ***Oliver Twist*** (1837-39 in *Bentley's Miscellany,* 1838 as a book). Yet this list of joint works, while imposing, is misleading. If one excludes the merely minor, *Oliver Twist* was the second and last work by Dickens illustrated by Cruikshank.

The truth is, there had been intermittent friction between the rising young author and the established illustrator. In part the friction had to do with haste and pressure—late copy, delayed plates, clashing schedules, and the like; in part it had to do with differences over the suitability of subjects for illustration. But these were difficulties more or less common to such collaborations; they were irritants rather than confrontations.

Yet a true and decisive confrontation had occurred early in their relationship. In October 1836, Macrone was busy with plans to publish the Second Series of *Sketches by Boz*. He had arranged for Cruikshank to illustrate this series as well, but there had been a delay with the text, and when Macrone was ready to move forward again, Cruikshank was busy with another work, thus necessitating another delay, this time until Cruikshank was free. After explaining his predicament to Macrone in a letter, Cruikshank added a few remarks: "I did expect to see that Ms. [of *Sketches by Boz* Second Series] from time to time in order that I might have the privilege of suggesting any little alteration to suit the Pencil but if you are printing the book all that sort of thing is out of the question. Only this much I must say that unless I can get good subjects to work upon, I will not work at all." Cruikshank's comment, though tactlessly phrased, was really a plea for a most limited privilege of occasional suggestion—a privilege which other authors sometimes allowed him. But Dickens viewed the matter in a different light. When he saw Cruikshank's note, he exploded scornfully (?19 October 1836):

> I have long believed Cruikshank to be mad; and his letter therefore, surprises me, not a jot. If you have any further communication with him, you will greatly oblige me by saying *from me* that I am very much amused at the notion of his altering my Manuscript, and that had it fallen into his hands, I should have preserved his emendations as "curiosities of Literature". Most decidedly am I of opinion that he may just go to the Devil; and so far as I have any interest in the book, I positively object to his touching it.

Dickens' fury was so great that he went on (quite unreasonably) to question whether the Second Series required any illustrations at all. Then he suggested that if the book did need illustration, Hablot Knight Browne ("Phiz"), who was currently illustrating *The Pickwick Papers,* should be the artist. Dickens eventually calmed down, but he sought thereafter (when not thwarted by heavy work loads and inflexible deadlines) to supply Cruikshank with completed copy, or better still, with proofs. By such means he could forestall Cruikshank's penchant for proffering unwanted advice.

Dickens' reactions are revealing. They demonstrate that from the very beginning he regarded his conceptions and his writings as inviolate; that he would accept no unsolicited suggestions and tolerate no interference. The episode is a comment on Cruikshank's claim, a claim he advanced publicly only after Dickens' death, that he was responsible for much of *Sketches by Boz* Second Series, and that he originated most of the characters and much of the action in *Oliver Twist.* Though Cruikshank was mistaken in this belief, he did sometimes contribute more than illustrations to a work in progress. He liked to regard himself as a creative partner in such a work, and he often plied his co-worker with suggestions and advice. Some authors (such as William Harrison Ainsworth) were glad to have such help and even to follow occasionally where Cruikshank led. But Dickens had a much different conception of the relationship between author and illustrator. He thought an illustrator should graphically render what

Frontispiece from Cinderella.

the author had written. Thwarted by Dickens' intractability on this score, Cruikshank gradually transformed his chagrin—a compound of frustrated desire, baffled will, and unappreciated advice—into a dream of actual achievement. In constructing this fantasy, Cruikshank was simply indulging a lifelong tendency to enlarge and exaggerate his accomplishments, a tendency that sometimes caused him to confuse aspiration with achievement, suggestion with fulfillment, and contribution with sole authorship. . . .

By July 1853, then, Dickens' personal relationship with Cruikshank had partly cooled and partly lapsed. From jovial parties and warm confidences, the friendship had dwindled into divergent interests and antagonistic criticisms. The professional relationship had long been severed, and though each man undoubtedly respected the other's genius, when each thought of his past working relationship with the other, he must have thought also of friction, frustration, and dissatisfaction. Yet there had been no open break, and in July 1853 each man regarded the other as a friend, albeit an eccentric or an unregenerate friend, as the case might be.

Thus matters stood when Dickens, amidst the roses and the vistas of Boulogne, came upon Forster's review of

Cruikshank's *Hop-o'-my-Thumb.* What Dickens brought to that reading on the personal level was a conflicting tangle of emotions and opinions. He mingled positive interest in Cruikshank and admiration for his art with skepticism concerning his views and irritation at his tactics. Yet when he read Forster's review his primary reaction was shaped not by years of Cruikshankian amiabilities and Cruikshankian crotchets—though these played their part—but by larger considerations. His reaction was dominated by his profound conviction (at the moment perhaps an intuition rather than a reasoned argument) that Cruikshank was tampering with the sources of imagination and creativity.

This is corroborated not simply by what Dickens later wrote, but by the disparity between Forster's review and Dickens' immediate response. Forster's review was full of praise and acceptance. He hailed Cruikshank's entrance into fairy land. No artist living, he thought, was better equipped by temperament and skill to be "court painter to Oberon." He then went on to describe the illustrations in *Hop-o'-my-Thumb.* His enthusiasm was boundless. Words such as "delight," "charming," "exquisite," and "genius," sprinkle the page. The illustrations, he asserted, were amongst the best that Cruikshank had ever drawn. He went even further: "more perfectly illustrated such tales never have been, and never again are likely to be." He continued by pointing out that Cruikshank occasionally introduced his own moral precepts into the tale, but this, Forster felt, was no fault. Quite the contrary. Such editing "can . . . do no harm—for such morals are not here obtruded in any dull way—and in the opinion of many it may be very likely to do good."

Dickens took a far different tack. What caught his attention were the intruded morals, their incongruity and their subversiveness. Then and there he determined to protest "half playfully and half seriously" against Cruikshank's editing, and then and there he wrote, in the letter already quoted, for a copy of Cruikshank's *Hop-o'-my-Thumb* and for an ordinary version of *Cinderella,* so that he could prepare himself for his reply and write it as soon as *Bleak House* was completed. When Cruikshank's little booklet did arrive, it confirmed and intensified Dickens' fears and angers.

As chance would have it, even Cruikshank's cover (all unwittingly on Cruikshank's part, of course) touched sensitive areas of Dickens' inner life. The cover portrayed a fearsome ogre watching over two scenes of parental abandonment. These scenes, captioned respectively, **"The Father proposes to lose the Children!!!"** and **"They Leave Hop 'o my Thumb and his Brothers in the Wood,"** depicted parents in the very act of plotting against and betraying their innocent children. Such a cover was calculated to arouse Dickens' profound sympathies and fears. His feeling that his own parents had rejected and abandoned him was perhaps the most shaping emotion in his life. His works are filled with unnatural parents, tender references to *The Children in the Wood* (another fable of parental abandonment), and terrifying evocations of being lost and parentless in roaring

streets. But more than this, the figure of the neglected or orphaned or outcast child—another projection of his profound sense of childhood abandonment—recurs with obsessive power in his writings.

Cruikshank's cover was thus a call to Dickens' deepest feelings about the sanctity and violation of childhood, and the fairy tale Cruikshank was about to recount (and indeed all fairy tales) had long since become symbols to Dickens of that sanctity and that threat. More than this, all fairy tales stood quintessentially for the saving grace of childhood imagination and childhood escape, and in a larger perspective, for the saving power of all imagination and art, a power that Dickens held to be sacred and inviolate. Cruikshank's text prostituted that power; Cruikshank (so it seemed to Dickens) manipulated the vulnerabilities of childhood and the privileges of art for narrow and fanatical ends. Cruikshank's marvelous illustrations captured the fears and fantasies and fulfillments of childhood. But the more wonderful the art, the greater the violation in making it serve purposes subversive of art itself.

In *Hop-o'-my-Thumb,* Cruikshank's art was a means of promulgating his text; for Dickens, that text was profoundly subversive. First of all, Cruikshank played fast and loose with the fable itself. He eliminated the central episode of how Hop saved himself and his brothers by tricking the ogre into murdering his own daughters (an episode that had powerfully and fearfully impressed Dickens as a child), imported into *Hop* the "Fe Fi Fo Fum" of *Jack the Giant Killer* (another episode that had fearfully gripped Dickens' imagination), and tampered with a multitude of lesser matters. Alone, these changes would have evoked Dickens' dismay rather than his anger. But Cruikshank had also sprinkled the story with the most prosing moral precepts and examples, the kinds of intruded morals that Dickens had hated as a boy and inveighed against all his life. Nor had Cruikshank limited his advocacy to rules of conduct; he had dragged in pronouncements on religious instruction, popular education, and free trade. It was just the kind of pervasive didacticism that Dickens had always regarded as dreary and deadening, the antithesis of fancy and imagination. Cruikshank was constantly intruding remarks about "nasty tobacco," "betting and gambling," the virtue of "perseverance," and the need "to admit foreign grain" into domestic markets. Cruikshank was remorseless. Hop and his brothers learned to wash themselves "in cold water (which they did winter and summer, because it is most refreshing and healthy to do so)"; to forego "much eating at supper"; and to avoid picking their teeth with a fork. They had also been taught by their "dear mother" to "go to bed early, which they all did, like good children, without any grumbling or crying." And every night good little Hop-o'-my-Thumb was always the first to say, "I'm ready to go to bed, mother."

From Dickens' point of view, Cruikshank's didacticism was doubly subversive. It intruded a prosing note that was totally alien to the spirit and tone of the fairy tale. But more important, it imported into the world of the fairy tale the anti-fairy tale. Enticed by Cruikshank's compelling illustrations, the child would enter the fairy-tale world only to find that it contained the same prosing precepts that nagged at him from the pages of his insufferable copybooks or his improving moral tracts. To Dickens, Cruikshank's text was a fraud. It would turn children away from the fount of fancy and imagination at the very source.

This was bad enough—in fact it was insupportable—but Cruikshank had gone further. He had infused **Hop-o'-my-Thumb** with an outrageous teetotalism. The ideology ran through the entire story. Drink was responsible for the poverty of Hop's father (who had been a rich Count before he turned to drink), for the deprivation of the family, for the abandonment of the children, and for most of the other sins and lapses in the story. Even the ogre's downfall was caused by drink, for he had imbibed so much on the night he had Hop and his brothers in his power, that they were able to escape and ultimately to steal his seven-league boots. The story had a happy, teetotal ending. When Hop brought his father before the King, the King rewarded his old friend (for the King and Count had been old companions) by making him Prime Minister. As Prime Minister, the erstwhile drunkard discovered that "strong drinks were hurtful to all." Accordingly he passed a law to "abolish the use of all intoxicating liquors; the effect of which law was, that in a short time there were very few, if any, criminals in the land; and the only paupers, or really poor, were those sick or aged persons who were unable to do any sort of work, for all the people in the land were industrious, and the country was rich."

This, Dickens thought, was Whole Hoggism with a vengeance. The entire notion would have been ludicrous had it not been aimed at children and had it not affronted Dickens' most profound beliefs. For in addition to violating Dickens' views concerning the crucial role of literature in childhood and the saving power of fairy tales, Cruikshank was intruding false notions concerning the causes of remediable social ills. He was now (to Dickens' way of thinking) introducing to the most sensitive areas of Dickens' belief the errors that Dickens had found in **The Bottle** and in **The Drunkard's Children**. The origins of poverty and crime, the intricate gestation of neglectful or rejecting parents, the ravaging inception of ignorance, cruelty, and despair—all these and more, in the gospel of Cruikshank, were simply by-products of "strong drinks." Dickens' childhood experience and his lifelong endeavor cried out against this notion. And Dickens' commitment to fancy and imagination cried out against transforming the child's bright birthright of fairy tales into prosing homilies and teetotal tracts . . .

Hop-o'-my-Thumb was the first story in a projected Fairy Library which would ultimately consist of a whole series of fairy tales rewritten and illustrated by Cruikshank. If Dickens' article damaged sales, the entire project might be jeopardized. Cruikshank was also about to launch a new monthly periodical entitled **George Cruikshank's Magazine**. This periodical and the Fairy Library were an attempt by Cruikshank—as it turned out his last really concerted attempt—to recapture his lost audience and his lost standing. The first issue of the new magazine appeared in January 1854, the second—and last—appeared the following month and contained **"A Letter From Hop-O'-My-Thumb to Charles Dickens, Esq. Upon 'Frauds On The Fairies,' 'Whole Hogs,' Etc."** Cruikshank's reply also contained a woodcut illustration showing Hop-o'-my-Thumb driving three enormous hogs—obviously gigantic Whole Hogs—back to *Household Words.*

Cruikshank's reply was rambling and discursive, at times defiant, combative, even abusive, at other times plaintive, humorous, even friendly. Cruikshank, writing in the guise of Hop-o'-my-Thumb, accused Dickens of going out of his way to find fault with him. Dickens was a man of "remarkable acuteness," but he had made a "great mistake" in allowing his "extraordinary seven-league boot imagination" to mislead him as to what the old fairy tales were. Dickens' article was "Much Ado About Nothing." For the text of a fairy tale is not fixed, and to "insist upon preserving the entire integrity of a Fairy tale" is like "shearing one of your own 'whole hogs,' where there is 'great cry and little wool.'" Cruikshank's editing was essential and salutary. He had simply removed the immoral and depraved elements from *Hop-o'-my-Thumb.* As for the temperance coloring, Dickens had an "evident contempt, and even hatred, against that cause." "I take the liberty of telling you," Cruikshank went on, "that it is a question which you evidently do not understand." Cruikshank concluded with a request and a rejection. "I have therefore to beg, that in future you will not drive your 'whole hogs' against us, but take them to some other market, or keep them to yourself if you like; but we'll none of 'em, and therefore I take this opportunity of driving them back."

Cruikshank caused his magazine reply to be printed also as a separate penny pamphlet. When, about the same time, he came to publish the next of his rewritten fairy tales, **Jack and the Bean-Stalk,** he did not continue the controversy directly, though he did make the giant a depraved individual who drank himself tipsy every night and ravaged the countryside as a result. But in *Cinderella,* the third installment of the Fairy Library, also published in 1854, Cruikshank alluded directly to the controversy. In a note at the end entitled **"To The Public,"** he admonished Harriet Beecher Stowe for describing him as "an old man, with grey hair"; reproved a reviewer for criticizing his setting of **Jack and the Bean-Stalk;** and advised would-be readers who might fall into "absurd mistakes" such as the aforesaid reviewer fell into or "such as my friend Charles Dickens has fallen into," to buy and read his penny-pamphlet reply to Dickens. (In later issues of this note, Cruikshank had his reference to Dickens reset so that "my friend Charles Dickens" became "Mr. Charles Dickens.")

As for the text of *Cinderella* itself, Cruikshank seemed bent on out-parodying Dickens' parody. When the King ordered fountains of wine in the streets to celebrate Cinderella's marriage, Cinderella's godmother "begged that his Majesty would not carry out that part of the arrangements," for "drink leads also to quarrels, brutal fights, and violent deaths." When the King replied that such violence is only committed by those who take too much, the godmother replied that "the history of the use of strong drinks . . . is marked on every page by *excess, which follows, as a matter of course, from the very nature of their composition,* and are [*sic*] always accompanied by ill-health, misery, and crime." The godmother then launched upon a page-long disquisition which praised the beneficence of the Almighty in making harmful liquors intoxicating, admonished the King that "so long as your Majesty continues to take even half a glass of wine a-day, so long will the drinking customs of society be considered respectable," and advised the King to "look at Cinderella, who has never taken any in all her life, and who never will."

Cinderella brought the Fairy Library to an abrupt halt. Whether this was the result of poor sales, hostile reactions, or Cruikshank's own decision, is not clear. What is clear is that *Puss in Boots,* the fourth and last fairy tale that Cruikshank rewrote for his Fairy Library—one suspects that it was conceived like the last two in 1854—did not appear until 1864. In 1865 the four fairy tales were collected in a single volume, Cruikshank retaining most of his earlier addresses and announcements and reprinting a further justification of his editorial practices. The latter defense, originally published with *Puss in Boots* in 1864 and entitled, **"To Parents, Guardians, And All Persons Intrusted With The Care Of Children,"** was based, for the most part, on the 1854 letter from Hop-o'-my-Thumb to Dickens. (The pamphlet version of that letter, Cruikshank explained, was now out of print.) Cruikshank, in effect, was making his controversy with Dickens a permanent part of his Fairy Library. His new reply contained few substantive changes. He reemphasized and reargued his position here and there, and he carefully pruned away all genial references to Dickens. . . .

For Dickens, Cruikshank was never a personal enemy. He was tiresome and irritating in his fanaticism, downright dangerous in his tamperings with the "nurseries of fancy," but Dickens latterly viewed him as eccentric and misguided rather than malicious, as an object of pity rather than hate. By the time their controversy erupted, Cruikshank had drifted out of Dickens' circle and in many ways out of Dickens' ken. The rose gardens of Boulogne were remote from the temperance meetings in Exeter Hall. As Dickens whirled through the wrenchings and the triumphs of his latter years, George Cruikshank became for him little more than an occasional flicker of memory on the fringes of his consciousness.

But for Cruikshank matters were otherwise. Dickens loomed large and inimical and puissant. Dickens was associated with the demise of Cruikshank's *Magazine,* the languishing of his *Fairy Library,* the failure of his attempts to recapture his lost popularity. Dickens had attacked the ideas behind *The Bottle* and *The Drunkard's Children,* had mocked Cruikshank's most cherished beliefs as Whole Hoggism, and had cruelly parodied his editing. Dickens had taken Cruikshank's ideas for many of the pieces in *Sketches by Boz* and for all of *Oliver Twist* and had made not the slightest acknowledgment. Dickens was petted and rich and famous while Cruikshank was poor and forgotten. Even the old days and the old times with Dickens were a reproach rather than a bond; they reminded him of his shameful excesses before he was saved by teetotalism. In his latter-day disappointment and paranoia, these oppositions and disparities waxed rather than diminished.

When Dickens died in 1870, Cruikshank was seventy-seven years old. He was still alert and vigorous, still valued by a circle of friends, but failure and disappointment had constricted and envenomed his outlook. Dickens now lay in Westminster Abbey, a resting place unimaginable in 1835 when Cruikshank read his first pages by Boz and etched his first illustrations for the *Sketches.* But Cruikshank's memories of Dickens were devoid of reverence or loss. The bright energy of the fledgling author, the triumphs of their early collaboration, the days and nights of boon companionship, the weeks of splendid strolling as amateur players—all were forgotten or of no account. Cruikshank's epitaph for his old companion was brief and unforgiving.

"I so hated the fellow," he said.

John Wardroper

SOURCE: An introduction to *The Caricatures of George Cruikshank,* Gordon Fraser, 1977, pp. 7-24.

George Cruikshank became a Victorian worthy—a spry and quirky one, it is true, yet still very far from the irreverent artist who had come to manhood in the time of the Regent. Although admirers cultivated him with biographies in mind and pressed him to write his life, he revealed little about that young man. He had renounced too much of him. But the work done in his twenties and thirties, his best work, survived unsuppressible and much sought after, to testify to his past vitality, and to remind him of the time when he had first heard himself called a genius.

He found that when printshop browsers came upon the zestful and sometimes scurrilous caricatures he had created an age before, they were inclined to think them the work of an earlier man of the same name. And indeed they were. But whatever he might think of the young Cruikshank, he was never a man to put up with being denied credit for work he had done. At the age of seventy, the one-time caricaturist and devotee of 'late hours, blue ruin and dollies', now aspiring painter in oils and teetotal campaigner, put on show in London a thirteen-foot-wide canvas, *The Triumph of Bacchus,* depicting the evils of drink in a dozen easy lessons. And round the exhibition hall he also put on display, from the vast hoard of his portfolios, more than a thousand drawings, etchings and engravings, some of them dating from his eighth year: to prove, as he said in the catalogue, 'that I am not my own grandfather'.

It was a self-censored selection. Cruikshank could not of course be expected to offend the proprieties of 1863 (and

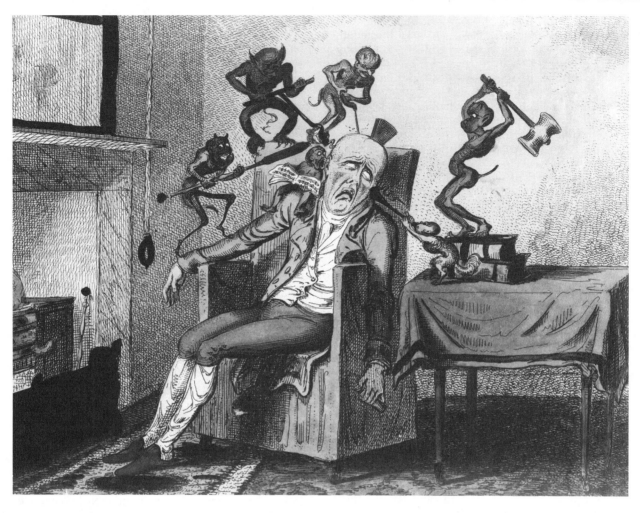

The Headache.

of his temperance associates) by exhibiting any Regency lewdness; but the selectiveness went much further than that. Although George IV had been dead for a third of a century, Cruikshank showed none of his rumbustious images of that gross Adonis and his outsize mistresses, nor any of the caricatures he had done in that reign on the radical side. This editing of his past was noticed. The *Art Journal* recalled in particular a famous series of anti-establishment woodcuts done by Cruikshank in 1820, and said, 'It will scarcely be credited that not one of these famous designs appears'. He had 'ignored the very existence of works that all admire and covet' and had 'done himself an injustice in his own gallery'. He had evidently gone further than some Victorians thought necessary in adjusting the evidence of his former less decorous self. It was a timid celebration by the man who had had the good fortune to be born soon enough to flourish as the last great master caricaturist of the Georgian era. . . .

From 1823 a growing proportion of his work was on a small scale, about three inches by two—a scale in which he had had intensive practice in his pamphlet wood engravings. The message, however, was no longer 'gunpowder in boxwood'. He was working to give pleasure at the fireside and in the nursery. In 1822-3 he did eight delicate etchings for *Peter Schlemihl,* the story of the boy who sold his shadow, and ten for the first English edition of the Grimm fairy tales—etchings that established him on the continent as well as in England as a masterly fairy-tale illustrator. He also did ten small etchings and eight wood engravings for a compilation by his friend William Clarke, *Points of Humour.* This book is notable as the occasion of the first long article in praise of Cruikshank, by Walter Scott's son-in-law J. G. Lockhart in *Blackwood's Magazine.* . . .

Cruikshank too had become by then a man for genteel smiles, though Thackeray does not admit it. He does not take his praise much beyond the 1820s. He calls Cruikshank 'the friend of the young especially', and recalls having as a boy given up tarts to buy Cruikshank prints: among them, when he was fifteen, the *Phrenological Illustrations,* 'which entire work was purchased by a joint stock company of boys, each drawing lots afterwards for the separate prints'. Gillray had hardly been 'the friend of the young', and many caricatures by him and his contemporaries, and by the early Cruikshank, were most questionable fare for children. Thackeray himself made this point in an article fourteen years later on the pleasant domestic art of John Leech, the *Punch* artist. Thackeray recalls from his childhood the portfolios of caricatures in his grandfather's house, and says, 'But if our sisters wanted to look at the portfolios, the good old grandfather used to hesitate. There were some prints among them very odd indeed; some that girls could not understand; some that boys, indeed, had best not see. We swiftly turn over those prohibited pages. How many of them there were in the wild, coarse, reckless, ribald, generous book of old English humour!' By this date Cruikshank had been several years a teetotaller and was not even creating many genteel laughs suitable for all the family. Good-hearted Thackeray complains gently: 'He has rather deserted satire and comedy of late years, having turned his attention to the serious, and warlike, and sublime . . . We prefer the comic and fanciful.'

Hilary and Mary Evans

SOURCE: in *The Man who Drew the Drunkard's Daughter: The Life and Art of George Cruikshank 1792-1878,* Frederick Muller Limited, 1978, 190 p.

He was a good man. And like all good men, he wanted to leave the world a better place than he found it. Luckier than most, he found himself endowed with a talent which could help him achieve this purpose, and so, for the seventy five years of his working life, he dedicated himself and his art to setting the world to rights. Even when he wasn't deliberately preaching, his pictures are loud with his unspoken comments, his approval or reproach, his anger or sympathy or hope.

Fortunately, both for himself and for the world he wanted to change, he was not only a good man but a good artist. If George Cruikshank the reformer had a message to get across, George Cruikshank the artist saw to it that the message was delivered with style and taste, discretion and wit. Even in his most blatant pieces of propaganda the moral is sugar-coated with art and, in return, his art is strengthened by this inner core of purpose. Without a sense of direction, his art could have been hesitant, diffuse, lacking conviction; assigned a definite job to do, it is confident, simple, self-assured. Without it, he would have been just one among the many competent professional illustrators of the day, ranked with Seymour or Onwhyn or Phiz. It is his sense of purpose which raises him above the rest.

This continuing sense of mission meant, too, that George Cruikshank the artist and George Cruikshank the man lived comfortably together in the same body. His work sprang out of his life, and in turn directed its course; his art was integrated with the other elements of his existence, never causing conflict. What the reformer wanted to say, the artist was happy to express. Self-doubt, trauma, hesitation of will—none of these seem ever for a moment to have disturbed either the steady progress of his career as an artist or his development as a man.

It was, up to a point, what the totalitarian ideologists prescribe—the artist putting his talents to work for Humanity, Art the Handmaid of Progress: from each according to his ability. The difference is that George the artist took his orders from George the man, not from some Humanity-in-the-abstract. If he believed profoundly in the social responsibility of the artist, it was because he believed in the social responsibility of *everybody,* whether artist or politician or greengrocer. But it was a responsibility which demanded personal initiative, not passive obedience to what others dictated. We know how angrily he opposed the police-state policies of the British government in the troubled post-Waterloo years; he would never have subscribed to any ideology which allowed Society to dictate either what a man should believe as a man or what he should express as an artist.

So the views he expressed were always his own. Insofar as he gave any thought to religious or political doctrines, he distrusted them. He had a lifelong suspicion of the Catholic Church in particular, but on patriotic rather than doctrinal grounds, and there is no evidence that he favoured any other sect except as a provider of a measure of social and moral stability. Nor, for all his activity in political controversy, was he ever a party man. Each issue was evaluated on its individual merits, not as a plank in some politician's platform. He was as turncoat in his allegiances as he was constant in the human sympathies which underlay them. Now radical to the point of revolution, now conservative to the point of reaction, he gave his support to whatever seemed best—not for a party, not for principle . . . but for people.

So, resolute to help the world, but treading no party line and obedient to internal impulses rather than external pressures, he was free to tackle in his own way the central theme that runs through all his art: the discrepancy between the world as it is and the world as it might be.

George knew both worlds and made them his own. He drew things as they too often tragically are: the waste of life in the gin shop; the violence of the mob, whether in rebellious Ireland or communist Paris; the tyranny of authority, whether vested in a Minister of State or a Parish Beadle. He drew lesser faults with a gentler tolerance: a housewife over-concerned for her polished fire-irons; servant girls gossiping on area steps; young men enjoying a midnight spree at the watchman's expense. But he also drew the world as it might be, and occasionally is: children playing peacefully on a suburban green; a theatre crowded from pit to gallery with cheerful playgoers; a Christmas party with the cake arriving in splendour. Whichever world he was drawing, the other was implicit in it. Look on this picture and on that, he invites us, and see how life is and how it could be. All we have to do is to choose between them.

But, all too often, we do not choose. We continue to waste our shillings in the gin-shop, our greed and cruelty continue to drive girls onto the streets and boys into thieving. Such obstinacy in choosing evil might make even the strongest-willed despair: if against stupidity even the gods strive in vain, what can a fellow-human hope to accomplish, however strenuously he deploys his talents? Luckily for George—and again, luckily for us—he found a third world to escape into, where he could forget both the world of reality and the world of the unrealised ideal. In this never-never world of fantasy, jolly Sir John Falstaff can drink his fill without dragging his family to ruin; Cinderella and her Prince can live happily ever after; and even the Fairies' revenge is not half as cruel as that of the Irish rebels.

In each of these three worlds George made himself at home, and makes each of them familiar to us in turn. But because, whichever world he was depicting, his theme remained the same—humanity—his three worlds are not distinct, they touch and overlap. Even in his most horrific scenes he reminds us what we have in common with the unfortunates who have been caught up in them: but for circumstance, the debauched drop-outs from the Gin-Shop could be sitting beside us laughing in the theatre gallery, the bloodthirsty mob could be sharing with us the delights of Greenwich Fair. George the artist prevented George the reformer from separating men into white sheep and black goats, for artists know all the shades of grey which lie between. So the father in the history of **'The Bottle'** is destroyed by his own weak nature: his downward career starts with a kindly human gesture. 'The Worshippers of Bacchus' sin through ignorance; it is their decent, praiseworthy wish to mark a happy domestic occasion to toast a bride, celebrate a christening, rejoice in a birthday which sets their feet on the fatal path. And in that picture which focuses his whole attitude to life within a single frame, The Outline of Society, good and evil touch and mingle; we are free to choose, no border guards prevent the good defecting to join the wicked, the sinner can always have second thoughts and return to grace.

Nor is his third world, his fantasy world, so remote that we must first pull up our stakes in the world of reality. We can escape for a little while as if spending an hour or two at the theatre, and return to the real world rested and refreshed. And in any case it turns out that its inhabitants aren't so unreal as they at first appear. Jack's Ogre is more easily outwitted than a tyrannical mill-owner or a corrupt politician; the witches are fearsome creatures, but no more so than the master of a workhouse. As for the fairies, you have only to open your library door quietly enough to catch them appraising your picture collection with their customary exquisite taste.

For, though the real world contains much to horrify and dismay, George loved it too strongly to leave it for long, nor would he encourage the rest of us to do so. His love of his fellow creatures and his affection for the strange ways in which we behave is vivid in every picture he drew—we are his single and lifelong preoccupation. Among all the thousands of his pictures, there is not one in praise of nature or God: no landscapes or studies of plants or natural beauty, hardly a picture of animals which does not also contain humans. We do not know why he gave up the Royal Academy classes he started attending at the

age of sixty, but perhaps he realised that they were concerned with every aspect of art except the one which concerned him: people, always people, were his only subject and only object. Art—art in the abstract—could only come between him and people, just as religious creeds and political dogmas would prevent him from seeing people as they really are.

And so, picking his way by the light of his own instincts, George avoided the rocks on which so many reformers wreck their good intentions. He isn't tempted to settle for textbook solutions and he isn't up in a pulpit, preaching. He's sitting beside us, clapping his hand on our shoulder, understanding our weaknesses but encouraging us to try and overcome them. He had a robust faith—no twentieth century words could replace that fine Victorian phrase—he had a robust faith in humanity; he never doubts that there is hope for you and me, despite our fondness for a drop of gin, our weakness for a pretty figure, our little prides and superstitions, even our bigotries and cruelties. He never lets us forget that it is not strength but weakness which makes man choose evil rather than good; his art encourages us to hate, not the cruel and bigoted people, but the circumstances which have made them so.

George didn't hate anybody. Even in his fairy tales, the giants and monsters are drawn more with pity than with fear and hate; in his moral drawings there are no downright villains, only victims of circumstance. The landlord who makes his living by selling the Demon Drink is to be pitied because he knows no better; Bill Sikes and Fagin are no less the playthings of fate than Nancy and Oliver.

Such attitudes could easily have made him a sentimentalist, but this danger too he managed to avoid. He was a tough-minded man, not evading the issues, always knowing the score. He didn't avoid the fact that drink can send a man's son to the thieves' kitchen and his daughter to the brothel, and he didn't fool himself, or us, into thinking things could be set right with a sanctimoniously pointed finger and a pious text. People are as they are, because the world is as it is: if we want to change them, we must first change the world. And so, all his life, George put his talents to work to change the world. . . .

Every piece of work which George produced, except for a handful of oil paintings towards the end of his life, was intended for reproduction; that is to say, it had to be compatible with one or other of the various printing processes then available. To ensure that his work was suitable the artist had also to be something of a craftsman. Even if he did not himself do the laborious donkeywork necessary to adapt his original drawing for printing, he had to have the technicalities of reproduction in mind while he made his drawing, and design accordingly.

The majority of George's work consisted of etchings; this is true both of his earliest work and of the work which he was to produce at the height of his career. Etching was a laborious process, and George was one of the very few great artists for reproduction to employ it consistently. . . .

He would start by making a rough sketch, perhaps scribbling alternative effects alongside until he felt he had got it all right. When he was satisfied with his design he would trace it carefully with a pencil on to thin or tracing paper. Next, he—or an assistant, meanwhile—would prepare the etching plate which, during his early career, would be of copper. The plate was heated, and on to it was rubbed a lump of wax-like resinous compound; there were various formulae, the one vital property being that it should be resistant to acid. The heat of the plate melted the compound sufficiently to spread a thin layer over the plate—this was called the ground. When the plate was covered all over, it was blackened by holding it over a candle flame or some equivalent.

George or an assistant would then take the plate and the drawing round to the printer (one of the reasons why it was professionally useful to live in the publishing quarter!). Plate and drawing would be placed together between dampened paper, and run through a roller press. The pressure would leave a faint silvery-grey impression of the drawing on the black ground of the plate.

That was the easy part. Now George would set to work to do the actual etching. For this he used a series of sharp steel needles of varying thicknesses, with which he cut through the ground to the copper beneath. As the ground was relatively soft, this wasn't physically difficult. The skill came in controlling the needle so that lines flowed smoothly, and in massing the numerous scratches which formed the shaded areas and created the subtle variations of tone called for by the original design.

When the image had been fully cut, the plate was dipped into a solution, usually of dilute nitric acid. Where the needle had exposed the copper, the acid would start to bite into the metal: elsewhere the plate was protected by the ground. So gradually the acid bit the artist's drawing into the plate.

The biting process could be halted at any time by removing the plate from the acid and rinsing it in water. If George wanted certain parts to be only lightly etched, he would varnish them over; then the plate would go back into the acid—perhaps after some further etching—so that other parts could be more deeply cut. This 'stopping out' process could be repeated as often as he wished. According to the strength of the acid, he might keep the plate in the bath for anything from one to one hundred minutes.

Then the plate went to the printer again. All that was necessary now was for the printer to coat the plate with ink, then wipe it off; this would leave ink in the cuts which the acid had bitten. When the paper was pressed onto the plate, the ink was taken up, to produce a perfect replica of the original. In transferring the drawing to the plate in the first place, the image would have been reversed; now that it was transferred from the plate to the printing paper, it was reversed back to the right way round again.

Later in his career, George took to using steel instead of copper plates. Steel is of course harder than copper, and

the acid used previously wasn't strong enough. But in 1824 a man named Turrell concocted a mixture of nitric and other acids, which enabled steel to be successfully used. The result was a deeper and finer line, because the acid didn't spread sideways in the cuts to anything like the same extent as in copper. This is what gives George's maturer etchings their delicate lines and subtle shading. The printer, too, appreciated the development, for the steel plates enabled him to achieve a much longer print run before the plates began to wear out.

Some of George's etchings were coloured—notably the big political prints of his Napoleonic series. The colouring was entirely hand done—colour printing didn't come in until nearly the end of George's career, and as far as is known none of his work was printed in colour during his lifetime. Hand colouring was a tedious business, often done by teams of girls on an assembly line basis, one doing the green, another the red, and so on: you can often see where they went over the edges of the artist's drawing. Under the circumstances, it is surprising how good the colouring often was.

For some of his book and magazine illustrations, particularly during the 1820s, George used wood engraving rather than etching. The great advantage of this, from the publisher's viewpoint, was that the picture could be reproduced on the same page as the text, because a wood block prints in relief like the typematter itself—the ink goes onto the sticking-up bits, not into the cut-in bits. It isn't possible to print the two kinds of print at the same time: a publisher using etched illustrations has to choose whether to cut the words as well as the picture, or print the sheet twice over, or print words and illustration on separate sheets. All these were done, but all were relatively expensive. To etch the words as well as the picture is a lot of hard work, and was done only when the picture was the dominant element and the words not too many—as, for example, on George's Napoleonic caricatures. Printing the sheet twice over was rarely done in Britain. The normal practice was to print the etched illustrations on separate pages, which then had to be stuck by hand into the book before it was trimmed and bound. This was how all George's maturer book illustration work was produced, but of course it added considerably to the cost of production. The publisher, therefore, had to weigh up whether the appeal of providing etched plates was sufficient to tempt the potential purchaser into the additional expense. In the 1820s the name of George Cruikshank wasn't perhaps well enough known, nor had the market for quality illustrated books been properly established and so, during this period, most of George's book illustrations consisted of wood engravings and it was not until 1840 that the etched plates were used to any great extent.

The wood engravings were made by drawing directly onto a piece of hard wood—usually pear or alder—which had been previously whitened with chalk. The rest of the work was done by the engraver, or 'cutter' as he was often termed. Cutting may not have called for the same creative imagination as did the initial drawing, but it was a longer job and required a high degree of skill, so it is not surprising that artist and cutter were generally paid about the same for their respective contribution. What the engraver had to do was cut away all the areas which George had left white, leaving his black portions projecting and, since the black portions were often small and delicate lines, the carving too had to be delicate. The thoughtful artist created his original drawing in the knowledge of what would subsequently happen to it, so that it was essentially a question of teamwork. A good engraver could make all the difference to the job, and in some cases—though we may suppose this happened rarely in George's case—he could positively improve on the original.

When the time came for printing, the wood block was locked into the printing frame together with the typematter, and words and pictures inked together to transfer the image to the paper.

Etching and wood engraving account for the bulk of George's work, but he did occasionally use other techniques. The celebrated plates which he and his brother Robert did for *Life in London* are hand coloured aquatints, a process originally intended to simulate water colour painting. It is essentially a variant of etching, which uses the ground itself, broken by heat to give a mottled surface, to print shaded areas which give the characteristic aquatint look. Outlines and any necessary detail are effected by etching in the usual way.

A few of George's drawings were reproduced by lithography, notably the contrasting prints **'Gin'** and **'Water'**. This is a flat surface process which gives almost perfect reproduction of pencil and chalk drawings, and was generally used for large-format illustrated books. . . .

One other process used by George was a rare variant known as Glyphography, which was occasionally used during the 1840s but never became popular. George was probably the only major artist to employ it. However, the use he made of it for his series **'The Bottle'** and **'The Drunkard's Children'** is very impressive, and it is surprising that the process was not more extensively used. Some of the details of the technique are still obscure, but basically it seems that the artist drew onto a metal plate which had first been stained black, then overlaid with a white composition. As George cut through the white with his etching needles, the black showed through just like a drawing. When his drawing was completed, the white areas were built up with additional material, and a relief block made in the form of an electrotype—more or less a mould created by depositing metal into George's etched plate; when removed, it formed a metal relief block to be printed from in the usual way.

Comparing his performance in these various processes, there is not the slightest doubt that George was right to choose etching whenever he could. His work in all media is of interest, but those where it has to be interpreted by some other hand, no matter how skilful, lose a proportion of his individuality, whereas his etchings remain utterly

distinctive. His wood engravings for, say, Hone's *Every Day Book* are very good, but not easily distinguished from the work of Hone's other contributors: whereas his best etchings are uniquely characteristic. . . .

[I]mmediately successful were his illustrations for popular tales translated from the German of Grimm, Chamisso and De la Motte Fouqué. Years later, Ruskin was to write of these etchings:

> If ever you happen to meet with two volumes of Grimm's German Stories, which were illustrated by Cruikshank long ago, pounce upon them instantly: the etchings in them are the finest things, next to Rembrandt's, that, as far as I know, have been done since etching was invented.

Praise indeed, and praise that was echoed by many other discerning critics. Writing in 1840 in the *Westminster Review,* Thackeray was to say, 'We preferred his manner of 1825 to any which he has adopted since.' This observation was made before George produced his finest book illustration, and it is not unlikely that Thackeray might have found reason to revise his judgement, yet it is one that is shared by many. William Bates, for instance, writing in 1878, says, 'Looking at these excellent etchings I am disposed to regard George Cruikshank as then at his best, and question whether he made any absolute advance after this early epoch'. Certainly, here in these fairy illustrations one can, perhaps for the first time, confidently recognise what might be termed 'the Cruikshank style'— for though he had many styles, the combination of fantastic detail within a satisfying harmonious framework which we discern in these etchings was to be the dominant characteristic of his work all his life.

If today we are more prone to admire his social commentary than his flights of fancy, this is perhaps simply the swing of fashion. Ours is a socially hypersensitive age, and it is his eye for the nuances and niceties of human behaviour which impresses us most. Personally, I have no hesitation in preferring his more mature work, and even among his work in the 1820s I would rather have such slight things as the series of street characters he did for the *Gentleman's Pocket Magazine* in 1827—modest, unobtrusive sketches but brilliantly observed. It was, after all, Thackeray again who said of George that he was 'a man of the people if ever there was one'. But it would be a mistake to overlook the importance of the Grimm illustrations in George's artistic development, for here is the 'pure imaginative outré' which Professor Wilson had called for. Fairy themes were to crop up intermittently throughout his life and inspire some of his most brilliant compositions—his very last etching was to be an illustration for a fairy story. . . .

Because of the reputation of his illustrations for Grimm's tales, George was asked to illustrate Sir Walter Scott's *Letters on Demonology and Witchcraft* in 1830. Later, George was to develop a 'fairy tale' style which might have been appropriate for this serious study of the paranormal, but in 1830 his illustrations are too whimsical for the text

Oliver Asking for More

An illustration for Oliver Twist.

and wholly out of key with Scott's measured consideration of his subject. Considered on their own, however, the etchings are fine examples of George's ability to give solid, tangible form to verbal accounts. If there are fairies, if there are witches, then this, we feel, is how they must be. They are credible creatures, and yet for all that, sufficiently not of our world to retain their fascination and mystery.

Another series of illustrations in the same genre are those George did for Sir John Bowring's **Minor Morals for Young People,** which appeared in three volumes from 1834 to 1839. Here again, his Wandering Jew is not to be compared with that created by Gustave Doré, nor his vampire with the legend which Bram Stoker's text was to evoke so shudderingly, but here is a Jew we might meet any day in the street, a vampire as the police might find themselves called upon to cope with. Like the fairies and the witches, they are creatures of substance—the Wandering Jew throws a shadow, the witches need barrels to support them in the water. George's fairies can no more flout the laws of nature than the rest of us. . . .

In the same year as he did his first Scott illustrations, 1836, George did his first illustrations for William Harrison

Ainsworth. It was the start of his most fruitful collaboration. Ainsworth, though little read today, was in his day so popular as to rival Dickens. He developed a formula of dressing up history as fiction in a sensational way which nevertheless managed to be respectable and even 'literary'—the best comparison in our times would be with a Hollywood version of history, broadly true to the facts but everything a few sizes larger than life, romantic sub-plots added to counteract any tendency of the central theme to overweigh the book and depress the reader. In novel after novel, Ainsworth took some eventful historical period—the Gunpowder Plot, the Reign of Henry VIII, the Great Plague and Fire of London—and fashioned it into fiction, or he would take the career of some notorious villain, such as the thief Jack Sheppard or the highwayman Richard Turpin, and weave a romantic fiction round his exploits.

It was Ainsworth's book about Turpin, **Rookwood,** which first brought him into contact with George. Three editions of the novel had already appeared without illustrations, and had proved an immense success; now his publisher, Macrone, ventured to see if he could milk the market further by issuing an illustrated edition. George was a natural choice, and the choice proved a wise one, too. Though his illustrations for this Ainsworth novel are far from being his best for this author, they are nevertheless very fine, and proved to the world that George was capable of more serious book illustration than he had hitherto produced. I dare say he surprised even himself.

Rookwood marks the turning point in George's career as an illustrator. That old bedevilling whimsicality is still in evidence, there is still just a shade too much of the former caricaturist in the faces and the gestures. But there is a new sense of sympathy with his subject, which tells us that the artist has let himself be governed not by his feelings for the particular situation, but by the spirit of the author's overall approach to his theme. There is, for the first time, a sense that illustrations can be more than a visual decoration to the author's text, that they can be a kind of alternative expression, a simultaneous presentation, in visual terms instead of verbal, of the author's vision. . . .

In 1833 there started to appear in the magazines occasional pieces over the signature of 'Boz'. They caught the attention of the more established Ainsworth, who introduced their author—a young unknown named Charles Dickens—to his publisher, John Macrone. Between them, they worked out the notion of a series of 'sketches' on various aspects of London life, since this seemed to be Dickens' forté. It was natural that they should think of inviting George Cruikshank to provide accompanying illustrations.

For Dickens at the outset of his career and George at a turning point in his, **Sketches by Boz** was a critical event. The first volume was published on February 7th, 1836, and was an immediate success. Today these pieces by Dickens, overshadowed by the greater works to come, tend to be less read than they should be. They are, despite their lightness of tone, astonishingly mature in attitude and sympathy, and leave the reader in no doubt that here is a writer of far greater potential than the typical 'comic' writer of the day. Dickens' text is superbly matched by George's etchings; it was the perfect collaboration. George's whimsical style, so wrong for Scott, is utterly right for Boz.

It was not only a successful collaboration, it was also a happy one. There were moments of doubt, inevitably. Professionally, George was a rapid and punctual worker, but he met his match in the young novelist, who dared to complain of him to Macrone, 'I think he requires the spur.' Later, when they were working on the second volume, Dickens heard that George proposed to make some amendments to his text. He was furious. 'I have long believed Cruikshank to be mad!' he exclaimed, and wrote to Macrone suggesting that a different illustrator be found. But he was reconciled, and after a while, as he got to know George better, he grew accustomed to the artist's peculiarities and perhaps came to see them as the inevitable accompaniment of genius. The working collaboration warmed into a friendship which was to be close for the next dozen years, and even then it was not broken by any quarrel but simply faded as their paths diverged.

Joseph Grimaldi, the greatest clown of his day, worked frequently at Sadlers Wells Theatre, just round the corner from George's home, and the two were well acquainted apart from George's love of anything to do with the theatre. Dickens, too, was passionately fond of the theatre, and no doubt accompanied George on evening theatrical visits. Author and artist were natural choices when Richard Bentley planned to publish the edited 'Memoirs' of Grimaldi. Dickens was editing Bentley's *Miscellany,* a monthly journal of popular literature, and George was also under contract to supply a large etching every month.

It was in Bentley's *Miscellany* that Dickens' first real novel appeared—for *Pickwick Papers* was more a thinly disguised series of sketches strung together. With *Oliver Twist* he established himself immediately as one of the leading novelists of the day. It displays a skill, a confidence and a maturity astonishing when we consider how little he had previously published, and how trivial most of that former work had been.

Oliver Twist inspired George to produce some of his most memorable illustrations. The London setting enabled him to use his intimate knowledge of London locations and London characters. He gave Bill Sikes and Fagin and the street arabs a vivid reality which, even today when his caricaturish style is out of fashion, remains the standard by which all other Dickens illustration must be judged. This is well evidenced by this observation by Arthur Waugh, a director of Chapman & Hall, who published the majority of Dickens' works:

> George Cruikshank, then in his forty-fourth year, was established as the most popular illustrator of his day. His work was in constant demand, and its reputation still survives with such vitality that there seem to be many people who have grown up under the belief that

Cruikshank was responsible for illustrating all Dickens's novels. The trade department of Chapman and Hall could bear ready witness to the persistence of this illusion. Again and again the inquiry is repeated. 'A bookseller has offered me a complete edition of Dickens,' some provincial enthusiast writes, 'which he claims to contain all the original illustrations. But on examining it, I discover that a large proportion of the pictures are by some artist named "Phiz": What I want are the original pictures by Cruikshank'.

Alas, *Oliver Twist* was to be the last fruit of their collaboration. Why, has been a matter for speculation ever since. On the whole, the working relationship between the two men seems to have been a happy one. Dickens did, it's true, object to George's proposal for the final plate in the novel, and suggest a replacement, but George seems to have provided it cheerfully enough, and there was no suggestion of a quarrel. It appears, in fact, that there were plans for George to provide the illustrations for the next Dickens novel, *Barnaby Rudge,* in 1839.

But at the same time as *Oliver Twist* was appearing in Bentley's *Miscellany,* his *Pickwick Papers* was coming out in parts. The early chapters had been illustrated by Robert Seymour, but this noted comic artist had shot himself midway through publication, for reasons which remain unknown, and the rest of the illustrations had been provided—after an anguished talent contest in which many contemporary illustrators were tried and considered—by the young Hablot Knight Browne, better known as 'Phiz'. I think it likely that, for all his respect for George, Dickens found the younger and less established artist more malleable, and preferred to work with him than with the less tractable George.

There was another aspect to his work with Dickens, a further instance of extravagant claims on George's part, but these will be best considered together with similar claims in regard to his collaboration with Ainsworth. I doubt if they were a factor in the question of who was henceforth to be Dickens' illustrator. The claims were not made until many years later, and the friendship between author and artist continued long after they had ceased to work together. Whatever its cause, the decision seems to have been motivated by professional rather than personal considerations.

What the world would have seen had it been George, not Phiz, who illustrated the later Dickens novels, is a tantalising conjecture. Splendid as Phiz's contributions certainly were, there is no doubt in my mind that George's would have been very much finer. His illustrations to *Oliver Twist* showed that he had the sympathy and the emotional range necessary to illustrate a writer of Dickens' breadth of vision, and his illustrations for Ainsworth were to show that he was acquiring a new technical virtuosity which vastly extended his powers of expression. We can only guess at what might have been, but we can be sure that it would have been the wonder of the world. . . .

Posterity has not been kind to the author whose contemporary popularity rivalled that of Dickens himself; a few lines dismiss him in the biographical dictionaries, and the judgments of scholars are rich in disparaging phrases:

> Even Dickens had his fine gold jewelled by Cruikshank. Ainsworth's tawdry rubbish—now all but forgotten, and soon to sink deep in the mudpool of oblivion—was illuminated with a false splendour by this great humourist.

(Walter Thornbury, *British Artists*)

That this is unfair is proved by the rapidity of the development of George's art during this period. An artist's skill is not improved in a vacuum; George's skill improved as a direct consequence of the challenge presented by Ainsworth's books. We may deplore the fact that it was these second-rate romances which received the full benefit of George's new maturity, but we must not overlook the possibility that it was precisely Ainsworth's high-pitched style, his dramatic scene-setting and eye for telling incident, which drew out George's latent powers to such stunning effect.

If Ainsworth is disparaged today, it is largely because he was an innovator who showed the way along which other and better writers were to follow. He was one of the earliest 'romanticisers'—with the perception to see that, from the flat and pedestrian chronicles of the life of that petty criminal Richard Turpin, the story of the Ride to York (a ride which, if it took place at all, was made long before Turpin's day) had the makings of a legend on a heroic scale. By highlighting the legend of Herne the Hunter in *Windsor Castle,* the ghost stories of **The Tower of London,** the marvellous escapes of **Jack Sheppard,** Ainsworth showed an instinct for the dramatic which struck an answering chord in his illustrator. George, too, had a love of the theatrical and the dramatic; he too liked to romanticise; to give, even to the most trivial incident, a myth-like quality. (For example, on page 108, he captions his scene not 'A gentleman desecrating a bright poker' but **'The desecration of *the* bright poker'**, raising the domestic accident to classic level.)

Apart from the earlier **Rookwood,** George's first work for Ainsworth was for **Jack Sheppard,** which appeared in the monthly parts of Bentley's *Miscellany* in 1839. **The Tower of London** followed in 1840, and **Guy Fawkes** in 1841. He was paid £40 a month for his plates, the equivalent of some £100 a week today, so that even if he had been doing no other work, George was assured of a very satisfactory income.

The quality of these illustrations is enhanced by the fact that he was now using steel plates instead of copper, and was discovering the added potential the harder metal gave him. To make any verbal comment on these illustrations would be superfluous to the point of impertinence—they are sufficiently eloquent in themselves. We don't need to be familiar with the text to appreciate the drama in each illustrated situation—every picture tells a self-evident story which even the illiterate can read. There is an object-lesson here for every artist who proposes to illustrate a book. The artist has, in a sense, humbled himself by setting aside his own inspiration and lending his art to that of the author, but he then discovers that what he gives, he gets—the author's text has called out unsuspected depths in the artist. Required to concentrate his imagination on a given situation—the instant where Jack Sheppard is discovered carving his name on the roof-beam, let's say—he is driven, unconsciously I'm sure, to empathise with the scene, transport himself into the situation, feeling, not as tacked-on embellishment but as integral elements in the scene, the hungry cat, the guttered-out candle, the handbills, the tools of the trade and all. What's more, all this humdrum detail serves, not to confuse the central subject of the picture, but to throw it into relief. In realising his author's text, the artist has realised his own art.

And if this is true of each individual picture, how much more impressive it is when we pass from one picture to the next, and see the dazzling breadth of George's new-found skill. From the meticulous detailing of the name-on-the-beam scene to the breathtaking audacity of Jack's confrontation with his mad mother, just two figures in a room, and then we come to the seemingly pedestrian diagramming of Jack's escape which builds up, as the sequence proceeds, to an archetypal comic-strip series—long before the comic-strip was invented! Even without the display of artistry in each individual plate, the virtuosity which could achieve such a diversity of treatment would be sufficient to guarantee George's inclusion among the world's greatest illustrators. . . .

George had always been at his happiest with the odd and the grotesque—drawing menacing ogres and long-nosed dwarfs with the same ease and familiarity as he drew pickpockets and parish beadles. As a boy of seven he had helped his father carry out a series of illustrations to *Baron Munchausen,* one of which is thought to have been the young artist's own design: it would have been one of his very first productions. And his very last etching was to be the frontispiece to a fairy tale.

There are many ways of delineating the supernatural, but they fall into two chief divisions. One school insists on the inhuman and monstrous aspect, emphasising the gulf which separates it from our everyday experience, stressing the other-worldliness of it all. For others, on the other hand, the weird and the wonderful are kept to human proportions if not to human size, so that the supernatural astonishes rather than alarms. George was emphatically of the second persuasion. His apparitions appear in human settings, there is nothing transcendental or ethereal about them and assuredly nothing mystical. They perform mischievous pranks on humans, in human settings, using human apparatus. They are not terribly frightening, they are often not maleficent so much as malicious. His human monsters are far more terrifying than his inhuman ones, Jack the Giant-killer's Giant is not half so awful as Oliver Twist's Fagin.

In 1853, the same year as he took up studies in the Academy Schools, he produced some work which demonstrated how little he needed what the academic teachers had to teach him. His etchings for the series of *Fairy Books* published by the faithful Bogue must be ranked among his finest productions, and among the most effective illustrations ever created for these well-known tales. Perhaps it is a pity that he was also allowed to provide the text, for he took it upon himself to edit the stories so as to make them illustrate the causes he held dear. In a paper entitled *Frauds on the Fairies,* in his magazine *Household Words,* his old friend Dickens gently mocked George for turning the protagonists of the nursery tales into spokespersons for temperance and other hobby-horses. In January 1854, in the second and final issue of *Cruikshank's Magazine,* George defended himself with the same good humour—and managed to score several telling points off his old friend.

But then as now, it was not for the words but for the pictures that readers turned to Cruikshank's *Fairy Books,* and we no more read them for their moral teachings than we do Perrault or La Fontaine. We may be the more inclined to forgive him when we recall that he was still a fresh convert to the temperance cause, and perhaps had not fully learned how to integrate it with the other features of his life. The *Fairy Books* are almost the only instance where his moral fervour is allowed to intrude upon work not specifically intended as propaganda.

He continued to produce a flow of work which, if not so great in quantity as earlier in his life, was still impressive by most artists' standards. It would certainly be irksome to mention all his work even at this stage of his career; mention of a few of the more interesting works must suffice. In 1850 he illustrated another picaresque novel, Smedley's *Frank Fairleigh,* with a series of etchings which show his ability to handle contemporary themes with the same relaxed mastery as he had brought to Ainsworth's historical romances ten years earlier. The grouping of the figures in **'The Results of giving Satisfaction'** has a balance which gives the picture tremendous power—yet the scene is so naturally conceived, so well integrated into the landscape and set off against the distant action, that the visual balancing of the successful duellist against his victim and surrounding friends appears the result of mere chance.

Also from this period is his view of Vanity Fair, for Bunyan's *Pilgrim's Progress.* George had first done some illustrations for the great nonconformist classic in 1816; later in his life he was to produce a series of twenty-five wood engravings which are of very slight merit. But this single etching, produced for an undated edition, succeeds better than perhaps most other scenes from the book might have done, because it found George on the familiar territory of the city street which he could people with the characters he knew so well—the actors, the street traders, the ruffians.

In 1852 he provided the illustrations for a work almost as uncharacteristic as Pettigrew's *Egyptian Mummies*—C. W. Hoskyns' *Talpa, or the Chronicles of a Clay Farm.* How George came to be illustrating a book which is described

as 'an agricultural fragment', I have no idea, but it drew from him some of the most inventive minor wood engravings of his career. No other artist that I know of ever tried to personify agricultural soil—even Arthur Rackham, who gave human faces to most natural things, never dared as much. And George's figure of Jack Frost, battering fiercely at the farmer's door, is a splendid creation, as is the 'iron horse' which may one day replace the horse-cab. . . . But though the railway rattles past the heron's pool, we have still much to learn from nature—the farmer can learn from the mole. In these *Talpa* engravings George is not, of course, being stretched to his greatest powers: but this only makes his performance the more impressive, bringing to each little sketch an inventiveness that gives each one a touch of his genius. Each illustration reveals the artist taking his subject, giving it thought, and adding an extra dimension which a lesser artist would not have bothered to look for. Here, on a small scale and so the more easily recognised, is 'the Cruikshank method' admirably demonstrated.

When we turn to 'Falstaff' we can see the same method operating on a higher level. The illustrations George did for his friend Robert Brough's *The Life of Sir John Falstaff,* in 1857, show the artist at the top of his form despite all his sixty-five years. Whatever he may privately have thought of Falstaff's drinking habits does not appear in this imaginary portrait which presents Shakespeare's character in uncavilling sympathy, no blame, no mockery, only a wholehearted salute from one enjoyer of life to another. . . .

[Cruikshank's] artistic talents were called for, in 1852, on behalf of a more serious form of slavery; he was asked to illustrate an edition of Harriet Beecher Stowe's *Uncle Tom's Cabin.* But the plight of the American negro, however sincerely George might sympathise with it in principle, was something too remote from his personal experience. His illustrations suggest a lack of personal familiarity with the situations he has to depict, and for once his imagination fails to provide what his knowledge cannot supply. In consequence, there is none of that sharpness of sympathy which comes from a first-hand acquaintance with the evil. It has been suggested that the disappointing quality of these illustrations is due to poor workmanship in the cutting of the blocks, but the fault lies deeper. The drawings themselves never rise above the level of competence—they lack fire and imagination.

Richard A. Vogler

SOURCE: "George Cruikshank: Caricaturist, Illustrator, and Reformer," in *Graphic Works of George Cruikshank,* Dover Publications, Inc., 1979, p. xviii.

It is important to remember that an artist like Cruikshank became the nineteenth-century exponent of a visual tradition in European religious and secular art which relates symbols and language in a unique way. Pictorial traditions tend to survive more pervasively in popular art forms like caricature than in almost any other kind of art. Emblem

The Doctor seizing Lawyer Murphy, from The History of Amelia, *by Henry Fielding.*

books as well as the hieroglyph and the heraldic device became a standard part of the visual vocabulary of an artist steeped in the tradition of caricature. The recurrent use, for example, of a dunce's hat in Cruikshank goes back to the basic iconology available to artists from the time of the Renaissance. Cruikshank is a late but direct inheritor of a very complex visual language that has steadily lost its power over the modern world. Furthermore, as an English artist working in a national tradition going back to Hogarth, Cruikshank produced art inextricably linked with language and a literary tradition, a reality that only recently has begun to be explored by scholars.

One feature of Cruikshank's artistic genius—so pervasive that it is often taken for granted—consists of his use of animism or the attribution of conscious life to inanimate objects. Perhaps the most pronounced example in this volume occurs in the composition, **"London going out of Town.—or—The March of Bricks & mortar!"**, but the phenomenon is found in numerous Cruikshank designs, including some of his illustrations for *German Popular Stories.* Closely related but different from animism is anthropomorphism or the humanization of that which is not human. This trait, found in a great number of works of children's literature going back to such classics as Aesop's fables, also finds full expression in Cruikshank's graphics.

The artist's French contemporary Charles Baudelaire said, "The special merit of George Cruikshank is his

inexhaustible abundance of grotesque. A verve such as his is unimaginable. . . . The grotesque flows inevitably and incessantly from Cruikshank's etching needle, like pluperfect rhymes from the pen of a natural poet." Very early in his career he manifests his own brand of distortion, both of bodily shapes and of the human face. There is something so characteristic about his use of the incongruous and the grotesque that to this day someone acquainted with his works can look at a particularly ill-featured face or misshapen body and declare it to be "Cruikshankian." The use of disproportionate size as well as bizarre, almost frenzied, exaggeration typifies his use of the grotesque and is often enhanced by his method of etching with its nervous, squiggly, almost surreal linear quality. He is often seen at his best when he does a kind of composite design that constitutes a theme and variations, such as "A Chapter of Noses." . . .

[I]t is appropriate to say a few words about the immediate delight found in Cruikshank's works. Although there is much to ponder and study in his graphic art, it is not necessary to *understand how* his art works to appreciate his genius. Rather, we should approach his art ready to enjoy it just as the child is delighted when he hears his favorite fairytale, recites his favorite nursery rhyme, or sings his favorite song. In Cruikshank's works we are universally confronted by teeming life devoid of escapist or elitist views. The artist is most at home when using the anarchic power of comedy to attack political chicanery and social wrongs, to expose pomposity or threadbare ethics, to attack false morality, or to show man's ubiquitous struggle to combat his circumstances. Cruikshank's characters, both his recognizable London nineteenth-century types and his more universal representations of stalwart individualism, will live forever in his graphic art because they awaken in us, his viewers, a liberating sense of our own identity. But perhaps his greatest feat is stripping away smugness and self-satisfaction and cutting down his characters to Cruikshankian size. His pencil and etching needle provide a summation of permanent human qualities, a mirroring not only of frailties, conceits, self-indulgence, and deceptions but also of resourcefulness, muddling-through determination, ineffable verve, and unabashed humanity. Ultimately we recognize in George Cruikshank's human comedy the ability of his art to cleanse with mirth and laughter the wounds of injustice abounding in an imperfect world.

Roy Porter

SOURCE: "Illustrator General," in *New Statesman & Society,* Vol. 121, No. 4105, October 9, 1992, pp. 28-9.

No cartoonist lacerated his victims with such Scarfeian savagery as the alcoholic and finally demented James Gillray. Nothing was sacred: radicals, reactionaries and royals—all were mercilessly flayed. If ever Swiftian misanthropy was embodied in political art, it was through Gillray's scabrous pen.

George Cruikshank took over where Gillray left off (out of homage, he even bought his work-table). And many of his early political prints featured in a splendid bicentenary exhibition organised by John Wardroper in association with the Cartoon Art Trust overtly echo Gillray's designs. Cruikshank's dissipated Prince Regent is Gillray's extraordinary "Voluptuary Under the Horrors of Digestion" gone still further to seed. But the young Cruikshank was also his own man, with techniques and visions distinctively his own. If Gillray's strength lay in an immediacy of gruesome and nauseating physical detail (Boney literally as a cannibal, carving Europe up), Cruikshank, by contrast, was more literary. He did not go for gut reactions.

Rather, his finest creations told stories, enacted puns and parodies, and translated ideas into images. **"The Political House that Jack Built"** (the nation's jerry-built institutions) reduced the jobbery and corruption of the Establishment to nursery-rhyme nonsense; equally radical, **"A Free Born Englishman"** showed John Bull in 1819, shackled and starving, lips padlocked.

Early Cruikshank hit hard. **"Princely Amusements or the Humors of the Family"**—Prinny and the other royal dukes enjoying a genteel domestic orgy, groping their mistresses—makes *Spitting Image* look positively pious. **"The Royal Shambles"**, a satire on Louis XVIII, shows he could be equally rude about continental royals.

After this coruscating start, it is tempting to treat the last half-century of Cruikshank's career, prolific and brilliant though it was, as somewhat anti-climatic. He more or less abandoned the genre of the political cartoon and stopped ridiculing the royals—he was at one point bought off with a £100 bribe from Windsor. He became the leading book illustrator of the era, working with Dickens on *Sketches by Boz* and *Oliver Twist,* and later with Ainsworth. He developed a taste for whimsy, sketching charming if facetious stituation-comedies (cabriolets collapsing, comic cats causing chaos in the kitchen). And, in a manner remniscent of Edward Lear, Lewis Carroll and even Richard Dadd, he grew preoccupied with doodling fairies, hobgoblins and other fantasy figments.

Cruikshank remained a perceptive observer of London high and low life. But, overall, there was a downward descent into the frivolous. And, as Wardroper stresses in his excellent catalogue introduction, he grew "strongly conservative", swiping at easy targets, like votes for women. Abandoning radicalism, Cruikshank became "non-political"; that is, observes Wardroper, an upholder of the status quo. Why the change?

Times had changed. It had been easy to give butcher Bonaparte a drubbing, or to expose the callous massacre of Peterloo ("Britons, Strike *Home*"). The more workaday parliamentary politics of the 1840s and 1850s offered fewer sitting targets. The Regent could be vilified, but not Victoria: the juvenile Queen was satire-proof. In any case, under Victoria, the stifling moralism of public taste dictated prudence. Obscenity and scurrility would have proved unacceptable; the humorist had to cultivate self-censorship.

And all the signs are that, by then, he wanted not to muck-rake, but to raise the tone, to win acclaim as an artist and public edifier. With success and mellowing years, Cruikshank dropped his former radical friends, and lived it up with literary London: Dickens, Bulwer-Lytton, the young Thackeray. There was a Cruikshank who craved a quiet life, basking in popularity and prosperity. But there was also another Cruikshank who turned vehement Victorian moralist. For in his fifties, the caricaturist took the pledge. He became an ardent temperance crusader, and vice-president of the London Temperature League.

His most memorable late efforts show the evils of alcohol, above all **"The Rival Fountains"**, or **"Gin and Water"** and **"The Bottle"**, a Hogarth-inspired sequence featuring a drink-ruined family going down the slippery slope, the father ending up a maniac, the daughter turning to prostitution. Yet the contrast with Hogarth is revealing. Hogarth's morality sequences, like **"Marriage à la Mode"**, are always double-edged, with a socio-political sting in the tail. **"The Bottle"**, by contrast, moralistically blames drink, while saying nothing of the social evils driving people to the solace of the bottle.

Cruikshank's two public faces (humorist and moralist) hint at a deeper split. For behind the apparently happily married Victorian worthy, radiating bourgeois bonhomie in Mornington Crescent, lay the classic double-life: a mistress, Adelaide Attree, and ten natural children, just a stone's throw to the west, off Albany Street. Now *that* would have been a subject for a cartoon! A pity Cruikshank, widely accused of indulging the vanity of endless self-portraiture, could never have engraved his double life for posterity.

Yet there is an enormous amount to savour in this lively exhibition, not least joyous scenes of common life (sailors carousing, prize-fighting) and sardonic social commentary on the metropolis: developers in Islington, the Southwark private water company spreading cholera throughout the capital, and the Great Exhibition. The Victorian cartoonist was not just a political commentator; his job was to create all the images, doodles and likenesses today provided by photos, TV, newsreels and graphics. Cruikshank was master of them all. This exhibition reveals him as the illustrator general of his age.

Amy Baker Sandback

SOURCE: "George Cruikshank, In Appreciation of A Knowing Smile," in *The Print Collector's Newsletter,* Vol. XXIV, No. 3, July-August, 1993, pp. 96-8.

Whether the noble savage in a romance by Rousseau, or the holy fool of a Dostoevski novel, or in more recent terms, a child's revelations in a Bruno Bettelheim case history, the wisdom inherent in a naïve sensibility is an enduring theme. In each instance the sophisticate turns for relief and/or insight to those considered more "natural" and more in touch with truths that are obscured for most of us. A connection with "the other" has also been an aspect of society's understanding of the arts, and it is certainly a part of my response to the graphic images of George Cruikshank. Apart from being a mirror of three eras of English society, 200 years after the artist's death these lively images continue to be a link to an animated inanimate world we still recognize with an understanding that has little to do with intellect and more to do with instinct.

Cruikshank's life corresponded to a period of rapid social, technological, and industrial change like our own time. He was born in London in 1792 and began his long career toward the end of the zesty Regency, was most prominent at the dawn of Victorian moralizing in the mid-1830s, and produced temperance tracts late in life, dying in 1878 at the height of British self-assurance as a world power. This is also the period that saw the development of modern book illustration. New ways of reproducing "pictures" and a general public with better education and more money to spend enlarged from a few to the many the readership for publications. The successful bookseller had now to satisfy a less scholarly audience—readers of tomes having been outnumbered by those looking for somewhat lighter entertainment—and to this end illustrated books proved to be a marketable solution, particularly if the pictures were clever and plentiful.

Journalists, humorists, and graphic artists gradually transferred their attention from the erratic production of tracts and broadsides tied to specific events, as brilliantly rendered by the likes of William Hogarth, Thomas Rowlandson, and James Gillray, to the profession of regularly providing materials for more formally published books and journals.

At one time or another, and in one role or another, Cruikshank was a star in this publishing world, supplying a journeyman's assortment of whatever was needed. You could say that he was born into the trade and cradled in caricature. As the son of a caricaturist living just off Fleet Street, he learned his craft from practical experience rather than from a course of study at an academy in the better parts of town. While Cruikshank was still quite young, Gillray's publisher Mistress Humphrey thought enough of his ability with an etching needle to commission him to finish some of the ailing master's late prints, where he added, some say, more than a few lines to the compositions. By 1823 he was the busiest illustrator in London, critically and financially successful, a man-about-town, popular in literary and artistic circles. The great John Ruskin himself was to claim that the quality of George Cruikshank's etchings rivaled Rembrandt's, a boost to his reputation that the proud artist accepted with grace. Yet he was never to lose his wonder at the doings of man and beast no matter how sophisticated his experience or his companions.

Characteristic of his talent was his special skill in turning odd bits of daily life into personalities. ***Three Courses and a Dessert,*** a humorous book written by William Clarke, published in 1830, is a prime example of this alchemy. In the illustrations listed on the "Bill of Fare" (i.e., table of contents) we are offered such treats as a rendering of an oyster, well contented and well attired with a pearl tie tack, which in June 1840 William Thackeray was to characterize in his "Essay on the Genius of George Cruikshank" for *The Westminster Review* as "cool, gentle, waggish, and yet inexpressibly innocent and winning." Or, if you prefer, there is the chance to observe the conversation of three lemons, each with a sour expression, or to share the smug superiority of a mushroom that sits slit-eyed on a mount. Having been endowed with special importance by the artist's pen, these beings are in no way intimidated by the gaze of a mere human reader. The eatables either ignore you or, like the pipe smoking "toad in a hole," stare directly out at you from the comforts of the bookplate. Various animals—a dog in an apron, a duck with an umbrella on a rainy day (as opposed to a man without), as well as two uppity water pumps and a stick that talks back to its owner—are part of the meal. We recognize only too well the pompous self-importance of our peers in the nonsense of the rendering, and what is truly remarkable is that the items on this menu lose nothing of their oysterness, or lemonness, or pumpness, in the artist's humanizing of their persons. At the end of the introduction is a weeping/smiling alligator (or is it a stand-in for the artist?) who asks our indulgence from behind a witness stand. The illustration is accompanied by the following cry for our understanding: "having thus, perhaps rashly, presented himself at the bar of public opinion, conscious as he feels of his own demerit, he can only throw himself on the liberality of his judges, and plead for a lenient sentence." A full pardon is granted by the audience, since Cruikshank had a natural talent not only to point a finger but to charm.

Cruikshank had a fashionable following for such light-hearted fare and besides Ruskin could count Baudelaire among his admiring fans. In the essay "Some Foreign Caricaturists" the French poet-critic wrote: "A verve such as his is unimaginable, nor indeed would it be credited if the proofs were not before our very eyes in the form of an immense *oeuvre,* a numberless collection of vignettes, a long series of comic albums—in short, of such a quantity of grotesque characters, situations, scenes, and physiognomies that the observer's memory quite loses its bearing. The grotesque flows inevitably and incessantly from Cruikshank's etching-needle, like pluperfect rhymes from the pen of a natural poet" (tr. Jonathan Mayne, *The Painter of Modern Life and Other Essays,* 1965). As Baudelaire observed, Cruikshank's output of this kind of image was enormous, if uneven, and all of it was wholehearted in its energy.

When one thinks of the most brilliant of his mature projects, however, one turns to his images for ***Oliver Twist*** by Charles Dickens. A good text always seemed to work like a springboard for Cruikshank's imagination, and over the course of his long career he illustrated books by such writers as Defoe, Fielding, Goldsmith, Smollett, Sterne, and the popular novels of his friend William Harrison Ainsworth. But in the full-page illustrations for the Dickens classic, published in 1838, Cruikshank is at his very best with all aspects of his considerable wit and talent well employed. It is not just the comic figures of Mr. Bumble and Oliver or the somewhat less pleasant Fagin that tell the story but the carefully rendered room, table, chair, fierce dog, or playful kitten that surround them; it is the light given off by the warming fire or the cold hopelessness of the prison cell that fills in the texture of the story. This may be a fictional world, but in the illustrations it is convincingly real. Whatever the terms of the collaboration—opinions differ on Cruikshank's contribution to the text—Cruikshank took the fine raw stuff of the story and spun another kind of gold in the images. We are convinced this is how it was and this was the way the characters actually looked, as if the artist had been there taking it all in like an early photojournalist.

Only in late productions like the tabloidesque melodrama *The Drunkard's Children* (which he also wrote) are Cruikshank's addenda intrusive, yet even here the thin ties of a bonnet and the soft stuff of a girl's dress against the arc of the massive stone bridge are telling. Whether of objects or people, the illustrations usually seem to have been created not from the artist's but from the subject's perspective; old shoes, bent trees, the ivy on the wall, as well as humans, all make or imply judgements and seem to have past histories that shape the moment set down on the page. As a result, we are carried along by the sincerity of these beings, just as we are by the tall tales of young children, convinced not by the facts of the matter but by the wholehearted ardor of the telling, and by the deeper universal truths that lie just below the surface.

This being the case it is not surprising that tales of the supernatural proved to be Cruikshank's stock in trade, one he counted on in good times and bad. As early as 1824 the elves in the Brothers Grimm *German Popular Stories* delighted not only the shoemaker but young readers and their parents. He did illustrations of devils and witches for Sir Walter Scott's *Letters on Demonology and Witchcraft* (the same year he created the repast of *Three Courses and a Dessert*), and *The Ingolsby Legends,* issued in three volumes between 1840 and 1847, is replete with the blackest of his many devils. His last project, done in 1875 and published in 1877, a year before his death, was the frontispiece for Mrs. Octavian Blewitt's *The Rose and the Lily,* the lily in question looking up from under its pad at a swarm of fairies that fly above a graceful rose at the river bank.

Cruikshank is a very knowing visual storyteller because he is able to be instinctively and disturbingly near the bone, as all true children are in their perceptions. I began to take an interest in Cruikshank's fantasies with thoughts about the animism in his drawings of animals and objects, but after a longer look it seems that while such intellectualizing is of modern interest, it is far from his spirit. A particularly talented changeling spirit, with remarkable abilities to surprise us by appearing as the soul of a lemon or the very heartbeat of a "little person" or an invisible eyewitness to events, is his kin. It is a kind of transformation of self rather than an academic or spiritual attitude that informs the graphics and allows him to appear to record (rather than create) an event or a character. Said to be a vain and difficult man, prone to hard drink and wrapped in a thin skin, he had an actor's ability to lose himself in a part and to perform for his audience with a child's openness. We should know better than to allow ourselves to be taken in, yet we suspend informed reason and accept talking lemons or the physiognomy of Fagin as they are drawn because we feel them to be true. There is no higher praise for an illustrator than the ability to achieve this kind of magic on the printed page.

Additional coverage of Cruikshank's life and career is contained in the following source published by The Gale Group: *Something about the Author*, Vol. 22.

Anne (Louise) de Roo

1931-1997

New Zealand author of fiction books.

Major works include *Cinnamon and Nutmeg* (1972), *Mick's Country Cousins* (1974), *Scrub Fire* (1977), *Traveller* (1979), *Jacky Nobody* (1984).

INTRODUCTION

Anne de Roo is best remembered for her young adult novels that incorporate the history, culture, and geography of her native New Zealand. The landscape of that country plays a role in each of de Roo's books, whether it is about a Maori family living by the sea, children lost in the bush, or a farm family raising sheep in the hills. Critics have praised the author for her characters' highly developed sense of the natural world and for accurately depicting life in the New Zealand countryside: Barbara Britton remarked that de Roo captures the "details of strenuous farming life." Although sometimes faulted for endings that are unrealistically tidy, the novelist also received acclaim for her sensitive, natural description of characters and the complex relationships between them. As Britton commented on *Mick's Country Cousins*, "All the characters are realistically drawn—the 'good' people have their weak, silly moments and the graceless [character] has affection somewhere inside him. This is an extremely good novel, full of comprehension of difficult feelings." Judith Aldridge, too, found de Roo's representation of family life accurate and insightful. She wrote of *Cinnamon and Nutmeg*, "The relationships within the family are well portrayed in all their joys and misunderstandings."

When asked by *Something about the Author*, de Roo said that she identified herself as "a New Zealand writer, principally concerned with the building up in a young country of a children's literature through which children can identify themselves and their roots, whether European or Maori." By making the conditions of life in New Zealand such an important element in all of her novels, de Roo made strides toward her goal.

Biographical Information

Born in Gore, New Zealand, de Roo received her B.A. from the University of Canterbury in Christchurch in 1952. The author spent twelve years living in the United Kingdom; de Roo told *Something about the Author* that the experience "enabled [her] to return with a new perspective and a new and deeper appreciation of the natural beauty of New Zealand's forests, mountains, and sea." Before turning to writing full-time in 1978, the author worked as a library assistant and librarian, a governess, and a secretary.

Major Works

The novel *Cinnamon and Nutmeg* centers on Tessa, a tomboy who revels in helping her father around the farm. Tessa feels that her favored status is threatened by the new baby boy in her family, and the fears of losing her place in the family, sadness over the recent loss of a sheepdog, and a new teacher who teases her all contribute to Tessa's decision to set off by herself into the hills surrounding the family farm. While wandering, Tessa discovers an orphaned wild goat kid that she names Nutmeg; later she discovers a prized calf wandering alone and names her Cinnamon. Tessa raises these two animals with love and a little help from her cousin, but she soon realizes that the calf must belong to someone. As the story develops into a mystery, and Tessa and her family must discover the true owner of Cinnamon, de Roo creates a portrait of the farming community and of the complicated family relationships of her characters. The family portrait de Roo draws becomes even more complex in the novel's sequel, *Mick's Country Cousins*. In this book, the focus is on Mick, a half-Maori cousin of Tessa's whose father has abandoned the family. Mick is sent to live on his cousins' farm when his brother proves to be incorrigible, and he also begins to act out of control. Mick feels that his cousins wanted another field hand not a family member, and he rebels by deliberately mismanaging his chores. He realizes he is wrong when his brother escapes from his detention school and attacks his aunt; Mick comes to realize that his aunt has never been anything but kind to him, and that the family does accept him after all. *Scrub Fire*, too, is a book about family relationships, this time primarily about siblings. The novel chronicles a camping trip into the bush that Michelle, Andrew, and Jason take with their aunt and uncle. Because of their uncle's incompetence, a bush fire starts, and the children must flee. They soon realize they are seriously lost and have no idea whether the adults are safe. Michelle takes charge, creating a fantasy for the family: she is the queen, and they are her subjects. Over the course of the twelve-day ordeal, though, Andrew comes through with wilderness knowledge and Michelle learns to appreciate her brothers in new ways, even as they struggle to survive. M. Hobbs commented, "The book is not only about survival, but growing up, learning humility and mutual respect, patience, and thoughtfulness."

Traveller and *Jacky Nobody* also feature the New Zealand landscape, but these are historical novels that also reflect the cultures that have shaped the country. In *Traveller*, Tom Farrell is an Englishman who comes to New Zealand in the 1850s to take the post of cadet on a sheep farm; accompanying him is Harriet Wills, betrothed to

Tom's future boss. When the two arrive in New Zealand, though, they receive the news that their employer and fiancé has died, and the two must amend their plans. Harriet stays in the port town to set up shop, while Tom heads inland to his farm. On the way he saves a sheepdog from starvation, and Traveller becomes his constant companion. Because of the dog, Tom also begins a profound friendship with an escaped convict. "Folk history and landscape combine in a strongly evocative tale of a remarkable animal with a convincing influence on human affairs," wrote Margery Fisher of the novel. *Jacky Nobody* also takes place in the nineteenth century, but this novel addresses the Maori culture in New Zealand. Jacky is an orphan boy raised by missionaries; when he discovers that he is actually the son of an elite Maori woman and a British sailor, the boy joins up with Chief Heke, a Maori warrior. Jacky describes the haka, a war dance, and the Maori attack to bring down the British flag. The title character is also there to narrate the retaliation of the Red Coats and the burning of the settlement; the novel is an accurate historical account of events that helped create modern New Zealand.

Awards

De Roo was awarded the ICI Bursary in 1981, and her storybook *Jacky Nobody* received an AIM Children's Book Award in 1983.

TITLE COMMENTARY

THE GOLD DOG (1969)

The Times Literary Supplement

SOURCE: "The Portuguese in Brazil," in *The Times Literary Supplement,* No. 3513, June 26, 1969, p. 693.

The Gold Dog is a spaniel pup bought with gold patiently panned by Jonathan Grey. . . . The scene is Marsten, a small town in Otago which once knew the excitement of a gold rush but is now asleep—until, that is, the children decide to try prospecting themselves and set off to explore Nugget Creek and Dry Bread Gorge. It is Miss de Roo's first book. The plot creaks a little and the writing is uneven but one gets a real sense of a close-knit isolated community.

MOA VALLEY (1969)

The Times Literary Supplement

SOURCE: "Away from It All," in *The Times Literary Supplement,* No. 3536, December 4, 1969, p. 1394.

Anne de Roo's second book, *Moa Valley* is set in similar country to her last, the still partly unexplored hinterland of southern New Zealand. . . . Miss de Roo tames her wild country. Her explorers are on holiday; even Mr. Peacock's obsession with moas is a hobby, not a way of life. . . .

Moa Valley is . . . a holiday adventure in the Ransome tradition. Caves are a cliché of this type of story, but these are caves with a difference—glow-worm caves under the bush of a remote part of New Zealand—and the finding of such caves is a real possibility. It was indeed only in 1955 that an amazing new one was found near the famous Waitomo Caves in the North Island. Earthquakes come in very useful and even the trek after the extinct moa is an almost reasonable proposition when one remembers that the *takahe* was spotted in 1948 and the *kakapo* in 1961, when both were thought to be extinct. New Zealand is welcome fresh territory for the traditional type of children's story, and this one has some well-differentiated characters and natural dialogue to add to the pleasures of its setting. There are some longueurs when the children are trapped in the valley and are slowly, stone by stone, finding a way out through the caves, and the geography of the whole area is a little confusing; one would welcome a more detailed sketch-map. [Altogether], this is a better book than Miss de Roo's *The Gold Dog* and one looks forward to more New Zealand stories from her.

BOY AND THE SEA BEAST (1971)

The Times Literary Supplement

SOURCE: "Sense and Sensibility," in *The Times Literary Supplement,* No. 3618, July, 2, 1971, pp. 763-64.

Boy and the Sea Beast is a human and dolphin story; such tales, like mermaid legends, have the problem of element: they must end in parting, death, or the dolphinarium. "Boy", the only male in a family of sisters, becomes the special companion of a dolphin in the bay.

> "He's beautiful," said Em, looking past Boy to where Thunder was leaping in graceful curves. "Boy, however did you manage to tame him like that?"
>
> "Tame him?" said Boy. He thought that over, "But I didn't tame him, It was more like—well, more as if he tamed me."

His games with the dolphin become too much of a tourist attraction, and to save his friend the boy loses him away to a small uninhabited island—"a nice island, just the right size for a boy". But not as he finds for a lifetime, or even a week. If the running human thread of the book is that old man-to-man, father-and-junior theme, let it pass; it does not affect the validity of the dolphin's portrait.

J. Murphy

SOURCE: A review of *Boy and the Sea Beast,* in *The Junior Bookshelf,* Vol. 35, No. 4, August, 1971, p. 241.

Boy-at-last is as his name suggests the longed-for son of a Maori family after several girls. His father has gone off to sea because he cannot stand all the women in the house, and has said he will only return when Boy-at-last is old enough to be his companion. This the child longs to prove. The two grannies live with the family in a Maori settlement at the north of North Island. These two old ladies are great characters, Grannie Rua the traditional Maori with painted chin and Grannie Tahi who has her own motor boat and works in Rachel's Bay, the English town nearby.

When Thunder, the dolphin, appears in the bay Boy determines to tame him and thus prove to his father he is grown up. How he and Thunder become a tourist attraction and how the family is finally united again form the plot, but what I found so fascinating was the insight one is given into the lives of this famous race. Miss de Roo manages to make them real, humane and dignified.

Barbara M. Booth

SOURCE: A review of *Boy and the Sea Beast,* in *School Librarian,* Vol. 20, No. 2, June, 1972, p. 181.

Once they are introduced to Anne de Roo and her stories from New Zealand, children of primary school age will look forward to seeing her new titles. This one will satisfy their desire for an adventure story featuring a boy with whom they can identify themselves as he strives to grow up to be ready for his father's return.

They share Boy's games and escapades and listen with him to his grandmother's traditional Maori stories. When one of the stories seems to come true and a great sea-beast enters the harbour, frightening all the villagers, it is Boy who makes friends with the dolphin, for such it is.

Anne de Roo writes well and her stories will hold the attention of all children who are rightly encouraged to read them.

CINNAMON AND NUTMEG (1972)

Judith Aldridge

SOURCE: A review of *Cinnamon and Nutmeg,* in *Children's Book Review,* Vol. II, No. 6, December, 1972, p. 185.

The main plot and characters of this book set in a New Zealand farming community are credible and lively. The reader can readily sympathise with Tessa's resentment towards the baby brother who seems a future threat to her position as father's right-hand man. The relationships within the family are well portrayed in all their joys and misunderstandings. Tessa's discovery and rearing of a goat-kid, and later a prize calf, make engrossing reading, especially for readers between nine and thirteen. The farming life of the community is effectively sketched in too, without sentimentality.

In unravelling the mystery that surrounds the parentage of the calf, however, Anne de Roo introduces less satisfactory characters and incidents, particularly an incredible lawyer and a very poor villain. The revived romance between the lawyer, Sanderson, and Tessa's aunt appears as an unnecessary tidy conclusion, and its superficiality accords ill with the realism of the main story in which emotions and maturing experience are depicted thoughtfully and vividly.

Kirkus Reviews

SOURCE: A review of *Cinnamon and Nutmeg,* in *Kirkus Reviews,* Vol. XLII, No. 2, January 15, 1974, p. 55.

When she's rejected by her father after the birth of a new son and teased by the new, citified teacher Jenny Wren, Tessa's credentials as a problem heroine are well established. But these agonies soon give way to the difficulties of caring for two hidden orphans, the wild kid Nutmeg and the calf Cinnamon, and later of tracking down the mysterious reasons why the purebred calf remains unclaimed. Tessa is isolated from everyone except her secret pets, but someone—like sophisticated cousin Jan on a week-long visit, or sympathetic Aunt Helen—always shows up conveniently to intercede with the grownups. The biggest mystery for readers may be in figuring out where all this is happening (New Zealand), and despite the inclusion of two individual animal babies, the story lacks seasoning.

Denise M. Wilms

SOURCE: A review of *Cinnamon and Nutmeg,* in *Booklist,* Vol. 70, No. 20, June 15, 1974, p. 1153.

Twelve-year-old Tessa Duggan, whose newborn brother seems to be getting everyone's attention, defiantly goes into the dense and forbidden New Zealand bushland near her father's farm. There, she stumbles upon two motherless babies: a wild goat and a beautiful calf. Tessa's farming know-how and the sensitive instincts of her young cousin Colin save the orphans' lives; but soon it is clear that the owner of the extraordinary calf must be found. Through an engaging chain of events in which figure Tessa's citified aunt, the aunt's childhood sweetheart, and some unethical neighbors, the mystery is solved. A rather lengthy story with the happiest of endings, believable as experienced through its ingenuous heroine.

Zena Sutherland

SOURCE: A review of *Cinnamon and Nutmeg,* in *Bulletin of the Center for Children's Books,* Vol. 28, No. 4, December, 1974, p. 60.

Set in New Zealand, a rural story in which a child's loving care of pet animals is the predominant note. Although the book suffers slightly from a plethora of characters, it has a sturdy plot and an appealing theme, good dialogue, and a brisk pace. Tessa is the younger daughter of a New Zealand farmer; her sister is rather prim and Tessa revels in being her father's helper. She's a bit jealous of a newly-born brother and turns all the more eagerly to a lost calf and a kid she finds; knowing her father won't let her keep Cinnamon and Nutmeg, she hides them in an abandoned house but worries about who the real owner of the calf is, since the animal is clearly of superior stock. Tessa's honesty in looking for a possible owner involves her in the uncovering of dishonesty on the part of a neighboring farmer and in the reunion between another neighbor and an aunt who had been engaged in their youth. Although there's a pat all-threads-tied note to the ending, it is satisfying and logical.

MICK'S COUNTRY COUSINS (1974)

Barbara Britton

SOURCE: "Under dogs," in *The Times Literary Supplement,* No. 3796, December 6, 1974, p. 1376.

Mick, a half-Maori New Zealander of thirteen in **Mick's Country Cousins** is a problem child hardened by neglect and inclined to see his brother Kevin's tearaway existence as vaguely glorious. But he has good basic qualities—a sense of kindness and loyalty—and, when Kevin is sent to a detention centre and he himself is removed to the care of relations on a farm, his problem is how to adjust his attitudes. His cousins are the subject of an earlier book, **Cinnamon and Nutmeg;** like that one, this book is full of details of strenuous farming life, while the people and animal relationships are so complex that they almost demand genealogical tables. All Mick's thoughts and actions have the sharpness of truth: he leads prize cattle astray, lets sheep into the wrong pasture, accidentally lames a horse, and his muddled reasoning for doing so is at once to revenge himself on his relations for being patronizing (some really are), to be kind to the animals in his ignorant layman's way and to nourish a fantasy-life previously fed on tough-guy films. But his intelligence and genuine feeling for the beauty and dependence of animals lead to self-discovery, even more than the mild treatment from his aunt and uncle who give him freedom, time and space to sort him self out. And his loyalty to his new relations is strengthened when brother Kevin escapes and attacks the aunt who has always been gentle with Mick. All the characters are realistically drawn—the "good" people have their weak, silly moments and the graceless Kevin has

affection somewhere inside him. This is an extremely good novel, full of comprehension of difficult feelings.

Margery Fisher

SOURCE: A review of *Mick's Country Cousin,* in *Growing Point,* Vol. 13, No. 7, January, 1975, pp. 2557-60.

The misery of Mick, the half-Maori hero of **Mick's Country Cousins,** is both believable and serious. Mick's father has long left the family, and Mick and his older brother are so far out of control that their mother does not oppose the decision of the court to send Kevin to an approved school, while Mick goes on an indefinite visit to his Aunt Helen at Riverlea Homestead. The boy's aggressive state of mind has made him far more conscious of his mixed race than anyone else is and he has made up his mind that these relatives of his only want him as an extra hand on the farm. Sullen and uncooperative, he listens willingly to the lies of Warren Howarth, whose father has been in trouble over the Riverlea herd (in **Cinnamon and Nutmeg**); but though he does enter into Warren's plans for revenge, his conscience is too active to let him go far and he realises in the end that he has been accepted simply as a member of the family. The conclusion of the story is somewhat bland but the state of mind of the boy is totally convincing and raises all kinds of questions about adult responsibility and the helplessness of the young, within an open-air, active and attractive story.

A. R. Williams

SOURCE: A review of *Mick's Country Cousins,* in *The Junior Bookshelf,* Vol. 39, No. 1, February, 1975, p. 60.

Miss de Roo seems another natural among several recent winners from New Zealand and Australia. Like **Cinnamon and Nutmeg, Mick's Country Cousins** "establishes in a relaxed way a whole way of life in a farming district". It goes further: it portrays in depth the psychology of a boy, half-Maori, bound for juvenile delinquency and with a perfectly enormous chip on his shoulder about "them", and a brother who is a real "villain". Sent to a farm run by country aunt and cousins, Mick causes all sorts of trouble in his efforts to "show" them, although he still enjoys enormously the physical aspects of farming. Miss de Roo makes it seem easy, but characterisation of this sort, the creation of an apparently "impossible" boy, without making the reader feel it is being "put on" is no cinch. The portrait of Mick, at such length, is quite something. You cannot help being convinced by Mick any more than you can resist the pastoral scene.

C. E. J. Smith

SOURCE: A review of *Mick's Country Cousins,* in *School Librarian,* Vol. 23, No. 1, March, 1975, p. 50.

Mick, a Maori half-caste semi-delinquent, is paroled into the custody of the Sanderson family of Riverlea Homestead, Taranaki, New Zealand, whom we met in ***Cinnamon and Nutmeg.*** Against a background of sheep rearing and shearing, horse riding and cattle showing his social values are adjusted until, in the final chapters, he can break away from his hero-worship of his fully delinquent brother, Kevin.

Family, farm and wider environment are drawn with affection and conviction, illuminating that interdependence of person and function that Mick needs to learn.

M. H. Miller

SOURCE: A review of *Mick's Country Cousins,* in *Children's Book Review,* Vol. V, No. 1, Spring, 1975, p. 22.

Mick is declared uncontrollable. He is half Maori, hasn't seen his father in years, and his big brother leads a gang. Mick's aunt and uncle, who run a sheep farm, offer to look after him. Gradually, Mick loses his resentment and racial self-consciousness amid the natural life of the animals and the countryside. He sees through big brother and discovers what is really important, what really satisfies him.

It is a good idea, but Anne de Roo has made the basic error of the moral novelist. She has a worthy message to deliver and has written her book with the purpose of delivering it. Little of the writing springs from a genuine involvement with character and situation. The story is actually quite interesting and has plenty of variety; the novelty of the New Zealand setting helps to maintain interest, but there is an awful lot of conversation and the author has a poor ear for speech.

Although the writing has little sparkle in it, the setting and action are realistic and the book could be a worthwhile read for boys or girls of eleven up.

SCRUB FIRE (1977)

M. Hobbs

SOURCE: A review of *Scrub Fire,* in *The Junior Bookshelf,* Vol. 42, No. 2, April, 1978, p. 101.

This original variation of the *Swiss Family Robinson* theme is set in the New Zealand bush. Fourteen-year-old Michelle's fears about the compulsory treat of a camping holiday given by a childless uncle and aunt to her and her two brothers are fully justified. A sudden fire raised by their uncle's ignorance of the bush separates them from the grown-ups, and Michelle's attempt as eldest to take charge sees them lost in the wilds, though the elder boy reveals unexpected knowledge of bush craft which at first helps them survive. They have also the problem of nursing the delicate youngest child who runs a high fever. Events are

highly dramatic, with several near-rescues and unexpected difficulties, and finally crises of despair which the rapidly weakening older pair have to overcome by mutual support and a fantasy story about their "kingdom". The book is not only about survival, but about growing up, learning humility and mutual respect, patience and thoughtfulness. Michelle's new awareness of beauty in nature is conveyed well to the reader too.

Judith Goldberger

SOURCE: A review of *Scrub Fire,* in *Booklist,* Vol. 77, No. 2, September 15, 1980, p. 113.

Three town-raised children, separated from their aunt and uncle by a sudden blaze that destroys their campsite and makes them run in panic from safety, are the focus of an engrossing story of struggle and survival in the New Zealand bush. The bush, at first nearly as foreign to the children as it will seem to American readers, gradually becomes a familiar, if inhospitable, entanglement. The author does seem to underestimate children's mentalities in occasional silly-sounding dialogue and too naive reactions. But the detail of the characters' 12-day ordeal, meshed skillfully with their growing courage and understanding of each other, makes this a difficult book to put down.

Patricia Manning

SOURCE: A review of *Scrub Fire,* in *School Library Journal,* Vol. 27, No. 3, November, 1980, p. 72.

A proffered camping trip with an aunt and uncle is irresistible to her younger brothers, but 13-year-old Michelle must be coerced into going. She is to look out for shy, 12-year-old Andrew and sickly, younger Jason. She watches in horror as inept Uncle Don sets the New Zealand scrub on fire in his first attempt at outdoor cookery; in the panicked minutes afterward, the children are separated from the adults and each other by racing sheets of flame. The children find one another again, but are hopelessly lost, and through the next 12 days they manage not only to survive but to make their way across a range of hills to safety and rescue on the other side. De Roo spends time on details; the children grow gaunt with hunger, experience pain, and reach their physical limits. New Zealand flora and fauna lend credence to her tale, but are not so obtrusive as to turn off American readers. The title recalls Southall's *Ash Road* and Gee's *Firestorm,* but the briefly described fire only serves to separate the children from adults; it is really a survival story.

Margery Fisher

SOURCE: A review of *Scrub Fire,* in *Growing Point,* Vol. 19, No. 4, November, 1980, pp. 3781-84.

Courage may take many forms. When three children are lost in the New Zealand bush after flying from the danger of a careless picnic fire, fourteen-year-old Michelle assumes the right of the oldest to lead the way to safety. Andrew, two years younger, is bookish and quiet, small Jason delicate; both boys willingly join in the game of crowning their sister as queen and acting as her devoted subjects. In fact it is Andrew who proves most capable of finding food and shelter: a secret love of the country has extended his town-bred knowledge of weather and direction. His is the courage of tenacity and good sense, Jason's of endurance, while as for Michelle, is she any less brave because she enjoys, at least for a time, the fantasy of ruling over a strange land? The initial event described in **Scrub Fire,** unexpected and alarming, brings for the children days of very real danger from starvation and exposure, since they have wandered far from any reasonable area of search. Though the author does not suggest that any one of them is scarred by the experience, there is certainly a subtle shift in their relations to one another as a result, and the background of hillside, bush and river acts as an accompaniment to their changing moods and their responses to the natural world they had approached in a spirit of light-hearted ignorance.

Kirkus Reviews

SOURCE: A review of *Scrub Fire,* in *Kirkus Reviews,* Vol. XLVIII, No. 21, November 1, 1980, p. 1394.

A two-week camping trip in the New Zealand bush goes awry when Aunt Celia and Uncle Don prove to be duffers, a campfire turns into a scrub fire, and 14-year-old Michelle, and her brothers Andrew (12) and Jason (9), find themselves lost in the wilderness. The book demonstrates the change in their relationships through their experiences, and otherwise is virtually plotless: what's at stake in fact is chiefly Michelle's character—uninterested in the trip and the outdoors at the start, ignorant and bossy, she does come to appreciate Andrew's quiet competence, the self-sufficient camaraderie the three briefly attain, and their need in some respects for their parents. In short, she becomes—without preachiness—a bigger and better person. To survive, Robinson-Crusoe-like, and maintain some sort of order, the three set up a make-believe royal court: Michelle is Queen, Andrew is Prime Minister, Jason is first Chief of Police and then, promoted; Crown Prince. And their make-believe is attractively and intelligently played out. But like Jason's illness, the most crucial development here, it's in no way involving; we're always on the outside looking in, following a situation in which we're waiting to see not whether they'll come out alive (which of course they do), not even why no one seems to be searching for them (which we learn about, in elaborate detail, at the close), but how Michelle will handle the next contretemps. And since she's not sufficiently rounded to be sympathetic *despite* her flaws, that's a very limited lure—leaving the relative unfamiliarity of the New Zealand wilderness setting as the book's main attraction.

Zena Sutherland

SOURCE: A review of *Scrub Fire,* in *Bulletin of the Center for Children's Books,* Vol. 34, No. 5, January, 1981, p. 91.

Michelle, fourteen, is the oldest of the three Seton children who are taken into the New Zealand wilderness by an aunt and uncle who are delighted by the idea of camping; Andrew and Jason, twelve and nine, are thrilled, but Michelle goes with sullen reluctance. A brush fire set off by inept Uncle Don sends Michelle running off on her own; later reunited with her brothers, she hopes that the two adults are safe. The Setons are not, they are quite lost. The rest (and major) part of the story has a Robinson Crusoe appeal, as the three children learn to cope with the wilderness; Michelle is resourceful, but it is Andrew's camping experiences and knowledge of survival techniques that carries them through the ordeal and back to safety. The setting, the danger, the self-reliance mustered by the children, are all appealing aspects of a story that is well enough written to sustain pace and interest despite the narrow scope.

TRAVELLER (1979)

Margery Fisher

SOURCE: A review of *Traveller,* in *Growing Point,* Vol. 17, No. 6, March, 1979, p. 3474.

Lost on the Canterbury Plains on his way to a cadet's job on a sheep station, in the scarcely explored New Zealand of the 1850s, young Tom Farrell is supported on a hazardous journey by the sheepdog which he rescues from starvation and which, finally, brings him to brief acquaintance with the notorious sheep-stealer and explorer James Mackenzie. Folk-history and landscape combine in a strongly evocative tale of a remarkable animal with a convincing influence on human affairs.

Marcus Crouch

SOURCE: A review of *Traveller,* in *The Junior Bookshelf,* Vol. 43, No. 4, August, 1979, pp. 216-17.

A story of pioneering days in New Zealand, Tom Farrell has sailed from England to take up work as a 'gentleman' cadet on a sheep farm in the hinterland of the new country. With him travels Harriet Wills who will marry Tom's boss, and Harriet's pet dog Bobby. But when they come into port sad news awaits them. Mr. Burford has been drowned, Harriet has no husband and Tom no master. Neither is prepared to abandon the adventure at this stage. Harriet scandalises society by setting up in business, and Tom makes the long and hazardous journey into the interior to find his farm. On the way, having lost his guide, he saves and is saved by a sheepdog to which he gives the name of Traveller. His destiny and that of the dog will be tied closely during his stay, as will that of George, the escaped convict in whose character the contradictory qualities of the new land are neatly illustrated.

It is a hard life. Folly or carelessness are quickly repaid by nature, if not by the tough men who hack a living out of a reluctant territory. Strangely, the predominant quality in this story is compassion, and the key to the action the relationship which grows up between Tom and the convict. Through this, Tom's compassion extends to another and more notorious criminal and in the last moments of the story he willingly parts with his most precious possession, the dog Traveller.

Miss de Roo is not the easiest of writers. There is plenty of action, but the course of it is not always clear, and the reader is called upon to contribute his unfailing attention. But the appeal of the land is so strong that one willingly gives more than the usual amount of surrender to the writer and her theme.

Gordon Parsons

SOURCE: A review of *Traveller,* in *School Librarian,* Vol. 28, No. 1, March, 1980, p. 54.

Stories about boys and dogs have a head start in the fictional stakes. Set in the New Zealand of the 1850s, Anne de Roo's novel relates the adventures of Tom Farrell, out from England, determined to prove himself in a hard pioneering world. Traveller is a mysterious sheepdog Tom befriends. This highly intelligent animal repays the debt in full as Tom establishes himself in the skills of sheep farming. The author knows her native country and its history. She peoples her world with credible characters and centres the novel on the strange and often tense relationship between Tom and a young, embittered escaped convict who takes much longer than Traveller to respond to human concern and respect.

BECAUSE OF ROSIE (1980)

Shirley Toulson

SOURCE: "In a Strange Land," in *The Times Educational Supplement,* No. 3340, June 20, 1980, p. 44.

Anne de Roo has a [gentle and human], though . . . unlikely, tale to tell. It works because one will believe almost anything about the past. *Because of Rosie* is set in New Zealand in the 1870s, and concerns four orphan children and their cow, on the run from their dreadful Uncle Prendergast. With all the luck and ingenuity of Robinson Crusoe, the children build themselves a house in the bush of the Manawatu plain; a task that would have been quite impossible without the help of the local Maoris, and a starving Norwegian carpenter whom they nurse back to life. They have half a dozen words of Maori, and no Norwegian, at all, so all communication is achieved through gesture and music; yet they are closer to these people than to their uncle, no matter how much they talk to him.

Elaine Moss

SOURCE: "Dreams of a Surrogate Mother," in *The Times Literary Supplement,* No. 4034, July 18, 1980, p. 806.

There are many ways in which the author can distance the agonies children endure; humour is Betsy Byars's chosen path, time is Anne de Roo's. *Because of Rosie* is set in New Zealand at the end of the nineteenth century and tells how a family of orphans survived in the wild after the death of their parents. Hypocritical Uncle Prendergast would have done his Christian duty by his sister's children—but his disrespect for their dead father leads them to run away.

The character studies of stubborn Will, the fiery eldest, sensible motherly Ellen, Sarah Jane who longs to be able to read, and mischievous Sam are perhaps rather more convincing than the story. For certainly the children, despite catastrophes, had more good fortune than seems probable—friendly Maori neighbours and an English scholarly recluse at hand—when, after a long journey they tried to establish a home for themselves and their only possession, Rosie the cow. This pioneer story is attractive in an undemanding way, but not in the same class as Laura Ingalls Wilder's American epic of the same genre.

JACKY NOBODY (1984)

Bill Boyle

SOURCE: A review of *Jacky Nobody,* in *Books for Keeps,* No. 36, January, 1986, p. 16.

Set in New Zealand's Bay of Islands in the 1840s, the story centres on the Maori rebellion of that period. Jacky, an orphan brought up by missionaries, witnesses Chief Heke's warriors dance their haka, or war dance, in defiance of the British. With his friend Noah, he chronicles, in this well told story, how Heke destroys the flagstaff flying the British flag, and the inevitable arrival of the Red Coats to suppress the uprising. Events do not quite work out with this predictability, and Jacky is last seen surveying the smoking settlement, shells falling from the offshore British gunboat. An incomplete conclusion which hints at a sequel to continue this interesting and unusual story.

Additional coverage of de Roo's life and career is contained in the following sources published by The Gale Group: *Contemporary Authors New Revision Series,* Vol. 51; and *Something about the Author,* Vols. 25, 84.

Jamaica Kincaid

1949 -

(Born Elaine Potter Richardson) West Indian born American author of adult and young adult novels and short stories.

Major works include *At the Bottom of the River* (1983), *Annie John* (1985), *Lucy* (1990), *The Autobiography of My Mother* (1995), *My Brother: A Memoir* (1997).

Major works about: *Jamaica Kincaid* (Diane Simmons, 1994).

INTRODUCTION

Jamaica Kincaid has been praised by critics for the terse yet lyrical quality of her writing. Sybil Steinberg of *Publishers Weekly* described Kincaid's work as "sensual, surprising, vibrant, and candid. Her characters are deep wells of emotions that we can draw from again and again." Although her work is fiction, Kincaid draws extensively on her own childhood, youth, and family history while exploring relationships between parents and children, discovering one's self as a person, the influence of history upon individuals, and the meaning of "home." Writing in *World Literature Written in English*, Patricia Ismond remarked, "[Kincaid] has lived most of her adult life away from [Antigua]; but it is to this childhood experience that she returns to find the possibilities of a creative adjustment to a world and time so different in its ethos." Diane Simmons wrote in her literary analysis, *Jamaica Kincaid, that* "Kincaid's work is about loss, an all but unbearable fall from a paradise partially remembered, partially dreamed, a state of wholeness, in which things are unchangeably themselves and division is unknown."

While Kincaid writes autobiographically, her work is fiction. Kincaid told Donna Perry in an interview for *Backtalk: Women Writers Speak Out*, "One of the things I found when I began to write was that writing exactly what happened had a limited amount of power for me. To say exactly what happened was less than what I knew happened." She uses her memories as a basis, but she enhances her memories with her art, giving her writing movement, atmosphere, and vitality. For example, in *Annie John*, Annie's illness corresponds with a rainstorm, enhancing the scene with a dramatic evocation of her situation.

Although Kincaid does not specifically target a young adult audience, her protagonists are all young girls facing their emergence into adulthood or young women fighting the ties of family and environment, themes that speak particularly to young adults. Her appeal is two-fold, in the poetry of her words and in the familiar situations her young protagonists face. Describing *The Autobiography of My Mother* as "Not innocent, not reverential . . .

[but] lyrical, brave, defiant," Hazel Rochmen of *Booklist* was also describing the body of Kincaid's work.

Biographical Information

Born Elaine Potter Richardson on the island of Antigua in the West Indies, Kincaid was an only child until the age of nine. She learned to read at age three and a half and continued to be precocious throughout her schooling. When the first of her three brothers was born and she was no longer the center of her mother's attention, she began to cause trouble in school, for which she was punished by having to memorize passages from Milton's *Paradise Lost*.

Her mother apprenticed her to a seamstress because, despite her intelligence, it was understood that she, with the double jeopardy of being both female and poor, would not be able to attend university. Kincaid claims that she would have preferred to stay in Antigua, attend university, and become a librarian or teacher, but in poor families only boys received such opportunities. As soon as she turned 17, she left Antigua and came to the

United States to work as an *au pair* feeling that she had no other choice if she was to have a future.

Over the years she held several jobs, completed her high school degree by attending a community college, and moved to New York City. In 1973 she changed her name to Jamaica Kincaid, partly because she wanted anonymity for her writing and partly just because she liked the way it sounded. An introduction to George W. Trow, writer of the "Talk of the Town" column for *The New Yorker*, was instrumental in establishing her as a writer. He often quoted her in his column, and eventually introduced her to *New Yorker* editor William Shawn who became Kincaid's mentor, one of the most important and beloved influences in her life. In 1976 she became a staff writer for *The New Yorker*, eventually writing "Talk of the Town" herself. In 1979 she married composer Alan Shawn, William's son, and moved to Vermont where he serves on the faculty of Bennington College. They have two children, Annie and Harold.

Major Works

Kincaid's first book, *At the Bottom of the River*, is a collection of short stories, but, according to Gregory MaGuire of *The Horn Book*, they "resonate one with another as poems in a cycle." Set in the Caribbean, the stories are based on Kincaid's memories and interior landscapes, less traditional narratives than they are portraits of character and personal perceptions. Although some critics found the book uneven and frustrating, all were enthusiastic about the beauty in Kincaid's use of language, and of her success in evoking and expressing complex emotions. A reviewer for *Publishers Weekly* wrote, "The voice—incantatory, lyric, rhapsodic—is closer to the condition of poetry and music than to fiction in any of its ordinary registers."

Greeted by a reviewer in *Publishers Weekly* as "fulfill[ing] the promise of [her] previous book," *Annie John* was Kincaid's first novel. Each of the chapters first appeared individually in *The New Yorker* and recount the biography of the narrator, Annie John, as a child on Antigua. The book follows Annie from age 10 through her early adolescence, and ends with her, a young woman of 17, leaving the island to attend nursing school in England. The story focuses on Annie John's turbulent relationships with her mother and with two schoolgirl friends. A critic for *Kirkus Reviews* commented that this novel is "poetic without a single intrusive image, emotional without a trace of hysteria, evocative without a bit of self-conscious exotica . . . truly capturing the agonizing give-and-take of parent/child love that goes delicately, yet irrevocably, awry."

Drawing once more from her own childhood experiences, Kincaid wrote *Lucy* as the diary of a 19-year-old West Indian girl. Lucy has come to New York, angry and unforgiving of her past, to work as a *au pair* for a satisfied yuppie couple with four daughters. She describes their family life, and the dissolution of the marriage, as a detached observer, while experimenting with and exploring her own sexuality and sense of herself as an individual. A true coming-of-age story, Lucy tries to "invent" herself while contemplating the failures of the people around her. Kincaid was once again hailed by critics for her vivid and poetic style. In her review in *Publishers Weekly*, Sybil Steinberg said, "Lucy's is a haunting voice, and Kincaid's originality has never been more evident."

In *The Autobiography of My Mother*, Kincaid's utilizes the life story of a Caribbean woman to explore the effects of slavery, colonialism, sexuality, and skin color on the identity of one woman and, by extension, a people. Hazel Rochman, in *Booklist*, described this book as "a novel of contained fury . . . The sentences twist and turn with surprise and bitterness. More argument than novel, it's the drama of the personal voice that makes it a spellbinding narrative."

Kincaid was inspired to write about her brother when she found out he was dying of AIDS. The resulting book, *My Brother: A Memoir*, has less to say about the brother she hardly knew than about her relationship with her mother and about the visits she made to Antigua to help nurse her brother. Critics praised the lyric beauty of her writing. In her review for *Booklist*, Donna Seaman said, "Honest, unapologetic, and pure, this is an eloquent and searching elegy for the dead and a prayer of thankfulness for the living."

Awards

Kincaid received the Morton Dauwen Zabel Award from the American Academy and Institute of Arts and Letters in 1983 for *At the Bottom of the River*. She also received the Lila Wallace-Reader's Digest Fund annual writer's award in 1992.

AUTHOR'S COMMENTARY

Donna Perry

SOURCE: "Jamaica Kincaid," in *Backtalk: Women Writers Speak Out*, Rutgers University Press, 1993, pp. 129-41.

Q: Could we start by talking a bit about **Annie John**, your first novel? I know that the situation is autobiographical. How do you translate what has happened in your life into fiction?

A: A lot of what happens in **Annie John** were things that actually happened to me. But one of the things that I seem to do in writing is [that] I often take a lot of disparate events, and, I don't know how, but sometimes they make a kind of psychological sense that I couldn't have foreseen or I can't see until I'm writing. I would say that everything in *Annie John* happened—every feeling in it happened—but not necessarily in the order they appear. But it very much expresses the life I had. There isn't anything in it that is a lie, I would say. For instance, the story of the long rain and the girl's illness. Both really happened—I had whooping cough when I was about eight or nine—but in the book the girl is older, about fifteen. These feelings and some of the things that happened—like the bathing of the pictures—happened when I was about nine.

Q: Why did you choose to write fiction instead of autobiography?

A: Because autobiography is the truth and fiction is, well, fiction. In an autobiography, for instance, I could not have had the long rain coincide with the girl's illness. One of the things I found when I began to write was that writing exactly what happened had a limited amount of power for me. To say exactly what happened was less than what I knew happened. Mr. [William] Shawn used to say I was a terrible reporter. I like the idea that when something happens it has a more powerful meaning than the moment in which it actually happens. When I started to write these autobiographical things I was told, "Oh, why don't you write a sort of autobiographical reminiscence about life?" but I wanted something more than that. I could see that if you put it in a sort of straightforward memoir that it would have a sort of bitterness that I didn't want—that wasn't the point. The point wasn't the truth and yet the point *was* the truth. And I don't know how to explain that.

Q: So you were after something more universal?

A: More universal. Yes. But at the time I did not know that, and now I make it a point not to know that.

Q: Would you ever write a story about something that hasn't happened to you?

A: I don't know how to do that, no. I read sometimes that a writer says, "Oh, I overheard a snippet of conversation and I went from there." I can't do that. If I overhear something I have to totally internalize it. I can only find the thing inside me. If it's not there, then I'm not able to figure things out. It's not that I couldn't write about something that didn't happen to me, but I would have to find the emotion somewhere inside myself.

Q: I gave the book to a young woman from Jamaica who enjoyed it, but she didn't like the ending because Annie leaves home. Have you heard that reaction before?

A: That's happened a lot among West Indian girls who have read the book. Many teachers have told me that. One teacher in Queens [New York] said that the class split over it: The West Indian girls said it didn't have a happy ending, the other students—not West Indian—disagreed. I don't know if it is, but I have noticed that black

people don't like unhappy endings. Perhaps we have too many. This reality of life is perhaps hard for us to face. Another reality is that life is ambiguous; it has many meanings and many endings. Most endings in life, I have noticed, are not happy. Death, of course, is the most common one.

I wonder why it is that Africans like a one-party state. Even when they are not Communists, they insist on one party. They can't stand the idea of many opinions, where the one that is most popularly expressed is the one that will go, but that the other differences are accommodated also. It's as if we must all think alike or nothing, and we must all think happily. And this idea that it must be happy and it must be the same means that there is deception all the time. So, yes, the reality of the ending of *Annie John* is very disturbing.

Q: I see the central character in *Annie John* as an outsider in some ways. Did you think of yourself as an outsider then?

A: I didn't think of myself as an outsider because of my race because, for one thing, where I grew up I was the same race as almost everyone else. And I did not feel I was an outsider because of my sex. Many people were the same sex as me also. But still, I did feel that I was an outsider.

It is true that I noticed things that no one else seemed to notice. And I think only people who are outsiders do this. I must have felt very different from everybody. When I tell people there now how I felt then, they look at me with pity. For instance, I have a friend now who is a little bit older than I am, who grew up in the same area I did. Our families were not acquainted—her parents are practically aristocrats, my parents are peasants. But she and I have now become friends, and I can tell her all of these things that I noticed about her. But at the time I was little and observing her I wasn't observing her for any reason I knew of. I mean, some of the people I knew were, like her, from a different class—they had land and money—and most of the people I knew were like me, just from working people.

So why did I notice her? I remember an incredible number of things about her, and it was just from seeing her come and go. We weren't friends. We never spoke to each other. She has two sisters and a brother and I can even tell her what they were like. I just knew the kind of people they were then.

Q: Would you say that you grew up with a consciousness of class difference?

A: No. Not really. I noticed things that came under that heading, but I noticed other things also. I just noticed things, a lot of things. I had all this information about everybody. I can just imagine that if it had not worked out this way I would have been someone who would have caused enormous mischief, because I knew so much about everyone that I would either have spread rumors or engineered catastrophes, including the catastrophe of my own life, I'm sure.

Q: Getting back to something you said earlier about drawing from experiences in your own life, did the "Columbus in Chains" episode really happen to you—the incident in *Annie John* when you write under the picture of an enslaved Columbus the words your mother spoke about her father: "The Great Man Can No Longer Just Get Up and Go"?

A: Yes, but my mother had really said, "The great man can't shit." I had written that and it wouldn't go in *The New Yorker,* so I changed it. Then I left it that way for the book because I realized that it had a more profound meaning, and now I can't exactly remember why. But I thought about it for a long time—I had a long conversation with my editor at the time because "shit" was not a word that appeared in *The New Yorker* then—appropriately, I have now come to feel.

The two incidents [hearing her mother and writing the caption] happened separately in real life.

Q: That section seems to be the part of *Annie John* that most clearly reveals a political consciousness. Do you agree?

A: I think that's the first place I began to know how to express it. I think in the things I just wrote [in 1988 and 1989], it becomes clearer, and it becomes clearer, also, to me, how to express it. But the typical reality of someone like myself in a place like Antigua is that the political situation became so normal that we no longer noticed it. The better people were English, and that was life. I can't say that I came from a culture that felt alienated from England or Europe. We were beyond alienation.

It was amazing that I could notice the politics the way I did, because most of those who took notice did so in some sort of world context, like the man who became prime minister. But I took notice of it in a personal way, and I didn't place it within the context of political action. I almost made a style out of it.

Q: Speaking of political consciousness, why did you write *A Small Place*? That's a very political book.

A: I really wrote it as a piece for *The New Yorker.* Mr. Shawn, the former editor, loved it and bought it; then Bob Gottlieb, the present editor, hated it [since the interview Tina Brown has become editor]. He said it was very angry. Not badly written. Angry. I now consider anger a badge of honor. It had a sort of traumatic history because it was so intimate. It was written for the readers of *The New Yorker,* whom I had come to think of as friends in some peculiar way. And then it was very much loathed by the new people.

I don't know how it is for most people—other writers—but I feel that I am sort of lucky or privileged to get to do this thing called writing, in which basically all I am doing is discovering my own mind. I'm very grateful that I am able to make a living at it, but that's all it is, discovering my own mind. I mean, I didn't know that I thought those things. I didn't go around saying them to myself. But then, somehow, once I had the opportunity to think them, I just did. I went to Antigua, and I began to see things again about it, and they turned into this article. So when *The New Yorker* didn't buy it, Mr. Shawn thought that it should be presented as a book, all by itself. He was right of course, as usual.

Q: I felt when I read *A Small Place* as though it was a kind of turning point in your writing, a growth in political awareness in some way, and that your works to follow would be different. Is that so?

A: Yes. I thought it was a turning point in me. I wrote with a kind of recklessness in that book. I didn't know what I would say ahead of time. Once I wrote it I felt very radicalized by it. I would have just thought of myself as a liberal person until I wrote it, and now I feel that liberal is as right as I can go.

Q: There's a lot of anger in it.

A: Yes, that's right, and I've really come to love anger. And I liked it even more when a lot of reviews said it's so angry. The *New York Times* said that the book didn't have the "charm" of *Annie John.* Really, when people say you're charming you are in deep trouble. I realized in writing that book that the first step in claiming yourself is anger. You get mad. And you can't do anything before you get angry. And I recommend getting very angry to everyone, anyone.

As I wrote it I realized that I had all this feeling and that it was anger. I wanted it to be crude and impolite—and all the other things that civilized people are not supposed to be. I no longer wanted to be a civilized person. Really, for me, writing is like going to a psychiatrist. I just discover things about myself.

I can see that *At the Bottom of the River* was, for instance, a very unangry, decent, civilized book, and it represents sort of this successful attempt by English people to make their version of a human being or their version of a person out of me. It amazes me now that I did that then. I would never write like that again, I don't think. I might go back to it, but I'm not very interested in that sort of expression anymore. Now, for instance, I've become very interested in writing about sex, or smells. I'm interested in being not a decent person.

Q: You said earlier that if you hadn't become a writer you might have caused a lot of mischief because of what you knew. Did *A Small Place* cause mischief? Were there repercussions in Antigua?

A: Not really. I think people thought it would and they talked about it. There's a section of the book that very much describes the reaction of Antiguans to the book. It was sort of a great event, and now it's just part of what happened that someone wrote this book and said these things that we—they—all know happened. There wasn't anything in it anyone learned, except that someone would make an attempt to tell the world about them. They have always seen themselves—we see ourselves—as little, insignificant people that great things happen to: slavery, America, the British, whatever. They never really thought that any of us could just stand up and say to the world the things that we know about ourselves.

So the world looking at them has become part of their everyday life. And I think the government was a little afraid that it would hurt them at first, so they sort of banned it, but then they were reelected by an overwhelming majority.

One thing Antiguans said about *A Small Place* is, "It's true, but did she have to say it?" No one says that it's a lie; the disagreement is, did I have to say it.

Q: In the book you mention that the library was closed. Has it been reopened?

A: No. But you know, yesterday I was reading an article about a newspaperman in Zambia who writes satirical articles about his government and he said that there isn't one bookstore in Zambia. There isn't a library or anything. So there is this incredible, almost conspiratorial effort on the part of the people who rule in the black Third World to keep any institution of learning out of their country. Mobutu, apparently, simply closed the universities when the students protested against him.

Q: Do you see this as similar to what happened in China [during the Tiananmen Square demonstrations]?

A: To some extent, but the Chinese want their students to be educated—in their own way. It's quite a big difference; the Chinese don't mean to do away with education. The Africans and the West Indians don't make that fine a distinction. They just don't want any opposition. The fact is that a lot of the things that are considered essential to having a nation are not in existence in black Africa or in the West Indies. We had better health and education under colonialism.

Q: The saddest part of *A Small Place* is that after colonialism many things in Antigua seem worse than they were under the British.

A: It's absolutely true; it's not an exaggeration. In the hospital in Antigua—the children's ward—most of the children are there because they suffer from malnutrition. And Antigua has the highest standard of living in the eastern Caribbean. I have no idea, by the way, what that means, but that's what they say. You do see people with a lot of things. Everyone has a car, everyone has a television. They have cable television, and they get something like thirty channels from North America. It

has all of what looks like prosperity. My mother, who lives in a tiny house, has a refrigerator and a better television set than we do. It's really quite remarkable.

Q: Could you talk about **"Ovando,"** a short story of yours that appeared in *Conjunctions* [vol. 14 (1989)]? As an allegorical portrait of the horrors of colonialism, that work seems to continue this concern with domination.

A: I can only say that story is something that I stopped because I realized I didn't know enough to go on. As I go around the world I understand it better and better. I think in some way I am very interested in domination. I suppose we all are. I feel that, in particular, my own history is so much about dominion; in fact we were called "the dominion," and all the colonies were "the dominions." So when I started to write **"Ovando"** I thought I was going to write a grand work about the question of dominion.

The other insight I have into history is that it's a bit like musical chairs. When the music stops some people are standing up and some people are sitting down, but at any moment you don't know if it will be you among the stand-ups or the sit-downs. I feel as though, if I am among the people sitting down, I always will identify with the people who are standing up—that my knowledge of my history tells me that I have to always make room on the chair for the people standing up. In writing **"Ovando,"** I was trying to understand how, for some people who found themselves sitting down, it would become important to try to remove the apparatus for the game to continue—so that they would never again be standing up.

Q: Do you see this as the situation of the colonizing countries like Europe and the United States?

A: Yes. On the other hand, we know that every relief also bears its own prison. If you remove the apparatus for the game to go on, then permanently sitting down is its own prison.

I realized that in order for me to finish **"Ovando,"** I would have to understand more about the reality of someone like Christopher Columbus than I know now. His journals are in Seville and you can go and read them. I really need to know more about these explorers themselves. I need to be older.

All these people are very admirable when you think of what they did—these "great men." People thought the world was flat. A very poetic idea.

In some ways, these explorations to the New World were very touching. I realize that one of the things that is bound up in this horrible thing that happened (slavery—the domination) is the great curiosity in every human being. I mean making maps, building a boat—there's something really extraordinary about it, very moving, when you think of these people just going somewhere without knowing what really they would find. It's not like going to the moon at all, which has this incredible support. It had an individual element that was admirable or inspiring.

But, of course, by the time they made their discoveries, everything admirable about them becomes lost.

Q: They became the conquerors?

A: Yes.

Q: At the end of **"Ovando"** you say that "a true and just sentence would be imbued with love for Ovando." That suggests that you think it would take a great-hearted person to understand Ovando.

A: It's a funny thing. I grew to understand that, too.

Q: **"Ovando"** seems very medieval. I kept thinking of Barbara Tuchman's *A Distant Mirror* [1978] and the cult of the Black Death. Were you suggesting parallels with the medieval period?

A: Yes. When you read the history of what the Europeans left behind, it is a record of disease and incredible suffering, poverty.

When I hear people talking about the "Great Western Tradition," I think, wait a minute, what are they talking about here? All I see is a tradition of incredible cruelty and suffering and injustice—not to mention murder, complete erasing of whole groups of people. Everybody is always looking for a way out. And what was their way out? The New World. Start fresh. But of course you can't. There's no such thing as a fresh start.

Q: Can you talk a little about your writing process? How do you write?

A: I read about writers who have routines. They write at certain times of the day. I can't do that. I am always writing—but in my head. I just finished writing a book [*Lucy*] about a month ago. I started it when Harold was three months and then I finished it when he was a year and six months. It will be published in the fall. It will be some stories that have appeared in *The New Yorker*. I don't know how I did it. I wrote in between things. I have to figure out how things will go—what we will have for dinner, how the children's lives will be, Allen's life, my life. I sort of expect that I'll figure it out.

I think I have to have a great deal of domestic activity to write. I am essentially a person very interested in domestic life and very interested in things that we think of, either in a good way or a bad way, as women's things. I know a woman and she comes to see me in the morning and we sit at the kitchen table. We just sit and talk. That's not how I write, but in a way it is. I sit with this woman and we sort of arrange the world. We talk about Bush. We talk about the Russians. We talk about Nicaragua. We talk about the homeless. We sort of settle the day—the world.

Then, about 11:00, I say, "Well, goodbye," and I go off to my office—a room at home. And I do whatever I do.

I may do absolutely nothing but read the newspaper and then for fifteen minutes I write a paragraph or maybe a sentence or a page. I can't tell how it may go. But that's how I write. I sort of think about it as part of my domestic life. In fact, I think I reduce everything to a domestic situation. I wouldn't be very interested in putting the world in the way the world is actually arranged. If I actually ran the world, I'd do it from the kitchen. It's not anything deliberate or a statement or anything, that's just how I understand things. It's arranged along informal lines. I don't like formality. I realize, for instance, that I would never live in a house with a dining room. I couldn't stand a room in which you only ate.

When I was little I had this great mind for history. And I never really understood it until I realized that the reason I liked history is because I also reduce the past to domestic activity. History was what people did. It was organized along the lines of who said what and who did what, not really unlike how the society in which I grew up was organized. The idea that things are impersonal occurrences is very alien to me. I personalize everything.

Q: That personalizing is what enabled you to make the connection between Columbus and your grandfather.

A: That's right. You see, I reduce everything to a domestic connection. It's all the great men who have been humbled. Finally.

Q: What difference have your children made in your life? You described the domestic arrangements that make writing possible—your friend who comes over to help out—but I get the sense that motherhood takes a lot of time.

A: Absolutely. I have two children: Annie, who is named after my mother and Allen's grandmother, and Harold, who is named after Allen's father's brother. Annie is five and Harold is a year and a half.

I don't mean to be one of those people who says everything happens for the best, because when you hear someone say that you are listening to a defeated person. But I have these two children, and yet I wrote one book in a year and three months. There was a long period after I had Annie that I didn't write at all. I don't know if I didn't have time to write or if I was gathering. You know there is a fallow period that one gets frightened of. You think, "Maybe I'll never write again." I never felt that way. As long as I can have some way of earning a living or doing something, I don't worry too much about it. I think, "Well, I haven't quite figured out how to say what I want to say."

That was true after I wrote **Annie John.** I wanted to say something but I didn't know what, and it turned out to be **A Small Place.** And then I planned to write a book after that, but I got pregnant and couldn't write. Then I had Harold. And then, just to earn some money, I started to write the first story of this new book. I didn't mean to write the whole book at all. And then within a year and three months I finished it.

Q: Is it harder to write now that you have children?

A: It's hard to write now, but it was hard to write before. I feel incredibly free—I feel I could have more children, I feel that I can write. I don't feel writing is cut off for me because I don't feel having experience is cut off from me. I think somehow if I didn't have the children I might feel that way. But, you see, being so interested in domestic activity, having children can only add to my feeling of domestic life. I am beginning to see their life as going out into the world, whatever it is. But I can only see that from the kitchen table.

Q: When do you let other people read your work? Does your husband read what you have written when you think it is ready?

A: He reads it daily [she laughs]. Probably I couldn't be a writer without Allen. When I'm writing, every night before he goes to sleep, he reads. It's not quite a joint project, but I really depend on him as a reader.

The way I wrote **Annie John** was that I would get up every day and I would say to him, "Well now, today I'm going to do . . . " and I would say pages and pages of how I would write. And he would say, "Oh, that sounds good," or, "Well, but what happens when this . . . ?" And I would say, "Oh, but this. . . . " Then, just as I told him, I would go into my room and write, and later I would show him what I had written.

He's not a writer, but he is very interested in writing and very interested in me, I must say. He's great fun to be married to. It's wonderful to have this great companion, in every way.

The terrible thing about traveling is that he doesn't like to travel, and so I travel alone. It is a great loss because I have all these experiences, and usually when we have these experiences we just chatter, chatter, chatter all the time. And when I'm alone there's no one to talk to. So then we just have these huge phone bills.

Q: These stories [in **Lucy**] seem harder edged than **Annie John.**

A: I think they are more frank. I think that after writing **A Small Place** and seeing the reaction to it, I realized that people couldn't stand a certain sort of frankness. But I knew that what I wanted to be, more and more as a writer, was frank about what the lives I wrote about were really like, as frank as I could express or as I could know. I didn't know if that would be possible, but that was what I wanted.

In the context of that, I'm still very conscious of art, of making something, and I'm always very interested in the

right word. I want to use the word that would best express something. But yet I wanted to be very frank and to be unlikable within the story. To be even unpopular. In the last two stories I wanted to risk more.

As I go on writing, I feel less and less interested in the approval of the First World, and I never had the approval of the world I came from, so now I don't know where I am. I've exiled myself yet again. In fact, the world that comforted me and made me a writer is now the world where I don't care about their approval: *The New Yorker.* I used to care about *The New Yorker.* I used to feel I had a personal stake in it. Now it's just another thing owned by someone with a billion dollars. Like everything else in the world.

Q: Yet they are still publishing your stories, aren't they?

A: Yes. I'm shocked. They bought all of them.

Q: This couple whom you describe in your last stories— Lewis and Mariah—seem like readers of *The New Yorker,* actually: white, upper middle class, politically left of center, city dwellers. But they also seem somewhat vapid to me. Is this your idea?

A: Yes. Well, you have to read the other two to come because the couple divorce. I really was an au pair, and I was writing about my own experience. The other people are incidental; they are not anyone I actually knew. I went out of my way to make the other characters not like people I actually knew.

Q: On a recent trip to the New York Botanical Garden [in the Bronx] I found a place called Daffodil Hill, a hill covered with daffodils that reminded me of the garden where the wife takes the narrator in the story **"Mariah"** [from **Lucy**]. Was that the place you had in mind?

A: No. I had never been to a specific garden; I just imagined it. This story of the daffodils did not really happen. But it is amazing to me that there is such a place and so it could have happened.

Q: Were you really forced to memorize Wordsworth's "I Wandered Lonely as a Cloud," the poem where he praises the daffodils?

A: Every colonial child has to do that. It's a two-edged thing because I wouldn't have known how to write and how to think if I hadn't read those things. I wouldn't have known my idea of justice if I hadn't read *Paradise Lost,* if I hadn't been given parts of *Paradise Lost* to memorize. It was given to me because I was supposed to be Satan. The last chapter of the book I have written has a lot of things about that. The book is called **Lucy,** short for Lucifer.

Q: So in this work, as in **Annie John,** there is some of what really happened and some manipulation of what really happened.

A: Like **Annie John,** everything happened but not necessarily in this way. I want the truth. I begin to understand this thing about the mind, and I'm sure it's not just true of me. I'm always shocked to see that things are more neatly connected than we think. I really manipulate the facts, but within the manipulation there is no lie. I believe I can safely say that—that in everything I say there is the truth.

I arrange things in a way that I can understand them, but it isn't completely fiction; it is, in fact, not in my imagination. I have no imagination when it comes to that. It's as if you were given a broken plate and you rearranged it into a pitcher. The rearrangement wouldn't deny the fact that the plate and the pitcher are made of the same stuff. I use the same material, but I make it into a different thing, something new.

In these stories, the place and the girl herself aren't named. It is New York, but it could be anywhere. I didn't want to specify because I didn't want any preconceptions about the place. She doesn't even name the island she comes from.

Q: Your stories seem seamless—both these new ones and the parts of **Annie John.** How do you account for the particular shape they take?

A: I just write, and things come to a crest, and that's how it is. My mind works in this way—its sort of like a puzzle. I know where the pieces are, but I don't want to fit them for myself or for the reader. I just write.

Q: It sounds like **Lucy** has an unhappy ending, too.

A: Yes. The last two stories are very painful, even for Allen.

Q: What contemporary fiction writers do you read?

A: Do you know any of the French West Indian writers? They are amazing. There is a collection of Caribbean women's writing, *Her True-True Name,* that is amazing [ed. Pamela Mordecai and Betty Wilson, 1989]. The French writers are much more frank, much more exciting. You can see the French influence in *Wide Sargasso Sea* [by Jean Rhys 1966] and *The Orchid House* [by Phyllis Shand Allfrey 1953]. *The Orchid House* is very good. I can understand if someone would think it was deeply flawed if they don't know the story, but I think it's very good.

If you don't know something intimately, you might not know if it is good. I'm supposed to write an introduction to a work by Zora Neale Hurston, but I don't know what to say. I think that I do not appreciate her as some people [do] because I have not had a certain kind of experience. The language makes assumptions about things that I just don't understand.

These French writers are also unbelievably bold about sex, and of course, sex is everything. The world starts at the crotch, essentially. And it's not that people are a slave to the crotch, but they are a bit. I once read an article about AIDS in Africa and the writer said that the reason

AIDS is spreading so fast there is that Africans are sex-positive. I thought this was a wonderful phrase. For example, prostitution was not known in Africa until Europeans came. An African woman would have many lovers, but there was no money exchanged. A man would bring a gift, but it wasn't in exchange for the sex. It was to show affection. And I think there's something like that where I come from, and so almost all the most basic arrangements are made on that basis: no exchange, just a gift.

I'm just about to get to this in my own fiction, this commodification of relationships. The commodifying of things is what I wanted to discuss in **"Ovando."**

Q: Before we end, I want to ask you about the role *The New Yorker* has played in your development as a writer. How important was it?

A: I don't think I would have become a writer if it wasn't for *The New Yorker*—the old *New Yorker,* that is. Not the thing that still calls itself *The New Yorker.* It was writing for them—for Mr. Shawn, really—that helped me learn how to write. I'm very grateful to him for that.

Allan Vorda

SOURCE: "I Come from a Place That's Very Unreal: An Interview with Jamaica Kincaid," in *Face to Face: Interviews with Contemporary Novelists,* edited by Allan Vorda, Rice University Press, 1993, pp. 80-104.

AV: Caribbean writer Derek Walcott, while writing about your work, stated that, "Genius has many surprises and one of them is geography." In what ways has geography both helped and hindered you as a writer?

JK: I can't say it has hindered me at all, and, if it has, I don't know of it. It seems to me that it has been more of a help since I can find nothing negative to say about the fact that I come from the place I'm from. I very much like coming from there. It would be false for me to take pride in it because it's an accident, really. It just seems to be sort of happenstance that I was born in this place and happenstance that I was born with black skin and all the other things I was born with. All that aside, the fact that I was born in this place, my geography has been, I think, a positive thing for me. I experience it as just fine. I am not particularly glad of it, as I say. The reality of my life is that I was born in this place. I find it only a help.

I can't say what it would have been like if I had been born a white Englishwoman. Actually, I think I *can* say. It seems as if it would have been quite wonderful because whenever I was growing up and looked at white Englishwomen, they seemed to have a life denied me. This isn't to say if I had been born a white Englishwoman I wouldn't have been perfectly miserable. They didn't seem perfectly miserable; they seemed rather privileged and had all the things I couldn't have. I think I just made the best of what I had. What I had was my mother, my father, my mother's family, my father's family, all of that complication, my history, which, as far as I know, began on boats. I'm part African, part Carib Indian, and part—which is a very small part by now—Scot. All of them came to Antigua by boats. This is how my history begins.

AV: The critic and black studies scholar Henry Louis "Skip" Gates, Jr., has stated about your work that "she never feels the necessity of claiming the existence of a black world or a female sensibility. She assumes them both. I think it's a distinct departure that she's making, and I think that more and more black American writers will assume their world the way that she does. So that we can get beyond the large theme of racism and get to the deeper themes of how black people love and cry and live and die. Which, after all, is what art is all about."

I agree with Gates' comment, but is this a conscious attempt by you not to overtly claim you are a black, female writer? Also, do you mind that you are still stereotyped as a black, female, Caribbean writer?

JK: No, I thought what Skip said was very revealing for me because I did not know that I had been doing that. I come from a place where most of the people are black. Every important person in my life was a black person, or a person who was mostly black, or very deeply related to what we call a black person. So I just assume that is the norm and that it is the other people who would need describing. I assume most of the people who are important to me, and not last among them is my own self, are female. When I write about these people it would never occur to me to describe their race or their sex except as an aesthetic. I wouldn't say, "She has two eyes." I assume everyone has two eyes, and the only reason I would mention the eyes is if it were a superficial decision. It's not conscious at all that I leave out a people's race. Race is important, but the thing I know deeply is that when you say someone is white or black—in my case I never say anyone is black because I assume that to be the norm—because everybody has an idea of what that means. I never say people are white. I describe them. When you get to know people, you don't describe someone as "my wife that white woman." Or that man we just met [Kincaid is referring to a strange fellow who interrupted the taping of the interview for half an hour to pontificate his unusual views of the world], would you say, "He is a white man?" No, because what you would say is that he's a very intrusive person and that he was somewhat boorish, except we were sort of interested in his lunacy. So you look at him and immediately identify him as someone who is intrusive, and then from there you pick up on certain characteristics, but the least thing about him is that he's white.

To answer the second part of your question about being stereotyped, I think for the people who want to do it that it must be a very convenient way, but it really belittles the effort being made. When I sit at my typewriter I'm not a woman, I'm not from the Caribbean, I'm not black. I'm just this sort of unhappy person struggling to make

something, struggling to be free. Yet the freedom isn't a political one or a public one: it's a personal one. It's a struggle I realize that will go on until the day that I die.

I'm living rather an ideal life. I think we all want to live a long life in which we attempt to be free. It's a paradox because the freedom only comes when you can no longer think, which is in death. You don't want to die, but you want to be free, and that's the outcome of the freedom. Perhaps I should say this is only a very personal view. In the meantime you struggle to make sense of the external from the things that have made you what you are and the things that you have been told are you: my history of colonialism, my history of slavery, and imagining if that hadn't happened what I would have been. Perhaps I would have been an unhappy woman in pre-European Africa. Who knows what I would have become? That's what I struggle to understand about myself.

It's not connected to the shell you see sitting at the typewriter. It's connected to the inner thing. Whatever I may say about being black, Caribbean, and female when I'm sitting down at the typewriter, I am not that. So I think it's sort of limited and stupid to call anyone by these names. The truth is, would we say John Keats is a white man who was a poet from nineteenth-century England? No, we just say he is John Keats. You think of these people in terms of their lives, and so that's what I'm saying. When you think of me, think of my life. My life is not a quota or an action to affirm an idea of equality. My life is my life. If it helps people to get to something I've written I'm glad, but, on the whole, I wish these terms would go away. Is my work any good? That is what I wish to know. . . .

AV: There is a litany of items in **"Girl"** (from *At the Bottom of the River*) from a mother to her daughter about what to do and what *not* to do when it comes to being a nice young lady. Is this the way it was for you and other girls in Antigua?

JK: In a word, yes.

AV: Was that good or bad?

JK: I don't think it's the way I would tell my daughter, but as a mother I would tell her what I think would be best for her to be like. This mother in **"Girl"** was really just giving the girl an idea about the things she would need to be a self-possessed woman in the world.

AV: But you didn't take your mother's advice?

JK: No, because I had other ideas on how to be a self-possessed woman in the world. I didn't know that at the time. I only remember these things. What the mother in the story sees as aids to living in the world, the girl might see them as extraordinary oppression, which is one of the things I came to see.

AV: Almost like she's Mother England.

JK: I was just going to say that. I've come to see that I've worked through the relationship of the mother and the girl to a relationship between Europe and the place that I'm from, which is to say a relationship between the powerful and the powerless. The girl is powerless, and the mother is powerful. The mother shows her how to be in the world, but at the back of her mind, she thinks she never will get it. She's deeply skeptical that this child could ever grow up to be a self-possessed woman and, in the end, she reveals her skepticism; yet even within the skepticism are, of course, dismissal and scorn. So it's not unlike the relationship between the conquerer and the victim.

AV: What is the connection in the story **"In the Night"** between the jablesse and her night-soil father with the woman she wants to marry? Is the woman a jablesse?

JK: No. That story is really a portrait of night in Antigua. I don't remember it as being a story about a particular person. It's a portrait of a character within twenty-four hours.

AV: Why does the narrator skip from one sex to another in such stories as **"In the Night"** ("Now I am a girl, but one day I will marry a woman."), **"At Last"** ("Sometimes I appeared as a man."), and **"Wingless"** ("I myself have humped girls under my mother's house.")?

JK: In a way I can't answer that because I wouldn't want to explain it very much. I think when I was writing those stories I really wanted to disregard certain boundaries, certain conventions. These were stories written in my youth. (I think of the time before I had children as my youth.) These are stories in which I had endless amounts of time to consider all sorts of things and endless amounts of silence and space and distance. I could play with forms and identities and do things then that I can't do now because I don't have the time to plumb that kind of depth. They were attempts to discard conventions, my own conventions, and conventions that exist within writing. I still try to forget everything that I've read and just write. That was what that was about, and it really doesn't bear close interpretation from me. The reader would have to do that.

AV: You depict the most ordinary events. In the book *At the Bottom of the River,* are you trying to show that the most ordinary events can become extraordinary?

JK: Oh, yes! I think there is no such thing as an ordinary event. I believe everything is of the deepest significance. If you could isolate an event, it would lead to profound things. For example, if you would trace the ancestry of everybody who has crossed this room you wouldn't be able to do anything else.

AV: A number of your stories such as **"What I Have Been Doing Lately,"** **"Blackness,"** **"My Mother,"** and *Annie John* (where the girl is sick and hallucinates over some pictures she is trying to clean) incorporate a type of magical realism. Are these phantasmagoric scenes derived from Latin American writers such as Borges or García Márquez, or even possibly Lewis Carroll?

JK: If it went back to anyone, it would be Lewis Carroll. Borges is the kind of writer when I read I'm just absolutely in heaven. I wouldn't say the same thing is true of García Márquez. I like reading him, but I don't feel it's the most wonderful thing like when I read Borges. The truth is, I come from a place that's very unreal. It's the reason for its political malaise, because it will not just look at the thing in front of it and act on it. The place I come from goes off into fantasy all the time so that every event is continually a spectacle and something you mull over, but not with any intention of changing it. It is just an entertainment. It's just some terrific thing you told yourself that happened today. I wouldn't say that I was influenced by these other writers you mentioned, because, for me, it's only an accident. It's really the place I grew up in. I'm not really a very imaginative writer, but the reality of my background is fantastic.

AV: You were born in 1949 as Elaine Potter Richardson, but in 1973 you adopted the pseudonym "Jamaica Kincaid." Was this name bestowed on you by George Trow of the *New Yorker,* and how was it chosen? You also stated that changing your name was a way of disguising yourself so you wouldn't have to be "the same person who had all these weights."

JK: No, by the time I met George Trow I had already changed my name. I wasn't that young. It's really more of the second question. I wanted to write. No one I knew had ever written. I thought serious writing was something people no longer did. By the time I discovered it was still being done, I didn't know how I could do it as the person who left home. I thought, and I think I would have been correct, I would have been judged pretentious. I would have been judged as someone stepping out of the things that had been established for me. I would have been laughed at. I didn't want anyone who knew me to know I was writing. I thought quite possibly my writing would be bad. The choosing of the name is something that is so private—because it also involves a lot of foolishness—that I can't even begin to tell you. It would involve remembering worlds of things that I remember quite well, but I'm no longer sure how to interpret what I was doing. I remember what I was doing, but I don't quite understand why I was doing it. So I'd rather not quite figure that out.

AV: If you don't want to answer the question directly, that's fine, but why "Jamaica" instead of "Antigua"?

JK: You see, you're trying to give it a logic that it did not have at the time. I was playing around with identities. When you're young you don't know how old you'll get to be and you feel every moment is *the* moment. In my case, there were many possibilities and that is the one I settled on. I had no idea anyone would one day be asking me how it all came to be or I would have made better sense of it at the time. I wanted to write, and I didn't know how. I thought if I changed my name and I wrote and it was very bad, then no one would know. I fully expected it to be bad, by the way, and to never be published, or heard from again. So I thought they'd never get to laugh at it because they wouldn't know it was me. So I changed my name. It was done one of those nights when you're sitting up late with friends who were trying out identities. If you saw photographs of me then, you would see how easy it was to do that. It was around this time I had started to write. When I started to get published no one ever called me Elaine. I'd always been unhappy with my name. You can almost say I became a writer just so I could change my name. . . .

AV: *Annie John* appears to be an autobiographical novel. You have also stated (*New York Times Magazine*) that "lying is the beginning of fiction." Do you think fiction works best when reality is mixed with fiction?

JK: Well, I certainly can't make a fast rule about it and say that about everything. It seems to be that those things are true for me, so far, and I don't know what I'll do in the future. How I've written, so far, is to exploit my personal experiences. I have no idea of writing as an objective exercise. I only write about myself and about the people connected to me or the people I'm connected to.

I, for instance, could not write a marvelous novel as far as I know. I could not write even a very bad novel about someone living in Houston, Texas. I would not know how. I can only write about the things I know. I happen to be that sort of writer. The process of fiction, for me, is using reality and then reinventing reality, which is the most successful way to do what I do.

The part about "lying is the beginning of fiction" was true. I used to be accused when I was a little girl of having a strong imagination, and that was why I was a liar. I lied all the time. It was a way, I thought, of protecting my privacy. They tried to beat it out of me, sometimes literally, by giving me a spanking—no, a beating! (There is great cruelty to children in the West Indies.) I was always mistrusted. The only thing I was accused of was that I had a good memory. I never forgot anything that happened. I would hear people telling something that happened, and they would leave out, in my opinion, the crucial parts. Every part was crucial. If someone left something out, then I would tell what happened and they'd look at me in amazement. So my memory was considered an act of treachery, and I was asked not to have such a good memory. Essentially, I would be told that I should just forget certain things that happened. It was considered one of my greatest faults, but I'd remember everything and then I would invent things. For instance, if something happened, such as a little smoke coming out of a building and the fire truck came, then I would say, "Oh, it was the biggest fire you ever saw, and hundreds of fire trucks had to come." I was incapable of just describing something as it really happened. I would remember that it had happened, and I might exaggerate the details, but other people would forget it happened. So that is essentially what my fiction is. It really happened, but the details became exaggerated.

AV: Antigua appears to be paradise on the outside, but an evil lurks, embodied in the basket of green figs balanced on Annie's mother's head. The basket has a snake hidden within. Is this a biblical or a Conradian evil or something else altogether?

JK: It would be biblical, although these things are very unconscious, or subconscious. I did not know how much until very recently, when I began to just read my writing out loud and eventually just collected the images of my writing. I began to realize how my writing and my use of images are based on my own understanding of the world as good and evil as influenced by two books in the Bible, Genesis and Revelation. If that's all any writer has been influenced by, it would be enough. My understanding of the world is influenced very much by those two books, which were my favorite books to read from the Bible. I used to read the Bible as a child just for fun. I really loved reading it, especially Revelation, which I could not get enough of. I used to make myself afraid just by reading it. Do you know that part where it is the end of the world and they turn into rocks? I took it literally.

It became very real to me. So I'm very influenced by the first book of the Old Testament and the last book of the New Testament. Everything in between is just sort of picturesque, but the beginning and end are the real thing. I did not know how much of an influence those biblical images had on my writing and understanding of the world until very recently.

It also turns out that there are recurring images of Lucifer, whom I apparently identify with, from *Paradise Lost,* which I did not know. I did not know how much I was rooting for the Devil.

AV: Would you also apply Lucifer's comment from *Paradise Lost,* "Better to reign in Hell, than serve in Heav'n," to Antigua's colonial situation?

JK: Yes. It is better to reign and to have self-possession in hell than to be a servant in heaven. You know how people would say, "Better red than dead"? I'm someone who would never say that. I always say, "It's better to be dead than to live like this. It's better to risk dying than to live as a slave." Always I say that.

AV: Is Annie John's love for Gwen supposed to be a substitution for her mother's lost love? Or are these lesbian tendencies?

JK: No, they weren't meant to be. I think I am always surprised that people interpret it so literally. The relationship between Gwen and Annie is really a practicing relationship. It's about how things work. It's like learning to walk. Always there is the sense that they would go on to lead heterosexual lives. Whatever happened between them, homosexuality would not be a serious thing because it is just practicing. The stories in *At The Bottom of the River* about the relationships between women are not meant, at least in my mind, to be homosexual. They were meant not to observe the convention of men and women, because I was trying to do away with certain conventions. I don't know if it comes up anyplace else, but Americans rather like to have things very much defined or to have things very much be what they say they are. The question of sexuality in these stories is not meant to be dwelt on because that is not the main thrust of them.

AV: There is a scene in **Annie John** where the narrator sees her reflection in a window yet doesn't recognize herself because she "had got so strange." Do you see yourself, both as a person and as a writer, still changing, or have the changes become less noticeable with age?

JK: By nature, I'm the sort of person who is never the same. Sometimes it's disturbing to me, because I find myself in a moment I like very much and wish I could stay that way, but I don't. I change very much. I'm still changing, but I don't always like it because it is not always convenient.

AV: Annie John's request to make a new trunk indicates she wants to start her own life, while the recovery from her illness as the long rain stops indicates she has moved from adolescence to womanhood. Is this correct?

JK: I think it is, but, again, at the time I was writing it, I wasn't conscious of these things as you point them out to me. If I were an objective reader, I'd be able to see it. I was writing these stories, and I was far less conscious of things than I am now. The sickness in the long rain actually happened when I was seven years old, with whooping cough, and I would get delirious. It's actually to that moment that I trace my fear of rodents. I was lying in my bed when I looked up and, around the edges of the ceiling that had this boarded mantel, I thought I saw hundreds of rats running around in a circle. I thought there were hundreds of them, but I think there was only one. I was powerless to do anything. I put that incident into the teenage life of the girl and made it a period of transition. I exaggerated the details.

AV: In **A Small Place,** you criticize tourists who go to Antigua to "escape the reality of their lives," which implies that tourists are an unthinking lot, and that tourists and their ancestors have profited from using Antigua. Isn't this a generalization that is both unfair and discriminatory?

JK: Not at all. If you think it's unfair and discriminatory, try it the other way around. Imagine that your existence depended on people who are very different-looking than you and whose differences seem to give them privileges that you cannot even imagine. Just imagine the situation in reverse. For example, in Vienna they depend mostly on tourism. You and the Viennese look alike, so that alienation just isn't there, but even if you're a tourist among people who look like you, they resent it. I can tell you there are differences in going to Vienna and going to Antigua. If you don't go to Vienna for fun, you can also go to experience all of the cultural benefits and gain a

deeper understanding of the Western world. If you go to a place like Antigua, it's to have a rubbish-like experience. You want to forget who you are for the moment. You're not interested in these people. You're not interested in their culture, except in some sort of anthropological way that offers you psychic relief. They have nothing of value you want to bring home. It's an escape, a moment to forget who you really are. If you think there isn't anything wrong with it, then try living it and you'll see how quickly you want to shoot every tourist you ever meet. It's deeply wrong. . . .

AV: What has been Antigua's response to your book **A Small Place**? I can't imagine the government looks upon you favorably.

JK: I think about that all the time. I imagine that I'd be shot. I haven't been back since the book was published. I wanted to go this year, but I didn't want to be separated from my children. I booked a flight the day the war in Iraq started; yet I didn't know how it would turn out, and I decided not to go. Now I don't have the time. God knows if they would shoot me, but it's a criminal place. I wouldn't be surprised if they had henchmen who would do it, because politics in the West Indies is very tribal. People take their colors very seriously. They divide themselves into people who wear red and who wear blue.

My mother is a blue. I'm nothing. When I was growing up, we were reds. Then my mother joined the party that broke away, and they are blue. She takes it so seriously. For example, I bought her a red T-shirt and she said, "No, I could never wear that." Even though she was visiting me in the United States, she brought her loyalties with her. This makes you think there isn't any hope for people in Antigua who think like this.

AV: The character Lucy appears to be similar to Annie John, except she is a few years older. Did you consider keeping the name "Annie John" for this character?

JK: I don't consider it a continuation because I would never write like that. It's a continuation only in the sense that it's about my life and it's the same life I'm writing about, but they weren't meant to be the same person at all. In any case, a key to Lucy is the name Lucifer and so she couldn't be called Annie at all. It's a very shallow—though understandable—connection to make, because the reader isn't me and in my mind, observing what I'm doing. I'm not interested in making the thing whole. I'm interested in parts of things. When Annie left her mother, that was it. We're not going to hear from Annie again. We're not going to hear from Lucy again. You might very well hear about a woman's life in the metropolitan area of the world, whether it's London, New York, Toronto, or wherever.

You might very well hear about how this life turned out, but to say it's a continuation of Lucy would be a mistake. Very, very crucial to understanding Lucy is her name. I think most people in America have such a different background than I do that people in America, especially in universities, are so obsessed with race that they miss the crucial things about Lucy. The great influences on that young woman's life are Genesis and Revelation and, strangely enough, *Jane Eyre.* I think all sorts of things escape American readers.

I suppose my writing is as mysterious to an American reader as someone like Zora Neal Hurston is to me. She's a woman who wrote in the twenties, part of the Harlem Renaissance, who had a very brilliant career and then died a maid in poverty. It's one of those stories which either you think is an American story or you think it is a racial story, but those are things that to really understand what I'm trying to do you'd have to know. Lucy is a very moralistic person, and she's very judgmental, because her view of the world is very much shaped by a nineteenth-century view.

AV: The scene in which Lucy tells her dream to Lewis and Mariah is uncomfortable because the couple looks at the dream from a Freudian and sexual viewpoint, whereas Lucy interprets it as meaning she has accepted them into her life. Did you have something like this happen to you in real life?

JK: Well, that I will not say. The scene really explains itself, because the people had become real to her. If you show up in someone's dream, it means they are finally real to you. It's a cultural gap. I tried to show that Lucy did not understand it; she only reports what happened in her dream. Of course, I understand it, but Lucy doesn't and isn't quite clear about it. Lucy doesn't know who Dr. Freud is, and it's said with a certain simplicity. I think it's the sort of thing I wouldn't have been able to write five years ago. I wouldn't have been able to separate the knowledge I have of Freud from the knowledge I did not have.

AV: There is the contrast between the island girl, Sylvie, who has the teethbite mark on her cheek, and Mariah, who "looked blessed, no blemish or mark of any kind on her cheek or anywhere else." Lucy does not identify with pleasant-smelling Mariah; she prefers to have a powerful odor. Why is Lucy, as well as Annie John, so iconoclastic? She seems to rebel against most things that are good, yet she has no reason to act this way.

JK: I think it's that "reign in hell, serve in heaven" problem again. A person like Sylvie seems more self-possessed to her. Even in her embryonic consciousness-raising, she knows that it's better from a feeling of self-possession to be Sylvie rather than Mariah, spiritually speaking. There's something sad about Mariah and, ultimately, defeated. She's the victim among the conquerors, whereas Sylvie is the victor among the defeated.

Later on, Lucy develops sympathy and grows to love Mariah. Lucy is the sort of person who, no matter what happens to her, would never identify with the victors. Lucy is naive, but she is not stupid.

Mariah is a lovely person. She didn't think the world would turn on her. What undoes Mariah is trusting in human nature, but this is not possible for Lucy, who trusts and mistrusts at once. It's not the sort of thing Mariah would understand, because she thinks love is all. Lucy thinks love is fine, but she doesn't look upon love as an absolute reality.

AV: Mariah shows Lucy the daffodils in the garden, but Lucy wants to kill the flowers. Why do so many of your characters have such negative, conflicting feelings?

JK: Let me answer that in a roundabout sort of way. My husband and I went to Paris last September on a boat. We sailed on the *QEII,* and after we arrived at Southampton we spent a couple of days in London. Every time I go to England I almost have a nervous breakdown. I have such conflicting feelings of England. I love it, and I hate it. It's not possible for me to be a tourist. I realize I'm a visitor, but when I go to England, what happens is that I also confront my past.

AV: It's ironic the English were waiting on you.

JK: Yes, that's true, although there weren't many English waiting on me. They were Pakistani, Irish, and Africans, but not many English were waiting on me. So we stayed in London and took a train to Dover where we were going to catch a ferry. We were getting to Dover, and I couldn't believe what my eyes were seeing: the White Cliffs of Dover! I had yet another nervous breakdown that was quite like Lucy and those daffodils. I had heard so much about those white cliffs. I used to sing a hymn in church that was about longing to see the White Cliffs of Dover over and over again. Things like that permeate my memory, but these things have absolutely no value to me. I hardly know the names of any flowers growing in the West Indies, except the hibiscus, but I know the names of just about all the flowers in England and I also can identify them. There is something very wrong here when I know the name of each flowering bush growing in England, but not in Antigua. I know the White Cliffs of Dover, and I've yearned for them. I could have lived a millennium without ever seeing them. So there is something wrong there, just as it would have been false for a person like Lucy to love those daffodils. Daffodils do not grow in tropical climates. I know a poem about daffodils, but I did not know a poem about hibiscus.

AV: Was there resentment after seeing the White Cliffs of Dover?

JK: Yes, of course there is resentment.

AV: But aren't the White Cliffs really amazing?

JK: They *are* amazing. They really are amazing.

AV: Lucy identifies with the French painter Gauguin, who found his homeland to be a prison and wanted something different. The two are much alike, even though Gauguin escaped to the islands while Lucy left the islands. Do you feel much in common with Gauguin, whose painting *Poèmes Barbares* is the cover picture for **Lucy**?

JK: I hesitate to say I identify with this man. I must say, as I was writing parts of **Lucy,** I was reading one of his journals called *The Intimate Journals of Paul Gauguin.* I found it a great comfort because he was so unrelenting of himself. He was very selfish and very determined; yet there are two things that struck me in that book. The first thing that struck me is his account of his friendship with van Gogh, which is the most hilarious yet cruel thing I've ever read. I never have laughed so much in jest. He describes van Gogh cutting off his ear, and you are just aghast because it's all very astonishing. The second thing was when he asked Strindberg to write an introduction to one of his shows. Strindberg wrote back a very long letter saying why he could not do it because he disliked Gauguin's work. So Gauguin used the letter as the introduction even though the letter stated what was bad about his paintings. Gauguin wasn't afraid to use someone's negative view of his work. He wore it as a badge. I rather admire that.

So I think the criticism I most value comes from people who do not like my writing. There's almost nothing that makes you feel more superior than the people who don't like you.

AV: The narrators or main characters of your fiction seem to have a cursory or dispassionate regard for sex (such as in the chapter titled "The Tongue" in **Lucy**). What was your viewpoint of sex as a young woman, and how has it changed as you've grown older?

JK: Good heavens, I don't think I could answer the first part of the question, although I must say Lucy rather enjoys it. What Lucy doesn't want is to be possessed again. She has just escaped a certain possession from her mother, and she doesn't want to be possessed again. I think at the end of the book she wishes she could be possessed and loved, but she can't at this point in her life. I suppose what she is saying is that she wishes time would pass quickly to allow herself to be consumed.

AV: Your writing style in **Lucy** is somewhat unusual in that you often start a passage, but before it is fully developed, you digress to a previous experience. For example, there is the party at Paul's where Peggy disapproves of Paul, but then you digress to the story of Myran and Mr. Thomas on the island.

JK: It's not anything deliberate, but last night after my reading someone said they really admired the way I had done that scene. It sort of leads you to explain how something was written, but I've come to understand there is no such thing in writing as a technique. Quite often you invent what you're doing while you're doing it, and it would be quite wrong to apply that style to all my writing. I was not aware of any special thing when I did that. I did that in **Lucy,** and that was it, but I have no intention of using it again. If it were to turn up again, it would be because I felt that was what was needed.

AV: With each book, your characters gain both insight and maturity with age, culminating with the ability to possibly love. Will your next book develop along these same lines, or do you plan to take off in a different direction?

JK: I really cannot say. For me, writing is a revelation. If I knew what it would be, then it would be of no interest for me to do it. When I sit down to write, I will reveal to myself what I already know. I already know all of this. I know how it works, but I haven't quite said it yet. The minute that I'm conscious of it, then it's of no interest. When I sit down to write it, it will become conscious to me. I will know it, and then I will move on. So I don't know what will happen. I don't know how it will work.

Moira Ferguson

SOURCE: "A Lot of Memory: An Interview with Jamaica Kincaid," in *The Kenyon Review,* Vol. XVI, No. 1, Winter, 1994, pp. 163-88.

MF: *Do you remember the first time you wrote? What was your inspiration and starting point?*

JK: I was in college and thought I would be a photographer, and I used to write out my photographs. If there was an inspiration, if there was a moment when I thought, "Oh, something could be done; somehow my thoughts could be written down," it must have been the moment I saw a French film called *La Jeté,* and I was reading Alain Robbe-Grillet. That was a big inspiration. And I began to write poems. I began to write of my photographs—what I would take and [how] I would set them up. I would look at what I had written down, and that is how I would take the photograph. I would write down what I thought the picture should feel like. And I would try to take a picture of what I had written down.

MF: *You pick some of that up in* **Lucy,** *about how you reverse the gaze with the camera . . . to stop people coming in on you by coming back on them.*

JK: Yes. That's true. I am thinking of that period of my life, and I look back.

MF: *Are you the first member of your family to write?*

JK: Yes, I do think I am the first person from Antigua to write and perhaps the first woman from that country. It is very odd. West-Indian writing until very recently was all men and then, for some reason, it is now mostly women. It is so funny. Like everywhere, everywhere it's mostly women who are writing anything interesting.

MF: *Do you think that parallels the resurgence of black women writers in this country—Alice Walker and Toni*

Morrison were two of many examples. Or do you think it's a coincidence?

JK: I don't know. Paule Marshall is really another generation. No, I think it must be a coincidence; I don't think American women have much that we can draw from. I mean the use of language is very different, and their concerns are much different. A much different sensibility. For instance, I think that American black people seem to feel—almost—that being black is a predestination in some way. They have a kind of nationalism about it that we don't have: black nationalism. Because they are a minority, they are more concerned with their identity being extinct, whereas we don't feel that way. Everybody is black. I mean, we don't think white people are permanent [laughs]. We don't feel permanent, either, but that feeling of "there will always be white people sitting on top of black people"—we don't have, I must say. Black nationalism in this country is very much because there is an acceptance, in some way, of how the majority of the population have thought about black people. There is very much an internalization of that. Why else have "black pride"? I mean there is no reason to be particularly proud of something you can't help. It is not an effort you made and you became black. It is just the way you are. There is nothing particularly pleasing or displeasing about it. I am speaking as an individual asking a group of people to behave the way I behave. But if you could somehow let them understand that their view of you has nothing to do with you and it remains with them, they are so befuddled. But I believe that is a very West Indian trait. They have never really buckled, maybe because they are a majority. It is still very peculiar to hear West Indians talk about racism because it is all borrowed. There is and was racialism, but on the whole they rejected it. They are sort of strong black people in the West Indies. What is actually on the mind of the West Indies is that American corruption, American money, has undermined more than anything the British Europeans did.

MF: *What made you decide to begin your fiction with an experimental style?* **At the Bottom** *is very deep and moving and thick imagistically and not as accessible as, say,* **Annie John.**

JK: It wasn't anything deliberate—it was how I felt the book had to be written. I was younger. I had no children. I had all the time in the world. I could spend a year writing one of those tiny stories, which I did. I strangely enough had no access to the simplicity and straightforwardness of **Annie John** and the simplicity, straightwardness, and complication of **Lucy** when I first started to write. The access I had to my writing was what turned out to be **At the Bottom of the River.** I could only speak like that then.

MF: *Do you know what prevented you from having access?*

JK: No. I didn't even know that I didn't have access to it. I think I never know what I have access to until I start to write. I don't really think I know how to write because

I think I can't write until I sit down at the typewriter. Every day I get up and I say, "I really can't write," and I write. But I feel I don't know how to write.

MF: *Did you have preconceptions about how hard writing was?*

JK: No. If I had preconceptions I would have not have done it. I thought I had no choice. It was that or die. I don't know how to do anything else. Essentially I don't know how to take orders. I don't know how to subject myself. I mean, for instance, I could never ever say "my boss," the words. "My boss" could never cross my lips. . . .

MF: *Early on in your career you moved from journalism to fiction, back and forth. Were there clear differences for you in those forms of writing?*

JK: None. As far as I am concerned I am only happy to write. Often the voices flow into each other because I am at a point where if I am writing supposedly different things, a fiction piece and a non-fiction piece, I often have just the same concerns. I am so happy to write that I don't care what you call it. When I first started to write, I thought, "I'm really not a writer because I don't have those distinctions, and the distinctions are what you would find in an English literary person." The whole point of the existence of someone like me is I'm not an English [literary] person. So I don't really care. When people think of falling standards, they must be thinking of people like me who just sort of usurp all the boundaries and just mix them up and just cross borders all the time. We just have no interest in the formalities. We are not interested in being literary people. We have something to say that is really urgent.

MF: *So it's a polyphony of voices, and they're all just speaking different ways about a multitude of things?*

JK: Yes, a multitude of things, sometimes the same thing in a multitude of voices. The important thing is to say that I think we feel—people like me must feel—and I don't want to speak for everyone, but I wouldn't be surprised if people in my position—you know, color, sex—just feel it's urgent. We have got to say it now. You don't know how long it will be that you can speak, maybe tomorrow you may be shut up again. You have got to say it now. So these drawing-room conversations and literary largesse and experimentation, we don't have time for it. Just however it gets said, just say it right now.

MF: *Can you say something about the evolving voice of resistance in your texts?*

JK: The development of my political consciousness and my ability to express it is really what you see. I was really not able to do more than I did in "Columbus in Chains." [A chapter of **Annie John**] And then by the time I wrote **A Small Place,** something had really matured. It gets more and more so. The thing I am working on now is even more. . . . I really understand a lot more than I did.

MF: *Is it fiction? Can you say a word about that new work?*

JK: It is fiction, and yet I am writing something about gardening, and so the thing from it has spilled out into gardening. For instance, it has dawned on me that gardening is one of the original forms of conquest. I mean elemental. You conquer food. You place it in one place. Also the idea of gardening is you stay in one place so you conquer your space. But apart from that, gardening, as we now know it, almost all of the flowers out there are the result of conquest. It just dawned on me that all the things that are not hardy come from warm climates, that they are perennials in the southern clime. Hibiscus could only grow up here. I actually have a hibiscus in the garden. It hasn't flowered this year. It is hardy and has to be well protected, but most annuals are perennials somewhere else. They just grow in the other place. But they are the result of conquest. I have sort of been writing that in the work of fiction I am doing, and yet I am writing something about gardens so that has come up. It has dawned on me, for instance, that I don't know the names of the flowers where I grew up, except for hibiscus and frangipani and oleander, because I come from poor people who would not have gardened for beauty but for food. So gardening must be a function of wealth. Gardening for no other reason than how it looks cannot be a function of anything else. The dahlia, for instance, is named after a Swedish botanist, I think, Anders Dahl. Yes, a lot of flowers are. Zin. Zinnias I think are named after a Mr. Zin and so on.

MF: *So you think that gardens are a bit like stolen property, a natural version of the Rosetta stone in the British Museum?*

JK: It's a version of it. There's a difference, though, because there is not one dahlia. It really is a form of theft and conquest. And it is not that you shouldn't have it, but it is not yours. What is incredible is how the conquered world would take the identity; for instance, "Dutch tulips." What is "Dutch tulips"? It is not native to Holland. Or cocoa isn't native to the Dutch. Or tea isn't native to England. Things like that. It gives them identity. Dutch chocolate is the best chocolate, but there isn't one cocoa tree that can grow in Holland. But what is so interesting, though, is that when people in the conquering position take things, it doesn't threaten their identity. But the weaker people *feel*—that's why they clutch or hold on so tight and define them narrowly, really leading even more to their defeat. Things are the things about themselves so they have all these cultural crises, cultural nationalism. But it didn't bother the Dutch at all to take a flower that didn't grow in their country and just take it on so that now the world thinks of tulips as Dutch. And it adds to the Dutch. But we can't do that; we don't do that. More and more people who look like me cling to their narrow definitions of themselves. They will not take anything that doesn't have some sort of phony or some kind of

ancestral image—to Africa or anywhere else. But it is really a sign of defeat when you cling so much. What you ought to do is take back. Not just reclaim. Take—period. Take anything. Take Shakespeare. Just anything that makes sense. Just take it. That's just fine.

MF: *So do you, would you position yourself in the Caribbean writing tradition?*

JK: Well, that's a very funny question. I speak as somebody from the British Caribbean. What tradition is that from? That is from English tradition. You know most people, especially people from my generation, had an education that was sort of an English public-school education. We got kind of the height of empire. They were trying to erase any knowledge of another history, another possibility. So we learned Shakespeare, the King James version, Wordsworth, Keats. That's the tradition. I'm of the English-speaking-people tradition. British people, English people. Not the Scottish, not the Welsh. English. I was reading a book by a woman from Zimbabwe and it said that it was truly an African novel that doesn't owe any debt to English writing. And it is not true at all. The book reminds me of Jane Austen in its humor and its kind of irony and its mannerisms. There is no "African novel." The tradition of novels is not an African form, as far as I can tell. But what is so wrong with that? This woman has written a novel that draws on Jane Austen. Jane Austen and her people would not hesitate for one second if they found something in Zimbabwe that they liked. They would just take it. And so she could take Jane Austen. [The book] is called *Nervous Conditions*. It is a fabulous book, borrowed from Jane Austen, and who cares? It is a fabulous book. Take. It's OK. So the world is ours. A lot of people say to me, "You must have had a lot of storytelling and your writing has come out of storytelling."

MF: *The anansi tales?*

JK: No, none. My writing does not come from that. My writing, if I owe anybody, it would be Charlotte Brontë. It would be English people. It would be Virginia Woolf. It would be Wordsworth, it would be Shakespeare, it would be the King James version of the Bible. I had never read a West Indian writer when I started to write. Never. I didn't even know there was such a thing, until I met Derek Walcott. He said "Do you know—?" I had never heard of them, so I can't remember who he said. And I said no. And he made a list of people for me to read. There was not one woman on it, by the way. And that is how I knew there was such a thing as a West Indian writer. I did not know. So I do not come from the West Indian writing tradition, and there is no such thing. There might be, eventually, but we are of the English-speaking tradition. You know you read [George] Lamming, and some part of it is like reading a nineteenth-century bore. It is so formal—the language—and his writing would be of absolutely no interest except that he is who he is. It's very boring, formal writing; but because of who he is, he is a black man from the West Indies and is very well educated. He is very smart, and he is telling us something that we have not heard before, a point of view we have not heard before. That is what is interesting. But the writing itself is of no interest.

MF: *So in terms of what you just said, what sense would you have of your progress and development as a writer from* **At the Bottom** *to your ideas right now about fiction concerning gardens? Do you see a lot of shift, peaks, and troughs? How do you see your development as a writer?*

JK: I look back at the years I have been writing, and I think—I have written too little. I have written four very very small books. It seems not enough—that is the only thing I can say. But it is so much for me; writing is really such an expression of personal growth. Another way I think I am not a real writer [is] because it is not a career for me. I don't know how else to live. For me it is a matter of saving my life. I don't know what I would do if I didn't write. It is a matter of living in the deepest way. I can only do this. I would just be crazy. I would just walk around and torment people. I have a friend, and I call him up all the time—we are very good friends and we talk about everything. But I just call him up, and I talk about my garden, and he said, "Why don't you write about gardens?" And I thought, "Yes, and so I am writing about gardens," but I didn't know. That's how I would have been if I hadn't become a writer. I would have been insane, and that's the truth. I would have had nervous breakdowns upon nervous breakdowns. I would have been one of those people. I mean I am really lucky. It's very much part of my being. It's the way I feel life is good. It's the way I feel connected. You know, sometimes I feel this is who I really am. I would have been somebody's mother, no matter what. I would have been somebody's wife, no matter what, I suppose. It was more likely I would have been somebody's wife and most likely I would have been somebody's mother. But it is not likely at all that I would have been a writer.

MF: *So how did it happen then?*

JK: Well, I just don't really know. I think about it and I think, "Well, this is very odd." I really don't know how it happened. . . . I just said I was a writer. I couldn't write but I said, "I'm a writer," and everyone said, "Yes, you're a writer," and I just started to write and that was that. I really don't know how it came about.

MF: *Growing up, did you recite narratives in your head? Rehearse conversations?*

JK: Yes, I did that. I still do that, but I actually never connected that to actual writing. You know, I used to see my mother talk to herself a lot. And I'm telling you something new. It has just dawned on me that I would see her doing things, and she would have these long conversations with herself. Usually I would see her doing it when she was washing or scaling fish or cooking. And it is possible she is a writer too. That is just what I would have done. Yes, so I used to do that. And also the other

thing is I used to daydream all the time and read all the time when I was a child and that was considered a really horrible thing. Everyone was very glad that I liked reading, and then it became this thing that I liked to do and didn't do anything else, so that became a problem. But I never really thought of writing as a child. I couldn't imagine writing because, first of all, I didn't know anyone around me who wrote. But the other thing is I didn't think people still wrote. I thought writing was something no one did anymore. One thing that everyone remembers about me until I wrote fiction was that I talked about my family obsessively, and people were very bored with it. In fact, some people who have read *Annie John* would just say, "Oh yes, you told me all about that." You know, it was not news to them at all.

MF: *At some point, was there a leap between thinking things internally and scripting them to your chums?*

JK: Well, I started to write for the *New Yorker* and then I would write "Talk of the Town." I remember the Fourth of July 1976 I wrote this very personal thing about America.

MF: *That's a very interesting piece. I think it is the first place I remember that you talked about your father's felt hat.*

JK: A recurring motif [laughs]. I was trying to write these personal things in "Talk of the Town." Then one day, it was after Allen and I met and we were living together and had just moved into this house, I just sat down one afternoon. I had been trying to write fiction, and I just sat down and wrote this thing called **"Girl,"** and I said to myself as I was writing it, "I don't care who likes it. I don't care if no one ever reads it or no one ever publishes it. This is what I am going to do." And I gave it to Mr. Shawn, and he was bowled over by it, I guess. It all looks clear now. But I really felt I was in the dark and would stay there. I mean again I had the sense of "I don't care, I would rather die than not write this way." This is how I would go.

MF: *That's an outstanding piece.*

JK: Well, it is my mother's voice exactly over many years. There are two times that I talked in my life as a child, as a powerless person. Now I talk all the time.

MF: *Do you see writing in any way as a form of political activism, or does that seem a view imposed on your texts?*

JK: When I write, I am thinking things that you would consider political but, really, I think—just to decide to get out of bed and breathe is a form of political activity. But when I am doing it, it is an act of survival for my own being. And were it not to have meaning to anyone else I would still do it. It's even wrong to impose on it . . . to say that I am politically active when I am writing. I am only politically active when I am writing if it is forbidden for me to write. If it is forbidden for me to write, then it becomes a political activity when I do it.

I suppose I don't know what a political statement would be since I am always very concerned with these issues. It is not as if at some time I am interested in tea parties and then suddenly I start to think about politics. I am always interested in how the powerful and the powerless relate. I realize that I started this with the mother and child, and it was only much later that I thought, "Well, that's what that's about." I am interested in the defeated and identify with the defeated even though I don't feel defeated myself. But I wonder sometimes when I think that everyone is so ashamed of defeat, but, you know, it is not your fault. People are always saying, "I am not a victim." Well, sometimes you are and it is not your fault. Actually, the great thing about being the victim is that you identify with the victim, and that may save you from victimizing. If you can keep in mind who suffers, it might prevent you from causing suffering, I think. I hope. . . .

MF: *Are you conscious of making history a part of your fiction?*

JK: Oh no, good heavens. That is so frightening. If I thought my writing was important in any way I perhaps would be afraid to do it. It is only important to me. I can't imagine it is important to anyone else.

MF: *And yet when it gets published it is everywhere.*

JK: Yes. But you know, I remember how much I loved books when the books would come. I love books still, obviously, but I am so used to having books. I go to the bookstore and spend hundreds of dollars on books, and I am so used to it. It's a thrill I take for granted, so it is not even really a thrill. It's just this wonderful thing. But when the books get published and sell a few copies, I can identify with it as the same as when new books would come to the library. God, I remember the librarian as this young, beautiful woman. It was one of the real shocks to me to see [when I returned to Antigua] that she had grown into this mature woman, and so it made me wonder how I looked. You know she caught me stealing books, but she would never say that. She used to be the cornerstone of a certain segment of society that money and corruption just usurped. This was a person that everyone had respect for. She is in many people's memories of their lives. But I bet you that is not true for children growing up now because the focus of life has changed. The focus is television and cable, you know. But she was like food for us. . . .

MF: *Do you see your writing, particularly your essays—* **A Small Place** *or* **"On Seeing England for the First Time"**—*as a form of opposition within a post-colonial space? Do you think of yourself as an oppositional critic?*

JK: No. But when you look at it objectively, that is what I am doing. But when I am doing it, I don't think that is what I am doing. Again I am getting something out of my head that if I don't will drive me absolutely insane. So I just do it. But I can see that is what I am doing. I mean I am not dense. . . .

MF: *Is it a coincidence that Annie John leaves Antigua about the time that Antigua gets associate status around 1967?*

JK: It is a coincidence, but that was when I really did leave home. I left home in 1965-66. So it is a coincidence. That book is very autobiographical. **Lucy** is very autobiographical. I think that what I am writing now is the first thing that isn't autobiographical. It is autobiographical in ideas, but not in situation.

MF: *Can you compare your treatment as a writer in Antigua with your treatment in the U.S.?*

JK: Oh, my God, there is no comparison. I think it is only because I'm accepted in America and made much of in America that people think of me. There is a reason why they should, but I don't really have a public there, I don't think. There are people proud of me, and I am really very grateful for that. Antigua is a very poor country, but it is not just that. The freedom to write I would not have had there—that's not political—it is just sort of cultural. People in Antigua do not like for you to speak the truth. In fact, a lot of people have said that in Antigua about **A Small Place.** They say it's true, but did she have to say it? So that's everything. I couldn't write there.

MF: *So coming here was an enabling experience?*

JK: Oh, yes, it was like taking an enormous purgative. And I am just still on the toilet. [laughs]

MF: *I notice that your books do not valorize U.S. values. You expose sham rather than valorizing.*

JK: I am not one of those people who just come to America and vote Republican. I would never ever do such a thing. It is just a part of human existence, isn't it, not to want to try to disguise reality. It is so painful; Antigua is not the only culture that lies. We live in one that lies. Everybody lies. You go to places like Germany where people lied to themselves during the holocaust; even as they were participating in things, they lied. People lie. The lies in this society are susceptible to reason and to truth. You can argue about it. You know it is not true and you can say it is not true. So for me, a culture like this is a relief. I am not attached at all to what I come from. I am glad not to be of it anymore even though it is very much a part of me and I can never be without it. I don't deny that. I am glad also to know something else. And I suspect one should always know something else on the whole.

MF: *Has your writing been autobiographical?*

JK: My writing has been very autobiographical. The events are true to me. They may not be true to other people. I think it is fair for my mother to say, "This is not me." It is only the mother in the books I've written. It is only the mother as the person I used to be perceived her. But I don't mind. I don't know what to do, I mean, you have to understand I find any such interest in my work peculiar. I don't know what to make of it. There is no reason for me to be a writer without autobiography. There is none at all. I have no interest in writing as some sort of exercise of my class. I am not from a literary class. For me it was really an act of saving my life, so it had to be autobiographical. I am someone who had to make sense out of my past. It is turning out that it is much more complicated than that when I say my past, because for me I have to make sense of my ancestral past—where I am from, my historical past, my group historical past, my group ancestry. So I could not be a writer the way that grand men used to be writers, like Dickens, or grand women. I had to write or I would have died. I can't think of anything else I could have done. I had to express myself in some way. I am not very good at drawing. I am good with words. I had to be able to do this. I am not good with logic like mathematics. I am never good at that. I don't like it.

MF: *In terms of the autobiographical dimension, does it sometimes happen for you that what you thought you wrote opens up later—so that the unconscious element is even wider than you thought?*

JK: Oh, absolutely. Oh, yes. In my first two books, I used to think I was writing about my mother and me. Later I began to see that I was writing about the relationship between the powerful and the powerless. That's become an obsessive theme, and I think it will be a theme for as long as I write. And then it came clear to me when I was writing the essay that became **"On Seeing England for the First Time"** that I was writing about the mother—that the mother I was writing about was really Mother Country. It's like an egg; it's a perfect whole. It's all fused some way or other.

MF: *Why was it important for you to portray strong female protagonists, ones who will not knuckle down or capitulate?*

JK: I notice this really in the literature of women not from the center of the world, if we think of the center of the world as Europe and then the periphery of where people of color come from. I notice it in the writing of women of this generation in Africa and the Caribbean. Every one of them is just an outspoken young woman, strong, who is aware of feminist rhetoric. But not really. I mean it is only feminist rhetoric because we know what feminism is. But there are women who are just terribly aware of the injustices done to them within their own cultures. It is astonishing. It just has this incredible truth. We haven't talked to each other. We just know this.

MF: *It crosses national boundaries.*

JK: Yes, in African writers and the Caribbean writers, the women are very very strong. Yes, and it is not phony. It is not borrowed. The strange thing is that the Americans, the women from the center of the world, lack that sense of self-invention or renewal, self-discovery. They don't

have that, unless of course they are a repressed group like the black women in America. But the white women in America and European women, you know, they don't have that at all. Duras is not like that. Her women are weak, they are abused, they are crumbling, and, of course, Jean Rhys—her women always crumble—even in the *Wide Sargasso Sea.*

MF: *What do you attribute that difference to?*

JK: Even as they are oppressed within their group, they are still of the privileged. I think that change for them would be very threatening to their status because when we rebel we want the whole thing washed away, turned upside down. But they can't do that because they would lose something too. Let's face it—a white woman earns more money in this society than a black man. She earns less than a white man, but she earns more than a black man.

MF: *So it is an investment in race or class.*

JK: Well, it's an investment in self-interest. It is your own self-interest. That sort of sweeping anger and that sort of let's-rip-it-out. They are sort of decaying, they sort of enjoy writing about decay in some enjoyable way. I'm thinking of Ann Beattie, who is a wonderful writer. . . .

MF: *I wonder if it is to do with people feeling they have nothing to lose versus people feeling they have a lot to lose? They become marginal if they do what you are doing.*

JK: Yes, like Adrienne Rich, who is someone who wants the whole thing out kit and caboodle. Yes. Mary Daly, the theologian. They are marginalized. They are identifying with an outside oppressed group, so they want the whole thing. But the writing becomes an exercise about writing, an exercise about ideas, which is fine, but great thinkers thought because it was necessary—it wasn't an exercise in thinking. They were really trying to sort something out. And that is what we are doing. We are trying to say something. We want to say something new. It is not an idea. It is not an exercise. It's necessary.

MF: *Do you think the fact your protagonists stick up for themselves is related to your family background, to your upbringing?*

JK: Well, I remember when I was little, I was very weak. I was considered very brainy but weak, and I was always being beaten up. I would come home with my clothes in tatters and my face scratched up, and my mother would take me back to the person who had beaten me up and say "fight, fight," and I couldn't fight. I would just cry and cry, and I remember this went on for years. Because I came first in class, I remember girls trying to flush me down the toilet, and another time they pushed me in before we had flushable toilets. It was at the Moravian school; they had pushed me into the outhouse pot, and I walked home with my shoes, my little sneakers, squeaky with poop, and my mother had to wash me down in carbolic acid diluted in water and disinfect me. And I remember the day, I must have been eleven or so, when I beat someone up. One day a girl did something terrible to me, and I beat her up. I remember the feeling that *I won.* I beat someone up. I won that fight. Everyone was astonished. And no one ever tried to fight with me again, and I became a kind of leader. . . .

MF: *In* **At the Bottom** *and* **Annie John,** *there is a concentration on the mother-daughter relationship, and in* **A Small Place** *it shifts to an assault on colonialism. Is the anger at the mother in* **Annie John** *an actual fact, or a metaphor for that anger?*

JK: I came to see that. I am my own psychoanalyst [laughing].

MF: *Water plays a very important part, especially at the closure of your texts as well as all the way through. It seems to be associated in some ways with life and growing up; it cleanses, fertilizes dry ground, opens up radical possibilities. I wonder if you would comment on the importance of water. Your endings are all about water.*

JK: It's really true. But how could it not be important? I grew up in a place that I don't think is as big as North Bennington. It is ten by twelve miles, and it is this tiny island surrounded by two vast bodies of water, an ocean and a sea. At the same time we suffered constantly from drought. We could see water, but it was of no use to us. All we talked about—it didn't rain, it didn't rain, it rained too much. It would rain too much and it would tear up the earth. Where my mother comes from it rains nine months out of the year. It rains, it rains, it rains, and then it stops and then it rains again. So it is just water. It is all people know. They don't know land. In Antigua, in particular, you see this beautiful, beautiful sheet of water. You can't turn anywhere that you don't see this water, but you can't use it. It is like a kind of torment. It is a kind of hell. You would have to ration water, you would have to go to the public pipes at six o'clock in the morning, and you would line up for water. But all you had to do was just turn around and you could see the sea. Just water.

MF: *It does sound a bit like torture.*

JK: Yes, torture. But you know, no one ever wondered about it. I never heard anyone say, "Isn't this a great irony that we can see water but it is of no use to us? Isn't this a kind of punishment?"

MF: *But you use water to talk about creativity in your texts.*

JK: But in the meantime—this was a physical thing—I was reading things. I would read the Bible, so all the water images in the Bible were just sort of wonderful to me. You would have the flood. Things like that were always used as an illustration of something about our lives. This is how good God was, you see, because he first sent the flood but he saved people. Moses and the Red Sea. Jonah and the whale . . . just on and on. And

I suppose there must be lots of images of mountains. But they don't stay with me. Yes, it is just water.

MF: *So water was crucial.*

JK: Yes, it is not an accident. I remember when people began to point it out to me, I wasn't aware. It wasn't anything that I had to reach for at all. It's just a constant in my imagination. Water, water swallowing up people who went to sea and never were seen again. . . .

MF: *The other image, probably very different, that crops up a lot is the monkey. Sometimes the monkey seems combative, and other times, for example, when you make that statement about Lewis and his uncle—I wonder if you are talking about racism?*

JK: No. That's another thing that would be an image from Dominica. The monkey. People are always transforming themselves into monkeys.

MF: *What do you mean?*

JK: People would turn themselves into something called a *jablesse.* You would become a *jablesse.* You would run around in the mountains and you would see a light in the mountain and you would see a *jablesse.* That was sort of a half man and half beast. And the monkey was a sort of thing people would turn themselves into. As far as I can tell it wasn't racial. It is not a substitute for race. I think I wouldn't use a substitute for race; I would come right out and say it.

MF: *And then there was the one where the monkey throws the stone.*

JK: Yes, that really was true.

MF: *At the end of* **"On Seeing England for the First Time,"** *you say that you "wished every sentence, every thing I knew that began with England would end with `and then they all died, we don't know how, it just all died.'" I wonder if you would expand on that and say who died?*

JK: Obviously not literally. It would be quite a terrible thing, I mean there would be a lot of grief let loose from the world if a whole country of fifty million people just disappeared. It would be a grave hole in the consciousness of the world. I suppose what I mean by that is the deeds of this place. It just all vanished. I mean it is a sort of childish indulgence. You don't like something, and it just dies. You know how when you are a child you just say, "I wish you were dead"? Yes, but you don't want the actual baggage of the death. It's a bit like that. I just wish the whole thing would stop.

MF: *The whole imperial project would just stop? I think that comes across very clearly. In discussing* **"Ovando,"** *you have said that you were just about to get to the idea of the "commodification of relationships" in your fiction. I* *wonder if that idea was part of your discussion in the essay on England, or perhaps in your new fiction?*

JK: It could very well be. I gave up writing that because I realized that I didn't know enough. By that I mean how these relationships work. I know better now, and I could resume it. But, actually, I was glad I didn't do it because it was something that people might have believed was part of the Columbus business—not that I would care really. . . .

MF: *In* **At the Bottom,** *in* **Annie John** *certainly, and in* **Lucy,** *protagonists create their own power, claim agency, be their own person, as it were. It is very important in your texts, and I wonder if you would say a little bit about that.*

JK: I have come to think, come to question whether such a thing as always claiming yourself isn't a great sense of insecurity because if you are not sure, you are always saying "I am." On the other hand, I do come from this tradition of possessing and claiming yourself, because if you don't possess and claim yourself, someone else will. You keep declaring that you are in full possession, which is to say you are on guard. If you are not on guard, someone will come right in and take you. But, ideally, it would be great just to be Buddhist-like about it, just sort of *be.* I am. I am not declaring it. Really, I don't come from a subtle culture.

MF: *What do you mean?*

JK: It is all very declarative. People just declare, declare, declare. That is not to say they are being truthful. In fact, because they are lying, they declare it. So that's why I think it must be a sign of great insecurity just to keep declaring. Well, I mean you do that only because you are not sure.

MF: *What would you think of as a more "subtle culture"?*

JK: I really don't know enough about other people to say, "Oh, that is a subtle culture," because the other thing about subtlety is that often it is a repressed person. There is no win really. For myself, I would like to be confidently existing and to know that I am, without declaring it all the time. But, gee, I haven't done too badly declaring, but I do think it is tiresome. If I saw anyone else doing it, I would really think they had an inferiority complex, and it is possible that I do. . . .

MF: *When you wrote* **"Ovando,"** *were you thinking at all of your grandmother?*

JK: No, not really. I was thinking more of a universal idea of sin, the person who transgresses. I was thinking of something larger. I was thinking of all the people who had lost in that one person, the nameless narrator, and all the people who had won in that other person—Ovando.

MF: *Why is the narrator nameless and genderless?*

JK: Well, because the people who lose . . . they don't have names. People who lose don't have names; they don't have sex. They don't have anything except their loss. They lost, and the thing about this loss, it is a particular kind of loss. It is not the losing of the French and the British fighting a war against each other. This is a loss of the people who are sitting somewhere who are innocent. They lost for no reason at all. It was not their fault. That was what I was thinking of, and that is really why I made the person nameless. It is not meant to be an individual. It is meant to be a voice, a voice of loss. The winner can be an individual, the winner always is. The winners all have names. Also there is a feeling of rape, I think. . . .

MF: *In a recent interview, and I think you were talking about* **At the Bottom,** *you said, "I can't write like that anymore. That kind of writing," you said, "is impossible for me now. I cannot be that isolated, mentally or physically." Were you glad circumstances moved you in another direction?*

JK: Yes, yes. Strangely, what helped me develop other ways of expressing myself was having children. I wrote **Annie John** before I had children, and I wrote it as a sort of relief-release from **At the Bottom of the River.** I thought that once I wrote that I would go back to writing in that other way. And it hasn't happened, and I am now beginning to see that it probably won't happen again because I am not in that stage of development. For me it is all development. That was how I could say what I had to say then, but I don't need that anymore. My ideas have gotten more complicated, so I need to express them more clearly. Then my ideas were simple so I could express them in this sort of cloudy, difficult way. But I don't need that.

MF: *What were those ideas?*

JK: Well, they were the ideas of someone emerging, like being born. Embryonic, you know. This little child's expression and expectation. I was very influenced by Charles Kingsley. I no longer feel that way. I no longer understand the world in that way. That was a new kind of thing, and now I couldn't do it again. It is impossible to write like that anymore. I don't feel small and new. I feel big and not old but grown up. I feel stronger now than I did then. Absolutely.

MF: *Often the protagonist seems lonely and alienated. Do you think you'll continue that way?*

JK: No, I think actually the protagonist I am writing now, I have now, is perhaps lonely and isolated, too—I think yes—and more godlike. There's hardly any point in writing about yourself as an agreeable fabulous person in your society. Why bother? It would be very uninteresting. "Oh, I am so wonderful. Everyone liked me." I remember reading Rousseau's *Confessions.* It's so—Am I not great? He sounds just like my mother. I now am writing about a grown-up woman. It's exciting.

MF: *How old is she?*

JK: Well, it spans her whole life, so I think that by the time it ends, she will be seventy something.

MF: *That will be very different; I don't think you have talked about a very old person.*

JK: No, I haven't really written the life of a woman. It is very interesting to me to see all the works of these women, as I say, from the far corners of the world. They all start out writing about their childhoods. Everyone of them. You know in a way that you wouldn't say, really, of Virginia Woolf. She wrote about her own childhood in that memoir, *Moments of Being.* And Colette did too. I am thinking of fiction. It is not just women. Writers from the far part of the world write about their childhoods a lot. Every one of them. It is as if we have to start at the beginning. The best writing really among this group of people is about their childhoods. Think of Merle Hodge's book. It is as if we just have to go over what happened to us. The thing about it is that it is all filled with cruelty. I once said this to Merle, and she really captures it more than I did. I suppose my life wasn't filled with that as a child, was not filled with that kind of physical brutality, but there is a lot of physical brutality visited on children. She really wrote about that in *Crick-Crack Monkey,* the beatings, the constant humiliations. I think that's a legacy of slavery. It is very very common. I have done that, and I sort of would like to write about a full life, and I am doing it I think. Slowly, very very slowly.

GENERAL COMMENTARY

Patricia Ismond

SOURCE: "Jamaica Kincaid: 'First They Must Be Children'," in *World Literature Written in English,* Vol. 28, No. 2, Autumn, 1988, pp. 336-41.

The earliest phase of Caribbean writing, fighting to claim an identity for the black man, began with a sense of his damaged psyche. Among some of the writers who have emerged since then, there is a noticeable shift to another area of exploration. They seem intent on affirming the character and spirit that were being forged in the region even while its peoples underwent the ills and privations of the past. They search out this character in the substance of family relationships, the urgencies of caring, sacrifice and struggle experienced at close domestic levels, and fostering courage and human values. . . .

Kincaid, writing from the metropolitan world of New York, returns exclusively to the childhood experience of growing up in Antigua. She has lived most of her adult life away from that setting; but it is to this childhood experience that she returns to find the possibilities of a creative adjustment to a world and time so different in its ethos.

Jamaica Kincaid made an immediate impact on the literary scene when she first appeared in the early 1980s. . . .

The reader is immediately struck by the originality of Kincaid's work, an originality that comes both from the peculiar character of the experience she recalls as from her singular rendering of it. In the more accessible *Annie John,* she re-creates a vivid picture of the Antiguan setting in which she grew up. It is the typical small-island environment before urban times. The conditions and lifestyle around the capital town of St. John's are still provincial. There are wooden shingle houses, their yards equipped with the inevitable breadfruit trees and the heap of stones for bleaching clothes; kerosene lamps have not yet been replaced by electricity. The men earn a living as fishermen and small craftsmen (Annie John's father is a carpenter); the women are devoted to caring for their men and children and keeping house. The people still hold to their belief in obeah cures, superstitions and bush baths. At the same time, parents who are not too badly off strive to bring up their girls "to be a lady" according to the norms of Sunday school culture. Kincaid recalls the "manners lady" to whom one was sent for lessons in etiquette. . . .

[I]n Kincaid's case, home and setting were indistinguishable from each other, as this comment suggests: "I identified parental restrictiveness with the restrictiveness of my surroundings." This experience of home, as Annie John records, centred especially on the figure of her mother. Kincaid's memory clings to that focal experience of her mother, and her work deals extensively with growing up in that close childhood relationship between herself and her mother.

The attachment must have been all the more intense for one who remained an only child up to the age of nine. The prominent role of her mother in her life, however, also harks back to a common feature of West Indian family life documented by Edith Clarke in *My Mother Who Fathered Me* (1957). Clarke showed how the prevailing types of conjugal relationships in West Indian society conspired to place the onus of responsibility for children on the mother, and left the father relatively free of parental obligation. Annie John recalls being hastily gathered into her mother's skirts whenever they passed "one of the women that my father had loved and with whom he had had a child or children." The father of these removed connections did not "belong" as fully as she and her mother belonged together. Add to this the fact that boys were banished from the world of a lady-like upbringing and we get the background to a curious feature in Kincaid: the figure of the woman remains deeply impressed on her consciousness. The image of the other, what she idealizes as well as resists, always appears in the form of a woman.

The particular circumstances of her background, therefore, and no doubt qualities of her own temperament, helped to deepen the seminal bond between mother and child. Revisiting that childhood, Kincaid gives testimony of the powerful ties between mother and child in what must rank among the most penetrating studies on the subject so far. *Annie John* traces the various stages of her progress from childhood to adolescence in terms of this relationship with her mother. It began with the fullness of maternal love, care and nurturing in infancy. The experience of being "weaned," a sundering between herself and her mother, marked the passage to girlhood. So that growing up and beginning to fend for herself meant an experience of increasing disfavour with her mother, presaging a silent opposition and undeclared war between them. . . .

The child-mother relationship thus deepens into an ultimate significance in Kincaid's imagination. It is a paradigm of the struggle between the self and the other, the tug between the yearning for completion and all outside us that seem to resist it, provoking, as Kincaid tells us, the will to master or be mastered. Beneath this struggle lies the final need for union. Kincaid's journey thus recovers an authentic mythic level in **"My Mother"**: the loss of innocence and security, initiation into experience, and the struggle to regain that innocence.

Kincaid remains close to the child's modes of perception and language in these renderings. The roots of her style, as earlier noted, lie in the child's instinct for fantasy; the free play between its imaginings and the world of fact; its spontaneous connections between widely different spheres and categories; and the natural simplicity with which it does all this. We are almost in the presence of the writer-child, as one reviewer puts it. Kincaid seems to have retained the child-faculty intact. Repossessing it in her adult years, she authenticates and affirms the power of the imagination of childhood. What has crystallized in this child-language extends into a number of powerful visionary modes in Kincaid's hands. There are accesses of clairvoyance and divination, of the prophetic and apocalyptic in her work. In a piece entitled **"At Last"** from *The Bottom of the River* she reflects on the irreducible essence of things, despite the world according to science and technology. The passage in question attains prophetic, biblical force, while we still hear the voice of the child: "Will the hen, stripped of its flesh, its feathers scattered perhaps to the four corners of the earth, its bones molten and sterilized, one day speak? And what will it say? I was a hen? I had twelve chicks? One of my chicks, named Beryl, took a fall?"

The preoccupation with childhood lies at the core of Kincaid's work and represents a very special achievement. In exploring it, she renews our understanding of the meaning of innocence and the value and possibilities of our first world. . . . One must look closely at what she recognizes in this innocence. It is not a state free from stain and imperfection. Growing up in *Annie John* involves an openness and receptivity to all manner of emotions and impulses, creative and destructive—love, dawning cruelty, generosity, possessiveness, instincts of hubris. In other words, the child is fully in touch with the complex motions of her own nature and being. It is also the freedom of the child's natural curiosity, the intentness with which it relates to the world around it, animate and

inanimate forms alike. In Kincaid's testimony, the mother comes to contain and embody the world because of the totality with which the child lived that first relationship with her; and the struggle to be reconciled with her mother contained in embryo the struggle to be reconciled with life itself. . . .

Derek Walcott, in an early response to Kincaid's work, has this to say: "Genius has many surprises, and one of them is geography." Kincaid grew up in an environment which helped give her a firm grounding in human relationships and their tenacity, an uncluttered landscape which kept her imagination in touch with primal realities. Her own work is proof of the power of that landscape. In reclaiming these roots she makes an explicit disavowal of the universe according to the twentieth-century view—a system that can be calculated, programmed and mastered, where the human spirit is left very little space to breathe. . . . In the global scheme of things, Kincaid's native Caribbean, despite the brutalities of its past, is yet close to the state of childhood, and has the capacity to bring this message.

Diane Simmons

SOURCE: "A Paradise Lost," in *Jamaica Kincaid,* Twayne Publishers, 1994, pp. 1-10, 20-2.

At heart Jamaica Kincaid's work is not about the charm of a Caribbean childhood, though her first and best-known novel, *Annie John,* may leave this impression. Nor is it about colonialism, though her angry essay *A Small Place* accuses the reader of continuing the exploitation begun by Columbus. Nor, finally, is Kincaid's work about black and white in America, though her novel *Lucy* runs a rich white urban family through the shredder of a young black au pair's rage. Kincaid's work is about loss, an all but unbearable fall from a paradise partially remembered, partially dreamed, a state of wholeness, in which things are unchangeably themselves and division is unknown.

This sense of betrayal, which permeates Kincaid's work, is explored first in the treachery of a once-adored mother. In Kincaid's first book, the collection of surrealistic short stories *At the Bottom of the River,* a girl yearns for an impossible return to the perfect world that existed before the "betrayal" of birth and for union with a mother figure who will "every night, over and over, . . . tell me something that begins, 'Before you were born.'" But the yearning for a lost maternal paradise is inextricably linked to betrayal, and elsewhere in *At the Bottom of the River* the mother is shown methodically transforming herself into a serpent, growing "plates of metal-colored scales on her back" and flattening her head "so that her eyes, which were by now ablaze, sat on top of her head and spun like two revolving balls."

In *Annie John,* a more conventionally narrative coming-of-age book, the treachery of a once-adoring mother is spelled out. As the child begins to reach puberty, the mother suddenly turns on her. The mother, who had previously seen her daughter as beautiful and perfect, now sees the child as a mass of imperfection and immorality. At the same time that she imposes rules and regimens designed to turn the girl into a "young lady," the mother also communicates that this project is doomed, that no amount of training can overcome what she now perceives to be the girl's true nature, that of a "slut."

While betrayal by a beloved mother is a theme that echoes throughout Kincaid's work, this first treachery is matched by another, that of the British colonial power, which dominated the Antigua of Kincaid's childhood. The young protagonist of **Annie John** enjoys the prestige of being a top student. But approval and praise are withdrawn when Annie, in her growing awareness that she is the descendant of people whose enslavement was the result of European "discovery," treats a picture of Christopher Columbus with mild disrespect. As a child of the colonial system, Annie is faced with a dilemma similar to that which she has begun to face when dealing with her mother: both powers, maternal and imperial, demand childlike devotion and unquestioning trust, and both turn on the girl in retaliatory fury at the slightest hint of mature awareness. To be acknowledged, loved, and rewarded, then, she must betray her own maturing self. The result is a confusion about where the self really lies: "Sometimes, what with our teachers and our books, it was hard for us to tell on which side we really now belonged—with the master or with the slaves."

Like the betraying mother, the colonial system, in pretending to nurture the child, actually steals her from herself. In the colonial system imposed by the British on the Caribbean, wrote Craig Tapping, speaking of both **Annie John** and In the Castle of My Skin, George Lamming's novel of a Caribbean childhood, "the self is faced with extinction by the very processes of acculturation which all who nurture the child commend." Only imitation and blind acquiescence are acceptable, not the questioning gaze of an emerging intelligence.

The themes of betrayal and of an increasing anger at having been somehow trapped into turning against oneself explode in **A Small Place,** in which the author revisits her home, the island of Antigua, after an absence of 20 years. The island is now self-governing, but white tourists have replaced the departed British as the dominant group. As the tourists turn the islanders into holiday attractions, the islanders retaliate in kind, reducing the tourist into a dehumanized object. "An ugly thing," Kincaid wrote, "that is what you are when you become a tourist, an ugly empty thing, a stupid thing . . . and it will never occur to you that the people who inhabit the place in which you have just paused cannot stand you."

If the white tourists in Antigua are excoriated, the black inhabitants are not spared Kincaid's wrath as they, in some areas, act out the roles of incompetence and dishonesty written for them by the English and, in others, emulate imperial rapacity. The postindependence schools are so bad that Kincaid, with her preindependence education, is shocked. And the government of Antigua is so patently dishonest that "the answer on every Antiguan's lips to the question, 'What is going on here now?' is 'The government is corrupt. Them are thief, them are big thief.' Imagine, then, the bitterness and the shame in me as I tell you this." Once again the betrayer is, in part, the self.

In **Lucy** the themes of loss and betrayal are continued, though the title character is no longer in the Caribbean but has come to work as an au pair in a big American city resembling New York. The sense of loss may be even more powerful here than in Kincaid's other works, as the rich beloved contradiction of the childhood world is not only figuratively but also literally lost. Lucy—named, her mother has told her, for Lucifer—has been expelled from both the Caribbean and her mother's life. Warm, vivid Antigua has been replaced by the pale chill of a North American winter. Lucy's mother, source of all intelligence, power, beauty, and magic, has been replaced by Lucy's wealthy employer, the affectionate but sheltered and naive Mariah, who proffers books on feminism to help Lucy over her deep sense of loss and despair. In one way, Kincaid's young protagonist has, by leaving home, triumphed over her mother's wish to keep her forever infantilized or criminalized. Still, she is threatened by the mother's power. She keeps her mother's letters but does not open them: "I knew that if I read only one, I would die from longing for her."

If Lucy has not entirely freed herself of her mother, neither is she free of the destructive legacy of a colonial education. When Mariah, brimming with delight in the pale spring of the Northeast, introduces Lucy to her favorite place, a grove of daffodils, Lucy is filled with rage. She has never seen a daffodil before but had been forced to memorize a long poem about daffodils as part of her British education, an education that, as a matter of course, expected students to ignore their own lush flora and to study and celebrate a plant they would probably never see. Though Mariah's intentions are innocent, even loving, Lucy wants only to take a scythe and "kill" the flowers. Part of her fury is at how "simple" they look, as if "made to erase a complicated and unnecessary idea," the complicated idea of dominance. The colonial education, which has forced the girl first to love daffodils, then to hate them, creates a chasm between her and the well-meaning Mariah. "I felt sorry that I had cast her beloved daffodils in a scene she had never considered, a scene of conquered and conquests; a scene of brutes masquerading as angels and angels portrayed as brutes. . . . It wasn't her fault. It wasn't my fault. But nothing could change the fact that where she saw beautiful flowers I saw sorrow and bitterness. The same thing could cause us to shed tears, but those tears would not taste the same." Here, too, neither the source of suffering nor its redress is simple.

While the themes of loss, betrayal, and self-betrayal permeate these works, this is probably not what draws most readers to Kincaid's writing. Rather, readers are struck first by the language, which reviewers frequently describe in terms of poetry, demonstrating a "joy in the sheer sounds of words." Kincaid's language can be examined in a number of ways. It has been claimed as particularly "feminine," the "language of sounds and silence" of the nursery, "which stands before and beyond the rational signifying words of the father." Kincaid's style has also been described as "a successful example of [the] Afro-American rhetorical strategy [as] parody, repetition, inversion mark every single movement of Kincaid's narrative." **"Girl,"** the first piece in the collection *At the Bottom of the River* and Kincaid's first story to be published in the *New Yorker,* which later published virtually all of her fiction, is described as "a rhythm so strong it seemed to be hypnosis, aimed at magically chanting out bits of the subconscious. . . .

While the style may mesmerize, may have such power as to seem an end in itself, the careful reader begins to see that Kincaid's language may be the most powerful symbol of all for the themes of loss and betrayal in a world divided against itself. In this passage, as the proprieties of Europe are positioned against the sensualities of Africa, the voice of the nurturing mother suddenly wheels to attack as the sentence turns upon itself. A Kincaid sentence, as West Indian poet Derek Walcott wrote, constantly "heads towards its own contradiction." Finally, it may be that it is in Kincaid's sentences, if not in her stories, that a kind of resolution to the crisis of loss and betrayal is achieved. Here at least the contradictions are held in suspension.

The fact that Kincaid's work is so frequently its own contradiction may explain the difficulty critics have had in categorizing it. Intensely personal, psychologically dense, Kincaid's writing "does not fit in to any of the fashionable schools of Caribbean writing" that are preoccupied with racial and social identity. Nor can she be easily categorized as a black or feminist writer: Kincaid does not feel the need to "delineate" her world "sociologically," wrote black studies scholar and critic Henry Louis Gates, Jr. "She never feels the necessity of claiming the existence of a black world or a female sensibility. She assumes them both." The ability to make this assumption marks a "distinct departure," in Gates's view, and he compared her to another writer, Toni Morrison, who also assumes her world. With writers like these, "we can get beyond the large theme of racism and get to deeper themes of how black people love and cry and live and die. Which, after all, is what art is all about."

While none of Kincaid's fiction is formally described as autobiographical, it seems clear that her three fictional works, when compared with stories Kincaid has told of herself in her journalism and interviews, are based on the personal odyssey of a girl who began life as Elaine Potter Richardson in 1949 on the tiny island of Antigua, a girl who adored her tall, beautiful, intelligent Dominican mother but who somehow lost that mother's love, a girl who left the Caribbean to work as an au pair for an American family, and who, nurtured by the anonymity and freedom of New York City in the 1970s, reinvented herself as the writer Jamaica Kincaid.

Autobiography is the only sort of writing that really interests Kincaid. Asked to discuss the extent to which her work is autobiographical, she said, "I started to write out of this need, I suppose, to settle demons and settle scores and all sorts of things. So . . . I'm driven to write, so it has to be autobiographical. . . . I don't have any other reason to write. I'm not interested in things for their own sake. I'm only interested in explaining something for myself." While Kincaid said that everything she writes is autobiographical, it is "also fiction. It wouldn't hold up in a court of law."

While the novel *Lucy* is based on Kincaid's first years in the United States, the experiences and emotions of a young West Indian woman living in the New York City of the 1970s are also explored in nonfictional form in an article entitled "Jamaica Kincaid's New York," published in *Rolling Stone* magazine. In both works there is a conscious sense of self-invention. In the *Rolling Stone* piece Kincaid wrote, "My mother sees my life in New York as turning against her.. . . She must know that I couldn't have lost one self and found another and still pass for a nonlunatic in any other place but New York." At the end of *Lucy* the young woman sees that despite the intense longing she feels for her mother and the life she has left behind, she is becoming someone new: "But the things I could not see about myself, the things I could not put my hands on—those things had changed, and I did not yet know them well. I understood that I was inventing myself, and that I was doing this more in the way of a painter than in the way of a scientist."

Kincaid's stepfather was a carpenter, and her mother kept house. As an only child, they young Kincaid felt happy and loved. But when she was nine, the first of her three brothers was born and her mother's attention seemed to shift. At the same time, the young girl became gradually aware of the islanders' subservience to the British, a status others seemed to accept. She began to be seen as a problem in school and, as punishment, was forced to memorize long chunks of John Milton's *Paradise Lost.* If her precocity got her into trouble with her teachers, it did not necessarily endear her to her fellow students: "I was very bright; I was always being made fun of for it."

The accounts of her childhood that Kincaid has given in interviews and articles are not only of conflict and loss, for they are intermixed with memories of a place whose natural beauty sometimes takes on a kind of spiritual quality and of a people who so fully accept and internalize this quality that they need not recognize it intellectually or label it. . . .

While Kincaid seems to suggest . . . that dwelling amid great natural beauty imparts a spiritual quality to life, she also sees, in a later work, that the same beauty can be a kind of "prison": "What might it do [to people] to live in such heightened, intense surroundings day after day?" One thing it might do, she speculates, is keep them trapped in the moment, never able to step back to analyze or shape their own experience and therefore seldom able to control it.

The Caribbean of Kincaid's childhood, as seen through her interviews and journalism, is not exclusively female. There are gentle portrayals of a carpenter-father (the island's "second-best"), his shop where "everything was some shade of brown," and his convalescence from a heart condition, which happened simultaneously with his daughter's recovery from a case of hookworm. The two invalids would lie on their backs on the parents' bed, their feet on the windowsill in the sun, until Kincaid's mother came in and asked them to take their feet off the windowsill, and "we would do it right away, but as soon as she left we would put them back." Kincaid's father (i.e., stepfather) talked to her about his own father's work on the Panama Canal—as a child Kincaid had the impression that her grandfather had built the canal more or less by himself—and about the Americans, or, as he called them, the "Yanks." Kincaid's stepfather, who had worked as a carpenter on an American base in Antigua during World War II and who enjoyed American movies such as the Bing Crosby and Bob Hope "Road" movies, would tell his daughter "how funny and great and attractive and smart Americans in general were. . . . At the end of every story about Americans . . . he would say, 'Oh, the Yanks are a crazy bunch, but they have ideas, and you can't stop a man when he has ideas.' But the thing my father said about Americans that made me love them the most was, 'The Yanks are great. Listen, if a Yank ever asks you if you can do something and you can't do it, don't say "No," say "I'll try."'"

Kincaid's childhood world is not, then, exclusively female, but it is predominantly so, as demonstrated by the opening sentence of one of her earliest pieces of fiction, a story called **"Antigua Crossings"**: "The Caribbean Sea is so big, and so blue, and so deep and so warm, and so unpredictable, and so inviting, and so dangerous, and so beautiful. This is exactly the way I feel about all the women in my own family."

One aspect of this unpredictability and danger was the women's practice of obeah, an African-rooted belief, similar to voodoo. For believers, Kincaid said, "everything has a life of its own, it's chaotic, it's subject to all sorts of laws. [That is] one of the beauties and one of the attractions, it is subject to laws that not everybody knows, so you can do something to someone because only you know how it works, and when you do it to them, only you know what it is you are doing. The person you are doing it to then has to find out how it works to counteract. It's a secret. It's never done out in the open."

Both Kincaid's mother and grandmother were believers in obeah. Kincaid's grandmother, like the grandmother in **Annie John,** was married to a Methodist minister and followed his faith for a time but reverted to a belief in obeah after her son died, apparently as a result of a magic spell. And the obeah worldview was a reality to Kincaid's

mother as well: "She lived in a really spooky place where the things you saw were not real. You'd see lights in the mountains at night and it wasn't a star, it was a jablesse [a person who can turn into anything]. . . . [She] did have this experience I've written about, of throwing the stones at the monkey that one day caught the stone and threw it back at her."

Obeah practice occasionally touched the lives of Kincaid and her brothers. Once, after a schoolyard confrontation, the mother of a schoolmate threatened to put a spell on Kincaid so that she would drown herself. Kincaid was sent to stay with her grandmother on Dominica, since "crossing seawater is always a good way to get rid of a curse; the evil spirits couldn't follow."

In the world of obeah, Kincaid said, life is lived in the subconscious: "Instead of going for an hour on the couch, your entire life was on the couch, a world of nervous breakdowns." And while she "hated the whole thing," with all its secrets and secret relationships, at the same time, she seemed to lament what she sees as its passing: "Now the layer of obeah life doesn't work any more, doesn't exist any more. . . . I think it has to do with television . . . that world which turns out to have been quite rich is lost. So rich in your imagination, and imagination led to worlds."

The practice of obeah suggested a hidden reality behind visible reality; a similar effect was achieved by the imperial presence of England, which continued in Antigua through Kincaid's childhood. From the "Made in England" stamp on the box of breakfast cocoa, to the requirement on every school exam to "draw a map of England," to the brown felt hat her father wore, in imitation of an Englishman and in disregard for the climate, England was held up to the Caribbean child as the "real" reality, even if not quite visible from where she stood. . . .

The children were drilled in English history, but this is not what had the greatest impact: "There were other views, subtler ones, softer, almost not there, but these softer views were the ones that made the most lasting impression on me, the ones that made me really feel like nothing." These could be conveyed through a phrase such as "when morning touched the sky" or "evening approaches," for "no morning touched the sky where I lived. The morning where I lived came on abruptly, with a shock of heat and loud noises. . . . Evenings where I lived did not approach; in fact, I had no evening—I had night and day, and they came and went in a mechanical way: on, off, on, off." The conclusion that a child drew from this contradiction was that "we must have done something to deserve" a world that so clearly was not what the world ought to be.

Although the colonial education was clearly designed, as Kincaid now sees it, to "erase" the reality of the colonial child, this design was not commonly perceived. Kincaid's mother was at that time in her life, Kincaid says, an "Anglophile" who strove to give her daughter a "middle-class

English upbringing." Everyone around Kincaid seemed to accept English domination, and the doctrine that a thing could be "divine and good only if it was English." Yet Kincaid could not help seeing the contradictions: "When I was nine, I refused to stand up at the refrain 'God Save Our King.' I hated 'Rule, Brittania'; and I used to say that we weren't Britons, we were slaves. I never had any idea why. I just thought that there was no sense to it."

In *Annie John,* the young protagonist has a daydream in which she imagines herself "living alone in Belgium, a place I had picked when I read in one of my books that Charlotte Brontë, the author of my favorite novel, *Jane Eyre,* had spent a year or so there." Not only would going to Belgium allow Annie to emulate her writer-heroine, but Belgium was such a distant and unknown place that her mother would never be able to find her. In reality, the young Elaine Potter Richardson went neither to Belgium nor England, but took the short plane ride to America. Here, less in emulation of Brontë than Jane Eyre, she would trace the unlikely trajectory from servitude and obscurity to prominence and power. . . .

With *Lucy,* as with all of Kincaid's work, it is impossible to separate fiction from life, and the book "upset some of Kincaid's friends and colleagues," apparently because the wealthy, troubled family in the book closely parallels that of the writer Michael Arlen, who employed Kincaid in real life and later became her colleague at the *New Yorker.* Of the complaint that Kincaid has used her former acquaintances and colleagues, Kincaid told an interviewer that "the only person in the book who is drawn directly from life is Lucy, the title character. The others are composites." But, Kincaid adds, "I would never say I wouldn't write about an experience I've had."

Kincaid's most recent work of fiction, *The Autobiography of My Mother* ("But it's not that," she said) is set in the West Indies and narrated by the same young woman who tells Kincaid's story **"Song of Roland."** This latter story, published in the *New Yorker* in the spring of 1993, was the first of Kincaid's fiction to explore the West Indies from an adult's point of view, rather than a child's. The Roland of the title is a stevedore for whom the narrator develops a passion: "I bathed my face then between his legs; he smelt of curry and onions, for those were the things he had been unloading all day; other times when I bathed my face between his legs—for I did it often, I liked doing it—he would smell of sugar, or flour, or the large, cheap bolts of cotton from which he would steal a few yards to give me to make a dress." Since Roland is married, the narrator also comes to know his wife, for, says the narrator, "I could not have loved Roland the way I did if he had not loved other women."

In her recent nonfiction, Kincaid has continued to explore the question of "domination" and the relationship between the powerful and the powerless. In the bitter essay **"On Seeing England for the First Time,"** Kincaid, as noted earlier, wrote of her childhood, in which "England was to be our source of myth and the source from which we got our sense of reality, our sense of what was meaningful, our sense of what was meaningless." The children were so imbued with an idea of England, Kincaid wrote, that a large space inevitably opened up between that idea and the reality of England. For Kincaid, the space "had become filled with hatred and so when at last I saw [England] I wanted to take it into my hands and tear it into little pieces." Since she could not do that, she could only "indulge in not-favorable opinions," and so she finds everything about England ugly and smelly. She understands that she may be "prejudiced," but she also recognizes to her despair that her prejudice cannot have the same impact upon the English as their prejudice had upon her: "My prejudices have no weight to them, my prejudices have no force behind them, my prejudices remain opinions, my prejudices remain my personal opinion. And a great feeling of rage and disappointment came over me as I looked at England, my head full of personal opinions that could not have public, my public, approval. The people I come from are powerless to do evil on a grand scale". . . .

Even in success, the sense of irreplaceable loss and mysterious, hidden betrayal that has permeated Kincaid's work is not wiped away. "I had crossed a line; but at whose expense? I cannot begin to look, because what if it is someone I know?"

TITLE COMMENTARY

AT THE BOTTOM OF THE RIVER (1983)

Kirkus Reviews

SOURCE: A review of *At the Bottom of the River,* in *Kirkus Reviews,* Vol. LI, No. 19, October 1, 1983, p. 1062.

These ten short pieces, some of which have appeared in *The New Yorker,* suffer from being grouped together in book form here: there's a blurry monotony in Kincaid's prose-poem style (lists, litanies, fragments) and a limited range of imagery in her existential monologues. Still, her first collection is flecked with individuality and talent—especially in the more ironic sequences. **"Girl"** is a three-page list of remembered instructions from a Caribbean childhood. ("Wash the white clothes on Monday and put them on the stone heap; . . . always eat your food in such a way that it won't turn someone else's stomach; on Sundays always try to walk like a lady and not like the slut you are so bent on becoming.") Several sketches deal with the narrator's fragmented, abstracted images of a beloved, overpowering mother, one who can even appear in dreamlike exaggeration ("Sometimes I cannot see from her breasts on up, so lost is she in the atmosphere"); and this passionate, ambivalent relationship is also linked, implicitly, to the narrator's childhood ambitions, her future roles as lover and mother. ("I shall grow up to be a tall, graceful, and altogether beautiful woman, and I shall impose on large numbers of people my will and also, for my own amusement, great pain . . . Now I am a girl, but one day I will marry a woman. . . . ") Far less distinctive, however, are Kincaid's adult-voiced meditations on existence, death, identity—with a few passages that read (unintentionally) like Woody Allen parodies of philosophy, and with the most familiar sort of inspirational/poetic grapplings: "In the light of the lamp, I see some books, I see a chair, I see a table, I see a pen; I see a bowl of ripe fruit, a bottle of milk, a flute made of wood, the clothes that I will wear. And as I see these things in the light of the lamp, all perishable and transient, how bound up I know I am to all that is human endeavor, to all that is past and to all that shall be. . . . " When least abstract, when least derivative (Gertrude Stein and Beckett are only two of the heavy shadows here), Kincaid shows vivid promise in this slim (80 pp.) debut; too often, unfortunately, her Caribbean/literary musings seem precious and repetitive.

Publishers Weekly

SOURCE: A review of *At the Bottom of the River*, in *Publishers Weekly*, Vol. 224, No. 16, October 14, 1983, p. 45.

The speaking voice and perceiving eye in these 10 short pieces, most of which first appeared in the *New Yorker*, belong to a nameless, undelineated girl of indeterminate age living at an unspecified time on some Caribbean island. "Pieces," that evasive, omnibus term, must apply here, for they elude any of the usual categories. There is no narrative, no story, few characters, not a hint of line, plot, sequence, complication or resolution. The young, tremulously sensitive, blossoming girl takes in the newly created world, seen as if for the first time, through her nerve endings—sun and moon, flowers and all growing things, still and running water, household objects, color and distances, the phases of time, herself as an object in nature, a mother cast in generalized mythic terms, a father dimly and fleetingly seen. The voice—incantatory, lyric, rhapsodic—is closer to the condition of poetry and music than to fiction in any of its ordinary registers. "I feel," she says at one point, "—oh, how I feel. I feel, I feel, I feel. I have no words right now for how I feel." And so it seems at times—the work of a truly gifted, risk-taking, original new writer (this is her first book) who hasn't yet quite found the words and modes best suited to her highly distinctive sensibilities.

The Horn Book

SOURCE: A review of *At the Bottom of the River*, in *The Horn Book*, Vol. LX, No. 1, February, 1984, p. 91.

Although the book jacket calls the ten selections stories, they might more accurately be called pieces. They read aloud beautifully as dramatic monologues; they resonate one with another as poems in a cycle sometimes will. The author writes about being a woman in a world of exquisite beauty and profound mystery. Although the stories are set in the Caribbean, they rely on the memory and interpretation of interior landscapes as well as of exterior ones and achieve a sense of magical universality. From the simple and funny first piece, **"Girl,"** in which a mother lists the rules by which her daughter must live, to the complex cycle-of-life idyll at the end, the author deals less with traditional narrative and exposition than she does with the portrayal of character and perception. Never named, her protagonists speak in the first person, ordering and cataloging the world with Whitmanesque attention to detail; they remember, they weep, they understand, they pause in bafflement. The book will serve as a bridge and an introduction to difficult writers like Virginia Woolf; being brief, it is easy to read without frustration. But the author will be remembered by both adults and young adults for her own words, for the gentle authority of her own voice: "I claim these things then—mine—and now feel myself grow solid and complete, my name filing up my mouth."

ANNIE JOHN (1985)

Kirkus Reviews

SOURCE: A review of *Annie John*, in *Kirkus Reviews*, Vol. LIII, No. 2, January 15, 1985, pp. 54-5.

Rarely does a writer move as surely forward as Kincaid does in this plain, sharp, affecting first novel—which abandons the mannerisms and pretensions that made her debut story-collection, *At the Bottom of the River,* so uneven and frustrating. In eight short autobiographical chapters (most of which originally appeared in *The New Yorker*), narrator Annie John traces her childhood on the island of Antigua from age ten to seventeen—with the emphasis always returning, quietly yet in a constant interplay of warmth and pain, to Annie's relationship with her regal, demanding mother. In "Figures in the Distance," Annie becomes aware of, then fascinated by, death and funerals—lingering at the funeral parlor when she should be picking up fish from the fisherman; still, though punished for her disobedience and her lies, Annie receives her good-night kiss as usual from her mother . . . so all is well. ("It was in such a paradise that I lived.") Soon, however, as Annie gets older, the world changes subtly yet terribly: "Because of this young-lady business, instead of days spent in perfect harmony with my mother, I trailing in her footsteps, she showering down on me her kisses and affection and attention, I was now sent off to learn one thing and another." The years that follow bring a series of tiny yet dreadful mother/daughter skirmishes—Mother's search for Annie's stash of forbidden marbles, Annie's escalating lies and thieveries, Mother's sarcastic accusations—while Annie finds substitutes for her paradise-lost in passionate friendships: soul-mateship with schoolmate Gwen; a fiercer relationship—"pinching by her, followed by tears from me, followed by kisses from her"—with the dirty, strong, secret "Red Girl." And finally, after Annie recovers from months of mysterious, paralyzing illness, she sets off for nursing school in England—dreading the future but determined to leave her present life ("I especially never wanted to lie in my bed and hear my mother gargling again"), still torn between love and hostility right up to the last minute on the deck of the ship. Poetic without a single intrusive image, emotional without a trace of hysteria, evocative without a bit of self-conscious exotica: a model, in fact, of selective, invisibly artful autobiographical fiction—truly capturing the agonizing give-and-take of parent/child love that goes delicately, yet irrevocably, awry. ("I could not be sure whether for the rest of my life I would be able to tell when it was really my mother and when it was really her shadow standing between me and the rest of the world.")

Publishers Weekly

SOURCE: A review of *Annie John*, in *Publishers Weekly*, Vol. 227, No. 7, February 15, 1985, p. 86.

In this tersely written yet lyrical novel, which fulfills the promise of the author's previous book, *At the Bottom of the River*, a girl growing up in Antigua is distressed and confounded by impending adulthood. Annie John's anxiety begins when she acknowledges mortality after one of her peers dies. Her emerging womanliness also unsettles Annie, as does the emotional seesaw of love and guilt that binds her to her mother. As Annie matures, the security she feels in her mother's all-enveloping love gives way to resentment toward the older woman's autocratic demands, which Annie fails to recognize as guidelines to usher her through adolescence. Annie seethes when informed by her mother that they should stop dressing identically, and she scoffs at the piano and etiquette lessons her mother insists upon. Distraught over an encroaching "future full of ridiculous demands," Annie becomes a delinquent. She plays marbles, a pastime her mother explicitly forbids; she lies and steals for her slovenly friend; she deliberately defaces a textbook. Eventually, Annie's turmoil overwhelms her, and she must decide how to relinquish childhood and accept responsibilities. Kincaid's depiction of Annie is astute and poignant. At the end of this brief, affecting tale, Annie is aboard the ship that will take her to nursing school in England—and, we hope, into another Kincaid novel.

Kathryn Dunn

SOURCE: A review of *Annie John*, in *School Library Journal*, Vol. 32, No. 1, August, 1985, p. 154.

Although this novel is set on the island of Antigua, Kincaid's theme of coming-of-age is universal. The summer that Annie John turned 12, her close relationship with her mother changed, becoming shattered almost beyond repair. Annie John becomes secretive and deceptive as she sees people and does things that she knows would elicit her mother's disapproval. Mistrust between mother and daughter grows; communication stops. Years later, when Annie John finishes school and is ready to leave home, her problems with her mother are still not completely resolved. Interspersed with the story of Annie John and her mother are typical events in her life—best friends at school, her first menstrual period. This is a finely crafted novel that allows readers to feel and recognize the pain that Annie John is growing through.

The Horn Book

SOURCE: A review of *Annie John*, in *The Horn Book*, Vol. LXIII, No. 1, January-February, 1987, p. 102.

The background—the island of Antigua in the Caribbean—is exotic to American readers, but the author does not describe it in great detail, as she clearly has other concerns on her mind. Episodic in structure, the book covers a broad age span, following Annie John from the age of ten to seventeen, when she leaves for England to study nursing. Kincaid is stressing the similarities between a black girl growing up in an isolated community with girls everywhere, so her approach is introspective and focuses on personal relationships: choosing a disreputable best friend, beginning the separation process from a beloved mother. Emotional recollection—sometimes so intense as to seem surrealistic—rather than sensory, physical recollection is the hallmark of this book.

Romi Natov

SOURCE: "Mothers and Daughters: Jamaica Kincaid's Pre-Oedipal Narrative," in *Children's Literature*, Vol. 18, 1990, pp. 1-3, 14.

[*Annie John* focuses] on the painful struggle to separate from the mother that characterizes early adolescence for many girls, Kincaid evokes with intensity the wrenching many of us shudder to remember.

The simple yet richly sensuous language, the emphasis on an adolescent's point of view, and the immediacy of the subject matter make *Annie John* an appealing book for adolescents. Perhaps because *Annie John* was not written specifically with a young adult audience in mind, it lacks the preciousness and the superficiality of many novels aimed at the young adult market. Often in the adolescent "problem novel," issues are raised and then hurriedly resolved. Characters and plot tend to be secondary, the narrative forced, and the characters one-dimensional. By contrast, *Annie John* is a fully developed psychological study. And perhaps because the work draws so heavily on autobiographical material, *Annie John* feels authentic. Annie, the young heroine, is honest and engaging; the portraits of her parents, based on Kincaid's own mother and father, are complex and convincing. They love their daughter, but they ultimately fail her, as we all were failed by the imperfections of our parents. And if we ourselves are parents, we are doomed to fail our children as well. Although the pain we cause (and were caused) obviously can be survived, the story of the severing of the parent-child bond, particularly from the standpoint of the adolescent, is often one of betrayal and anguish. . . .

Annie John begins with a death and ends with the promise of rebirth. From the initial image of a child dying in a mother's arms to the final image of a "vessel filled with liquid . . . placed on its side . . . slowly emptying out," *Annie John* chronicles the child's psychological journey away from the mother toward adulthood. In her close attention to the severing of this most primal bond between mother and daughter, Kincaid offers a kind of anatomy. . . .

Like the writings of other contemporary black women, particularly the work of Paule Marshall and Alice Walker, Jamaica Kincaid's fiction focuses on the importance of continuity and community as they are preserved and kept alive by mothers, through their stories and through their connection with their daughters. Even though the intimacy between mother and daughter threatens at times to devour the newly developing spirit of the adolescent girl, it is an essential and integral source of nourishment, based as it is on connection, fluidity, and mutuality. *Annie John* is the story of the passion and power of that bond.

A SMALL PLACE (1988)

Kirkus Reviews

SOURCE: A review of *A Small Place,* in *Kirkus Reviews,* Vol. LVI, No. 9, May 1, 1988, pp. 671-72.

In a book as brief (96 pages), swift, and stinging as a viper's strike, Kincaid makes her nonfiction debut by turning her astonishing talents—seen in a short-story collection and a novel—to a subject that eats like salt at her wounded heart: the rape by white tourists of her native land, Antigua.

It's at these interlopers that Kincaid spits her lovely venom, adopting the rare second-person narrative form: "If you go to Antigua as a tourist," she begins, "this is what you will see." What she reveals is a land of ungodly natural beauty ("no real seawater could strike that many shades of blue at once . . . no real cloud could be that white"), external oppression and of an internal corruption, legacy of colonialisms, wherein, as everyone knows, "People close to the Prime Minister openly run one of the largest houses of prostitution" and "it is not a secret that a minister is involved in drug trafficking." For Kincaid, a prime symbol of the suffering is Antigua's public library, once housed in "a big, old wooden building painted a shade of yellow" and now, after the 1972 earthquake, housed in a "dung heap" above a dry-goods store;

meanwhile, native Antiguans wait for white members of the exclusive Mill Reef Club to decide whether to offer money to restore the old building. Kincaid rages not only at the library's fate, but at "what sort of place has Antigua become that the people from the Mill Reef Club are allowed a say in anything?" For are they not descendants of the "human rubbish" that colonized the land, and cousins of you, a tourist, "an ugly, empty thing, a stupid thing . . . pausing here and there to gaze at this and taste that . . . "?

At turns elegaic and vicious, self-pitying and proud, this electrifying work is a new classic in the literature of hate—and of love, for a tortured land and for the possibility, albeit dim, of changing things: "once you cease to be a master, once you throw off your master's yoke, you are no longer human rubbish, you are just a human being, and all the things that adds up to."

John Brosnahan

SOURCE: A review of *A Small Place,* in *Booklist,* Vol. 84, No. 20, June 15, 1988, p. 1706.

It is not with nostalgia but deep bitterness that Kincaid travels back in history and into her own past to address the current conditions in Antigua, the Caribbean island of her birth and childhood and the setting for her memorable novel *Annie John.* Since Antigua gained its independence from British rule in 1971, the local government has moved very slowly in promoting the livelihood and living conditions of its citizens. Those in power and the former colonialists, however, have prospered, and it is the dramatic contrast between haves and have-nots that Kincaid exposes in her trip back home. The book reveals what most white tourists would never see: latent discontent bubbling beneath the picturesque tropical surface, a blend of economic distress and new, more subtle racial tensions experienced by black residents in a highly volatile fashion. A bleak travelogue fueled by fire, passion, and love.

Paul Stuewe

SOURCE: A review of *A Small Place,* in *Quill and Quire,* Vol. 54, No. 10, October, 1988, p. 26.

A Small Place reads like a cross between a 1960s New Left tirade and a travel article, and the results are definitely small beer indeed. In meditating on why independence has done little to improve the quality of life in her native Antigua, Kincaid demonstrates little more than a pronounced ability to complain about—but by no means explain—history's unfair treatment of the island's black citizens. While understanding her sense of injustice, even the most sympathetic reader will likely conclude that her directionless discontents are part of the problem rather than a contribution to its solution. Although a decent piece of periodical journalism might possibly be quarried from *A Small Place,* its embarrassingly slight musings have no business appearing in book form.

Isabel Fonseca

SOURCE: "Their Island Story," in *Times Literary Supplement,* No. 4476, January 14, 1989, p. 30.

In a short book whose style owes more to the manifesto than the essay, Jamaica Kincaid condemns her native Antigua's tragic development, from its colonial past to the new tourism which has replaced it and which she sees, alarmingly, as identical.

Christopher Columbus discovered Antigua in 1493, and shortly thereafter the nine-by-twelve-mile island was settled in the usual ghoulish manner "by human rubbish from Europe". Kincaid asks us to question "why it is that all people like me seem to have learned from you is how to imprison and murder each other, how to govern badly, and how to take the wealth of our country and place it in Swiss bank accounts?" Unfortunately, she does not offer any explanation except to say that it is "mostly your fault". And now, in a perverse homage to the former power, the ruling élite has invited in a new species of "imperialist", the tourist—"an ugly human being from America (or worse, Europe)".

Kincaid's (laudable) purpose is to make the readers of this grisly tale as uncomfortable as possible. Her shrill, radically subjective method, however, serves only to alienate. She buries Antigua's sad and familiar story in a graveyard of clichés (for "only a cliché can explain you") and the result is a deadened and dogmatic prose which tells all but reveals little. Antigua is presented as a generic outpost of colonial memory. It is true that Antigua, like all of the Caribbean islands, has for centuries always been fought over and owned by foreign powers. What Kincaid does not say is that for more than twenty-five years Antigua, along with its own dependencies, Redonda and Barbuda, has had full internal self-government and the right to opt for full independence at any time without reference to—permission from—the British Government. Nor does she discuss what is probably a greater source of misery to the Antiguan people than a colonial past or a dependency on tourism: the fact that Antigua, unlike the other Leeward Islands, has no rivers. Rainfall is slight and the island suffers from severe droughts and, in turn, severe deforestation.

No one would question the gist of the story as Kincaid tells it. Who could doubt her when she says—or her propriety in saying—that "nothing can erase my rage—not an apology, not a large sum of money, not the death of a criminal—for this wrong can never be made right". More dubious, perhaps, is her characterization of all visitors to Antigua as stingy, incurious and contemptuous (not to mention "incredibly unattractive, fat and pastry-like fleshed"). Her idea of contemporary Britain is of a nation of retired officers, lamenting the lost empire: "the English have become such a pitiful lot these days, with hardly any idea what to do with themselves now that they no longer have one quarter of the earth's population bowing and scraping before them. They . . . should, at

least, be wearing sackcloth in token penance for wrongs committed. . . . " The force of her argument is further undercut by a curiously wilful scrappiness about such things as, for example, the food an overfed tourist might eat, which is supposed to convey the pervasive corruption of the island in a single bite: "A good guess is that it came from a place like Antigua first, where it was grown dirt cheap, went to Miami, and came back. There is a world of something in this, but I can't go into it right now." Her savage tone is also diffused by the shapelessness of the essay: she shifts from an attack on the Swiss (which they earn partly for being so clean and partly for harbouring blood-money), to rambling reminiscences of her childhood, notably of happy days spent stealing from the now destroyed public library ("once I had read a book I couldn't bear to part with it"). The book is full of inconsequential anecdote and *non sequitur.* It is hard, for example, to grasp why the library, which she remembers as the place where "you distorted and erased my history and glorified your own", should, more than any other place, come to symbolize her beloved "old Antigua".

Kincaid's disregard for both her reader and her subjects suggest that her central purpose in *A Small Place* is not illumination, but something more personal. She is trying, from her adopted home in the place most unlike Antigua except in size (the cold New England state of Vermont), to "work through her rage". However satisfying it may be for the writer, rage seems an ill-chosen idiom for the expression of anything one really wants to make understood—like the letters that one writes but should never send.

Gary Boire

SOURCE: A review of *A Small Place,* in *Canadian Literature,* Vol. 128, Spring, 1991, pp. 141-43.

Disquiet . . . is the primary and lethal effect of Jamaica Kincaid's all-too-brief *A Small Place.* This is a short, sad, and extraordinarily angry book that lobotomizes the touristic mindset of depoliticized readers. The perfect antidote to Cruise Brochures, *A Small Place* speaks about Antigua from within a context similar to that of Derek Walcott or George Lamming.

Kincaid addresses the peculiarly Caribbean aspects of decolonizing readers and writers; that is, how do you create a text that (1) resists economic and cultural imperialism; (2) seeks to dismantle a culture's self-representations as both delusive and mystifying; but (3) recognizes that these representations fulfil crucial economic and psychic desires of both local and overseas interests? More specifically, how do you convince European and/or North American readers (read maggot-white winter sunseekers) that their paradisical "getaway spot" is a third world ghetto? Worse, a ghetto that their culture and their own tourism has selfishly created and sustained through various shadings of historical, economic, and political imperialisms? The project is fraught with writerly risks from the outset; most liberal readers, after all, don't like to be caught with their politically-correct designer-swimwear down around their ankles.

A Small Place, in other words, is an intensely irritating and incontrovertibly honest book. Kincaid parodically appropriates that grand expansionist mode—the travel essay—for her own purposes of deconstructive "re-misprision"; throughout she exposes and re-exposes the more fungoid substructures that underlie those sustained images of blue lagoons and happy rhythm-laden natives. Behind the guise of a dispassionate travel reporter her narrator coolly itemizes corruptions in Antiguan political circles, examples of touristic ignorance, and specific forms of historical and economic exploitation. As in Findley's *The Wars,* Kincaid subtly deploys the open-endedness of that maddening word, "you", thus continually manipulating her readers into either complicity or hypocritical disgust. Unsympathetic readers will rightly foreground Kincaid's shrill arrogance—a kind of perverse Parnassian sneer against anyone unlucky enough to be a non-Antiguan and/or unwise enough to ever have been a tourist. But such a response would be unfair because partial. Despite its tonal or attitudinal coarseness, its pervasive self-righteousness, and Kincaid's own bizarre (and delusive) denial of self-implication, *A Small Place* is an important and sophisticated irony: a small hit of counter-power, delivered in a deceptively pedestrian idiom against a deceptively benign antagonist.

LUCY (1990)

Publishers Weekly

SOURCE: A review of *Lucy,* in *Publishers Weekly,* Vol. 237, No. 33, August 17, 1990, p. 50.

Kincaid has with this novel created an insouciant yet vulnerable narrator in the person of Lucy, a teenage girl from the West Indies who works as an au pair for a seemingly happy family in an unidentified city that one assumes is New York. Lucy is fascinated with her discoveries about American life—"At first it was all so new that I had to smile with my mouth turned down at the corners"—and with Mariah, Lewis and their four golden little daughters. Their pleasures in life intrigues Lucy, who observes, "Even when a little rain fell, they would admire the way it streaked through the blank air." Lucy has renounced her own family and past, but at the same time she paradoxically expresses culturally imbued views with arrogance. She sees the world around her with both awe and contempt, and maintains a unique dead certainty about how people are. Her own sexual exploits seem more mysterious to her than the deterioration of Lewis and Mariah's marriage, which she presciently and detachedly observes. This is a slim book but Kincaid has crafted it with a spare elegance that has brilliance in its very simplicity. Lucy's is a haunting voice, and Kincaid's originality has never been more evident.

Donna Seaman

SOURCE: A review of *Lucy,* in *Booklist,* Vol. 87, No. 3, October 1, 1990, p. 203.

Lucy Josephine Potter, 19, has left her home on Antigua for life as an au pair in a northern city, determined never to return. She is angry and unforgiving, slow to warm to her genuinely friendly and generous employer and the cold, alien environment. Lucy is critical and clinical, observing the failings of people and trying to "invent" herself. She explores sexuality, discovers the alchemy of photography, and watches the disintegration of her employer's marriage. Gradually, the source of her bitterness emerges—her intense relationship with her mother and her resentment at never having her intelligence recognized and encouraged, never being seen as an equal to her brothers. And it goes beyond that: Lucy is angry about racism, colonialism, about having to come to the U.S. as a servant. She is stunningly frank and indomitable, firmly following her path to wisdom. Kincaid continues to hone the poetic style of her acclaimed novel *Annie John.* Her prose is sensual, surprising, vibrant, and candid. Her characters are deep wells of emotions that we can draw from again and again.

THE AUTOBIOGRAPHY OF MY MOTHER (1995)

Publishers Weekly

SOURCE: A review of *The Autobiography of My Mother,* in *Publishers Weekly,* Vol. 242, No. 41, October 9, 1995, p. 75.

Kincaid's third novel is presented as the mesmerizing, harrowing, richly metaphorical autobiography of 70-year-old Xuela Claudette Richardson. Earthy, intractably antisocial, acridly introspective, morbidly obsessed with history and identity, conquest and colonialism, language and silence, Xuela recounts her life on the island of Dominica in the West Indies. In Kincaid's characteristically lucid, singsong prose, Xuela traces her evolution from a young girl to an old woman while interrogating the mysteries of her hybrid cultural origins and her parents, who failed to be parents: her mother died during childbirth; her often absent father, a cruel and petty island official, cultivates a veneer of respectability ("another skin over his real skin"), rendering him unrecognizable to his daughter. At 14, Xuela undertakes an affair with one of her father's friends, becomes pregnant and aborts the child. Experiencing that trauma as a rebirth ("I was a new person then"), she inaugurates a life of deliberate infertility, eventually becoming the assistant to a European doctor, whom she later marries. Xuela's Dominica, two generations after slavery, is a "false paradise" of reckless fathers and barren matrilinear relations, of tropical ferment, fecundity, witchcraft and slums, whose denizens resemble the walking dead. With aphoristic solemnity at times evocative of Ecclesiastes, Kincaid explores the full paradoxes of this extraordinary story, which, Xuela concludes, is at once the testament of the mother she never knew, of the mother she never allowed herself to be and of the children she refused to have.

Hazel Rochman

SOURCE: A review of *The Autobiography of My Mother,* in *Booklist,* Vol. 92, No. 7, December 1, 1995, p. 587.

The rage of Kincaid's essay *A Small Place* (1988) is distilled here into a novel of contained fury. A Caribbean woman tells of her search for identity in a wasteland destroyed by conquest and slavery. Her mother was Carib, one of the last remnants of a vanishing people ("My mother had died when I was born, unable to protect herself in a world cruel beyond ordinary imagining, unable to protect me"). Her father is part African, part Irish, corrupt and powerful; he doesn't love his daughter. She's without family, country, landscape, religion. Home is danger and treachery. History is defeat; it has left her people forever foreign, marginalized, other. And history cannot be overcome ("I then and now had and have no use for redemption." Alone, she's the archetypal hero whose search for her mother leads her to discover herself. She begins with her body, which she loves in all its sensuality, and she fuses the erotic with the deliberate conscious knowledge of who she is as an individual person, separate from any group or nation. Kincaid's language is stark, nearly monosyllabic, as the narrator makes herself in flesh and mind. The word not is used over and over like a beating echo for what is lost ("It was not nothing"). Absence is palpable. The sentences twist and turn with surprise and bitterness. More argument than novel, it's the drama of the personal voice that makes it a spellbinding narrative. Not innocent, not reverential, this disturbing story is lyrical, brave, defiant.

Doris Hiatt

SOURCE: A review of *The Autobiography of My Mother,* in *Kliatt,* Vol. 31, No. 2, March, 1997, p. 10.

This beautifully written, harrowing novel takes place on a small Caribbean island, Dominica. The narrator, Xuela Claudette Richardson, is the daughter of a father who is part African, part Irish, and a mother (who died while giving birth to Xuela) who was Carib, a small, little-respected minority. Xuela is unloved (her father deposits the newborn with the woman who does his laundry). He is a corrupt policeman who later marries and has another family.

This story of Xuela's childhood, her work, her sexual experiences, and her alienation seems more essay in mood than fiction. It is a dark tale of abandonment, of separateness. Xuela desires no children of her own and makes sure that she cannot have any. She marries an English doctor who loves her but for whom she has no love, and she has one lover for a brief time who is able to arouse her emotionally.

The author, herself born on the Caribbean island of Antigua, powerfully defines the differences between black and white, love and indifference, and the meaning of colonialism, all done subtly but powerfully.

MY BROTHER: A MEMOIR (1997)

Publishers Weekly

SOURCE: A review of *My Brother: A Memoir,* in *Publishers Weekly,* Vol. 244, No. 32, August 4, 1997, p. 53.

"I became a writer out of desperation, so when I first heard my brother was dying I was familiar with the act of saving myself: I would write about him." The result of Kincaid's self-preserving urge is a memoir that has less to do with her AIDS-afflicted, Rastafarian brother (whom she knew only slightly as an adult) than with recent visits to her native Antigua during which she helped her mother nurse him. It will surprise none of Kincaid's devotees that the memoir's dominant tone is measured rage, an attitude toward her family so passionate that it can make you wince. It's still shocking to read a middle-aged woman claim that she and her mother hate each other. And yet Kincaid is one of our preeminent prose stylists. Her exasperations, furies and regrets fall out with all the naturalness of spoken observations on the weather ("for young people are always beautiful until they are not, until they just are not") and sound just as believable. Although this memoir contains very little public grieving of the balled-handkerchief sort (Kincaid reserves that for her father-in-law and former editor at the New Yorker, the recently deceased William Shawn), it is all the more poignant for its austerity—and if it has "saved" Kincaid, it has also preserved her troubling, troubled family more credibly than perhaps any gentler book could have done.

Kirkus Reviews

SOURCE: A review of *My Brother: A Memoir,* in *Kirkus Reviews,* Vol. LXV, No. 16, August 15, 1997, p. 1279.

The death of Kincaid's brother from AIDS results in a book that is lyrically beautiful and emotionally forceful, but lacking a deep examination of its many themes.

Writing only a year after the death of her brother, Kincaid uses the event to reexplore issues that permeate her novels and other writings: family, race, and migration. *My Brother*'s flowing, stream-of-consciousness prose pulls readers along through the range of psychological changes Kincaid experiences as she grapples with her loss. From birth, Kincaid's brother Devon had been a source of trouble for the family: committing crimes, taking drugs, and being sexually promiscuous. The contrast between what her brother is at the time of his death (an unrepentant and fated man living in their native Antigua) and what Kincaid has become (a famous writer living in the US) paints a poignant tableau of sibling difference. What is most important here is the precariously complex and often emotionally violent relationships within families. At the forefront is the mother, a figure Kincaid finds herself unwillingly forced to wrestle with again as she attempts to care for the brother she left behind years ago. Distance is what pervades this world: distance from family, from one's origins, from understanding (it is not until after Devon dies that Jamaica learns of his homosexuality). The death of Devon and Kincaid's return to Antigua serve as metaphors for her belief that redemption and escape are finally impossible. But these ideas and the range of others Kincaid touches upon remain underdeveloped throughout the book.

Kincaid states, "These are my thoughts on his dying," and reveals the book's flaw: *My Brother* is a tirade of depression and confusion that fails to make sense of the maelstrom.

Donna Seaman

SOURCE: A review of *My Brother: A Memoir,* in *Booklist,* Vol. 94, No. 1, September 1, 1997, p. 5.

Kincaid's fiction seethes with an anger that not even the most gifted of novelists, herself included, can invent. The struggles over questions of identity and freedom her characters experience do, indeed, turn out to be variations of aspects of Kincaid's life, and the source of her rage—the trying circumstances of her youth and her mother's volatility and psychological ruthlessness—are finally disclosed in all their complexity and confusion in this unflinching memoir chronicling her youngest brother's death from AIDs. Kincaid hardly knew Devon. She was 13 when he was born, and he was only 3 when she left Antigua for good. She and Devon were essentially out of touch for decades, but as soon as he became ill and was hospitalized, Kincaid rushed to his side. She was able to make his last days comfortable and hope-filled by dint of her spontaneous and unexpected affection and, more practically, her ability to secure AZT, a drug not available on the island. Kincaid tells Devon's shadowy story and presents the hard facts about her adversarial relationship with her mother in language as solid and deliberately placed as smooth stones in a walkway. Circular and chantlike, her haunting tale is punctuated with recurrent mantras, especially the blunt admission, "I do not know." Honest, unapologetic, and pure, this is an eloquent and searching elegy for the dead and a prayer of thankfulness for the living.

MY FAVORITE PLANT: WRITERS AND GARDENERS ON THE PLANTS THEY LOVE (edited by Kincaid, 1998)

Alice Joyce

SOURCE: A review of *My Favorite Plant: Writers and Gardeners on the Plants They Love,* in *Booklist,* Vol. 94, No. 22, August, 1998, p. 1946.

It seems like everyone is gardening these days. After reading Kincaid's introduction to this enchanting anthology, it is readily apparent that the celebrated writer, for one, is utterly fascinated by the exhilarating enterprise of cultivating her own special landscape. Kincaid's fascinating compilation gives readers insight into which plants have stirred feelings of accomplishment, yearning, or sweet contentment in the hearts and minds of such notables as Colette, D. H. Lawrence, and William Carlos Williams, revealing their poetic ruminations on lilies, purple anemones, and Queen Anne's lace. In a more contemporary vein, Kincaid includes the delightfully entertaining musings of eminent individuals currently associated with the gardening world. Michael Pollan, Daniel Hinkley, and Nancy Goodwin are represented among the engaging essays and poems matching historical figures of some renown and today's gardening greats with their favorite flora.

Publishers Weekly

SOURCE: A review of *My Favorite Plant: Writers and Gardeners on the Plants They Love,* in *Publishers Weekly,* Vol. 245, No. 35, August 31, 1998, p. 57.

Author and gardener Kincaid believes that "[m]emory is a gardener's real palette . . . as it summons up the past . . . shapes the present . . . [and] dictates the future." For many, specific plants evoke specific memories; gathering 35 brief essays and poems that have been written throughout this century, Kincaid has compiled a bouquet of these plants and their corresponding memories. In "Lily," Colette remembers placing the eponymous white flowers around a statue of Mary, who "would be brushing, with the tips of her dangling fingers, the long, half-open cayman jaws of a lily at her feet." Czech writer Karol Capek writes in "Buds," published in 1929, that for him, even if he went out into the country, he would "see less of the spring than if I sat in my little garden" in Prague. Poet Maxine Kumin shares her appreciation of non-flowering plants and confesses that "nothing looks prettier to me than a well-tended flourishing vegetable garden." Ian Frazier, in "Memories of a Press-Gang Gardener," divulges how, after years of weeding gardens in his suburban childhood, he came to appreciate the activity, and when visiting "gardening friends . . . ask[s] what weeding needs to be done." In one of the strongest entries, "Marigold," Hilton Als admits hating that flower. During one childhood summer when his mother was ill, he recalls, he ate dirt from the marigold bed, to which his father devoted all his attention, and developed ringworm. Kincaid hopes that readers will draw some satisfaction from this collection, because a "garden, no matter how good it is, must never completely satisfy." In this she has succeeded, by presenting a book that is often beautiful, though some of its parts are not as radiant as others, and a few have yet to blossom.

Kirkus Reviews

SOURCE: A review of *My Favorite Plant: Writers and Gardeners on the Plants They Love,* in *Kirkus Reviews,* Vol. LXVI, No. 18, September 15, 1998, p. 1374.

Kincaid has assembled an impressively varied collection of essays by writers living and dead concentrating on the plants that hold a special, often almost mystical, attraction for them. These pieces are united not only by the writers' devotion to the challenges and (sometimes very subtle) rewards of some one particular species, but by the overriding emotion here: love. The Czech playwright and novelist Karel Capek celebrates the "mysterious 'Now!' of a garden," the moment unseen when buds emerge into bloom. Thomas Cooper, the editor of *Horticulture* magazine, celebrates the resilient geraniums, "one of the quintessential garden plants." Michael Pox's essay on "My Grandmother and Her Peonies" strikes a note frequently repeated in the collection: many of the plants that a gardener considers favorites have that status in part because they are entwined with the memories of those one has loved. Every garden is, in its way, a garden of memories. Kincaid nicely balances the collection between the more down-to-earth musings of horticultural writers (Graham Thomas on carnations, Ernest Wilson on the Silver tree, Katherine White on irises) and essays by writers far better known for their work in other genres (Marina Warner on roses, D. H. Lawrence on cyclamens, Elaine Scarry on columbines). An ingenious, varied, and pleasurable collection, certain to strike sparks of recognition in even the most modest gardener.

Additional coverage of Kincaid's life and career is contained in the following sources published by The Gale Group: *Authors and Artists for Young Adults,* **Vol. 13;** *Black Literature Criticism;* *Black Writers,* **Vol. 2;** *Contemporary Authors,* **Vol. 125;** *Contemporary Authors New Revision Series,* **Vols. 47, 59;** *Contemporary Literature Criticism,* **Vols. 43, 68;** *Dictionary of Literary Biography,* **Vol. 157; and** *Major Authors and Illustrators for Children and Young Adults 2.*

Marjorie Kinnan Rawlings

1896-1953

American author of fiction and nonfiction books.

Major works include *South Moon Under* (1933), *The Yearling* (1938), *Cross Creek* (1942), *The Secret River* (1955), *Short Stories by Marjorie Kinnan Rawlings* (1994).

INTRODUCTION

Author of the classic *The Yearling,* Rawlings is considered one of the leading regional writers of American literature. Writing in the *Dictionary of Literary Biography,* Victor Lasseter asserted that she "belongs to the tradition of such writers as John Steinbeck, Eudora Welty, and William Faulkner." Most of Rawlings's novels and short stories—and all of her most highly acclaimed works—are set in the scrub wilderness of northern Florida, where she made her home for more than half her life. Critics have focused most of their praise on Rawlings's sensitivity in depicting the landscape, flora, and fauna of the Florida bush, and her lively portrayals of the Florida "crackers," the poor rural whites who scraped out a living from the scrub.

In the 1930s and 1940s, Rawlings conducted research for her writings by living with rural families and joining them in the seasonal rounds of hunting, fishing, and moonshining. She gathered their stories and experiences and wrote her stories and novels in the dialect of the people of rural Florida, capturing both their speech patterns and their folk wisdom. Margaret Gillis Figh noted, "Her use of superstitions, sayings, and similes in the native vernacular has aided greatly in making it possible for Mrs. Rawlings to create a picture of [the 'cracker's'] everyday life and to reveal its significances. By this means she has portrayed both his stoical fatalism and his earthy humor, which enlivens even the grimmest poverty." Rawlings peopled her stories and novels with families living on the very edge of starvation, fighting the rough wilderness for what they needed to survive. Her characters are generally portrayed without sentimentality; they are complex individuals with strengths and weaknesses, who are at times serious and driven and at times joyful and lighthearted. But the people Rawlings writes of are most interesting for how they fit into their natural environment. The rural folk treat the natural world sometimes as an adversary, and sometimes as a healer and friend. Gordon E. Bigelow wrote that Rawlings believed "that a man can be happy only in the degree to which he is able to adjust harmoniously to his surroundings. The more natural those surroundings, and the more completely he is in harmony with them, the greater will be his happiness." For her, the Florida scrub and its inhabitants were intimately entwined, reaching a

balance quite apart from the rest of the world. Her writings reflect both her fascination and her respect for the people of the Florida hammocks, swamps, and scrub woods, interests which found their literary pinnacle in *The Yearling.*

Biographical Information

Rawlings was born and raised in Washington, D.C., but her love of nature and the rural life was shaped by childhood summers spent on family-owned farms in Maryland and Michigan. She was just seventeen years old when her father died, bringing her idyllic childhood to a close. Rawlings developed an interest in writing as a young child, winning a *Washington Post* short story contest at just eleven years old. She attended the University of Wisconsin at Madison, and upon her graduation in 1918 she moved to New York City; there she married Chuck Rawlings, a fellow writer. The couple moved first to Louisville and then to Rochester, New York, where Rawlings contributed to the *Times-Union* newspaper and had her own syndicated column, "Songs of the Housewife." In 1928 the couple took a vacation in northern Florida and fell in love with the area. Rawlings took the money left to her by her mother and invested in a seventy-acre orange grove and modest house at Cross Creek, southeast of Gainesville. Although she had written stories before, Rawlings was not successful at publishing her work. With the move to Florida, she found her ideal subject—the people and land of the scrub. Her first story from Florida, "Cracker Chidlings," was published in *Scribner's* magazine in March, 1930.

Rawlings, who was divorced from her husband in 1933, kept writing about the Cross Creek wilderness until she married Norton Sanford Baskin and moved to St. Augustine in 1941. Rawlings's failing health, complicated by heavy drinking, resulted in little publishable material from the last years of her life. She died in 1953 of a brain aneurysm.

Major Works

The one work for which Rawlings is best known is *The Yearling*, a novel that has been compared to Mark Twain's *The Adventures of Huckleberry Finn* and Rudyard Kipling's *Kim*. Protagonist Jody Baxter is twelve years old and the only surviving child of Penny and Ma; the little family must struggle to survive in the Florida wilderness of the post-Civil War era. Penny is a sensitive father and an excellent woodsman, and he brings Jody up to be attuned to the natural world and to face up to the hardships of their particularly difficult life. Ma is humorless and stern, made cold by all her years of hard work with little reward. Jody himself is dreamy, and although he accepts responsibility—helping in the garden, fishing or hunting with his father—he sometimes wanders off to play. *The Yearling* traces Jody's transition from boyhood to adulthood over the course of one extraordinary year. Jody and Penny hunt Old Slewfoot the bear, who preys on the Baxter's stock; during the hunt, Old Julia the hound is badly injured by the bear. And Jody is introduced to death when his crippled young neighbor and friend, Fodderwing, dies—Jody sits with his body through the night until his funeral the next day. A terrible flood ruins the crops the family relies on and is followed by a plague that kills wildlife and stock alike. But Jody's world also contains great beauty: he and his father witness the elaborate and mysterious mating dance of the whooping cranes, and the surrounding woods offer places of endless discovery for the boy. When his father shoots a doe leaving a motherless faun, Jody adopts the newborn as a pet, naming him Flag. He and the deer frolic together, sleep together, and share Jody's food. Jody loves the faun more deeply than he has ever loved anything, and though he tries to keep the deer out of trouble—and away from the life-sustaining corn crop—the climax of the book is inevitable. When Flag destroys the new corn a second time, Penny insists that the faun must be killed. The man is confined to his bed with a near-fatal rattlesnake bite, and Jody himself must shoot his pet. The moment is a defining one for the

boy, who briefly runs away only to return ready to face manhood. The book has touched millions of readers over several generations, and its status as a classic seems secure.

Rawlings wrote only one book specifically for children, *The Secret River*, published posthumously. In this simple story young Calpurnia journeys into the Florida scrub to try to find fish to help her family, fallen on hard times due to a shortage of fish. Deep in the forest the girl finds a beautiful river filled with catfish. She catches many of the fish, and brings them back to her family and community. She saves the day but is told by the wisest woman in the woods that she will never be able to physically return to the river, but that it will always be in her imagination.

Among Rawlings's other works are the novel *South Moon Under*, the semi-autobiographical *Cross Creek*, and a collection of short stories. *South Moon Under* tells the story of three generations of the Lantry family living in the scrub lands of northern Florida. The elder Lantry, after killing a government revenue agent, moved his family into the scrub from a settlement across the river; he resists civilization in order to be protected by the wilderness. The cycle is repeated when his grandson Lant kills the cousin who betrayed him and the young man thus exiles himself again to the scrub. Rawlings, who did extensive research for the novel, wrote of the family fishing, hunting, making moonshine, and eking out a living from the poor land. The Lantrys are completely outside of civilization, living by their own rules within the wilderness cycle. While Rawlings never lived completely as a "cracker," she did record her experiences with the people of the Florida wilderness in *Cross Creek*. Critics have compared *Cross Creek*, published in 1942, with Thoreau's *Walden*; both are autobiographical writings about withdrawing from society to live a rural, natural life. Rawlings's is the account of moving to the Florida scrub from Rochester, New York. In her new home she learns the novel flora and fauna, rebuilds her orange groves, and—most important for the author—she studies her neighbors to learn their habits, their lore, and their language. *Short Stories by Marjorie Kinnan Rawlings* includes many of the stories the author published in *Scribner's* and *Harper's*. These stories, too, focus on the Florida "cracker": they involve superstitions of the scrub families, adventures with alligators and "varmints," and the illegal attractions of moonshine. One story included in the collection is "Gal Young 'Un," about a widowed woman who marries Matt, a young man with questionable intentions. Soon after marrying, Matt sets up a still on the woman's property and brings a young mistress home with him, revealing himself as a gold digger and a scoundrel. Others of Rawlings's stories are more humorous, but nearly all are about the hard scrabble lives of the Florida settlers.

Awards

Rawlings won the Pulitzer Prize for fiction in 1939, for *The Yearling*. She also received two O. Henry Memorial awards for her short stories "Gal Young 'Un" and "Black Secret;" *The Secret River* was a Newbery Medal Honor Book in 1956.

AUTHOR'S COMMENTARY

Marjorie Kinnan Rawlings

SOURCE: "The Letters," in *Selected Letters of Marjorie Kinnan Rawlings,* edited by Gordon E. Bigelow and Laura V. Monti, University Presses of Florida, 1983, pp. 56-9.

Cross Creek
Hawthorne, Route 1
Florida

November 18, 1932

Dear Mr. Perkins:

I was bullying my husband last night into reading some of my chapters of **South Moon Under** as I worked on them. He threw down the manuscript and said, "I'm going to make a suggestion that will infuriate you, and I'm possibly wrong about it. Take out all your profanity. If you do this, you automatically open up a wide and continuous market for the book *among boys,* entirely distinct, an accidental by-product, from your mature appeal."

Of course, I was as shocked as if he'd suggested that I sell myself into slavery. I remember, out of the red fog that enveloped me, remarking caustically that possibly the book could become the first of a series, "The Rover Boys in Florida." I remember being soothed with copious draughts of native rye. When I came to, he went on to explain that he meant nothing of the sort. He said that the book, as an accurate picture of one of the last strips of American frontier, contains so much woods and river lore that would appeal to boys in the way *Huckleberry Finn, Treasure Island,* and some of Kipling, appeal to them, that it was a pity to cut off the book from such a group by what he considers the casual excrudescence [*sic*] of the profanity of Lant. He didn't mean, he said, to impugn the artistic quality of the book at all; that far greater, more artistic and mature books than I will ever write, happen here and there to contain a picture or a quality that makes boys devour them ignoring the mature angle altogether. Then I remembered your speaking of *Huckleberry Finn* in connection with the possibilities you saw in the river chapter, and I am ready to admit there may be something in the idea.

It sounds like an affectation to say that I don't particularly care whether or not the book sells. I just happen to mean it. I should rather have it considered good by people of discernment, than popular. But I do have common sense enough to be willing to broaden its appeal if the book is not harmed in so doing. I have possibly already

fallen between two stools as to its artistic unity. The mass of out-of-the-ordinary detail and native lore, may, if I am lucky, slip naturally along with the narrative. Or, it may obscure and defeat my basic conception of the cosmic conflict of man in general struggling against an obscure law and destiny. So for Heaven's sake, since this menace is already present, don't let me bring in a new one unless we're pretty sure of our ground. I mean, don't let's "purify" the book for an adolescent consumption that might never materialize, and ruin the book at the same time for the discriminating adult palate.

Now: I want you to think it over very carefully from both the publisher's and the artist's standpoint. I don't know you well enough to know which is dominant in you. But in spite of your betrayal of me by handing over the manuscript to the printer without being sure that it contained no atrocities, I trust you implicitly as an artist and a critic, and I shall accept your judgment in the matter without further question. I want you to answer two questions:

Is Lant's profanity extraneous and meaningless, as my husband claims it is in 75% of the instances? (He admits the effectiveness of such phrases as "the ring-tailed bastard," the "skew-tailed bastard" and such.) Or is the profanity, as of course I intended it to be, an amusing and vigorous part of my character? Typical changes occasioned by the deletion would be, for instance, when Lant is trying to roll the big dead alligator in his boat, "He sobbed, 'God damn you, you stinkin' bastard, I'll not leave go——'." Substitutes for "son of a bitch" and "bastard" would be "booger," "scaper," "scoundrel," "jaybird," "buzzard" and "jessie." There are three places that occur to me where Lant's profanity is an integral part of the story; where his mother accepts his son of a bitch and bastard without question, but objects violently to his "I'll beat your butt"; where she objects to his calling her sister's son a son of a bitch or a bastard but agrees with enthusiasm to the epithet taken up by the whole vicinity, "the pimp"; and where Lant objects to Kezzy's roughness of speech in front of the girl, Ardis.

The other question: is there so much else in the book that would be objectionable for boys from a parent's standpoint, that nothing is to be gained by toning down one character's language? I have already been talked into deleting one or two of the more medical bits of folk lore. I think such bits of lore as the doctor's comment on women in relation to child-bearing and the moon, Zeke's remark that "a woman in the house ain't a woman in the bed"—that type of thing would simply, I should think, go right over an adolescent's head and not be objected to by a Puritan parent. I may be quite wrong about that. That leaves such things as the quarrel about the out-house and the quarrel of the crazy man, Ramrod Simpson with "ol' Desus Chwist." My husband thinks that since the crazy man is not very much developed any way, in the story, that it would be as effective to replace Jesus with the devil—(always a neat and tasty change.)

Well, you figure it out. Mechanically, the changes would be quite simple. *Don't* let me emasculate either character or story to a very problematical end. *Don't* let me turn a rough woodsman into a Boy Scout! But you will see the thing absolutely clear, and I have a queer feeling there may be something in it.

This is the last time I'll be tugging at your coat-tails to have you answer questions. I hope to be quite done this week and go off hunting on the 20th with the whole thing off my mind. You will receive the last installment not later than Wednesday the 23rd. . . .

Very sincerely,

Marjorie Kinnan Rawlings

GENERAL COMMENTARY

Margaret Gillis Figh

SOURCE: "Folklore and Folk Speech in the Works of Marjorie Kinnan Rawlings," in *Southern Forklore Quarterly,* Vol. XI, No. 3, September, 1947, pp. 201-09.

In her books dealing with the Florida Cracker Mrs. Rawlings has created a regional fiction whose strength rests upon its sympathetic portrayal of the humor and the tragedy of the backwoods. During her years at Cross Creek she has been close to traditional sources, and her ear has become remarkably attuned to the popular speech. Hence she has been able to write fiction that has its roots in the folk morality, customs, and beliefs. She realizes the inseparableness of the Cracker and his native setting, and she has shown in her books how his thinking has been molded through many generations by his primitive environment. Her use of superstitions, sayings, and similes in the native vernacular has aided greatly in making it possible for Mrs. Rawlings to create a picture of his everyday life and to reveal its significances. By this means she has portrayed both his stoical fatalism and his earthy humor, which enlivens even the grimmest poverty.

Although these beliefs and sayings are the same in essence as those of English and other Old-World ancestors, their imagery is that of the Florida scrub country. The natives of this section, like all isolated groups, have created their own myths around the forces which they have to battle against and the other aspects of their lives which arouse their emotions. They fight against the external forces of weather and wild beasts. They wrestle with illnesses which they do not understand. Life is hard, but they take it as their part and go on. And they are always ready for "a good time" in spite of their struggles against almost overwhelming odds.

Mrs. Rawlings devotes a major portion of *Cross Creek* to recounting her experiences in becoming acquainted through everyday activities with these Crackers and their way of life. In listening to their folk tales and sayings, in hunting, fishing, and working with them, she has become a part of their community and has achieved an understanding of it that has enabled her to weave into her fiction the many threads of its folk wisdom. . . .

Mrs. Rawlings has introduced the folk element into her work through describing customs such as fence raisings, frog hunting, cane grindings, peanut boilings, and log rafting. She shows the Cracker "making his crop," "marrying his wife," and "burying his dead;" but it is in recording his backwoods vernacular that her real claim to distinction lies, and his activities are most vivid when he is talking about them. Her best characterizations are made when her people express their folk wisdom and illuminate it with North Florida imagery.

As long as Mrs. Rawlings deals with the scrub country, her work gives a valid interpretation of life as it is lived by the average backwoodsman, but when she changes her scene to the North Carolina mountains, as she does in *Mountain Prelude,* or to other sections as in her stories which have appeared in magazines during the past four or five years, her writing loses its spontaneity and degenerates to the uninspired level of popular periodicals. She can write about this scrub country, because she has based her work on a sound artistic foundation. She has made use of regional material, not merely to exploit the quaint or the odd, but to show how life has been molded from generation to generation by an environment. Her characters are individuals, but they bear the stamp of North Florida upon their faces, in their speech, and in the workings of their minds to such an extent that they are symbols of their community and embody the essence of its folk spirit. The use of folklore has contributed greatly to this end. And in turn, Mrs. Rawlings has been of service to the folklorist in that she has unearthed much hitherto unrecorded material and has preserved it in its own rhythmic language pattern.

Gordon E. Bigelow

SOURCE: "Marjorie Kinnan Rawlings' Wilderness," in *The Sewanee Review,* Vol. LXXIII, No. 2, April-June 1965, pp. 299-310.

In January of 1943 the *Saturday Evening Post* ran a feature article entitled, "Marjorie Rawlings Hunts her Supper; Menu: Alligator, Turtle, and Swamp Cabbage." With the story went a series of photographs showing her in picturesque outdoor activities—spearing crabs at night on Salt Springs Run, gigging frogs from an air boat on Orange Lake. The article illustrates how much she had become in the public eye a kind of great white huntress, complete with breeches, boots, and bird dogs. Actually the view is as partial as the view Whitman wished to propagate of himself as one of the roughs, by publishing in the first edition of *Leaves of Grass* an engraving of himself wearing workman's clothes. In both cases the truth was more complicated. But public willingness to see Mrs. Rawlings in this light, and her own ironic willingness to be pictured in this light, are testimony to how prominent a part the wilderness has played in her best-known writings.

Looked at from another side, she was a true sophisticate, a brilliant Phi Beta Kappa from the University of Wisconsin, an experienced Hearst reporter and feature writer, who, until she came to Florida to live in 1928, had spent most of her thirty-two years in cities. The little citrus grove and shabby farmhouse which she bought at Cross Creek were irresistible to her precisely because they were located four miles off any paved road, between two great shallow lakes whose perimeters were still jungle, and because the handful of people living nearby were all of the earthiest, least sophisticated sort. From the moment of her coming she showed a steady fascination for the "wild," for the subtropical exotica she saw all around, and she recognized at once, in the Florida crackers and their way of life, a true remnant of the frontier, living on into the twentieth century. Her fascination with place and folk became a passion to observe and record, at first in the spirit of a reporter who has run across rich new feature material, but she soon found herself with a strong personal commitment to this country, and her writing began to take on the aspect of literary art. She brought to Florida an already deep interest in nature, which she said she learned as a child from her father on a farm he owned just outside the city of Washington. She brought a gift for observation sharpened by her years as a newspaper woman, and she brought one of the sharpest ears for vernacular speech of any writer in contemporary American literature. In 1931 she made the first of a number of prolonged visits in the Ocala Scrub, living with cracker families who became her lifelong friends. The Big Scrub at that time was not a wilderness in the strictest sense, but it was wild enough to have many deer and an occasional black bear and to be virtually without human habitation except on its perimeter, wild enough to convey a strong sense of the true wilderness.

This encounter with a relatively unspoiled nature and with the life of the Florida cracker put her in touch all at once and at a number of points with the American past, with that peculiarly American encounter with primal nature along a sharply contrasting line of civilization known as the frontier. As a result her writings reflect some of the most deeply imbedded attitudes and experiences of the American people, and belong to a main current of American culture flowing from Crèvecoeur and Bartram in the eighteenth century, through Cooper, the transcendentalists, and Whitman in the nineteenth century, to Faulkner in modern times.

Throughout her writings the wilderness theme is closely associated with a developed doctrine concerning the relation of man to his environment. She believed, briefly, that a man can be happy only in the degree to which he is able to adjust harmoniously to his surroundings. The more

natural those surroundings, and the more completely he is in harmony with them, the greater will be his happiness. Different kinds of places appeal to different kinds of people. When she came to Cross Creek she brought with her a Scottish terrier, Dinghy, and a cat named Jib. Dinghy, she said, hated the Florida backwoods from the first sandspur under his tail, was miserable until he was taken back to the city; the cat loved the jungle from the first moment and throve on the wildness. Mrs. Rawlings makes it clear that her own reaction was like the cat's, and she implies that the cat was somehow good because he loved the wildness of the Creek, the dog somehow bad because he hated it and preferred cities.

As Bartram had done in the late eighteenth century, she described for her generation the natural wonders of Florida, the great springs, the tropical rivers, the limestone sinks, the alligators, and the floating islands. She botanized habitually like Thoreau, naming in her books virtually every wild shrub, tree, and flower, and most of the tame ones, in her part of the state. To a lesser extent she did the same with the birds and "varmints." She had the same sensitivity as Thoreau to the flow of the seasons, and, as he had done in *Walden,* used a cycle of the seasons as one of the main organizing devices of her book **Cross Creek**. She said she could tell the stage of spring by the particular scent of the citrus, as Thoreau had said he could do by noting which flowers were in bloom, "for the seasons at the Creek are marked, not by the calendar, but by fruits and flowers and birds." As he had been drawn to the Maine woods to satisfy his hunger for the brute and untamed element in life, Mrs. Rawlings was drawn to the deeper wild of the Big Scrub, which lay only twenty-five miles away across the Ocklawaha River. After her first stay of nearly two months in the scrub, she wrote to Maxwell Perkins, her editor at Scribner's: "I knew these people were gentle, honest. I knew that living was precarious, but just how hand-to-mouth it is, surprised me. I was also astonished by the *utter lack of bleakness or despair,* in a group living momentarily on the very edge of starvation and danger. . . . I found a zestfulness in living, a humor, an alertness to beauty, quite unexpected, and of definite value to record. . . .

"These people are 'lawless' by an anomaly. They are living an entirely natural, and very hard, life, disturbing no one. Civilization has no concern with them, except to buy their excellent corn liquor and to hunt, in season, across their territory with an alarming abandon. Yet almost everything they do is illegal. And everything they do is necessary to sustain life in that place. The old clearings have been farmed out and will not 'make' good crops any more. The big timber is gone. The trapping is poor. They 'shine, because 'shining is the only business they know that can be carried on in the country they know, and would be unwilling to leave. . . . It is quite simply a part of the background, a part of the whole resistance of the scrub country to the civilizing process. The scrub, as a matter of fact, has defeated civilization. It is one of the few areas where settlements have disappeared and the scanty population is constantly thinning. . . . "

What her letter describes is a people living precariously on the fringe of a wilderness area which had felt the ravages of civilization, but had successfully preserved itself against them. Her account reminds one of eighteenth-century theorists like Rousseau or Chateaubriand, who claimed that virtue would most abound in men who lived in a state of nature. These crackers living in the scrub seemed actually to *be* such people: they lived an "entirely natural life," if a very hard one; they were gentle, honest, had a zest for life and a feeling for beauty—no depraved Tobacco Road degenerates these. They were law-breakers, but only for forgivable reasons: because they must live; because they loved their wild country so deeply they would be unwilling to leave it and would do whatever they must to remain in it; because their law-breaking was part of a resistance to civilization. She undoubtedly meant it when she said that she could live their life easily, including the breaking of the law, because the life in the scrub was so "peculiarly right," but her own participation has the air of a little girl playing at a fascinating game. This was a game she could play seriously, but as much as she admired the crackers and their ways, she didn't have to play the game for keeps, and they did. The thing she had to do was to return to her own somewhat different compromise with civilization at Cross Creek and write about what she had found in the Big Scrub.

Her experience there provided the basic substance of her first novel, *South Moon Under,* in which she depicted these people and their life in great detail, sometimes coming so close to describing actual persons and events that one or two of her moonshiner friends later told her they had uneasy moments wondering if her descriptions might not lead the authorities straight to their stills. Her treatment of the place and the people was remarkably truthful, if one allows for an emotional bias in favor of her friends which led her to emphasize their better qualities. She was drawn to them because their lives, though full of privation and danger, were in harmony with the forest and for that reason full of a grace and dignity she had never found in city life. In a sonnet published in *Scribner's* magazine about this time she said that now that she had left cities, they all seemed to blur into one, and what she chiefly remembered from them were things irrelevant to cities, geese flying swiftly south in November, the murmurings of rain, moons setting, suns rising. One could summarize her attitude by saying that it resembles in many ways what Lovejoy and Boas have called: cultural primitivism—"the discontent of the civilized with civilization."

South Moon Under chiefly reflects contemporary times in the scrub; her other greater novel of the scrub is *The Yearling,* which deals with a period fifty or sixty years earlier, the 1870's and '80's, before the partial despoiling of the wilderness. The Baxters in this book are the first settlers on their pine "island"—pioneers literally, and their condition of life follows a classic frontier pattern which lies deep in the soma of every American: the simple cabin in a forest clearing, a split-rail fence surrounding the few acres wrested from the wilderness and planted to corn and beans, a pig or two, a cow and an old horse in a small barn near the cabin, the simple fare from the fields supplemented by game from the forest, most artifacts made by hand, most operations around the place performed by hand or with primitive machinery, as one would expect in a pre-industrial way of life where there was little money, and little commerce except by barter. The only thing one misses is the redskin with his tomahawk lurking in the undergrowth outside the clearing.

If her account of the frontier is in many ways typical, it also conveys a sense of the particular place and time—alligators, Spanish moss, water hyacinths, the Ocklawaha River steamers. The book's air of truth comes from that same combination of accurate reporting and lived experience sifted through a highly charged creative consciousness which she had employed in *South Moon Under.* She did careful "research" for *The Yearling,* as she had done for the earlier book, obtaining many details of the old ways and the lore of hunting from three old hunters who were already in their eighties when she knew them, men who had actually lived in the scrub when it was still an unspoiled wilderness, so wild that wolves roved in packs and panthers were so much a threat that it was unsafe to dress out a beef and try to pack it home alone, even in broad daylight. She lived with the families of these old men, went hunting, fishing, and prowling with them, and listened by the hour to their stories. What they told her, added to what she had learned in writing *South Moon Under* and what she knew now from experience, provided her with the means to create a vivid sense of the life of the early frontier in the Big Scrub.

On one side Mrs. Rawlings was a true romantic in her treatment of nature and the frontier, stressing strangeness, uniqueness, and the distance of a nostalgically conceived past. Her own attitude is nicely caught in a remark she quotes from a cracker mother speaking to her young son at a church supper where bear meat was being served: "Now son, you savor this good. This here's bear meat, and what with things changin' outen the old way, and the bears goin', you're like not to never get to taste it again." This was exactly how Mrs. Rawlings felt about the wilderness and the old ways.

But on another side she was a thoroughgoing realist. "I know you think I put too much emphasis on the importance of fact in fiction," she wrote to Perkins after *The Yearling* was published, "but it seems to me that this type of work is not valid if the nature lore behind it is not true in every detail." Because she wished to tell the whole truth, the nature she depicts has not only idyllic beauty, as in the episode where Jody Baxter makes his fluttermill at Silver Glen Springs; it also has terror, as when Penny is struck by the rattlesnake, and an inscrutable cruelty, as when the great storm destroys the Baxters' crops and floods the scrub country so that the wild creatures are drowned by hundreds.

She strikes a similar balance between romance and realism in her woodsman-frontiersman, who has been depicted in a variety of ways in literature, from savage mountain man to squalid, malaria-ridden poor-white. The most pervasive view, which long ago achieved the proportion of a myth, is the one given by Cooper in Natty Bumppo of *The Leatherstocking Tales*. Natty has the Indian's virtues of physical courage, endurance, great strength, and the power of instinctive action, as well as the white man's "gifts" of pity, humility, deference to womanhood, and a strong sense of personal honor. Cooper leaves no doubt that this man is a paragon of physical and moral virtues because he has grown up and has been able to live at an ideally simple level in the great forest, far from the corrupting influences of civilization.

There is no developed figure in Mrs. Rawlings' fiction of the white savage, nor are there more than brief glimpses of the degenerate clay-eater; but several figures, chiefly Penny Baxter in *The Yearling* and Lant in *South Moon Under,* remind one of Natty in their prowess as hunters, in their readiness, their ability to meet crisis. They have little book learning, but are wise in the ways of the forest; they have the same quiet humor, the sensitivity to beauty, the gentleness. But each of these characters is also individualized: Penny is diminutive in size from having been worked too hard on meager rations as a boy, and he is a farmer as much as he is a hunter; Lant is lean and gangling and is a moonshiner as well as a gifted woodsman. Both remind one of R. W. B. Lewis' "hero in space," the man like Natty Bumppo or Huck Finn who lights out from the territory when the irritants of civilization become too great. Penny Baxter went to the scrub to live because his spirit had been bruised too often among men. "The peace of the vast aloof scrub had drawn him with the beneficence of its silence," she wrote in *The Yearling.* "Something in him was raw and tender. The touch of men was hurtful upon it, but the touch of the pines was healing. Making a living came harder there . . . but the clearing was peculiarly his own. The wild animals seemed less predatory to him than people he had known. The forays of bear and wolf and wildcat and panther on stock were understandable, which was more than he could say of human cruelties." This is a classic statement of the romantic doctrine that nature can heal the human spirit which has been hurt by life in cities, and one detects in it a personal note. Mrs. Rawlings' move from Rochester to Cross Creek was her way of lighting out for the territory, and she went for the same reasons that Penny went to the scrub. Lant's desire for elbow room in *South Moon Under* is shown more by a holding operation than by an active flight, by his refusal to leave the wilderness he loves, even if he must resort to illegal means to stay there. Lant is only one example of a recurrent figure in Mrs. Rawlings' stories, a young man who is left without resources, but who makes out by pluck and ingenuity—trapping, fishing, moonshining—whose life in the open is hard, but who never considers turning to the city to find readier means of support.

Several critics have pointed out a fundamental contradiction in *The Leatherstocking Tales,* whereby Cooper shows an obvious fondness for Natty and for his free and virtuous life in a wilderness Eden, but also allows Natty to be sadly mistreated by civilization and eventually driven to flight. Otis B. Wheeler has suggested in a happy twist of Eliot's phrase that Cooper suffered a dissociation of sensibility where Natty was concerned, that his heart was with Natty, but his head was on the side of civilization. Mrs. Rawlings exhibits this same ambivalence in her fiction. She applauds Penny Baxter's flight from the town into the wild scrub, and she gives him in his role as hunter and woodsman many of the attributes of Natty Bumppo, those virtues which are the result of living close to nature. But she also makes Penny a knowing and hardworking farmer, who successfully fights off the incursions of wild creatures and holds the wilderness at bay as the agent of civilization. Thus he falls squarely into the image of the idealized agrarian freeholder, which has been so pervasive in American culture since the eighteenth century. Penny chiefly displays his hunting prowess when he pursues Old Slewfoot as an aroused farmer avenging the slaughter of his stock. As an independent, self-reliant yeoman farmer living in a great forest, he is representative of a frontier condition midway between the savagery of the mountain men and the corruptions of sophisticated society, of that agrarian middle ground esteemed by Crèvecoeur and Jefferson as the ideal condition for human happiness. To this frontier, so intimately associated with the American dream, Mrs. Rawlings obviously has strong attachments, both theoretical and emotional.

Like Cooper, she objected to civilization because its law curtails a man's freedom and because it destroys the wilderness and the beauty and virtue which are part of it. She also saw civilization as a sickness of the sort which Penny flees to the Big Scrub to escape. Shortly after *The Yearling* was published in 1938, Mrs. Rawlings took a week's cruise in the Bahamas, which attracted her as possible material for another book. "The poor people on some of the islands are up against the same struggle as the scrub people," she wrote to Perkins, "except that the sea and the wind are the adversary, instead of the land. I like to see people bucking something solid instead of their own neuroses. Of course, neuroses have become somethings to reckon with—I suppose it is too late for humans to turn back to the basic simplicities, the soil, the prehistoric struggle for food. . . . "

This call for a return to the basic simplicities emphasizes how much her own passion for nature was combined with a protest against the blight which industrial civilization casts on the human spirit, a protest virtually identical to that of the transcendentalists of the last century, a protest shared by many other major writers in this century. In theory, her ideal escape from the gray sickness of civilization would be to a wilderness idyll like that of Hudson's *Green Mansions,* but her doctrine of harmonious adjustment to environment allowed varying degrees of compromise with this ideal, the most likely being an agrarian life of the sort she tried out at Cross Creek. In such a life, as in the wilderness proper, one is "bucking something solid," and is able to honor that atavistic sense of attachment to earth which she said all men have, and which they ignore only at peril to their happiness. Her feeling for the earth led her to a sense of identification with the whole process of life, a mystic, half-ecstatic awareness that birth, growth, and death are one, and good. In *Cross Creek* she describes a wild sow giving birth to her litter under a magnolia tree in the hammock land near Orange Lake, then makes this remarkable statement: "The jungle hammock breathed. Life went through the moss-hung forest, the swamp, the cypresses, through the wild sow and her young, through me, in its continuous chain. We were all one with the silent pulsing. This was the thing that was important, the cycle of life, with birth and death merging one into the other in an imperceptible twilight and an insubstantial dawn." Then she ranges the statement on a cosmic dimension. "The universe breathed, and the world inside it breathed the same breath. This was the cosmic life, with suns and moons to make it lovely. It was important only to keep close enough to the pulse to feel its rhythm, to be comforted by its steadiness, to know that Life is vital, and one's own minute living a torn fragment of the larger cloth."

She meant Cross Creek in a real sense to be her Walden Pond or, better still, her Brook Farm, the place where she would achieve that holy harmony of mind and muscle which would produce the highest kind of human happiness. She soon discovered, as Hawthorne did at Brook Farm, that the writing demanded precedence, and as soon as she was able to hire others, her own labors at the grove became either supervising or puttering, while she submitted more and more to the anguish of the typewriter. But during the first three or four years at the Creek she grubbed enough in the earth to feel the pulse of life in her garden and grove and knew it to be the same as the pulse which she had felt beating in the forest.

Like Faulkner's Ike McCaslin, she became convinced that the land cannot be owned but only used under God's suzerainty, that the curse which lies upon it comes from the greed for ownership. And like a good eighteenth-century physiocrat she says in the final chapter of *Cross Creek:* "It seems to me that the earth may be borrowed but not bought. It may be used, but not owned. It gives itself in response to love and tending, offers its seasonal flowering and fruiting. But we are tenants and not possessors, lovers and not masters." In this spirit, she consigns her Cross Creek property after her death to the redbirds, to the wind and the rain, to the cosmic secrecy of seed.

Thus one finds himself using the words sylvan, bucolic, pastoral—rather than brute, savage, untamed—to describe Mrs. Rawlings' wilderness. Hers is a jungle with most of its fangs drawn; the predators—wolf, bear, or aborigine—have either been eliminated or are rapidly being destroyed, so as to leave predominantly a wilderness of flora, along with the comfortable lesser fauna to give one the thrill of encounter with the brute. One seldom meets the categorically savage and primordial which were so important to Faulkner: the hot rank stench of a great bear rearing over one with paws outstretched, the great buck whom one salutes with "Oleh! Grandfather, Chief." Hers is also a wilderness which contains or borders upon plowed fields, and her attitudes toward wild nature are almost inextricably enmeshed with agrarian attitudes, and both of these come from an essentially mystic insistence upon a holy harmony between man and earth, between man and the life of the cosmos. Both of these are parts of a protest against the "strange disease of modern life," and a plea for a return to simpler, more natural ways. The extraordinary beauty of her wilderness she conveys in language of extraordinary beauty, a gift to her readers of which one could predict that the wilderness which can heal them is to be found less and less in nature and more and more in books like hers.

Gordon E. Bigelow

SOURCE: "The Long Road Up," *Frontier Eden,* University of Florida Press, 1966, pp. 1-2, 158.

Marjorie Kinnan Rawlings belongs to the great renaissance in American fiction between the two World Wars. She was a meticulous artist with high standards who worked hard and, though her output was modest, her best work has an excellence which tempts one to the word "classic"; but she was so surrounded by other literary giants that her accomplishment has been obscured by theirs. Her major themes and attitudes place her squarely in one of the mainstreams of American culture, and yet she belonged to none of the literary schools or groupings of the period in which she wrote, unless it is to the regionalists and their rediscovery of the beauty and worth of the American scene as a subject for literature.

As a protégé of Maxwell Perkins, the great editor at Scribner's, she belonged to a literary elite which included Wolfe, Hemingway, and Fitzgerald, all of whom she knew. In terms of age she might have qualified as a member of the Lost Generation for her birth year was 1896, which made her three years older than Hemingway, a year older than Faulkner, and the same age as Fitzgerald and Dos Passos, but for several reasons she remains distinct from them all. As a female, she missed military service in World War I and the European exile which was its sequel for so many American writers and, though she was a dedicated writer from an early age, her literary career was slower getting started by a full decade than for most of her distinguished contemporaries. Her important writings appeared during the thirties and early forties but reflect very little of the prevailing naturalism or social consciousness of those years. She wrote of poor-whites in an exotic, semitropical setting, with unusual candor and lucidity but without showing them as the victims of corrupt capitalism or as depraved moral degenerates. Her books have little of the iconoclasm or pessimism of the time; without being sentimental they are mainly affirmative in tone. Though she made little use of sex, physical violence, or sensation, her books enjoyed an enormous popular success, selling so well in the years just before World War II that she became something of a national celebrity. Her writings brought her a number of awards and honors, including the O. Henry First Prize Award in 1933, the Pulitzer Prize for fiction in 1939, and three honorary doctorates; her best-known novel, *The Yearling,* was translated into thirteen languages and acclaimed as a literary masterpiece in many parts of the world. Since she was chiefly a plain-spoken writer, not a conscious symbolist except in her last novel, she has attracted little attention from critics interested in ironies, ambiguities, and symbol-chasing. . . .

Within her limited range Marjorie shows the uniqueness and the authority of the true artist. All her writings have the important virtue of readability, and in this respect she belongs to the older great tradition of Twain and Howells rather than to the modern school which began with Henry James. She will probably continue to be more a reader's writer than a critic's writer since the special virtues of her books are more readily experienced than described. She may not have notched as high nor as big a blaze on the pine tree of literary fame as she hoped, but the mark that she made was deep and will last.

SOUTH MOON UNDER (1933)

The Christian Science Monitor

SOURCE: A review of *South Moon Under,* in *The Christian Science Monitor,* March 4, 1933, p. 8

Marjorie Kinnan Rawlings has found a hitherto undeveloped field of fiction in the Florida scrub. Here she has encountered a people of uncouth speech and primitive standards of living—a slow, simple, peaceful, limited people, whose surroundings have nevertheless developed in them certain positive skills and wisdoms. They know the woods and the river and wild creatures. They are able to be almost entirely self-sustaining. They have learned in considerable measure to live at peace with mankind and with nature, and get some joy out of apparent meagerness.

The lives of a few of these people have furnished Mrs. Rawlings with the material for her novel, *South Moon Under.* She has written of the Lantrys, who left what seemed to them like civilization in the pine woods settlements and crossed the river to live in the scrub. In the fertile strip that lay between the scrub and the river Lantry built his cabin. He cleared and fenced 25 acres, tilled his land, and supported his family. They in turn grew up and some of them cleared other land in the scrub and made some sort of living. Lantry's favorite daughter, Piety, lived on with her father after she married, and her son Lant grew up under his grandfather's tutelage to know and love the scrub.

Times, however, were harder for Lant than for his grandfather. The land had been worked over too long. All the cypress logs he could cut had been sold. The price for furs from the woods and alligators from the river had gone down. And government men made distilling a hazardous business.

The search for a livelihood resolves itself into a sharp conflict. It brings Lant into conflict with the law, and it marks the end of a period in the life of the scrub. (Mrs. Rawlings has said that the scrub is more thinly populated now than it has been for 50 years. "The imaginary family of *South Moon Under* is placed on the site of one of the many abandoned clearings.")

In writing about the Lantrys and their neighbors, Mrs. Rawlings has not rested content with reproducing their curious lingo and describing their way of living. Beneath the idiosyncrasies of their life she has tried to penetrate to their way of thinking, their emotions and their codes.

Three things are especially to be noted in the author's work. One is her skillful use of conversation. It is all in poor-white lingo, but each person speaks it with a difference. There is a variation in each generation, and a difference between those on the settlement side of the river and those in the scrub.

Another point of excellence is her zest in picturing her people when they are merry. A fence-raising, a frolic, a cane-grinding when everybody turned out for fresh cane juice and fun—such scenes she is able to write about with a crescendo of mirth. These people knew how to enjoy themselves.

And in the third place, she writes best of all about the wild life of scrub and river. It is evident that she, too, loves the peace and isolation of the place. In the last few years she has come to know it intimately, has been lost in it, has voyaged by small boat the full length of its river boundaries.

There is a good firm body to this book because the author understands so much more than the superficial details of the scene, and because she has succeeded in getting the whole thing—surface beauty and strangeness, and the underlying strong pulse of life—into her book.

Jonathan Daniels

SOURCE: A review of *South Moon Under,* in *The Saturday Review of Literature,* Vol. IX, No. 33, March 4, 1933, p. 465.

Not the South moon lost under the earth but still darkly potent, nor the drama of men and persistent fear make Marjorie Kinnan Rawlings's new novel the splendid book that it is. She has written a vigorous story of murder and hiding, but, better than that, she has drawn in terms as lush and slow as the scrub grows a country and a people fresh in literature and rich in reality.

Her country, the Florida scrub of high pines and impenetrable stunted oak and myrtle rising from infertile sands and the surrounding tropical swamp of twisting water and bright flowers and bell-bottomed cypresses, is new in print, but the same implications of life in isolation lie in its tangle that have been drawn upon in the numerous stories of the coves and hollows of the Southern mountains. Her people, the Lantrys and Jacklins of the scrub and their piney woods kin, are related to the tradition of Southern and mountain whites who have been drawn in terms as diverse as dripping sentimentality and stark degeneracy. Mrs. Rawlings escapes both. In drawing her country and her Lantrys she has looked at the inhospitable earth and found it full of strangeness and beauty, and at the men and women of an old breed and seen in them dignity and the instinct that life, hard as it may be, is good. Also, and more profoundly, she has given her people an absolute integrity with their earth.

Her story is simple and familiar. Like the beginning of a circle of fate she begins with the Lantry who comes, driven by hidden fear, from the murder of a revenue officer in the Carolina mountains to the piney woods of Florida. The same fear drives him to the scrub where his brood, born of a querulous piney woods wife, takes root in the thin soil. They breed and die, plant and root and go back into the more profitable and more precarious business of making whiskey. The book ends with the first Lantry's grandson driven by the same fear after murder that made his grandfather a hunted man all his days. But behind him, as behind his grandfather, lies the scrub, impenetrable, inhospitable, but the way of escape and the symbol of hope for a man hunted.

This story Mrs. Rawlings has written well, but it is not her chief preoccupation. Chiefly she is interested in drawing the scrub and the people who live in it. She presses neither the country nor the people to the service of her plot. Slowly and with fine detail she has drawn the three generations of Lantrys who are the chief figures of the book, the great red-bearded grandfather, his daughter, Piety, who, of all his children, embodied his integrity and his spirit; and her son, Lantry Jacklin, the true child and man of the scrub.

For these and around them, Mrs. Rawlings has created a world. She lingers as lovingly over the intimate details of their lives and the hard struggle for existence as she does over deer prancing in the moonlight or pale orchid water hyacinths blooming beside young Lant's loaded raft. In a sense the three generations represent not only a return of fate but also stages of acclimatization to the scrub. For Lantry, entry into the scrub is a step deliberately made; Piety grows into womanhood there; but the boy, Lant, born there, is a part of it. He knows all the craft of the savage in the forest, the ways of plants and beasts and fish, how to wring subsistence from its apparent forbiddingness. He learns from an old native all the secrets that a man can know of it, and with a half wit who is always berating "dat ol' Desus Chwist" he floats the valuable sunken cypress logs to market. Also he learns the lucrative but dangerous business, for which the secretive country seems almost created, of illicit distilling. The scrub is his life, and if it leads him to the murder of his cousin after that cousin has broken the prime moral of loyalty, it also brings to him the love of a woman as tenacious, as overwhelming, and as simple as the scrub itself.

In drawing her characters Mrs. Rawlings has enlivened them with a strong masculine humor, racy and native. Neither in tragedy nor in fun is there any false note of primness about her people. Piety's conversation with the old country doctor about the hookworm and Lant's embarrassment when his piney woods girl comes to visit and his mother recalls his lazy postponement of building a back house are incidents from which Mrs. Rawlings draws stout laughter. More excitingly amusing is the treatment of the outlander who came and committed the crime of fencing his land. Mrs. Rawlings has not loaded her story with folk verse, but the few she quotes are excellent, as the mock blessing offered at the fence raising:

> Good God, with a bounty
> Look down on Marion county,
> For the soil is so pore, and so awful
>   rooty, too,
> I don't know what to God the pore
>   folks gonna do.

Readers will welcome the freshness of Mrs. Rawlings's scene, but it is not mere new scene that gives her book its great distinction. What makes it one of the really fine books of the year is that the scene and the characters are drawn with a richness and vigor which makes them wholly alive. It is a book full of life, and of insistence that life with "love and lust, hate and friendship, grief and frolicking, even birthing and dying" is a choice thing. Out of that insistence in these simple people grows dignity and integrity and a strength equal to the irresistible growth of the scrub itself.

The Times Literary Supplement

SOURCE: A review of *South Moon Under,* in *The Times Literary Supplement,* No. 1651, September 21, 1933, p. 628.

Marjorie Kinnan Rawlings may have taken the title of her novel, **South Moon Under,** from a passage in which a boy watches animals disporting themselves under the moon, and goes on to reflect that they were mysteriously affected by it even when it was below the horizon. The subject is some such lunar system as a whole, rather than the courses and aberrations of particular members of it. The characters attract and repel one another as if the determining factor were propinquity; it is as if an unseen power, while allowing them self-expression, kept them to orbits demanded by the pattern; they refrain from any self-assertion that might distort it—accepting birth and death as if it were predetermined rising and setting.

The orbits in which they move are in the Florida scrub with a swift, deep-banked river running through it; and the story begins with the moving of the farmer, Lantry, together with his wife and five children, from the settlement on one side of the river to the dense scrub on the other, where his newly built cabin is the only habitation for ten miles. It is fear that has driven him into the solitude; for, when making moonshine whisky many years before, he had killed a revenue man, and he was haunted by dread of a pursuit that was without substance in fact. Apart from this shadow the figures in the story are solid. The author has drawn an isolated community that makes its own rules and sees to it that they are observed. That the settlers are members of one body is the first impression to be gathered, for they assemble from over the river to help Lantry with his fencing. To set against this good fellowship they have their own ways of ridding themselves of those who offend against their code. Through Lantry, through his children, and, later, through his grandson, we are enabled to see the trees and animals of the scrub, and to follow the trapping and other callings by which the men and women meet their simple needs. The author is to be congratulated on the solidity and consistency of the impression given and on the artistic self-control with which she has adhered to her scheme of proportion. In the end the grandson also takes to making moonshine whisky; and the note of the last page is that of the first—the note of fear. There has been a cycle, and history has repeated itself.

GOLDEN APPLES (1935)

Henry Seidel Canby

SOURCE: A review of *Golden Apples,* in *The Saturday Review of Literature,* Vol. XII, No. 23, October 5, 1935, p. 6.

There is a tenderness in Mrs. Rawlings's novels of the Florida orange country that may outlast the psychopathic hate with which other Southern writers have lifted the despised Cracker into literature. Her books explain, what is a mystery in others, why the poor white loves his soil, why, indeed, he is worth writing about at all except as a psychological phenomenon. Florida, a country made distasteful by its advertising, becomes again in her stories the land that stirred Bartram's imagination, and through him Coleridge. The hammocks, the lakes, the rivers, the ibis, are an atmosphere, a spiritual environment, beautiful, difficult, inescapable, like the so different Wessex of Hardy.

And, with no trace of sentimentality, she has a gift for the idyllic. Her Luke and Allie, orphans left on their own resources in the wilderness, are like the strong sour fruit and delicate blossom of the wild orange. The sap of the wild hammock runs in them also. The bloom and frost and recovery of their dangerous contacts with life are part of a rhythm of nature which the orange tree knows.

This novel has a theme much more metaphysical, and incidents more melodramatic, than this cycle of nature, but it is the brother and sister, the sun and frost, that make it good. Tordell, the remittance man from England, who comes to live with them on his family's land where they have squatted, is an interesting variant of the villain seducer who learns through his own mistakes what it is to have a heart. Dr. Albury, who compensates by good deeds

for spoiling his half-mad son, Camilla who fights for her great orchards like a mother against the kidnapping frost, and the Crackers of the settlement, are right enough. And they all serve to expound the thesis of the novel, which is that not even love can protect against injustice and frustration, but only the sense that vitality goes on past the individual, past the hope, and past the defeat, making experience still worth while for the strong-willed, clear-sighted, who have escaped. It is a sound thesis, yet I could wish that Mrs. Rawlings had not labored it. It is implicit in Luke who, after his sister's death in a premature confinement, takes a poor-white half wit to wife so that his bodily needs will not interfere with his passionate will that sweet oranges shall grow upon the stubs of the sour wild orange of the wilderness. It is implicit in Allie, with her hair like fur and her tawny skin, fragile, unblaming, a willing sacrifice. The "furriner" and the orange people from the planted lands, and the metaphysics of love and compensation, cumber a story which so long as it is simple is superb.

The Nation

SOURCE: A review of *Golden Apples,* in *The Nation,* Vol. 141, No. 3677, December 25, 1935, p. 750.

Golden Apples promises to become one of the minor best-sellers of the current season. It concerns a young Englishman who comes, broken in spirit, to the "hammock" country of central Florida and there undergoes what the blurb-writers like to call a spiritual regeneration. This glorious consummation develops from his gradual realization of Life, vital, pulsing Life, as it is lived by the share-croppers of the region. The book pretends to realism; but one looks in vain for more than passing reference to the meanness and squalor of an existence miserably eked out. Mrs. Rawlings reasons in the manner of successful writers before her: share-cropping is rustic and earthy, all that is rustic and earthy is necessarily wholesome-and-real, the spectacle of a share-cropping community is therefore just the thing to regenerate a broken-hearted English gentleman. The novel is given over to the staples of petty fiction—tempestuous passion, primitive kindliness, *et al.* It is trite and quite harmless.

THE YEARLING (1938)

Jonathan Daniels

SOURCE: A review of *The Yearling,* in *The Saturday Review,* Vol. 17, No. 23, April 2, 1938, p. 5.

There comes a moment everywhere when ceasing to be a boy may be a tragedy like dying. But the story of that moment has never been more tenderly written than by Marjorie Kinnan Rawlings in this novel of Jody, the boy of the Florida hammock country, and Flag, the faun, who grew together out of a frolicking youngness to the bitter realities of maturity.

It is a story sad enough; one, indeed, which might easily fall into the bathos of youth's own humorless seeing of its incomparable despair. But Mrs. Rawlings wisely has not written in the solemn terms of tragedy. Rather her book of the Baxter family is crowded with comedy of character, with full-bodied folk wisdom, and with the silence and the excitement, the ultimate noise and accumulated natural history of the backwoods hunt. These Baxters are a stout folk: Penny Baxter is a mighty hunter though a runty man, and he is also the shrewdly sensitive father of Jody and husband of Ory. She is the unamused realist concerned with the scant commissary and her two males. And Jody is, beyond his dreams, a boy like that faun which he saved from starving in the woods as thick with hunger as with life.

Alone such a family, so sympathetically created, might have seemed another group of the pretty, poetic poor, written out of squalor into the condition of the philosophers and of content. But they are bound to reality by the encircling scrub about the "island" of their clearing and by the neighbor Forresters, great, rough, fighting, frolicking frontiersmen, who are mean enough to trap an unliked neighbor's hogs but as ready to give him quick, big-muscled aid in trouble. Such humans in the scrub are only a few of Mrs. Rawlings's characters: there are close beside them old Slewfoot, the bear, Flag, the faun, pigs and cows, horses and dogs, even the thick rattler which struck in the dark to lay Penny Baxter low, the dancing cranes and a whole zoölogy of creatures driven and dying in the highwaters of tropical storm. Indeed, Mrs. Rawlings's picture of this aftermath of storm, of the huddled and violent death of the beasts and varmints, of the plague of black tongue which followed among the survivors, and of man's greater difficulties in a stricken wilderness, carries the book beyond the dimensions of a tender little legend of a lost childhood and adds strength and meaning to that legend.

Mrs. Rawlings has written a wise and moving book informed with a love of all living kind. It falters occasionally into sentimentality. When she writes of the town beyond the scrub, of lavender-scented Grandma Hutto and her sailor son Oliver who loved the yellow-haired girl—whom Lem Forrester did not mean he should have without a murderous mauling—the book sometimes seems artificial and shaped for trivial story. But in the wilderness, on the hunt, in the storm, in the face of impending hunger and encircling jungle, her people are real and living. Certainly they are never mere bush beaters for local color. Isolated, they are not remote. As Mrs. Rawlings writes we are all there in the scrub; and beyond the sanctuary of boyhood and the security of clearing, struggle and burden, fear and weariness await us all.

William Soskin

SOURCE: A review of *The Yearling,* in *New York Herald Tribune,* Vol. 14, No. 31, April 3, 1938, pp. 1-2.

With Tom Sawyer, Huckleberry Finn and the lesser members of the fraternity of young boys in American literature well in mind, it is quite possible to maintain that Jody Baxter, son of the farmer and huntsman, Penny Baxter, in Marjorie Kinnan Rawlings' new novel, *The Yearling,* is the most charming boy in the entire national gallery. He may lack some of the sense of mischief and the adolescent wryness which have endeared Mark Twain's kids to our hearts. But Jody, roaming in the scrub forests of Mrs. Rawlings' favorite Florida country, living close to his animals with a sensitive emotional understanding of them, learning the subtleties of life which a child in sophisticated communities can never know, and reflecting that wholesomeness in his own spirit, has a gayety and a bubbling humor which run far deeper than that of any of the famous adolescents of our literature.

Jody is a young, laughing St. Francis in his own small world, and his unspoken conversations with his fawn, his dogs, his bear cubs, with the growing things and the deep pools and strong-flowing streams of Florida, are a communion with some spiritual core of the world. His story, as Mrs. Rawlings tells it, opens windows wide for the reader, and lets in sunlight and fresh breezes just as surely as an older St. Francis did for another world.

I find it difficult to convey the special importance of the history of this perky young Jody, for his quick, gentle humor, his intuitive intelligence and his bright courage, without resorting to an unbecoming effervescence of adjectives. I feel, however, that if it were possible to withdraw my own son from his social curriculum of modern learning, athletics, strictly supervised play, his carefully cultivated hobbies and his controlled psychological adjustment in progressive schools, and to give him the hunger and the live appetites that Jody knows, the pragmatic wisdom of Jody's days of hunting, loafing, farming, worrying about subsistence and exulting in the victories over wild life, the benefit of daily living with a sensitive huntsman and a farmer such as Jody's admirable little father, and the tonic of contact with a stern, hard, realistic and yet lovable mother such as Ma Baxter—I would do it. *The Yearling* is an education in life that is far removed from our dreary urban formulas; but it is fundamental and close to our own secret hopes, for all its romance and its frontier environment.

First of all, however, *The Yearling* is a novel. Out of its leisurely, beautifully composed record of a year's living on the meager Baxter clearing in the Florida brush, there emerges the story of Penny Baxter, who was either brave or crazy to withdraw from the towns and start a farm in the heart of a country populous with bears, wolves, panthers and rattlesnakes. Penny is a generous man of good sensibilities and an excellent neighbor, but he wanted the peace of the aloof forest and the beneficence of its silence. He had been bruised too often by fellow-men. "The forays of bear and wolf and wild-cat on stock were understandable, which was more than he could say of human cruelties."

His land, an island of long-leaf pines which was a landmark in the rolling waste that was the scrub, nourished him healthily, for it healed his bruises and made a self-reliant, clever hunter of him, a quiet man, less violent than the huge Forrester brothers who drank and swore and let their violence loose upon the neighboring land, and fought with their fists and hunted cruelly and sat naked in their house in the night, singing and swilling in whisky. He had brought the buxom girl who became Ma to the farm in his thirties, and she had borne him children who had died. Jody was the only surviving child—and he had something of a young faun's spirit about him, a dreaming remoteness which, alternating with his vast boy's appetite and his sudden spurts of sentimental affection, made him a puzzle to Ma.

But Penny understood him thoroughly out of his memories of countless afternoons of a faun in his own childhood, and Penny had grown into the kind of father who could serve as a hero for Jody—whether he was tracking down the villainous black menace of a bear, Sluefoot, who raided the farm stock, or outwitting the burly Forresters in a game of sharp trading, or creeping through the brush with the boy so that they might secretly observe a company of whooping cranes dancing a cotillion to their own strange music that was part cry and part singing.

Penny it is who shields Jody from Ma's sternness when the boy goes off honey-hunting or exploring the dream-like gardens of the forest instead of sticking to his chores. Occasionally, too, Penny plays on Jody's weaknesses. When he twits the boy about a little girl named Eulalie, Jody is furious and denies he has a sweetheart.

"If you say that again, Pa, I'll jest die," Jody exclaims, and that is a peculiarly good example of his pungent, earnest way of talking. When he returns one day to find venison cooking and the kitchen all fragrant as a result of Penny's hunting that day, he addresses his mother: "We got us a shootin' Pa, ain't we, Ma?"

Jody has a way with his Ma, but he is even more successful with his Grandma, who is an elderly, slight, charming flirt of a woman, whose femaleness made all men virile. Grandma lives in a little house by the river, in a cloud of fragrance made up of the sweet lavender on her clothing, the dried grasses in the fire-place jar, the honey in the cupboard, the cookies and fruit cakes and the smell of the soap she used on Fluff's fur and the pervasive scent of the garden, and above it all, the smell of the river that was a whirlpool of odorous dampness and decaying fern.

It is no wonder that Jody finds it hard to be a grown-up, responsible fellow in these rhapsodic sensory wanderings of his. Sometimes it is the smell and the terribly fine fragrance of roasted bear and deer meat in the forest—this only a little while after his heart and stomach have sickened at the bloody cruelty of the hunt. Sometimes it is the smell of the calf, of the earth he hoes, of the stream she fishes. Sometimes it is the curious, strange smell of other people's houses—like the Forrester's. Often there is the smell of tragedy and violence—of bears and wolves raiding their farm and destroying months' stores of food,

or the smell of the land after a terrifying storm and flood, when the dead bodies of animals float by on the roads and when plague strikes them and the game may not be eaten.

It is on one of the dangerous days, when Penny is struck by a rattlesnake during a hunt and when he kills a deer in a fury of hunting violence after the accident, that Jody finds the love of his life—a young fawn. A day or so later, when Penny was recovering from the poison, Jody makes his way back to the spot and carries the fawn home. And from the moment be teaches the wobbly little fawn to take milk and asks his Ma to smell him—"Look at him, Ma. Lookit that sleekity coat. Smell him"—and makes the fawn a member of the Baxter family wandering about the house, leaping along during the hunting treks, sleeping with Jody and . . . playing with him, this story of a boy and an animal becomes one of the most exquisite I have ever read.

Out of this landscape of life in the Florida scrub, woven closely with unforgettable portraits of native people in their kitchens, in their churches, in ceremonies of birth and death, in their tragedies and their virile battles against the elements, Mrs. Rawlings draws a story with a tragic climax—that of the end of youth. It is because we have known the innermost recesses of Jody's heart and the intimacy of his dreams that the ultimate need to kill the fawn becomes a drama of overpowering proportions. It is written with a thorough poignance, and yet with a fine sense of detachment and of the normal flow of life that leavens all such tragedies of youth. As a result of the death of the fawn young Jody comes eventually to know that his yearling days are over, as are his pet's, and Penny tells him that "you've seed how things goes in the world o' men. You've knowed men to be lowdown and mean. You've seed ol Death at his tricks. You've messed around with ol' Starvation. Ever' man wants life to be a fine thing, and a easy. 'Tis fine, boy, powerful fine, but 'tain't easy. . . . I've been uneasy all my life."

We will be grateful, all of us, for this lovely story, and Mrs. Rawlings, I hope, will realize that gratitude.

Edith H. Walton

SOURCE: A review of *The Yearling,* in *The New York Times Book Review,* April 3, 1938, p. 2.

Already published by Marjorie Kinnan Rawlings are two novels and innumerable short stories about the isolated, backwoods people who live in the wild heart of the far-flung Florida scrub. Her name is identified with the region. When one hears the term Florida Cracker one thinks at once of her work. For all that and despite her previous accomplishment, Mrs. Rawlings has written nothing even comparable in excellence to **The Yearling.** A feeble plot, superimposed arbitrarily, was the weakness of **South Moon Under** and especially of **Golden Apples.** In **The Yearling,** however—which is merely a simple chronicle of one significant year in the life of a 12-year-old boy—Mrs. Rawlings has not allowed herself to be hampered by plot requirements. Character and background are her sole consideration; in a narrative of moving beauty she has achieved complete integration between them.

Penny Baxter, his wife and his son, Jody, own land on a pine island high set above the arid scrub. All around them is the forest, given over to wild creatures; though there are towns within trading distance, the Baxters' only neighbors live four miles away. The Forresters, however, have six mighty black-bearded sons to oppose against the wilderness, whereas tough, wiry little Penny must fight his battle alone, with only Jody to help. It is a hard battle. Added to the usual hazards of farming—crop failure, drought and storm—there are marauding beasts to contend with and game to be patiently tracked. On Penny's skill as a marksman the family welfare depends. Plenty or semi-starvation may hang on a single shot.

Undersized as he is, Penny has a sturdiness and sweetness of character which even the Forresters respect. Dogged, crafty and tireless when it is necessary for him to kill, he will injure no living creature except in self-protection or when it is needed for food. This sensitiveness Jody inherits. Like his father, he has an instinctive feeling for beauty, an instinctive passionate love for the strange, wild scrub. Now that Jody is 12, the two are boon companions, hunting and fishing together, practicing innocent deceptions upon Jody's grim-faced Ma. Heavy, unimaginative, soured by a hard life and the death of her other children, Ma Baxter is a dampening influence in the household despite her basic kindness of heart. As pert little Grandma Hutto once told Jody tartly, "Your father married a woman whom all Hell couldn't amuse."

From April to April, then, one follows the life of the Baxters, watching Jody grow in endurance and resourcefulness, coming to share emotionally the flavor of his adventures. Almost plotless in the formal, conventional sense, the story catches one up into the rhythm of wilderness living. Its crises become as important as they were to Penny and Jody. The pursuit of old Slewfoot, the vicious, thieving bear; the great storm, with its aftermath of flood and pestilence; the attack of famished wolves upon the Baxters' enclosure; the occasional, exciting trips to Volusia, the river town—out of such simple episodes as these Mrs. Rawlings has fashioned a tale which in effect is remarkably dramatic. As well, there is the spicy recurring comedy of the Baxters' relations with the Forresters—who are at one moment kindly neighbors, at another lawless brutes.

Essentially, however, the kernel of the story is young Jody's passion for his tame fawn, Flag. Having long craved a pet—"something with dependence to it"—Jody acquires the baby fawn when it is still teetering unsteadily on absurd, fragile legs. Against his mother's will, he shares his food and his bed with it, and trains the merry, impudent little creature to follow him about everywhere. Jody and the fawn soon become inseparable. They race and gambol together in the forest; Flag is the boy's playmate,

his treasure and his friend. In his happiness, Jody does not realize, as the seasons swing round, how big Flag is growing, how troublesome and wild. The fawn is a yearling now, almost fully grown, just as Jody himself is no longer really a child.

For a time, understanding as he does his son's love for the fawn, Penny is patient with Flag and endures his depredations. There comes a moment, however—the climax of the novel—when tolerance can stretch no further. Too large now to be restrained, the fawn—not once but twice—destroys the precious crop of young tender corn, and faced with so serious a menace, Penny not unreasonably decrees that Flag must die. For Jody there follows a nightmare of heart-break and rebellion which culminates bitterly in his running away from home. When he returns, humbled and forlorn, Jody is a different person. He knows, in his new maturity, that Penny acted as he must. He has learned to face sorrow and inescapable necessity. His father can spare him no longer. The heedless boy, Jody, has died with Flag, the fawn.

With this climactic episode, *The Yearling* reaches a peak of poignance and tragic power. The incredulous agony of Jody when, despite all his safeguards, the fawn for a second time destroys the vital crop is depicted so very movingly that it becomes almost unbearable. The only scene in the book which can match it is the death and funeral of Fodderwing, the fey, crippled little Forrester whom his rough brothers adore. Wisely, however, Mrs. Rawlings does not and need not depend upon such high points in her narrative. The thing about *The Yearling*—its great claim to distinction—is that it is able to make so much of simple, homely events. The zest of a hunting expedition, the stir of Spring in the forest, a suddenly glimpsed dance of grave, stately cranes—it is out of material as humble as this that the texture of the book is woven.

Certain virtues one expects from Mrs. Rawlings. She has, for example, a marvelous ear for the flavorsome cracker dialect; she makes one see and smell the lonely, arid scrub. Never before, however, has she created a set of characters who are so close and real to the reader, whose intimate life one can share without taint of unconscious patronage. In most books of this kind, including the author's own, the backwoods folk of the South are distressingly quaint and alien. They belong, seemingly, to a different race, a different world. Penny and Jody, however, for all their lack of schooling, have a natural, sensitive intelligence which one respects and responds to from the start. They are people of worth and dignity, inarticulate but wise. *The Yearling*—and this is the best tribute one can pay it—is nothing so narrowly limited as a "local-color" novel. Rather, it recasts with unusual beauty the old, timeless story of youth's growth to maturity.

Forrest Reed

SOURCE: A review of *The Yearling*, in *The Spectator*, Vol. 161, November 11, 1938, p. 824.

I am rather surprised to find that *The Yearling* has been a best-seller in America: I should not have expected it to be a best-seller anywhere. To begin with, the only female character of importance is the middle-aged, well-meaning, but fault-finding Ma Baxter: secondly, the hero is her son Jody, a boy of twelve: thirdly, from start to finish animals play at least as prominent a part in the novel as humans. The scene is Florida; the people are poor and illiterate—struggling to make a living off the land, struggling against the encroachment of tropical forests and their inhabitants—bears, panthers, wolves. I definitely liked the book: indeed it would have been strange had I not done so, for Jody is very much my kind of boy, and I could check all his feelings by my own. Therefore I knew that they were neither falsified nor exaggerated, though they might be unusual. It is the story of a friendship—on the boy's side demonstrative in its expression, and passionate in its intensity. On the other side are grace, charm, beauty, affection; but also something tricksy and elusive. Had the yearling been a dog, not a fawn, there would have been a truer reciprocity. The fawn is a day old when Jody finds him close to a slain doe, his mother; and he is a young deer when, twelve months later, the story ends. The last scenes are painful, yet their cruelty is of a kind that could only have been inspired by pity. "It's life that goes back on you," says Jody's father, and the words appear to sum up admirably the teaching of Miss Rawlings' novel.

Obviously the author is a lover of animals. There is killing in the book, but it is done in self-defence or for food, not for sport, and there are many scenes of quite another nature—the scene of the old lonely wolf returning in the moonlight to play with the bulldog, the scene of the beautiful and fantastic dance of the cranes. Jody's father is fond of animals; his mother emphatically is not. In the boy, however, the father's sympathy is intensified, is far more emotional, so that Ma Baxter, had she known the word, would probably have called it morbid. "He did not believe he should ever again love anything, man or woman or his own child, as he had loved the yearling." On this note the tragedy ends, and, with his temperament, the prophecy may very easily prove true. Yet not a hint of sentimentality enters into Miss Rawlings' treatment of Jody or the beasts. She is here too sure of her ground. On the other hand, it does now and then weaken her presentment of the father. The novel has little grace of style, but it has an original theme most sympathetically and understandingly developed.

The Times Literary Supplement

SOURCE: A review of *The Yearling,* in *The Times Literary Supplement,* No. 1925, December 24, 1938, p. 813.

This novel has had this past summer a considerable American success, but it seems at first so localized in interest, and so slow in movement, that one wonders for some while whether and how it will survive transplantation. The scene is the, even in literature, unfamiliar "hammock" country of inland Florida half a century ago or more, covered by thick forests still plentifully inhabited by dangerous and other wild animals. The people of the story are the three Baxters—the small but tireless Penny, the practical and hard because hard-driven Ma, and their only surviving child, the twelve-year-old Jody, already done with schooling and (if with boyish lapses) his father's right-hand man on the crops or out hunting. The two go out together after bear, panther, deer, and even wolf and alligator; they visit and fight with their rough neighbours the Forresters; they go to the village and call in more friendly fashion on Grandma Hutto. Jody has fever, Penny is bitten by a rattler, rain and flood destroy the crops, and plague kills the animals which are no less a source of food.

So life goes on from day to day, yet as one reads one finds that out of these incidents a very solid sense of both place and character is built up in one's mind, and against the harder, harsher background the story of Jody's love for his pet fawn Flag, rescued from the forest after Penny had killed the mother, runs like a thread of bright and delicate beauty, cool and innocent as Jody's own clear outlook on the world. Through Flag, Jody is destined to learn how hard and harsh the world can be. This concluding episode is tenderly and deeply moving, holding something of the tragedy of the breaking of all childhood dreams, but if it is here that Miss Rawlings moves most surely from localism to universality, her earlier pages also provide some moments of authentic and appealing loveliness—glimpses of wild animals, of scenes in the forest, of father and son in happy, unperturbed companionship.

WHEN THE WHIPPOORWILL (1940)

Edith H. Walton

SOURCE: A review of *When The Whippoorwill,* in *The New York Times Book Review,* April 28, 1940, p. 6.

More, even, than most regional writers, Mrs. Rawlings has exploited a single section, a single landscape, and has barely looked beyond its confines. In *The Yearling,* in *South Moon Under,* in various short stories which are here published in book form, she has devoted herself almost entirely to the backwoods people of the wild Florida scrub, whose life she knows so well. Steadily, too, her work has improved—not so much in deeper knowledge of that life as in her own attitude toward it. Always marvellously familiar with the folkways of her characters, their pithy dialect, their peculiar brand of humor, Mrs. Rawlings is less and less inclined to emphasize their quaintness at the expense of their humanity. This is one reason why *The Yearling* was so greatly superior to her two earlier novels. Her Florida Crackers, these days, are people—not oddities.

When the Whippoorwill, to be sure, does not represent only or chiefly Mrs. Rawlings's later work. A collection of tales written over a period of a decade, it includes a diversity of moods and manners. Side by side with a group of supremely comic yarns—**"Varmints," "Alligators,"** the immortal **"Benny and the Bird Dogs"**—there are stories with the same tender and moving quality which so distinguished *The Yearling.* No matter what the tone, however, the average of this collection is quite astonishingly high, as much in its farcical moments as its sober ones. From this volume, even though it is a miscellany, one gets a picture of a whole way of life—led arduously in a semi-wilderness. One learns what these backwoodsmen are, or were, really like, what jests amuse them, what wisdom they have garnered. The separate stories fall into a larger pattern.

As to the stories themselves, the longest and most ambitious—it is really a novelette—is called **"Jacob's Ladder."** Very simple, and at times quite heartrending, this is a tale of a pitiful young couple who run off together from the piney-woods and who are met everywhere they wander by ill-luck, malice or injustice. All they ask is to earn a living, whether at fishing, trapping or 'shining they do not much care, but everywhere men or circumstances conspire to defeat them, and in their simplicity they cannot fight back. "There ain't nothin' left to try," Mart tells Florry. "There ain't no'eres left to go. We been a-climbin' ol' Jacob's ladder thouten no end to it." That there *is* finally an end, and a reasonably happy one, does not detract from the poignance or integrity of a story which is as limpid and unstudied as they come.

"Gal Young Un," which won the first O. Henry prize for 1933, is another of the longer stories. Its pattern, however, is more complex and somewhat more artificial. A gray, gaunt, upright widow, hidden away in the backwoods, is courted by a cheap young ne-er-do-well who desires her only for her money. Because she is infatuated, they marry, and at once he shatters the serenity of her setting by installing a still and bringing with him his flashy friends. Eventually he brings also a timid young mistress—who opens Matt's eyes to his essential cruelty and callousness. The struggle, then, is a queer, silent, dogged one between these three protagonists, with her background strengthening old Matt for final victory. **"Gal Young Un,"** in short, plays one more variation on the fable of the worm that turns. It is a good story, sharp, adroit, vigorous, but it has just a faint whiff of the synthetic.

As for the purely humorous stories, they beggar description. How convey, since they depend so much on the fruity tang of dialect, their crackling, comic homeliness? Mrs. Rawlings has a special genius for this kind of yarn, which seems much more artless than it is. **"Benny and the Bird Dogs,"** for instance, which has again and again been reprinted in various anthologies, is just about as funny a contemporary story as any I have run across. Its old scalawag of a hero cuts the fool in a really legendary manner. **"Varmints,"** too, which concerns a lifelong feud over one perverse and unnatural mule, has the same dry and salty quality. Add to these **"Alligators,"** and that faintly wistful comedy of marriage, **"Cocks Must Crow,"**

and you have a group of rip-roaring folk yarns which borrow from and improve upon the tradition of the tall tale.

Naturally, not everything in this volume is minted gold. I was not particularly impressed by either **"The Enemy"** or **"A Plumb Clare Conscience,"** and even **"The Pardon,"** though unquestionably effective, struck me as a little obvious, a little theatrical. On the whole, however, **When the Whippoorwill** is so far above the average of the usual casual collection of stories that Mrs. Rawlings has reason to be proud. With complete mastery of the vernacular, with an appreciation of their qualities which is at once tender and amused, she has presented a robust, self-respecting people as it seems they must really be. There is, in this volume, a minimum of the nostalgic and the patronizing. Simply, the author knows her Florida background, and cares enough for it to depict it truthfully and without flourishes. This is good regional writing—a phenomenon not so frequent as one might suppose.

Jonathan Daniels

SOURCE: A review of *When the Whippoorwill,* in *The Saturday Review of Literature,* Vol. XXII, No. 7, June 8, 1940, p. 6.

In ten stories of her own belated Florida frontier and one tender interlude with a grave boy in the Carolina mountains Mrs. Rawlings continues and sustains her warm and understanding treatment of hell-raising folks and rabbity shy ones, all of whom, except such cold trash as Trax Colton, make good laughter or show a half-secret tenderness more precious for the hiding. Though often in a poverty as hard as Florry Leddy and her man Martin found, and a loneness as complete and at last as bitter as Mattie Syles knew, they occupy a good world with standards which are sound as well as quaint.

There is sentiment to overflowing in Mrs. Rawlings's stories of rip-snorting old men and scolding women, of varmints, and of boy and gal young uns hungry in loneliness. Some of them come perilously close to sentimentality. But her stories are by no means all new cane syrup and Florida sunshine. There is meanness and injustice, and practically everything our welfare workers and welfare writers would associate with underprivilege. Her concern, however, is not with the economic and social order but with the human heart. She gives her characters dignity in bootlegging and integrity in the midst of undoubted malnutrition.

The literary race of her people is both familiar and long known. The Florida scrub folk are the same company that filled so many books about the Appalachian people, sharing a similar patterned poverty in a similar isolation. But Mrs. Rawlings has not only moved from the mountains to Florida in developing a locale peopled by persisting frontiersmen, she has also added a skill and a wisdom to the tales about them. These stories are fit company for her novels about the same people.

Brian Howard

SOURCE: A review of *When the Whippoorwill,* in *The New Statesman and Nation,* Vol. XX, No. 502, October 5, 1940, pp. 339-40.

[T]his is the best for air raids, and especially for those who entertain a natural, or acquired, nostalgia for "the deep South." The characters are nearly all drawn from those odd, simple people, the Florida Crackers. Sugar-cane cooking; night-fishing in the Gulf of Mexico; moon-shining; square-dancing—it is all there, deployed against the background of a sultry and poetic vegetation. The language has its charm, too. In **"Cocks Must Crow"** one suspicious woman introduces herself to another:

> "You're a widow, they tell me. Soda?"
> "Water. Water and whisky."
> "I never heard tell of a water-widow."
> "He was drunk as ten coots and fell in the water
>   and never did come up. A lake's as good a
>   burying-place as any."

Among others, **"Varmints"** is a good story about an eccentric mule, and **"Benny and the Bird Dogs"** has something pleasantly crazy about it that eludes definition. In **"Jacob's Ladder,"** which is really a short novel, the scene moves for a time to a remote corner of the Florida coast. If the author is to be relied on, this must be one of the most obsessing and desirable places in the world. Palms, pelicans, oysters, cypresses, oleanders, figs, unfamiliar fish, water-turkeys, fiddler crabs, and endless uninhabited islands to explore. Delicious.

CROSS CREEK (1942)

Katherine Woods

SOURCE: A review of *Cross Creek,* in *The New York Times Book Review,* March 15, 1942, p. 1.

The new book by the author of *The Yearling* is not a novel. But it could have been written only from a born novelist's sensitiveness and skill. *Cross Creek* is one of those unclassifiable books which weave the threads of personal experience and observation and acquaintance into a far-spun texture beyond the writer's individual existence or surface contact. Observation and acquaintance have become insight; experience is not mere event but response. The novelist's awareness has touched people and place and incident, and the result is beauty and laughter and poignancy and truth. So the understanding and artistry—both alike robust and exquisite—that told the story of *The Yearling* and of *South Moon Under* re-create the vital entity of the Florida back-country where Marjorie Kinnan Rawlings has found and made her home: the scene, the folk, the "creatures" of Cross Creek.

It is a tiny place, a bend in the road, a connecting stream between two lakes, in a remote land of fertile hammock and unfenced pasture and ancient wood and orange grove, four miles from the nearest village, considerably farther from a town. Its stable population consists of five white and two colored families, but a few derelicts are tolerantly received and looked after as they come and go, and a few strangers make tentative settlements now and then. Eagles nest in tall cypresses, egrets and ibis and great herons may be seen by the water, chameleons like tiny dragons enjoy old houses' domesticity, and in the marsh the grazing cattle seem half lost in water hyacinths. It is a land of primitive living, of necessitous toil, and of enchantment. When Mrs. Rawlings had sold her first Florida stories she could plant the old pecan field to more oranges in her seventy-two-acre grove; but in the early days of difficulty and question old black Martha brought the earth's word of comfort: "Ain't nobody never gone cold-out hongry here."

And Martha, ageless and sure, "like a dusty Fate, spinning away at the threads of our Creek existence," spoke, too, her own philosophy: "I reckon you know, you got to be satisfied with a place to make out. And is you satisfied, then it don't make too much difference does you make out or no." Tom Glissen, a next-farm neighbor, put his feeling with more concrete emphasis: "I wouldn't live anywhere else if I had gold buried in Georgia," Tom said. "I tell you, so much happens at Cross Creek."

It does. There are such obvious challenges, of course, as the desperate all-night struggle of a sudden freeze among the Winter oranges, or an outbreak of belligerence as when black Cissie's Henry poured buckshot into his sister Adrenna's all-but-worthless new man, or the search around the lake for the wayward Mr. Tubble, found asleep on a tussock close to a gallon jug. But subtler dramas, too, are all about. The carpenter Moe lives his sturdy, frustrated, proud and lonely life, and is Mrs. Rawlings's friend in mutual respect and untroubled equality. An invitation to a "pound party" brings the enlightening acquaintance of the Townsends, imperturbably poised and courteous, immune to education and resistant to all Public Health aids, delightedly buying an "ottymobile" with the piled-up earnings of $36 paid on Saturday night and as happily borrowing money for food on Monday morning.

But in the far stretches of wilderness where Mrs. Rawlings rode with a village friend—sixteen hours in the saddle—to take the census (across the River Styx that was not idly named), a piano sent the music of talented, loving fingers from a half-starved cabin in the piney woods; and there dauntless toiling pride could tell its story. The glorious inebriation of Mister Marsh Turner might set him to smashing any one else's furniture as well as his own, yet would leave him still a magnificent gentleman, recognized as such by those "infallible snobs," the Negroes, who always put the "Mister" before his name. Farce-comedy is played out in the drama of Mr. Martin's pig among the petunias. But the tragic compulsion of the black stranger 'Geechee's story is too heartbreaking to forget.

And as "so much happens" among the uninhibited, tolerant, brave and generous men and women of the Cross Creek country, so the country itself offers its adventure, and every season unfolds its special drama around the year. After the Summer's lush slow passage will come the strange leaden heat of the early Autumn days before storm, when all the Negro superstitions wake and spread with heavy vitality; and when rain and wind have ended their gigantic onslaught the superb Fall days are piled full of activity, and every family grinds its sugar-cane in its own mill and boils its syrup and its peanuts, too. The hard fights against frost have their own magic: "I have seen no more beautiful thing in my life than my orange grove at night, lighted by the fatwood fires." And there is a singing beauty of shared excitement in the fox hunts in the Summer moonlight (but it's the chase, not the kill, that is the adventure, and they are always glad when the fox goes free).

Incident aplenty was in the boat trip, with only another woman as companion, on the virtually uncharted (because always changing) reaches of the northward-flowing St. John's River, where the almost imperceptible drift of the water hyacinths bore the only witness to the difference between current and swamp; but it is the permeating response to nature that makes the story really thrilling. And all through this full-packed book which is far too sophisticated for any merely pagan philosophy, the birds and beasts that are this country's denizens are as alive as the people themselves, against the vivid life and beauty, the mystery and persistence, of this unfamiliar land.

In the flexibility of her response Mrs. Rawlings's style, like her mood, is always suited to her material; and she catches the community of land and people, so, in the strength and mirth and loveliness of her book. That wholeness of communication, of embodiment, is what gives *Cross Creek* its unique character and value: not alone its beauty, or compassion, or earthy understanding, but the integrated re-creation that is the fruit of them all. This is such re-creation as Isak Dinesen (though with more classic perfection) gave to the Kenya uplands in *Out of Africa,* and Marie Mauron (with sympathy not quite so complete) in *Le Quartier Mortisson* to Provence. This book of Florida needs no comparison, however; it is Florida, nothing else. Yet in a different sense it reaches out toward everything: in this sharp and tender recognition, man and the earth and its fruits and creatures are seen and felt as a universal whole. Earth gives itself to the love and toil and laughter of needy man—himself so strangely both free and fate-ridden. "But we are tenants and not possessors. Cross Creek belongs to the wind and the rain, to the sun and the seasons, to the cosmic secrecy of seed, and, beyond all, to time."

Louis B. Salomon

SOURCE: A review of *Cross Creek,* in *The Nation,* Vol. 154, No. 12, March 21, 1942, p. 346.

There is a deceiving simplicity about *Cross Creek,* a book of pleasant reminiscences of "a bend in a country road"

by the sharply perceptive author of *The Yearling.* By the time you finish it you realize that it is more than the story of the people and flora and fauna of a backwoods community: it is a way of life—a way that smacks of Thoreau, without Thoreau's asceticism, for the author, while believing that nature possesses the secret of happiness, loves all sorts of people, and records their peculiarities of temper and dialect with zest and humor.

"I do not understand," she writes, "how anyone can live without some small place of enchantment to turn to." She herself has found her small place among the colored folk, the white folk, the magnolia trees, the hogs, and the waters of the *Yearling* country, and in this narrative of her sojourn there she reveals herself again as an extremely sensitive observer, who sees much that others do not and feels keenly about everything. It is as if color and sound and happiness and sorrow were all heightened for her, and she translates this brightness and sharpness for the reader. It is hard to believe her assertion that writing causes her "great mental anguish," when her style is so natural, so apparently spontaneous, so full of quick humor and quick sympathies. The Florida she pictures is not the Florida of the resort folders; it is hard and crude, but being at least quiet and warless it has a good deal to recommend it just now, and *Cross Creek* places it before you with haunting charm.

Carroll Munro

SOURCE: A review of *Cross Creek,* in *The Saturday Review of Literature,* Vol. XXV, No. 14, April 4, 1942, p. 368.

Marjorie Rawlings raises oranges and good stories at Cross Creek. And, being a good novelist, she sees even more than meets the eye. Her *Cross Creek* more or less comprises the original research for a dozen novels, at least two hundred and sixty-five assorted short stories, and five and one-half serial stories suitable for publication in the very best women's magazines. Not that Mrs. Rawlings suitably disposes of any of the Cross Creek tales in a wholly pleasing and commercial manner as far as the women's magazines are concerned. Her eyes are too sharp for that; her romantic micrometer too accurately manipulated.

Cross Creek lies back yonder "t'-other side of the swamp. It's a bend in a country road, by land. . . . " And it's more than that. Cross Creek is sub-tropical, and it is lush. There are exotic birds and beasts about, snakes underfoot, oranges hanging on trees, five white families, two colored families, and assorted derelicts.

From time to time Mrs. Rawlings has been described as a "sophisticated city woman" who chooses to live in the Florida backwoods. It is a puzzling description. She is a good cook on her own admission. Although pardonably indifferent to rattlesnake hors d'oeuvre, she knows a thing or two about "hush-puppies" and blackbird pie. Not that such knowledge implies a lack of sophistication. Rather it would seem to be indicative of what Cross Creek does to some people.

Mr. Tubble winds himself up on a tussock with a gallon jug. Higginbotham breaks his heart in the snake market. 'Geechee drinks corn liquor occasionally, all the time. Mister Marsh Turner drinks corn liquor all the time, occasionally. Kate contrives to mix up her sweetheart and her man Henry in the same bed and gets routed out at the point of a Winchester rifle. It is fun. And hard work. For Mrs. Rawlings knows well enough that it takes more than a Dutch Oven to make a meal. And she knows that it takes first-hand experience as well as artistry to make a good book.

This book is certainly first hand. Mr. Martin's pig was shot by Mrs. Rawlings. It was her dog Mandy the neighbors poisoned. And it was Mrs. Rawlings who prepared the duck her friend Dessie shot on the wing with a .22 rifle. Incidentally, Dessie would appear to be quite an individual. Daniel Boone might have taken her to wife had she been his contemporary. Throughout the years at Cross Creek Mrs. Rawlings takes things as they come, whether a frost in her orange grove, or an unjust feud with Tom Glisson. She has a way with her. Never does she forget that human relationships are difficult at best. Nor does she forget that Cross Creek, and perhaps almost everything on earth " . . . belongs to the wind and the rain, to the sun and the seasons, to the cosmic secrecy of seed, and beyond all, to time."

Cross Creek is in a sense an unclassifiable book. It is not a "local color" book. Nor would it fit into, although it might nudge the category of "Florida, Flora, and Fauna." It is not even a good sociological report. The Floyd family negate that possibility. No competent sociologist would admit into his records the fact that the Floyds thoroughly enjoyed belonging to the underprivileged class. Rather, and for the lack of anything better, *Cross Creek* would seem to be pure Marjorie Kinnan Rawlings. It's an autobiography. And for the sake of the record, it is necessary to add that Mrs. Rawlings does not make herself out either quaint, or amusing, or gay, or tragic. In *Cross Creek* she reveals herself as a good cook and an artist. That is an accomplishment, indeed, for one woman.

THE SOJOURNER (1953)

Louis Bromfield

SOURCE: A review of *The Sojourner,* in *The Saturday Review,* Vol. 36, No. 1, January 3, 1953, pp. 9-10.

Marjorie Kinnan Rawlings's new novel, *The Sojourner,* is a good novel. It is a solid novel. At moments it has passages of inspired writing, although it never quite attains the fire and the feeling of the author's *The Yearling,* which was very popular with both critics and public some years ago.

I say this realizing that there is nothing more tiresome than for a reviewer to compare the current work of an author with some earlier book which had a notable success and then complain because it is not the same book over again. Once a novelist achieves one outstanding success, the pressure of publishers, reviewers, and public is all toward inducing him to write the same book over again; and when he does not do so, all three complain that the new book is not up to his usual standard. It takes a strongwilled writer to resist these pressures; and few have achieved it.

I do not compare Mrs. Rawlings's present book with *The Yearling* because I would like to see her write *The Yearling* over again, but because there seems to be something wrong either with novelists or with the public today—or with both—which makes most novels seem uninteresting, or at least less interesting than the novels of ten or fifteen years ago. In other words, I think that if *The Sojourner* had appeared ten or fifteen years ago it would have been acclaimed by reviewers and would have headed toward the top of the best-seller list at a time when the sale of a best seller mounted into hundreds of thousands. Today, few best sellers on the fiction lists reach a sale of a hundred thousand. . . .

In *The Sojourner* Miss Rawlings has told in good, sober prose what is virtually a Biblical story of a really good man and his tribulations. In some respects it is the story of all good men who are inevitably subject to becoming victims and whose greatness arises from their inward capacity to accept their victimization without bitterness or spiritual atrophy, I suspect that the story would have gained in strength if it had been, frankly and boldly, a contemporary story. The time and the place are both blurred, deliberately so; but it gives a remoteness to the characters.

It is the story of two brothers, one born in joy and the other in bitterness by a mother who eventually went mad. One was a plodder, one a brilliant, physically attractive waster. Mrs. Rawlings has followed in great detail the life of the plodder. The attractive wastrel leaves the pages of the book almost at once and, until the end, one hears of him only by rumor. From time to time one hungers for news of him. The author describes the wastrel admirably and then abandons him until we come upon him dying at the end of what appears to be a wasted life. We do not even know whether or not it *was* a wasted life or how the unmoral, attractive Ben himself regarded it. I think that at times, because of this lack of contrast, the good brother, Asahel, seems duller than he really was.

One does miss the lift of *The Yearling.* It was as if the earlier book were written out of the heart because the author *had* to write it. There are moments in *The Sojourner* which read like so many novels that appear today—as if the author felt that he must go ahead and finish it. Do not let me mislead you. Mrs. Rawlings is a skilled and able writer, and she has a good story to tell. The characters are, as they say, "well drawn," although at times one feels that she is laying on the whimsy a bit thick.

The Sojourner is a good book. It is a solid book. You will enjoy it if you are one of those who still finds time for reading anything beyond "condensations." But somehow, like most of the fiction appearing today, it seems to lack excitement and fire. . . .

Coleman Rosenberger

SOURCE: A review of *The Sojourner,* in *New York Herald Tribune,* Vol. 29, No. 21, January 4, 1953, p. 3.

In *The Sojourner,* a moving and beautiful book, Marjorie Kinnan Rawlings has written the story of one man's life, and in the selling has endowed it with a measure of significance for every man. Asahel Linden, whose story she tells, was a farmer, living out his eighty years from the 1860s to the 1940s, but the elements of his story are as timeless as the continuing search of mortal men for certitude and understanding and brotherhood.

Mrs. Rawlings' talent as a story teller—her ability to evoke character and mood, to create a narrative of sustained interest—is widely and affectionately known. This talent is abundantly evident in *The Sojourner.* Simply as a story it is an engrossing and engaging book.

This is in itself no small achievement. But to evoke characters who seem to move with a life of their own, to enrich these characters and their experiences with a degree of meaning and relevance beyond their time and place, without lessening their reality as individuals facing individual problems, is to test the limits of the novel as a literary form.

It is in these terms, it seems to me, that *The Sojourner* deserves to be considered, and in these terms it is a major achievement.

Mrs. Rawlings takes her title and her theme from the First Book of Chronicles "For we are strangers before thee, and sojourners, as were all our fathers; our days on the earth are as a shadow, and there is none abiding." She provides, if I am not mistaken, an explicit symbol in Asahel Linden's name. For I am told that the meaning of Asahel, one of those names in the Bible which occur but three or four times, is "God hath made."

Surely Mrs. Rawlings' Asahel—sojourner on earth, planting and harvesting the land with no title to it, inarticulate but hungering for communication, groping toward answers to man's ancient questions, coming to recognize good and evil in their many disguises—is man made by God.

Mrs. Rawlings' story of Asahel begins when he is twenty, standing with his brother and mother—"three unmourning mourners"—at the fresh mound of his father's grave. It closes sixty years later, with Asahel's own death. Yet the quality of Mrs. Rawlings' prose is such that there are no sudden breaks in the narrative. The events, often dramatic and sometimes unexpected, which are singled out

over the six decades, seem to move with the inevitability of the seasons. The sixty years of *The Sojourner* form as unified a whole as the twelve months of *The Yearling.* Only once, in the development of Asahel's eldest son, was I conscious of what seemed to me a discordant quality, and this may well be a deliberate effect to emphasize the direction of his development.

Asahel's lighthearted brother, who is seen but briefly at the beginning and at the end of the novel, remains throughout an important figure in the continuing effect which the image of him has upon the minds of the others. He leaves home to escape the dominance of his mother, and for her the hope of his return becomes an obsession which churns up all the evil of her nature. For Asahel, always profoundly aware of an essential loneliness of the individual, he is the embodiment of the fact that "Every man has lost his brother." For the girl that he had loved lightly and left behind, and whom Asahel loves deeply and marries, the loss is less for there seem no currents to be stirred very far below the surface of her warm gayety.

Asahel's wife is for him light and warmth in his isolation, but, oblivious even to the fact of that isolation, she can provide no fellowship or communication with him which might dispel it.

Seeing the qualities which develop in his children—the ruthless greed of the eldest, the vacuity of the second—intensifies his sense of separateness and adds a feeling of failure as a father. Then, with the youngest child, the starry-eyed and incorruptible Dolly, there flashes a flame of understanding and communication.

Asahel's affinity with others, too, the lost and lonely and wandering, who in their various ways maintained an integrity and dignity—the gypsies who camped each year on the farm, the old Indian who had seen his way of life destroyed, the sad-gay little hired man taken to drink, even the dark quiet man met briefly on the train—is presented with such compassion and beauty of language.

There are two pivotal scenes in the novel the emotional impact of which, I think, will be sharply felt by almost any reader. These, significantly for the theme of the novel, are scenes of birth and death. In the first, the tense fight for the life of mother and child, the reader is fully caught up in the sustained anxiety of the uncertain struggle. The second, the death of a child in snow, a scene which in less sure hands could scarcely have avoided the sentimental, is written with a poignancy which is not likely to leave any reader unaffected.

At the end of Asahel's long life—"so brief a sojourn, not even a full century"—we have in his reverie a summing up:

"He too, he recognized, had sought to find the unfindable. He had lost and sought a brother, and it was in the faces of all men he should have peered. He had been homeless, and knew that for such men as he there was no home, only an endless journey. He had sought to know the unknowable. He and his whole race, great, slow, grop-ing, God-touched children, would have to wait a long time, he supposed, for that, learning one lesson a millennium, sometimes forgetting it and having to begin all over. He himself, he thought humbly, had learned far too little. He had done much harm. He had known good from evil, and he had sat miserable and mute when the fight was called for. He had carried his standards into battle perhaps not quite too late."

The story of Asahel Linden, sojourner on the earth, is a luminous fable of man, affirmative and hopeful.

Frances Gaither

SOURCE: A review of *The Sojourner,* in *The New York Times Book Review,* January 4, 1953, p. 4-5.

Mrs. Rawlings' grove at Cross Creek, in Alachua County, Fla., earlier yielded books as reliably as oranges: from **South Moon Under** through **The Yearling,** so widely and justly loved, to a total of six in its first decade. It was as though their author knew, or needed anyway, no other soil, no other climate to nourish her talent forever. Certainly her readers, enchanted by a virgin world where an idyll of boy and fawn sprouted as easily as the green palmetto, coveted no transplanting. But now it comes to light that Mrs. Rawlings—even as Adam, whom the Lord God sent forth from Eden to till the ground from which he was taken—has of late been hard at work on an old farm conceived as somewhere west of the Hudson River valley. The result, after a long silence, is the present novel, **The Sojourner,** a Literary Guild selection for January. Moreover, by interior evidence of **The Sojourner,** she is as much at home there as her sojourner himself, who in all his life was never, with one brief exception, to travel farther away than he could go by sleigh in winter or light buggy in summer.

The elder Linden, having been a hard taskmaster, died unmourned in the Civil War decade, and perforce left his farm behind him. To his widow it was property to be used for power—both in life and even after. To Benjamin, her elder and only loved son, it was a jail to be swiftly fled as soon as the jailer was underground.

Ase, the younger son, left to deal single-handed with his bitter-tongued mother, the stark old house, the barn and its creatures, the winter fields (three hundred acres broad) and, more ambiguously, with Ben's careless, unfinished courtship, was conscious chiefly of his own inadequacy. Yet, prowling lonely in a freezing twilight, he was already seeing how such a slope might some far-off spring foam with peach bloom and apple and awkwardly composing a note: "Asahel Linden requests the pleasure of the company of Miss Nellie Wilson at the Grange dance, if not too late in asking."

The best of **The Sojourner,** to one reader at least, abide in the small indigenous particulars which just this author can so well supply. She knows how a man scans those autumn skies for the snow needed to save his winter wheat and, with him, the exact color of every kind of honey. Apple-blossom is as pale as April sunlight; clover, like the brook water under the willows; buckwheat, which comes latest, makes a red black comb, strong and pungent. She gives us the taste of Nellie's stupendous cooking, the fragrance of her kitchen. "Apple rings were drying in pans on the back of the slow-burning range. There was the smell of molasses cookies, of raspberry tarts, of butternuts, hickory and black walnuts, the spice of rose geranium Nellie had brought inside in fear of sudden frost . . . the freshness of clean starched curtains."

This is no mere embellishment of events as chronicled. Such details, by accretion, build a world compact and abundant to sustain all its indwellers: not only Ase, plodding about his chores and leafing through his encyclopedia, and pretty Nellie, busy as a wren beside him, but also their children, his greedy mother and what Nellie calls his cronies, from fiddling old Tim McCarthy down to wistful young Jan in the hired man's house. If Ase was never to own the land he worked but belatedly (and then for only so long as it takes to put a deed, sweat-grimed from a vagabond's pocket, into a clean envelope and post it) the reader is nevertheless full fed at last—unless, incurably nostalgic, he yearns still for Florida sun and life forever at morning.

THE SECRET RIVER (1955)

Ellen Lewis Buell

SOURCE: A review of *The Secret River,* in *The New York Times Book Review,* May 15, 1955, p. 28.

Although Marjorie Kinnan Rawlings' **The Yearling** has long been as much at home in the juvenile library as in the adults', **The Secret River** is the only story that Mrs. Rawlings wrote expressly for children. It is a strange, haunting tale which lends itself to different interpretations, according to age and temperament.

It is the story of Calpurnia, a child of the Florida forests, who, having heard that hard times have come because of a shortage of fish, sets out on a fishing trip of her own. She finds a secret river, of superlative beauty, makes a fine catch and on her way back through the dark woods she feeds a bear and a panther. Safely home, she has the satisfaction of knowing that she has "turned hard times into soft times" for her family and neighbors.

So far, this might be just an engaging tale of a child's make-believe adventure, set against a realistic, beautifully detailed background, but there is the enigma of the secret river. The wisest woman in the woods tells Calpurnia that she will never find it again but that she can always go there in her mind. Perhaps the river is a symbol of all the wonderful places created in the imagination.

Or, as suggested by the late Maxwell Perkins in a letter to the author, it was a real river, transformed by a child's pleasure in discovery into an enchanted place. Certainly this is not a story for realists who demand a definite answer, but for the imaginative it will have an indefinable quality of wonder.

Virginia Kirkus' Service

SOURCE: A review of *The Secret River,* in *Virginia Kirkus' Service,* Vol. XXIII, No. 10, May 15, 1955, p. 327.

A wistful and rather lovely story with significance for young and old comes from Marjorie Kinnan Rawlings' posthumous papers, a short piece she had been keeping in hopes of someday turning it into a full book. It is a simple tale of a little Florida swamp girl, whose folk poet's mind makes a dream reality. Calpurnia, the little girl, hears from her father that times are hard and that there are no fish to catch. Then she goes to Mother Albirtha, the wisest woman in the swamps, and is told of a secret river where there are many fish. So Calpurnia goes there to catch the catfish which she gives to animals and people on the way home, and brings good times to her community. Though she tries to find the river again she can never see it except in her imagination. Soft, woodsy pictures in black and white on brown are by Leonard Weisgard.

Helen Adams Masten

SOURCE: A review of *The Secret River,* in *The Saturday Review,* Vol. 38, No. 30, July 23, 1955, pp. 28-9.

The Secret River is the only complete work found among the papers of Marjorie Kinnan Rawlings after her death. The author's correspondence with her editor, Maxwell Perkins, shows that she had some idea of allowing this brief story to grow into a longer book. Had this happened this little masterpiece of the imagination of childhood might never have reached children, to whom it rightly belongs.

The beauty of the cypress trees, knee deep in water; the hungry, stoical people of the Florida forests; the child Calpurnia, who learns that "the secret river is in your mind. You can go there any time you want to," and her humorous little dog, Buggy-horse—all these are so real and appealing one regrets that this is the only book the author wrote for children.

Leonard Weisgard has done some of his most sensitive work in drawings that have a feeling for character and place and are quite perfect for the text.

A special kind of enchantment is inherent in this little book, which should have a strong appeal for anyone who has imagination or understanding of the magical things that happen to a child.

SHORT STORIES BY MARJORIE KINNAN RAWLINGS (1994)

Publishers Weekly

SOURCE: A review of *Short Stories by Marjorie Kinnan Rawlings,* in *Publishers Weekly,* Vol. 241, No. 11, March 14, 1994, p. 68.

Admirers of Rawlings's Pulitzer Prize-winning **The Yearling** and her other novels should welcome this first collection of all but two of her short works, most originally published in the *New Yorker,* the *Saturday Evening Post* and *Scribner's Magazine* between 1928 and 1953. The stories, some only a couple of pages long, are presented in order of publication and come together piece by piece like the blocks of a simple homespun quilt. From the early **"Jacob's Ladder"** to **"A Mother in Mannville"** and **"Fish Fry and Fireworks,"** Rawlings sharpened her storytelling skills and deepened her understanding of the backwoods world of her Florida neighbors and the African Americans who worked for them. She had a knack for setting each scene with a few homey details, putting the reader right inside the story. Dialect, colorful but always intelligible, was used to great effect. In **"Cracker Chidlings"** Fatty Blake critiques his neighbor's Brunswick Stew: "'I was born and raised in Floridy and I'm pertickler. I don't want to squirrel eyes lookin' at me out o' my rations!'" Tarr's introduction provides essential background to set these stories in the context of the time and Rawlings's efforts to face her own feelings about race. **"Black Secret,"** her last work on the subject, won an O. Henry Prize, as did **"Gal Young Un."**

Booklist

SOURCE: A review of *Short Stories by Marjorie Kinnan Rawlings,* in *Booklist,* Vol. 90, No. 16, April 15, 1994, p. 1513.

The previously uncollected stories of the writer who remains Florida's best, though Rodger Tarr, who has edited this collection in a nice piece of scholarship, says that Rawlings' literary reputation has been in steady decline since her death in 1953 and that her short stories are uneven. Perhaps, but they capture with great integrity and verve a Florida that no longer exists. And they don't seem dated. The best of them may be **"Gal Young Un,"** an O. Henry Prize winner in 1932 that seems, nonetheless, contemporary in its portrait of an independent woman who is exploited by a faithless drifter. And yet what appeals most through the years is Rawlings' ear for dialect, as in **"Varmints"**: "There's no woman in the State of Florida has got more patience with the varmint in a man than me. It's in his blood, just like a woman has got a little snake and a mite of cat."

Additional coverage of Rawlings's life and career is contained in the following sources published by The Gale Group: *Authors and Artists for Young Adults,* Vol. 20; *Contemporary Authors,* Vol. 137; *Contemporary Authors New Revision Series,* Vols. 74, 104; *Dictionary of Literary Biography,* Vols. 9, 22, 102; *Junior DISCovering Authors; Major Authors and Illustrators for Children and Young Adults; Something about the Author,* Vol. 100; *Twentieth-Century Literary Criticism,* Vol. 4; and *Yesterday's Authors of Books for Children,* Vol. 1.

Seymour Simon

1931-

American author of nonfiction and fiction.

Major works include *The Paper Airplane Book* (1971), *Einstein Anderson* Series (1980-1983), *Chip Rogers, Computer Whiz* (1984), *Space Photo* Series (1985-1992) and *Icebergs and Glaciers* (1987).

The following entry presents criticism of Simon's works from 1985 through 1999. For discussion of his earlier works, please see *Children's Literature Review,* Vol. 9.

INTRODUCTION

Seymour Simon is best known for his nonfiction science books which cover topics that include animal behavior, astronomy, physics, chemistry and computers. His natural curiosity and experiences as a teacher influence his writing style and provide him with ideas for his books, which are aimed at middle school students. In fact, quite often his books are inspired by questions of his or his students. Simon believes in the personal rewards of learning by doing. To that end, several of his books include simple experiments that readers can try on their own. Another common feature of his books is that they contain questions to make the reader think. Sometimes the answers are provided; other times the answers come about through activities or experiments. Several of Simon's books encourage children to explore their own immediate environments. In an interview for the *Lion and the Unicorn,* Simon stated, "To me, science is a way of finding out about the world." Critics point to Simon's clear, straightforward writing style that is both stimulating and to the point. They also commend his ability to lead children gradually into complex ideas. Simon is recognized as a scientist who successfully couples his enthusiasm with a knowledge of teaching skills to conceive authoritative and interesting books for children.

Besides nonfiction, Simon has also written several fiction books that focus on science and computers. While critics often note the lack of plot in these books, they also make note of his smooth writing style and his use of humor in the books. Even more, they praise his ability to introduce young readers to science and computers in a fiction format.

Biographical Information

Seymour Simon, born on August 9, 1931, in New York City, has always been interested in science. His interest in astronomy and technology started with the science fiction magazines he read as a child. He later attended

the Bronx High School of Science and was the president of the Junior Astronomy Club at the American Museum of Natural History.

In 1953, Simon received his B.A. from City College (now City College of the City University of New York). That same year he married Joyce Shanock and then spent the next couple of years in the U.S. Army. In 1955, Simon began taking graduate courses at City College, centering most of his studies on animal behavior. The observations from these studies he later used in books about animals for children. He continued taking graduate courses for five years.

After his graduate study work Simon became a teacher for the New York City public schools, where he taught science, creative writing, and other subjects to intermediate grade and junior high school students. Having always been a writer, he decided to submit some articles to *Scholastic* magazine while he was also teaching. *Scholastic* did not accept any of those articles, but they did ask him to write an article for the magazine about the moon. For the next few years, Simon taught school and wrote articles for *Scholastic*. In 1968, he published his first book, which was on animal behavior, as part of a curriculum supplement.

In 1979 Simon retired from teaching to focus on his writing. His earlier books had been "very curriculum-oriented," as Simon said in an interview for the *Lion and the Unicorn*. Although he felt those books were important, he wanted to write the type of book children would pick up on their own in the library. With extra time for writing, he turned a lot of his focus to fiction books that introduced children to science. During his career he has also reviewed juvenile science books and written occasional scientific articles for teachers.

Simon believes that science is finding out about the world, and he thinks it is important to interest children in science at as young an age as possible. In his interview for the *Lion and the Unicorn* he stated, "What I really enjoy is getting a letter from a child (or an adult sometimes) who tried out an experiment from one of my books and is writing to tell me about his discovery. When I can share his experience, it's as much fun as the first time I found something out for myself." He also pledged "to continue to write imaginative books about science, and continue to present them in ways that I think are interesting or novel."

Major Works

The Paper Airplane Book is one of Simon's most acclaimed books. In this book, Simon explains the principles of aerodynamics by using different types of paper airplanes. As readers learn about the different parts of the paper airplane and the effects each part has on the overall performance of the airplane, they also learn how real airplanes work. Critic Zena Sutherland, writing in the *Bulletin of the Center for Children's Books,* called the book "an exemplary home demonstration book," noting that "the author uses the process approach, suggesting variations on the airplane and asking the reader to consider *why* a certain effect is obtained, or which change is most effective for a desired result."

In the *Einstein Anderson* Series, Simon takes on the fiction genre. In these books, Simon uses the appealing character of Einstein Anderson who loves bad puns and solves mysteries (ten per book) through his knowledge of science. The series has been compared to Donald Sobol's *Encyclopedia Brown* books in that they invite readers to interpret a set of clues as well as to become knowledgeable about science.

Barbara Elleman, in a review for *Booklist*, wrote, "Related with spirit and peppered with puns, these will intrigue science buffs and offer entertaining possibilities for group presentation in the classroom."

Another popular fiction book is Simon's *Chip Rogers, Computer Whiz*. In this book the young protagonist solves mysteries with his computer, and exposes young readers to actual BASIC programming in the process. The solution to the mystery is contained not only in textual clues but also in an actual program which can be run on most computers. *Booklist* reviewer Denise M. Wilms called the book an "entertaining mystery" and concluded that "there's no denying its success at making the subject of computers approachable."

In the *Space Photos* Series, Simon returns to nonfiction. This series includes more than ten books, published two at a time, that include books on the Earth, planets, stars, and galaxies. Each book uses photos with concise text to explore space. Size of celestial bodies, origins of their names, and their characteristics are among the many things discussed in the books. Phillis Wilson, in a review for *Booklist*, says of *Mars* and *Uranus*, "Simon is again right on course. . . . Striking an effective balance in these books, Simon combines lucid, flowing text with spectacular photographs." And a review in *Publishers Weekly* calls *Galaxies* "fascinating and accessible."

In *Icebergs and Glaciers*, Simon continues his work in nonfiction. Using color photographs, Simon introduces readers to icebergs and glaciers and talks about their size, history, and movements. Betsy Hearne, in *The Bulletin of the Center for Children's Books*, wrote that "Simon's clean, compact writing . . . goes a long way toward covering a topic relatively untouched for this age group," and Jonathon Betz-Zall, writing for the *School Library Journal*, called Simon's book "lively and informative."

Awards

Simon has received several awards for his body of work. The National Science Teachers Association (during the period of 1972-1988) named more than thirty of his books as Outstanding Science Trade Books for Children. He has also won the Eva L. Gordon Award, American Nature Society, for contributions to children's science literature. Awards for individual titles include the Children's Book Showcase Award, presented by the Children's Book Council, for *The Paper Airplane Book* in 1972, and the Best Children's Science Book of the Year Award, presented by the New York Academy of Sciences, in 1988 for *Icebergs and Glaciers*.

TITLE COMMENTARY

HOW TO TALK TO YOUR COMPUTER AND *MEET THE COMPUTER* (1985)

Kirkus Reviews

SOURCE: A review of *How to Talk to Your Computer* and *Meet the Computer*, in *Kirkus Reviews*, Vol. LIII, No. 1, May 15, 1985, p. 40.

Of all the print generated by the computer boom, these introductions might be the most elementary. The first half of **Meet the Computer** simply points to the keyboard and screen; defines *input* and *program;* notes that programs can be stored on cassettes, disks, and cartridges; and takes "you" through a game of Space Mission that shows the computer in action. The second part goes a step beyond the obviously visible, taking "you" inside the computer to meet the CPU and its contents, a CPU chip, memory chips, and an output chip. "Now," says Simon in conclusion, "when you use a real computer at home or in school, you will know what it is doing."

How to Talk to a Computer talks in appropriate terms to kids, showing how "your friend" Anna responds easily to "Throw the ball to me," but a computer-run robot needs exact step-by-step directions. In the same mode, Simon uses a program for making a peanut-butter sandwich to demonstrate that the steps of a BASIC program must be numbered in the correct order. Introducing a second simple language, he demystifies a Logo program for drawing a square, explaining "FORWARD 100" as telling the Logo turtle to move forward "100 tiny turtle steps" and "RIGHT 90" as telling it to turn right 90 degrees. Unfortunately he doesn't explain the term 90 degrees, which is not necessarily understood at this level.

Overall, unimposing, orienting companions to a first encounter with computers, all the more approachable for [Barbara and Ed] Emberley's perky cartoons.

Denise M. Wilms

SOURCE: A review of *How to Talk to Your Computer* and *Meet the Computer,* in *Booklist,* Vol. 81, No. 18, June 1, 1985, p. 1405.

Computer literacy has a head start thanks to these two easy introductions to basic computer concepts and common terminology. In **Meet the Computer,** readers see the computer's principal external parts (a keyboard, screen, and processing unit), learn about internal mechanisms such as the chip and RAM and ROM memory, and find out how to input information or load a program that instructs a computer on what to do. **How to Talk to Your Computer** teaches some rudimentary programming concepts as well as some elementary BASIC commands. Both books have bright, colorful formats, although the accompanying cartoon drawings are sometimes a little too coy. Useful for school situations and for parents wanting to acquaint their children with home computers.

Susan Scheps

SOURCE: A review of *How to Talk to Your Computer* and *Meet the Computer,* in *School Library Journal,* Vol. 31, No. 10, August, 1985, p. 25.

Here are two companion volumes which give clear elementary introductions to the computer. **How to Talk to**

Your Computer explains how a computer knows what to do. Sequential thinking and the BASIC and LOGO languages are briefly introduced in text and illustrations. **Meet the Computer** shows what a computer can do. Large diagrams coupled with simple description provide an overview of a computer's innards and workings. The Emberleys' brightly colored cartoon robots, astronaut mice, computer parts and children—many highlighted with a black background—flow across the pages. The final two-page illustration showing children at work on several types of programs ties the whole together. Information is summarized on the last two pages of both books. Simon's two-volume introduction to computers is, to date, the only thorough presentation for the very youngest users. The eye-catching format and instructive illustrations are sure to please many a prospective young programmer.

YOUR FIRST HOME COMPUTER: BUYING IT, USING IT, AND KEEPING IT WORKING (1985)

Denise M. Wilms

SOURCE: A review of *Your First Home Computer: Buying It, Using It, and Keeping It Working,* in *Booklist,* Vol. 81, No. 18, June 1, 1985, p. 1405.

Rank (and presumably well-heeled) beginners will find lots of helpful advice in this elementary introduction to home computers. Simon first looks at what a computer is, defining its major parts and explaining its function. Then comes a look at how the average home computer is used for games or various educational programs, for word processing, or as a link to telecommunications systems. For readers who have decided to buy a computer, Simon urges shopping around and soliciting feedback from friends or user groups. He cites a few familiar brands as good value but doesn't go beyond that because of market flux (though recommended in this galley, the IBM PC*jr* is no longer produced). Services and software get quick overviews, and there is a simple introduction to BASIC programming and common computer terminology. Illustrated [by Roy Doty] with cartoon drawings, this is a useful primer for the completely uninitiated.

Edwin F. Bokee III

SOURCE: A review of *Your First Home Computer: Buying It, Using It, and Keeping It Working,* in *School Library Journal,* Vol. 32, No. 5, January, 1986, p. 78.

A brief overview of the basic components of a home computer with many sound suggestions about how to select a computer, what to do with it and how to keep it working. The writing is clear, and the glossary of computer terms will be helpful to anyone who is just becoming interested in computers. The cartoon-like illustrations are more decorative than informative. Because of the rapid changes in the computer industry, the information on specific computers and programs will become outdated very quickly. For example, Simon refers to the IBM PC Jr, which is no longer being produced. The main value of the book is that it advises children to give thought to their selection of a computer and suggests a variety of practical uses for the computer once the child has it at home. In terms of actual selection of a machine, though, students should be advised to check magazine reviews for the most current information.

E. Bruce Brooks and John D. Stackpole

SOURCE: A review of *Your First Home Computer: Buying It, Using It, and Keeping It Working,* in *Appraisal: Science Books for Young People,* Vol. 19, No. 2, Spring, 1986, pp. 37-8.

LIBRARIAN [E. Bruce Brooks]: The jacket flap claims that this book "takes the guesswork out of selecting an appropriate home computer," but this goal is not quite reached. The chapter order suggests the right method (pick an application, then a program, then hardware that can run the program), but programs mentioned are not evaluated or even described, and RAM requirements are not given, leaving the reader with a general principle, six brand names, and the suggestion to visit a computer club. The chapter on networks is effective, and obviously based on personal experience, but the other information chapters are not up to material available elsewhere. Chapter 1, on inner workings, is not as graphic as Neil Ardley's *Computers,* and Chapter 6 on BASIC, is inferior to Shelly Lipson's, *It's Basic.* Chapter 4, on care, omits telephones as a source of dangerous magnetic fields, is too relaxed about food and drink near the computer, and does not advise backing up disk contents.

SPECIALIST [John D. Stackpole]: This introduction to machines and their uses for neophytes is full of all kinds of good advice. Unfortunately the advice is rather general: "join a computer club" or "check with your friends who own one" or "deal with a reputable computer store." Well, yeah, o.k.; not that the advice is bad (indeed you would do well to do all those things and more, like try to rent what you might buy later) but it just isn't very specific. That really isn't the author's fault, either; the technology is changing too fast to say anything specific in a book—newspapers are about your best hope.

The computers being discussed are at the ATARI, Commodore, TRS-80, and Apple level; generally the ones most often thought of as "game playing"; they can do far more than that, of course, but not as much as the big boys can (IBM PC and its clones). *My* advice is get as much memory as you can.

A substantial scientific error pops up on p. 5 where microchips (transistors) are described as being made of "purified beach sand." Not so. It is the *impurities* in silicon that make transistors work.

Also it is not clear what age level the book is for—at one point the author suggests that the reader will learn about binary numbers in school. Yet how many high or junior high school kids have the 2-3 kilobucks needed to buy the hard and software described in the book?

Perhaps I am a little too hard on the book—I was in the process of selecting my first home computer (a PC clone) when the book came and it seemed to leave out the questions I was asking. Perhaps the nonspecialist reviewer will see things differently.

101 QUESTIONS AND ANSWERS ABOUT DANGEROUS ANIMALS (1985)

Kathleen Odean

SOURCE: A review of *101 Questions and Answers About Dangerous Animals,* in *School Library Journal,* Vol. 31, No. 10, August, 1985, p. 69.

Simon uses a question-and-answer format to present brief but fascinating information about animals which are, or are believed to be, dangerous to humans. His discussions of the dangers include examples of true incidents and false beliefs, and the answers also cover facts about the animal, such as size, habitat and distinguishing features. The layout is attractive, with frequent black-and-white drawings [by E. Friedman] more cartoon-like than scientific in nature. The one- to four-paragraph answers are written in straightforward, casual prose. A recurring theme is that humans present more danger to animals and other humans than do any dangerous animals. The index is skimpy, including many but not all of the animals discussed, and no other information, such as place names. . . . The Simon book, with its less demanding format and brightly colored, amusing cover, will be a popular addition on this appealing topic.

Dolores Allen

SOURCE: A review of *101 Questions and Answers About Dangerous Animals,* in *Science Books & Films,* Vol. 21, No. 3, January-February, 1986, p. 169.

This delightful and informative book answers 101 questions that children in grades three through six might ask about the habits and behavior of dangerous animals. The answers are brief, well-stated, and to the point. The simple illustrations and easy-to-read style will hold the interest of youngsters. The table of contents divides the animals by categories, and the sturdy binding should withstand rugged use in the classroom or in the home.

SOAP BUBBLE MAGIC (1985)

David Gale

SOURCE: A review of *Soap Bubble Magic,* in *School Library Journal,* Vol. 32, No. 3, November, 1985, p. 78.

After an inauspicious start of introductory pleasantries, Simon presents a variety of experiments relating to soap bubbles. In an easy-reader format, he asks questions that encourage children to make observations. More often than not, he then describes the results, although often without explanations of the causes or with incomplete ones ("Now you know why. Clear water has a stronger pull than soapy water."). Simon covers the effect of air movement on soap bubbles and bubbles' shape, cohesiveness, etc., but he does not use accurate terminology, instead calling *surface tension* "water skin," for instance. While use of easier terms may make the information more accessible to young readers, the lack of the correct terms will make later learning all the more difficult. Illustrations [by Stella Ormai] show a multi-ethnic group of young children playing with the bubbles, but they are rendered in murky yellows, pinks and greens. Budding scientists will enjoy the activities suggested here, even if the presentation does have its flaws.

Selina Bendix

SOURCE: A review of *Soap Bubble Magic,* in *Science Books & Films,* Vol. 21, No. 4, March-April, 1986, p. 226.

Interracial, nonsexist illustrations accompany a text designed to encourage children to think for themselves and experiment to find the answers to their questions. The experiments use simple, inexpensive home or schoolroom materials, some of them made by the child. Soap bubbles are used to introduce the concept of surface tension. Older siblings or parents may learn something new about the behavior of water surfaces as they help a young child with the experiments. The instructions include appropriate safety warnings and ways to avoid making a mess. The systematic approach will help a child to develop an organized approach to satisfying curiosity.

THE BASIC BOOK (1985)

Joanne Troutner

SOURCE: A review of *The BASIC Book,* in *School Library Journal,* Vol. 32, No. 5, January, 1986, pp. 76-7.

A brief introduction to the world of programming in BASIC. Readers are introduced to vocabulary and writing a simple program with a print statement. The concepts of GOTO and FOR/NEXT are also explained with examples written for a birthday party. The programs are written and the concepts are explained in a generic manner that enables the instruction to fit most popular microcomputers. The clever, colorful illustrations [by Barbara and Ed Emberley] enhance the material presented. Overall, this is an excellent introduction to computers that starts at a simpler level than most others.

Orville Ruud

SOURCE: A review of *The BASIC Book,* in *Science Books & Films,* Vol. 21, No. 4, March-April, 1986, p. 223.

The BASIC Book encourages and instructs the reader on entering BASIC programs on a microcomputer. The text is built around the story of a boy who is coming to the "Science Club" house for his birthday party; his friends want to surprise him with some messages on the microcomputer. Animation, color, and graphics are used to capture the reader's interest and to make instructions explicit. In following the instructions, the reader uses the microcomputer and gains experience with statements, line numbers, command words, NEW, PRINT, END, RUN, LIST, loops, GOTO, FOR NEXT, and INPUT. The BASIC programs are approached sequentially, and lists of the programs and sample outputs are displayed. The child following these instructions will need some outside help, however, since procedures for correcting mistyped letters and lines are not explained in the text. The dictionary on the back cover and the explanations of commands within the text provide a basis for learning BASIC and trying out various uses of it.

BITS AND BYTES: A COMPUTER DICTIONARY FOR BEGINNERS (1985)

Edwin F. Bokee III

SOURCE: A review of *Bits and Bytes: A Computer Dictionary for Beginners,* in *School Library Journal,* Vol. 32, No. 5, January, 1986, pp. 76-7.

Simon's picture dictionary contains definitions for 50 of the most common terms associated with computers. Each page is divided into two panels with a computer term, a short definition, usually a brief explanation and a humorous picture. The definitions are appropriate for children who are just becoming interested in computers. For example, "Crash—When the computer suddenly stops working" is accompanied by a cheerful picture of a puzzled boy looking at a blank computer screen. Words within a definition that are explained in another section of the book are printed in capitals but there is no pronunciation guide. A lively, colorful introduction to the subject.

Orville Ruud

SOURCE: A review of *Bits and Bytes: A Computer Dictionary for Beginners,* in *Science Books & Films,* Vol. 21, No. 4, March-April, 1986, p. 223.

Bits and Bytes is a dictionary of words commonly used by people who operate microcomputers. It is intended to help young computer users understand and properly use computer words, although the age level the book is most appropriate for is difficult to gauge. The words defined include: access, address, back-up, BASIC, bug, cartridge, chip, circuit, computer, CPU, data, disk, disk drive, display, file, GIGO, graphics, hardware, input, joystick, K, keyboard, load, Logo, memory, microprocessor, mouse, output, peripheral, port, processing, program, RAM, ROM, run, save, and word processing. Illustration and animation are widely used along with written definitions of each word. With its color and animation, this book appears to be designed for student in grades one to three. However, the language used and the subject content appear more appropriate for students in grades four to six. The open-column style and large print do make the text easy to read. Another asset is that when the definition for one word uses another word defined in the book, the word is capitalized so that the user can easily locate its definition; however, since this occurs for 45 of the 50 words defined, the reader may be kept busy going around this circular path for a final definition.

SHADOW MAGIC (1985)

Selina Bendix

SOURCE: A review of *Shadow Magic,* in *Science Books & Films,* Vol. 21, No. 4, March-April, 1986, p. 226.

This experimental approach to learning about light and planetary motion through the study of shadows would be particularly useful for an introduction to these subjects in a class of young children, although some of the experiments require more dexterity than most five-year-olds possess. The concepts could already be familiar to seven-year-olds with well-educated parents. The book encourages careful observation and analysis of cause and effect relationships that abound in the everyday world. The shadows in the illustrations exhibit more artistic license than is appropriate for the book's mission, but the illustrations of children are interracial and free of gender-role bias.

Barbara C. Scott and Clarence C. Truesdell

SOURCE: A review of *Shadow Magic,* in *Appraisal: Science Books for Young People,* Vol. 19, No. 3, Summer, 1986, p. 70.

LIBRARIAN [Barbara C. Scott]: Written in I-Can-Read format, **Shadow Magic** is a simple introduction to shadows. Shadows are seen as part of the young child's everyday life, as a method of telling time and as part of our natural environment. The book is most successful when it looks at shadows in a way that is personal and real to the reader. The child is encouraged to go outside and study the shadows of various objects, to look at the shadows of materials of various opacity and to experiment with casting shadow figures. The directions for making a sun clock are clear, and there is a brief explanation of the difference between sun time and the time on a regular clock.

In discussing the earth in relation to the sun, the book gives very brief explanations that are generally sufficient. Sometimes however, in the interest of short simple sentences, explanations are too brief to be meaningful. For example, the description of the variation in shadow length throughout the day is done with a combination of picture and text that may be too abbreviated for most young children to understand.

SPECIALIST [Clarence C. Truesdell]: **Shadow Magic** is probably most honestly described as a fairly average little book about shadows. Illustrations [by Stella Ormai] are nothing special and they are accompanied by a text to match. Perhaps we would be more favorably impressed were it not that there are a number of superior books on the same subject.

It is commendable that the author shows how to make a sundial out of a piece of cardboard and a nail. It is not so commendable, however, that the illustration on page 23 shows the nail sticking up no higher than about one inch. Children who take seriously this illustration, and try to make the sundial as shown, invariably suffer a great deal of disappointment over the inadequate shadow length and underwhelming shadow movement. In brief, the sundial as shown on page 23 leads to disappointing results.

The last 18 pages of the book are devoted to making some interesting shadows with your hands, your body, and various objects. It's all good fun, and that's what this book is all about. Not much of a science book by any means, so nothing useful will come of trying to review it as if it were.

TURTLE TALK: A BEGINNER'S BOOK OF LOGO (1986)

Kirkus Reviews

SOURCE: A review of *Turtle Talk: A Beginner's Book of Logo,* in *Kirkus Reviews,* Vol. LIV, No. 8, April 15, 1986, p. 640.

An appealing fifth book in this beginning computer series.

Key terms and commands are highlighted in red type and by the accompanying illustration. Terms such as "Showturtle," "Clearscreen," and "Wrapping Around" are clearly presented both in the text, with samples of how the command appears on a computer screen, and with the whimsical turtle character demonstrating. Simon indicates that the commands will work with any of the different computer Logo programs, even though what appears on the screen may be slightly different from the illustration in the book. He does not make it clear that some detective work may be necessary to integrate these instructions with those for a particular computer.

Still, an excellent introduction to Logo for the young computer user and for computer phobics of all ages. Glossary.

Joanne Troutner

SOURCE: A review of *Turtle Talk: A Beginner's Book of Logo,* in *School Library Journal,* Vol. 32, No. 10, August, 1986, p. 109.

Another excellent book in Simon's computer book series, this one introduces youngsters to the computer language Logo (based on the LSCI version of Logo). Concise explanations of the basic commands or primitives are presented. Youngsters are exposed to the concepts of degrees and how the turtle turns on the computer screen. The REPEAT command and the development of procedures are also introduced. Overall, this volume is a well-done introduction to the Logo language for children.

Eric M. Kramer

SOURCE: A review of *Turtle Talk: A Beginner's Book of Logo,* in *Science Books & Films,* Vol. 22, No. 2, November-December, 1986, p. 103.

I liked this book very much. It is written for children who have access to a microcomputer with the Logo language, and it explains the simplest (but most important) Logo commands in an enjoyable manner. Each command is introduced on its own page or half page, along with suitable drawings and cartoons to aid understanding. Students can easily follow the explanations. Older students could use this book by themselves as a first introduction to the use of Logo on any microcomputer, while younger students could start by reading along with a teacher or another student. I was pleased to find a useful glossary of terms—nearly complete with only 18 words in it, showing that even a potentially confusing computer language can be explained clearly with a minimum numbers of terms. The book covers such terms as clearscreen (CS), left (LT), right (RT), and all the necessary commands to move the "turtle" around on the screen. The book ends by explaining how to write a procedure, the key to designing beautiful shapes and writing simple programs.

STARS AND *THE SUN*
("Space Photos" series, 1986)

Denise M. Wilms

SOURCE: A review of *Stars* and *The Sun,* in *Booklist,* Vol. 83, No. 1, September 1, 1986, p. 68.

These two titles follow in the footsteps of their elegant predecessors, **Jupiter** and **Saturn.** Impressive, large color photographs and diagrams anchor both books, whetting readers' appetite for the textual information that surrounds them. In **Stars** Simon provides a sense of their vast numbers and distance relative to Earth. He also describes their life cycles, which leads to definitions of terms such as *red giants, white dwarfs, novas,* and *black holes.* To the question of whether somewhere there are other stars that might support planetary systems and Earth-like environments, Simon gives an "almost definitely yes" answer and notes scientific efforts to monitor space for signals from intelligent life. In **The Sun,** Simon labels this vital orb a medium-sized star, though its proportions by Earth standards are gigantic. He looks at the sun's structure and atmosphere; sunspots and the magnetic forces they project are described as well. By the book's finish, the sun's unimaginably large size and powerful life-giving force are quite clear. Both books show Simon's gift for reducing complex subjects to understandable proportions. He uses concrete analogies to make points that might otherwise be hazy and provides definitions for technical terms in context. These books are handsome and informative, musts for the science shelf.

Jeffrey A. French

SOURCE: A review of *Stars* and *The Sun,* in *School Library Journal,* Vol. 33, No. 4, December, 1986, pp. 95-6.

Simon continues his series begun with **Earth** and **The Moon** and including **Jupiter** and **Saturn** with the same format and level of success in this pair on the stars and the sun. The brief text and dazzling illustrations serve as a sort of picture glossary introducing the terminology of stellar objects. **Stars** presents constellations; the distance to, size, and temperature of the stars; the nuclear power source of stellar energy; binary systems, clusters, galaxies, and quasars; the possibility of other solar systems; and stellar evolution, novae, black holes, neutron stars, and pulsars. **The Sun** discusses the sun as a star; its distance from earth, size, and temperature; the solar system; the sun's hydrogen-fueled nuclear power; the parts of the sun and its atmosphere; eclipses, sunspots, prominences, flares, and the aurorae. Some may quibble that the wording of the descriptions of some very complex topics (e.g., nuclear reactions) is at times superficial, but such cursory treatment is necessitated by the texts' brevity and the limited background of their intended audience. A couple of illustrations are handled in less than stellar fashion: the color-coded coronagraph, while spectacular in itself, is said to "show different levels of brightness in the corona," but the meaning of these varying colors is not explained at all. Nor is there any explanation of the way in which the magnetogram shows the north and south poles of sunspot pairs. Most readers will overlook these limitations, though, and revel in the other photos as well as in Simon's writing, which, in its clarity, conveys an almost childlike sense of wonder at these objects. Like the earlier titles, this pair is sure to be popular.

Sally Cartwright

SOURCE: "Two for Budding Astronomers," in *The Christian Science Monitor,* July 10, 1987, p. 26.

For readers with imagination, **Stars** and **The Sun** by Seymour Simon are breathtaking.

For adults and for children old enough to think in terms of abstraction, enormous distance, and mystery, the text and photographs in these two books will evoke fascination and wonder.

Simon briefly describes what astronomers see today. He uses familiar, graphic comparisons, such as, "If the earth were the size of a golf ball, then the sun would be a globe 15 feet across."

In simple words he gives an idea of distance: "Imagine traveling in a space ship going 10 miles a second. Even at that speed, it would still take you about three and a half months to reach the sun. But it would take more than 70,000 years to reach the next nearest star, Alpha Centauri."

Simon has authored more than 100 science books for children, and his experience wears well.

The information is simplified but accurate. The writing is direct and clear.

It's not easy to approach nebulae, quasars, and black holes with everyday vocabulary.

Although he does not explore their complex significance, such as the relation of black holes to curved space and relativity theory, he does whet the reader's appetites.

The two books are elegant, with attractive large type, page-wide photos of full color, coated paper, and hard covers. Either volume would make an inspiring gift for a 12-year-old, and possibly for an occasional 10-year-old, were he or she an incipient and enthusiastic astronomer.

While the picture-book size of the page and print might suggest that these books are suitable for younger ages, Piaget and others have shown that this kind of abstract information, so distant from our daily experience, is rarely understood and appreciated by children under 12 years of age.

The rudimentary but expansive information in these books inspired me to read further, to question and probe until I plunged into the new physics from Planck and Einstein, to Heisenberg, Bohr, and Bohm.

Although Simon himself does not go so far, his books, touching new information discovered through our speed-of-light technology may invite an exciting range of thinking and speculation.

THE LARGEST DINOSAURS (1986)

Denise M. Wilms

SOURCE: A review of *The Largest Dinosaurs*, in *Booklist*, Vol. 83, No. 3, October 1, 1986, p. 275.

Sauropods, the largest of all the dinosaurs, are introduced in this picture-book explanation. Against an imposing array of black-and-white line-and-wash drawings [by Pamela Carroll], Simon explores the latest theories on what these animals looked like, how and where they lived, and what they ate. Six particular kinds are named: apatosaurus, brachiosaurus, camarasaurus, diplodocus, supersaurus, and ultrasaurus. Accompanying illustrations include both overall views of the species as well as conceptions of what physical details such as heads, feet, or tails may have looked like. An explanation of the mystery surrounding dinosaurs' extinction rounds out the presentation. Useful for students and browsers, this may also be read aloud to children unable to read it on their own.

Kirkus Reviews

SOURCE: A review of *The Largest Dinosaurs*, in *Kirkus Reviews*, Vol. LIV, No. 20, October 15, 1986, p. 1588.

The sauropods—that's what they're called, these largest of the large, and Simon memorably tells just *how* large these dinosaurs were.

Clear images (such as larger than a school lunchroom) make information about the lizard-footed creatures stick. Discussing six types—apatosaurus, brachiosaurus, camarasaurus, diplodocus, and the recently discovered supersaurus and ultrasaurus—Simon reports their measurements, eating patterns, herding habits, even their predators, if one can imagine such a thing. Woven throughout is the knowledge of experts, who still make pioneering discoveries in this field. Specific results of their work are listed; young travelers on vacation can check up on the fossils. Large, airy drawings add further accuracy.

Sure to be popular for its clarity, accessibility, and Simon's own happy fascination with the topic, this is a delightful addition to the dinosaur collection, and, like the animals themselves, it's big.

Cathryn A. Camper

SOURCE: A review of *The Largest Dinosaur*, in *School Library Journal*, Vol. 33, No. 3, November, 1986, p. 94.

An excellent complement to Simon's **The Smallest Dinosaurs. The Largest Dinosaurs** contains much basic information on six major sauropods. Simon's prose is clear and focused; children will have no difficulty gleaning facts from the two to three pages of information provided for each dinosaur. Pronunciations of the dinosaurs' names, explanations of what the names mean, and an index also help make this book accessible to children. . . . Simon's book explains recent changes in dinosaur theory, including a discussion of the Brontosaurus' name change to Apatosaurus, and the confusion over the correct Apatosaurus skull. Carroll's ink and wash illustrations give a clear feel for the size of these creatures, but their lack of color may lose the attention of children expecting full-color prehistoric dioramas. Still, this book will be well-used both by young researchers and dinosaur fans.

ICEBERGS AND GLACIERS (1987)

Publishers Weekly

SOURCE: A review of *Icebergs and Glaciers,* in *Publishers Weekly,* Vol. 231, No. 6, February 13, 1987, pp. 94-5.

Perhaps Simon's nonfiction for children is so successful because he gets readers involved in the natural world around them, with both arresting and accessible facts. In this new book, he tells readers that the largest glacier ever measured is 200 miles long and 60 miles across; but it's also "bigger than the state of Vermont or the country of Belgium." And those glaciers *move.* Simon also covers how ice fields form and become mobile, and why they are dangerous. Readers who put icebergs and glaciers in the same category as dinosaurs—from a time long ago—learn of the relatively recent tragedy of the *Titanic,* and that icebergs someday may be used as fresh water sources in deserts. The facts are coupled with clear, full-color photographs; the correlation between text and illustration is direct and obvious, making captions unnecessary. Simon suggests that readers take a look at landscapes around them—they may just see a place where a glacier has passed by.

Betsy Hearne

SOURCE: A review of *Icebergs and Glaciers,* in *The Bulletin of the Center for Children's Books,* Vol. 40, No. 7, March, 1987, pp. 135-36.

The combination of Simon's clean, compact writing with well-selected color photography and careful book making goes a long way toward covering a topic relatively untouched for this age group. After an explanation of the consistency of snowflakes, packed snow, and ice fields, the text describes the movement of glaciers by sliding or creeping, various processes of measurement, landscape alteration, geological effects of glacial movement, and the formation of icebergs. The graphics are impressive, from a blow-up of a single, exquisitely patterned ice crystal to a computer-colored photo of Iceland taken by satellite and revealing of the stark geographical contrasts in that country. A must for the science shelf.

Jonathan Betz-Zall

SOURCE: A review of *Icebergs and Glaciers,* in *School Library Journal,* Vol. 33, No. 7, March, 1987, p. 166.

This treatment of glaciers and icebergs is beautifully illustrated, and the text is clear and well-written. Simon describes the physical composition and properties of glacial ice, including new findings of how glaciers move: either by sliding on films of water or by internal flows—"creeping." He presents facts at a basic level, without much explanation or detail, and uses fairly simple vocabulary. Every spread is illustrated with beautiful color photographs, including one computer-colored photo of Iceland that shows temperature variations. Type is large, with lots of white space. . . . This one would almost be worth adding to collections for the spectacular illustrations alone, but Simon's lively and informative text makes the book even more impressive.

Margaret A. Bush

SOURCE: A review of *Icebergs and Glaciers,* in *The Horn Book Magazine,* Vol. LXIII, No. 4, July-August, 1987, p. 485.

Spectacular views of glaciers provided by glossy photographs, some taken by satellite and some computer enhanced, accompany Simon's informative explanation of the history, formation, and movement of glaciers. Mountain glaciers, ice caps, ice sheets, and icebergs are all described, and there is also mention of particular discoveries about the behavior of glaciers and some of the methods used to study these dramatic bodies of ice. Occasionally the pictured scenes become confusing since the photographs are not captioned; most are adequately identified or explained in the text, but a few provide more visual effect than information. Some use of white print on dark blue pages adds to the book's showy style. The slim, highly visual book belies a discussion that is well structured and clear, though by no means simple. Similar in appearance to the author's recent books on planets—*Jupiter* and *Saturn*—the volume is a welcome presentation of a subject sparsely covered in recent years.

V. H. Anderson

SOURCE: A review of *Icebergs and Glaciers,* in *Science Books & Films,* Vol. 23, No. 2, November-December, 1987, p. 103.

Here Simon has compiled a selection of striking aerial and ground-based photographs of glaciers, icebergs, and glaciated terrain for an oversized, hard-cover picture book directed toward the juvenile reader. One-half to full-page color photographs are the book's dominant feature. The text, in oversized bold type and relevant to each illustration, is easily followed. There is no glossary, but the text usually successfully defines terms as they are encountered. There is a problem in the explanation of the process by which snow becomes glacial ice: " . . . the weight of the snow and ice squeezes the grains of ice together forcing out the trapped air . . . The white of airy snow becomes the steel blue of airless ice." In fact, the residual air is entrapped within the glacial ice as tiny bubbles, and these bubbles of air are today being examined as representative samples of ancient atmospheric conditions. A question might also arise concerning the aerial image of Alaskan glaciers against a landscape of red-colored terrain. Is the non-ice-covered terrain of Alaska really red? What is needed is an explanation of "false color infrared imagery" so the reader could understand that the red hue reflects healthy, vigorous vegetation. (Another solution is to eliminate this particular illustration.) The treatment of icebergs suffers pictorially from too high a concentration on the unique tabular icebergs of Antarctica versus coverage of the much smaller pinnacled icebergs of the Northern Hemisphere. These icebergs, calving off the glaciers of Greenland, for the most part, are the more serious hazards to navigation in the shipping lanes of the North Atlantic. In addition, in the many illustrations of icebergs, no differentiation is made between the glacial ice of icebergs and the numerous floes of sea ice (frozen seawater) appearing in the same images. Generally, the book's treatment of glacial ice and glaciers and ice caps and ice sheets is more comprehensive than its treatment of icebergs.

MARS AND *URANUS* ("Space Photos" series, 1987)

Phillis Wilson

SOURCE: A review of *Mars* and *Uranus,* in *Booklist,* Vol. 84, No. 4, October 15, 1987, p. 400.

A highly acclaimed and award-winning science writer, Simon is again right on course with this duo, companion volumes to his *Jupiter, Saturn, Stars,* and *The Sun.* Striking an effective balance in these books, Simon combines lucid, flowing text with spectacular photographs. Skillfully rendered drawings are interspersed as needed. Mars, the author relates, has an orbit 140 million miles away from the sun; its year is 687 Earth days long. Because the planet shines with a reddish-orange color, it made the Romans think of blood and war; hence, the name Mars, after the Roman god of war. Mars has craters, mountains, plains, valleys, and Olympus Mons, "the largest known volcano on any planet in the Solar System." Are there any Martians on Mars? Simon answers the question briefly but leaves it open-ended. In contrast to Mars, Uranus, according to Simon, orbits almost two billion miles from the sun, taking it 84 Earth years to circle the sun once. Uranus was first recognized as a new planet in 1781, and astronomers named it after the Greek god of heaven and ruler of the world. *Uranus* includes descriptions and photographs of five of its named moons. Of special note is Miranda, which scientists think "has the oddest mixture of surfaces ever found in the Solar System." It is clear from Simon's presentation that critically significant advances in knowledge have been made through the *Mariner, Viking,* and *Voyager* spacecraft expeditions. A first purchase recommendation in the science book category.

Elizabeth S. Watson

SOURCE: A review of *Mars* and *Uranus,* in *The Horn Book Magazine,* Vol. LXIII, No. 6, November-December, 1987, p. 762.

On his journey through the universe Simon has stopped to explore two of the more fascinating planets. Mars is not only a planet that we have learned quite a lot about

through the *Mariner* and *Viking* probes but is also one more easily understood by young readers because of its many similarities with Earth. Uranus, on the other hand, is still largely unexplored in both science and children's literature. The most recent data results from a 1986 pass by *Voyager 2,* which found, among other things, two rings and ten moons that were previously unknown. From its strangely tilted position to its forty-two-year days and nights, Uranus is a mystery that is just beginning to be solved. Both books mention the historical view of the planets, cite the meaning of their names, and carefully place the planets within the solar system in relation to Earth and the sun. The photographs are mostly from those sent back by the spacecraft and show amazing detail which is clearly explained in the text. As with the other titles in the series, the information is distilled to produce sufficient facts for the beginner while mentioning aspects of the planet questioned by scientists or still in doubt that will encourage the more advanced reader to consult other books.

Jeffrey A. French

SOURCE: A review of *Mars* and *Uranus,* in *School Library Journal,* Vol. 34, No. 4, December, 1987, p. 82.

Continuing his series that includes *Earth* and *The Moon, Jupiter* and *Saturn,* and *The Sun* and *Stars,* Simon turns his attention to one of the earliest explored planets, Mars, and the most recently visited, Uranus. The text in each provides basic statistics on its subject (e.g., size, orbit, rotation, moons, rings, atmosphere, surface, etc.) as well as information on the exploration to date of each planet. Once again, although the texts are serviceable, it is the full-color NASA photos that are the main attraction. *Mars* includes Viking lander photos from the planet's surface and aerial shots of dry river beds and Mars' moons. *Uranus* features Voyager fly-by photos of Uranus and its five major moons, which actually show more detail than is possible on photos of the cloud-shrouded planet itself. Both books are visually striking and enjoyable reading. Even though the bulk of the information and photos in each is available elsewhere, both books are virtually essential purchases, *Mars* for one of the loveliest presentations of its topic and *Uranus* for its much-needed inclusion of the results of the Voyager fly-by.

GALAXIES ("Space Photos" series, 1988)

Betsy Hearne

SOURCE: A review of *Galaxies,* in *The Bulletin of the Center for Children's Books,* Vol. 41, No. 8, April, 1988, p. 168.

Part of an astronomy series that already includes books on the sun, stars, and four planets, this meets the challenge of conveying immensity by analogy. In describing the more than three hundred billion stars that make up the

Andromeda galaxy, for instance, Simon says, "If you were to count one star per second nonstop, it would take you more than nine thousand years to count the stars in that galaxy." The measurement of light-years gets similar treatment, with reference to time as well as distance: "The light from the Andromeda spiral that we see today first started on its journey more than two million years ago, when our ancestors lived in caves." Dramatic photographs, computer-colored against black backgrounds, show the shapes of spiral, elliptical, barred spiral, and irregular galaxies. Although a concluding statement asserts that the universe is without any boundary, the map that "plots the locations of one million galaxies" unfortunately undercuts this idea with a round frame. Outside of such nit-picking, this is a solid addition to children's understanding of scientific phenomena.

Publishers Weekly

SOURCE: A review of *Galaxies,* in *Publishers Weekly,* Vol. 233, No. 14, April 8, 1988, p. 93.

Like an afternoon at the planetarium watching a sky show, this is a step-by-step introduction to and description of the many galaxies in the universe. Simon, the author of many science books, uses 20 color photographs, most of which are from the National Optical Astronomy Observatories, to accompany the text. He includes discussions of the ways in which astronomers classify galaxies, black holes, smaller satellite galaxies such as the Magellanic Clouds and supernovas. The terms are explained within the text; however, a glossary might have been a nice addition. As fascinating and accessible as this book is, with its straightforward writing, the concepts may be difficult to comprehend for some readers in the designated age group. They may gain more by sharing Simon's splendid work with adults or older siblings.

Margaret A. Bush

SOURCE: A review of *Galaxies,* in *The Horn Book Magazine,* Vol. LXIV, No. 3, May-June, 1988, p. 374.

Beyond the planets of our solar system, several of which Simon has described in previous handsome volumes, are galaxies of unimaginable magnitude. Their unfathomable distance from the earth makes the striking photographs assembled seem quite miraculous. Several views of the Milky Way galaxy are followed by pictures of others in the Local Group—the Andromeda galaxy, the Magellanic Clouds, M104 (the Sombrero galaxy), Centaurus A, and others. In addition to these enormous star clusters, other galactic bodies are shown, such as the Tarantula nebula and Supernova 1987A. A few of these bodies can be seen with the human eye from points in the Southern Hemisphere, but most have been made visible through powerful orbiting telescopes. As in the earlier books, many of the pages juxtapose white print against the dark colors of the night sky while the more traditional black print on

white pages forms a dramatic contrast. The short, informative text describes the patterns, makeup, shape, size, origins, and relationships of the individual galaxies and galaxy clusters. This fine introduction to an awe-inspiring subject will surely stimulate interest in stargazing, further reading, and investigation.

VOLCANOES (1988)

Kirkus Reviews

SOURCE: A review of *Volcanoes,* in *Kirkus Reviews,* Vol. LVI, No. 12, June 15, 1988, p. 904.

Twenty-five altogether stunning full-color photos and a clear, concise text are melded into a masterful introduction to volcanoes. Simon discusses the four major types, their locations and sources, and the different kinds of lava they produce. Smoke, steam, fumes, fire, and lava are dramatically portrayed: the fusion of the visual image and the written text is outstanding. Familiar volcanoes are well represented with photos of Mt. St. Helens, before and after the 1980 eruptions, and Mauna Loa, the largest Hawaiian volcano. Less familiar are the eruptions in the sea near Iceland that in 1963 formed the island of Surtsey, and in 1973 added a 735-foot volcano to the island of Heimaey.

Excellent science writing, a pleasure to read and view.

Publishers Weekly

SOURCE: A review of *Volcanoes,* in *Publishers Weekly,* Vol. 234, No. 11, September 9, 1988, p. 134.

From ancient myths to modern headlines, volcanoes are among the world's most amazing phenomena. Simon, award-winning author of **Icebergs and Glaciers, Jupiter, Saturn, The Sun** and **Stars,** et al., explores the subject thoroughly. Using examples like St. Helens and the volcanoes of Iceland and Hawaii, the author is able to address all aspects of his subject: the history, nature and causes of volcanoes. But given the expert presentations and finesse readers have come to expect from Simon, this work seems more difficult than it needs to be, and lacks the forcefulness and clarity of his previous books. However, **Volcanoes** is a good choice for reading aloud and as a lead-in to discussions; the superb full-color photographs redeem any shortcomings of the text.

Mary A. Burns

SOURCE: A review of *Volcanoes,* in *The Horn Book Magazine,* Vol. 67, No. 1, September-October, 1988, p. 648.

Illustrated with photographs in color. Fiery rivers of lava and mountainous billows of smoke are surely the most evocative images associated with volcanoes and are conveyed with spectacular intensity. The dramatic photographs which are a common feature of other volumes by Simon are once again employed in conjunction with clearly stated explanations of the subject. The text is carefully constructed in relation to the photographs, serving more as extended captions than a fully developed essay. Actual eruptions of Kilauea, Mount St. Helens, Mauna Loa, and Surtsey are shown. Explanations of the causes, erupting behavior, location of volcanoes, and characteristics of the four major types of volcano are provided. The overview emphasizes geographical consequences and leaves the reader wanting to know more about the human losses and risks in the vicinity of active volcanoes. One very interesting scene features fire fighters spraying the encroaching lava during an eruption in Hawaii; but generally there is no real sense of the impact on humanity, making the boldly dramatic landscapes seem almost abstract. A potentially useful diagram of the earth's plates is confusing in its layout and lack of direct explanation. On the whole, however, the exceedingly handsome presentation is both appealing and compelling.

Stephen W. Zsiray

SOURCE: A review of *Volcanoes,* in *School Library Journal,* Vol. 35, No. 4, December, 1988, p. 118.

Simon presents information on volcanoes to young readers in an understandable text and colorful format. . . . [T]his book provides a general overview of the types of volcanoes found around the world. . . . Further, it can be used successfully to generate interest on the part of those readers reluctant to pick up nonfiction books, as Simon gives readers an armchair tour of some of the more impressive volcanoes around the world: Mount St. Helens, the undersea volcanoes in Iceland, and Mauna Loa in Hawaii. The book is graced with many illuminating color photos that bring the text to life. However, the illustration of the plates, or crust layers of the earth, is somewhat difficult to understand. . . . Still, this is a useful and attractive addition to science collections, as it is likely to become a favorite choice of young scientists.

HOW TO BE AN OCEAN SCIENTIST IN YOUR OWN HOME (1988)

Beth Ames Herbert

SOURCE: A review of *How to Be an Ocean Scientist in Your Own Home,* in *Booklist,* Vol. 85, No. 3, October 1, 1988, p. 327.

How can the budding ocean scientist get started when the nearest saltwater is hundreds of miles away? The answer is in the fascinating experiments in Simon's latest how-to book. Each chapter of this conversationally written volume poses a question; for example, "What is in sea water?" and "How can fresh water be made from sea water?" Following a quick

consideration of facts about the ocean, the book outlines an experiment that utilizes household items and a few pieces of special equipment, such as a lab thermometer. Both [David] Carter's carefully labeled illustrations of the experiments and Simon's explanatory conclusions help tie up loose ends. Although some landlocked readers may be disappointed that several experiments require children to be at the seashore, the book's thoughtful inclusion of a list of aquarium suppliers and a further reading list will augment young scientists' studies of the oceans.

Roger Sutton

SOURCE: A review of *How to Be an Ocean Scientist in Your Own Home,* in *The Bulletin of the Center for Children's Books,* Vol. 42, No. 3, November, 1988, p. 84.

Salt (sea and table) and water are the primary ingredients for most of the twenty-four projects and experiments in this collection; other materials and equipment should be readily available. While a few of the projects involve plants and animals, including brine shrimp (aka sea monkeys) most have to do with measuring salinity, waves, and currents, with bowls, aquariums and bathtubs providing stand-in service for the ocean. Instructions and diagrams are clear, as are Simon's explanations of the various phenomena. Good for science fair, as well as for those kids who just need a respectable excuse for playing with water.

Frances E. Millhouser

SOURCE: A review of *How to Be an Ocean Scientist in Your Own Home,* in *School Library Journal,* Vol. 35, No. 3, November, 1988, p. 122.

An updated version of Simon's ***Science at Work: Projects in Oceanography.*** The black-and-white drawings are by a different artist but similar, and the clearly-written instructions have been expanded and updated. The experiments are good ones, such as discovering the minerals in sea water and how it differs from salt water made from tap water and table salt; comparing the freezing point of fresh and sea water, and thereby learning why salt is sprinkled on icy roads. Simon also describes setting up and stocking a salt water aquarium as well as experiments to conduct by the shore and from a small boat. Organization is excellent. Each experiment is divided into three sections: the purpose of the experiment, the materials needed, and how to do it. The index will lead young scientists and librarians to specific experiments, especially during science fair season when many copies of this book will be useful.

STORMS (1989)

Kirkus Reviews

SOURCE: A review of *Storms,* in *Kirkus Reviews,* Vol. LVII, No. 3, February 1, 1989, p. 216.

A dramatic look at the formation of thunderstorms, tornadoes, and hurricanes, with spectacular, full-color photos on every page. The vividly written text also packs a punch: "In twenty minutes, a single thunderstorm can drop 125 million gallons of water and give off more electrical energy than is used in a large city during an entire week." Or: "Scientists say that the energy in a hurricane is equal to dozens of atomic bombs going off every second." Technical terms—including "downdraft," "updraft," "windshear," and "storm cell"—are explained clearly and concisely. Black pages with snaking streaks of lightning and white text add to the visual impact—and provide a sense of nature at its most awesome. This is science writing to capture the imagination.

Betsy Hearne

SOURCE: A review of *Storms,* in *The Bulletin of the Center for Children's Books,* Vol. 42, No. 7, March, 1989, p. 182.

Following the format of his stellar series on the sun, stars, and planets, Simon here taps a topic of private terror to many children who have not outgrown early fears of thunder and lightning. There's inherent drama in the information itself, and the book heightens this with bold color photos of cumulonimbus clouds (including a diagram to show air movements), storm cells, squall lines, hailstorms, gust fronts, lightning play, tornados, and hurricanes. The display is awesome, and the text respects it. Explanations are clear but never condescending; the science of radar, satellite, and computer tracking is as astounding as the ancient theory of Thor's chariot striking clouds. Children seeking material for reports will find the real power of facts.

Charles P. Arnold

SOURCE: A review of *Storms,* in *Science Books & Films,* Vol. 25, No. 1, September-October, 1989, p. 35.

Storms is a complementary addition to Simon's beautiful collection of award-winning science books for children. The half- to full-page glossary color photographs are sure to attract young readers as will the subject. *Storms* is an excellent way to introduce the science of meteorology to children. Severe storms are among the most awesome wonders of nature, for young and old alike, and, in many ways, they are still mysteries. Simon begins with thunderstorms, explaining what we know about them, such as the prodigious amounts of water and electricity they generate, how many there are, and their role in maintaining global temperature distribution. He also imparts facts about hail and how it forms, downdrafts, lightning, and thunder. The microburst, a phenomenon responsible for several aircraft accidents in recent years, is also mentioned. The intended audience may not be able to appreciate that there are 100 million volts in a single bolt of lightning or mention of temperatures five times that of the sun's surface, but these are minor objections. Tornadoes and their destructive winds and capricious behavior are presented about halfway

through the book. I think Simon could have created a little more interest here if he had mentioned that a small but important instrument-laden platform used to study these storms in the central plains is called "Toto" (after Dorothy's little dog in the *Wizard of Oz,* of course). And that the part of Kansas called "Tornado Alley" is perhaps the most prolific area in the world for tornado formation. Hurricanes are the last of the great storms presented, and they are given short shrift. There exist magnificent satellite photos of other hurricanes that make the book's depiction of "Alicia" pale by comparison; more attention could have been given to these. However, overall, I highly recommend *Storms;* it is another award winner for Simon.

WHALES (1989)

Betsy Hearne

SOURCE: A review of *Whales,* in *The Bulletin of the Center for Children's Books,* Vol. 43, No. 2, October, 1989, pp. 44-5.

Simon introduces toothed and baleen whales in a smoothly written text that can be read aloud as a picture book or alone by independent readers. The mammals' habits and habitat are capably covered, several species get detailed treatment, and kids will love the occasional Ripley's believe-it-or-not tone of information ("In one day a blue whale eats more than four tons of krill, about forty million of these animals"). However, the vivid comparisons sometimes lead to quirks of description as well: "Just the tongue of a blue whale weighs as much as an elephant" begs the question of how big and what kind of elephant; the callosities of a right whale should hardly be called "strange bumps"; and "carries" is a misleading term for gestation period, especially under a photograph where a sperm whale cow seems to be actually carrying her calf. In fact, the dramatically attractive photographs that characterize Simon's books are here sometimes obscure; features are hard to distinguish in pictures opposite a description of a whale's skull and body, for instance, or in the shots of a fin whale, minke whale, and blue whale. Other photographs and facts are beautifully clear, and the concluding appeal for saving this endangered animal is a moving one.

Ellen Fader

SOURCE: A review of *Whales,* in *The Horn Book Magazine,* Vol. LXV, No. 6, November-December, 1989, p. 794.

Simon wastes no time engaging the interest of his reader; in the first paragraph of this fascinating photo essay we learn that "the humpback whale is longer than a big bus and heavier than a trailer truck," and that "the tongue of a blue whale weighs as much as an elephant." Similar tidbits are scattered throughout this lively exploration of the characteristics and habits of several species of whales. Especially notable is the care Simon has exercised to choose unusual and stunning photographs to illustrate his lively text; whales fill every inch of space and seem barely contained by the edges of each page. The opening double-page spread of humpbacks feeding is one that readers will return to many times. Simon's affection for his subject is clear, and his final plea asking children to decide whether whales will be allowed to share the world with us in the future seems a fitting end to this tribute to the species. Up-to-date information presented in an eye-catching format.

DESERTS AND *OCEANS* (1990)

Kirkus Reviews

SOURCE: A review of *Deserts* and *Oceans,* in *Kirkus Reviews,* Vol. LVIII, No. 14, July 15, 1990, p. 1006.

Assembling 20 striking full-color photos for each title, Simon attempts to explain the hows and whys of landforms, tides, winds, and waves. The texts here are brief but not easy, introducing such specialized terms as "gyres," "tsunami," "fetch," "arroyos," "playas," and more. Some essential information appears only on the endpapers: worldwide locations of deserts and the major ocean currents. *Oceans* provides colorful computer-generated maps to show El Nino, the dramatic warming of cool waters off the coast of Peru that causes sea life to disappear; however, the graphics, although beautiful, need more explanation to be readily understandable to the novice. The text of *Deserts* is less technical; the photos here of rusty, rippling sand dunes and majestically sculptured rock formations are visually appealing.

Though their texts are not always clear, both books dramatically convey Simon's enthusiasm for earth's natural phenomena.

Kay Weisman

SOURCE: A review of *Deserts* and *Oceans,* in *Booklist,* Vol. 87, No. 4, October 15, 1990, p. 441.

Two more exceptional titles from a prolific writer, each with remarkable photographic illustrations.

Deserts concerns itself mostly with North American examples—the Great Basin, the Mojave, the Sonoran, and the Chihuahuan. Simon defines the term *desert,* discusses why deserts occur, and describes how their climate differs. He explains how wind and water erosion can create some unusual land formations, such as mesas, buttes, chimney rocks, and playas. He also mentions plants and animals common to these regions and their adaptations to life with infrequent water.

Oceans covers the geography of the ocean floor, major currents, and El Niño (a shift in the prevailing currents that causes severe climactic changes). Tides, tsunami, waves, coastal erosion, and marine life are also touched upon.

Useful for report writers and browsers alike, the two accounts are fascinating introductions to their topics.

Rosanne Cerny

SOURCE: A review of *Deserts* and *Oceans,* in *School Library Journal,* Vol. 36, No. 12, December, 1990, p. 119.

Excellent introductory titles. Simon presents clear, simplified explanations of natural phenomena with well-chosen full-color photographs that go beyond decoration, becoming integral parts of the texts. Spectacular photos of the deserts of the American southwest are used to show the various features from rippling sand, to wind-eroded rock formations, to the sparse vegetation characteristic of the area. There is a little information on how both plant and animal life have adapted to the harsh climate, and on the wonderful public lands such as Monument Valley, the Grand Canyon, etc. The maps on the endpapers show the major deserts (except for Antarctica), but the rest of the world's desert areas, while occasionally mentioned in the discussion, are not represented in the photo selections. In [*Oceans*], Simon explores the magnitude of the oceans and their impact on the Earth's climate. He includes good black-and-white diagrams of how tides work and how waves form and transfer energy. The endpapers are maps of the world showing how and where the major currents flow.

Ellen Fader

SOURCE: A review of *Deserts* and *Oceans,* in *The Horn Book Magazine,* Vol. 67, No. 1, January-February, 1991, pp. 89-90.

Simon explores two of Earth's important ecosystems—oceans and deserts—which, the author explains, respectively cover over seventy per cent and fourteen per cent of our planet's surface. A combination of generally crisp color photographs and clear graphs, diagrams, and maps makes each book an eye-catching learning experience. Even the endpapers contribute information in the form of colorful maps of the major ocean currents and of the locations of deserts throughout the world. Simon covers fairly standard material—how deserts form and change, the relationship between the moon and the tides, and the influence of the sea on climate. But for those who have wondered how plants and animals survive in a harsh desert climate or have difficulty understanding how waves form, Simon's brief, concise explanations will be appreciated. Visually stunning and exceptionally well-designed resources.

BIG CATS (1991)

Diane Nunn

SOURCE: A review of *Big Cats,* in *School Library Journal,* Vol. 37, No. 5, May, 1991, p. 90.

Simon returns to the animal world with a striking presentation of seven members of the cat family: those that roar—the lion, tiger, leopard and jaguar—and those that merely purr—the puma, cheetah, and snow leopard. An overview discusses characteristics inherent in all, and singles out those unique to individual species. Enough information is presented to satisfy browsers and to develop an understanding of the cats' hunting techniques and adaptations to specific environments whether grasslands, jungles, or snowy mountains. Care has been taken to include those that exist in many parts of the world and to dispel some myths about these mighty hunters. Concluding statements describe how many of the big cats have been hunted nearly to extinction and give suggestions on ways they can be protected. The format is large, spacious, and uncluttered, and the text flows with an energy that matches the strength of these animals. Full-page, full-color photographs are well chosen for their clarity and diversity as cats stare boldly, hunt for prey, or appear in gentle poses with their cubs. A book that commands attention and is as impressive as the magnificent beasts it features.

Kay Weisman

SOURCE: A review of *Big Cats,* in *Booklist,* Vol. 87, No. 17, May 1, 1991, p. 1719.

Simon opens with a brief introduction to these large and dangerous animals, noting their similarities (all are carnivorous mammals with sharp canine teeth, razor-sharp claws, and keen senses) and differences (they can live nearly anywhere in the world, from the snowy lands of the Arctic to temperate mountains and grasslands to tropical rain forests and swamps), For each of the seven felids covered, he describes size, habitat, food preferences, enemies, and unusual behaviors. Although only four are scientifically classified as "big cats"—the lion, the tiger, the leopard, and the jaguar (because they all roar)—three other large cats, the puma, the cheetah, and the snow leopard, are included as well. Several of these beasts are endangered, and the author urges governments to set aside wildlife preserves and pass stronger laws to protect them. Using an oversize format similar to that of his *Whales,* Simon offers a clear, succinct text illuminated with stunning, large color photographs of these graceful felines.

Betsy Hearne

SOURCE: A review of *Big Cats,* in *The Bulletin of the Center for Children's Books,* Vol. 44, No. 10, June, 1991, p. 251.

Stunning color photographs face every page of Simon's continuous text, which includes an introduction to the big cats and a look at each species: the lion, the tiger, the leopard, the jaguar, the puma, the cheetah and the snow leopard. Basic facts such as the *Felidae* family's keen night vision are consistently and smoothly presented, with only an occasional lapse in organization, as when a

description of the lion's range interrupts the discussion of the characteristics and advantages of living in a pride. The combination of action shots—one tiger is caught midspring out of the water—and the author's practised, informal style will win the attention of young readers, with whom Simon charges the future of the big cats. The picture of a lion leaning into the sunset, right next to the discussion of the animals' endangerment, and an endearing photo of a leopard cub on the last page make it hard not to consider the message.

Barbara C. Scott and Harold J. Gray

SOURCE: A review of *Big Cats,* in *Appraisal: Science Books for Young People,* Vol. 25, No. 1, Winter, 1992, pp. 61-2.

LIBRARIAN [Barbara C. Scott]: The strong, handsome faces of the big cats stare out from the cover and the title page of this dramatic book. As the reader picks up the book and leafs through the pages, he or she is captivated by the beauty of these large beasts and slightly repelled by the graphic evidence of their hunting skill. The big cats have always fascinated people, and in this new work by Seymour Simon, readers can satisfy their curiosity about these powerful creatures.

Simon begins by talking about those characteristics that the big cats share with one another and with all members of the cat family. He then describes seven different members of this family: lion, tiger, leopard, jaguar, puma, cheetah and snow leopard. Simon's text is detailed enough to make distinctions among the seven, but simple enough to keep the young reader's interest. As is usual in his books, each double-page spread consists of a large photograph and its accompanying text. Unfortunately, the photographs are somewhat uneven in their quality, and this detracts from the overall impact of the work. There is no index, which is not much of a drawback since there are only eighteen pages of text and the animals under discussion are easily identified. Towards the end of the book, Simon begins to alert the reader, in a variety of ways, to the important message that many of these cats are endangered species. This book will not sit on the shelves. Its subject is popular, and its message is vitally important.

SPECIALIST [Harold J. Gray]: This book is filled with excellent, full color photographs complemented nicely by text placed on alternate pages. Simon writes in a very readable, flowing style. The coverage of information is adequate for readers at this level, and is generally accurate. There is a nice mixture of basic biology, ecology, zoogeography, and conservation presented throughout the work. The book begins with a general overview of the big cats, and then presents details on the tiger, lion, leopard, jaguar, puma, cheetah and snow leopard. Unique characteristics for each of the cats discussed. It will be a very useful source of facts for the young student. The author also discusses concerns about wildlife conservation, an important message to present to our youth.

There are only a few flaws that prevent me from giving this book an excellent rating. Some of the text may be difficult for the typical five- to six-year-old reader tackling the book alone. Simon makes one misleading statement in suggesting that the "sensitive hairs in this jaguar's ears can pick up the sound . . . " A typical reader will interpret this literally and believe that hair can be used for sound reception. Finally, there is a feeling of non-parallel construction in the treatment of each species that was slightly awkward for this reviewer. For instance, cubs are discussed for only three of the seven species. Otherwise, this book is highly recommended.

SPACE WORDS: A DICTIONARY (1991)

Publishers Weekly

SOURCE: A review of *Space Words: A Dictionary,* in *Publishers Weekly,* Vol. 238, No. 30, July 12, 1991, p. 67.

Simon's latest is an informative journey through the universe—a pictorial catalogue that presents illustrated definitions of terms related to space travel and exploration. Explanations of such concepts as the Big Bang theory of extraterrestrial life are simple and concise; the language is comprehensible and not too scientifically sophisticated for its audience. [Randy] Chewning's watercolors offer a palette bold enough to stimulate interest yet warm enough to help demystify some of the subject matter. Although billed as a dictionary, more distinct alphabetical divisions and perhaps phonetic pronunciation keys would make this a better beginning reference tool.

John Peters

SOURCE: A review of *Space Words: A Dictionary,* in *School Library Journal,* Vol. 37, No. 10, October, 1991, p. 112.

A picture dictionary of 75 astronomical and astronautical terms and people, illustrated with simple pen-and-ink drawings painted with bright watercolors. Simon tries to cover far too much here; although many definitions are models of accuracy and clarity, some are startlingly simplistic, such as "space: Everything beyond Earth's atmosphere" or just confusing ("zodiac: A circular band in the sky around which the sun, moon, and planets appear to move"). Obviously, the author had to pick and choose from a vast vocabulary, but his choices are sometimes hard to understand: *"Explorer I"* but not *Sputnik;* "dwarf star" and "red giant" but not the rest of the main sequence; "mission control"; "Milky Way" *and* "Milky Way galaxy"; "nova" *and* "supernova." Chewning's pictures are visually appealing, but not always trustworthy; the asteroid belt isn't nearly as dense as shown, and a neutron star, described as "about the size of New York" is plainly much larger.

Stephanie Zvirin

SOURCE: A review of *Space Words: A Dictionary,* in *Booklist,* Vol. 88, No. 5, November 1, 1991, p. 515.

Brightly colored paintings will lure children right into Simon's latest book, an *A*-to-*Z* on space that begins with *Apollo* and ends with *Zodiac.* While the arrangement presupposes some knowledge on the part of the reader, it is still a useful catchall of core information about people, planets, programs, and space-related devices and phenomena, which Simon explains in a simple, clearly stated sentence or two. The handling of cross-references is awkward, but, fortunately, there are only a few.

EARTHQUAKES (1991)

Ellen Fader

SOURCE: A review of *Earthquakes,* in *The Horn Book Magazine,* Vol. LXVII, No. 5, September-October, 1991, p. 614.

Simon's cogent examination of earthquakes will go a long way toward answering young people's questions about the topic. Subjects discussed include the causes of earthquakes and how faults are formed, the different ways earthquakes are measured, and the kinds of damage that can result because of an earthquake. The format of this brief volume resembles many of Simon's recent books, such as **Storms** and **Oceans,** employing a liberal amount of either white or deeply colored paper to draw attention to the maps, illustrations, and the numerous photographs; the art dramatically pictures many scenes of destruction, including Mexico City in 1985 and 1906 San Francisco. Suggestions of what to do if caught in an earthquake conclude an informative survey.

Will Kyselko

SOURCE: A review of *Earthquakes,* in *Science Books & Films,* Vol. 27, No. 8, November, 1991, p. 239.

Earthquakes examines the when and where of earthquakes, how they happen, the damage that they do, and how they can be predicted. Text and pictures interact. Brief statements in large type on one page describe the full-page color photographs on the facing page. Not only do the photos fill that page, but several times they spill across the gutter to fill a quarter of the text page. The impact of the photos is in their size and content—for example, the full-page picture of railroad tracks twisted and bent into ribbons of steel and left sliding down a dip-slip fault like sagging wires, the result of an earthquake near Seattle. The text is factual, appropriately subdued against the pictures of destruction. Yet it is active, as we learn when we read that the San Andreas Fault "winds, . . . dives, . . . [and] slashes" for hundreds of miles through California. Facts are presented in a way that is easy to visualize: "Yet a million times each year—an average of once every thirty seconds—somewhere around the world the ground shakes and sways." The artwork is clear and colorful. Particularly appealing is an illustration showing the buildup of stress along the boundaries of tectonic plates and the catastrophic release of that energy.

Martha B. Mahoney and Ron J. Kley

SOURCE: A review of *Earthquakes,* in *Appraisal: Science Books for Young People,* Vol. 25, No. 2, Spring, 1992, p. 42.

LIBRARIAN [Martha B. Mahoney]: *Earthquakes* is another single concept book created by Seymour Simon. The text begins with a description of an earthquake. Then follow statistics about the frequency of earthquakes worldwide, their causes, instruments for measuring them, and their effects. The photographs of the seismograph show a drum with lines being made by a needle that is sensitive to minute movements of the earth's crust.

Major earthquakes are pictured and described. One map shows where earthquakes have occurred in the world and another shows the earthquake zones in the continental United States. An explanation is given of why earthquakes occur on fault lines. Finally, the reader is given hints as to what to do in case an earthquake does occur.

An index would help readers using this book for research. I think many will read this book because of the interest in this potentially destructive force.

SPECIALIST [Ron J. Kley]: Some of the book's illustrations are neither captioned nor identified in the accompanying text. One illustration, purporting to explain a "dip-slip fault," is seriously misinterpreted and contributes to the confusion, rather than providing enlightenment. The rather provocative term, "Ring of Fire," is introduced without any clue that might explain its meaning. The earth's mantle is described as being composed of "melted rock"—a somewhat ironic error inasmuch as it is the transmission of the earthquake waves through the mantle which demonstrates the great rigidity of mantle rock. Then, after featuring pictures of land, homes and schools torn asunder by earthquakes, and after citing casualty figures running in the tens of thousands, the book blithely advises readers to "remain calm and don't worry" if they should have the misfortune to be caught in such a calamity.

At the price of nearly $1.00 per page of text, this book offers far too little substance and far too much error and confusion to be a worthwhile purchase.

MERCURY AND *VENUS*
("Space Photos" series, 1992)

Kirkus Reviews

SOURCE: A review of *Mercury* and *Venus,* in *Kirkus Reviews,* Vol. LX, No. 3, February 1, 1992, p. 190.

In the same large, square format as Simon's earlier books on other planets, a clear, concise text draws on the latest findings and the best of recent color photos. Venus has her special charms—the hottest planet in the solar system, covered with clouds of sulphuric acid, with bizarre surface details—all emerging from photos and radar maps taken from earlier Russian expeditions and NASA's Magellan spacecraft, which is still orbiting Venus. Our sister planet? Not even human siblings exhibit such diversity, and why this is so is an intriguing puzzle. Simultaneously published: *Mercury,* an equally fine contribution to science collections (though, like the planet itself, less bulky—only 24 pages).

Carolyn Phelan

SOURCE: A review of *Mercury* and *Venus,* in *Booklist,* Vol. 88, No. 14, March 15, 1992, pp. 1353, 1356.

Following the same handsome format he used in his previous books on individual planets, Simon here turns his attention to Mercury and Venus. Each book begins with an earthbound view of the planet, starlike in the evening sky, and includes full-color diagrams, composite photographs, and artists' conceptions of the planet. The eye-catching design and illustrations make this series stand out from others on the subject. As usual, Simon presents basic information clearly and offers perspective on how we learned about Mercury and Venus. Useful as resources for children studying the planets, these books also have the potential to lead students a step further in their enjoyment and understanding of astronomy.

Zena Sutherland

SOURCE: A review of *Mercury* and *Venus,* in *The Bulletin of the Center for Children's Books,* Vol. 45, No. 9, May, 1992, p. 249.

Like earlier books in this excellent astronomy series, these two volumes are distinguished for the beauty of the color photographs (from space probes) and the clarity of informative diagrams and continuous texts. Simon is adept at arranging scientific material in a logical way that makes it accessible; his writing is clear, succinct without being terse, and always illustrative of good scientific principles: objective, distinguishing between fact and conjecture, and making it clear that scientific knowledge is built on the continuing input from many sources and is perennially subject to change as new data accrue.

SNAKES (1992)

Paul B. Shubeck

SOURCE: A review of *Snakes,* in *Science Books & Films,* Vol. 28, No. 3, April, 1992, p. 84.

Seymour Simon's very brief, but informative, volume on snakes is written for upper elementary and junior high school students. For the most part, it is easy reading, although a few technical terms are included. (The pronunciations of some are given.) For every page of text, the facing page contains a full-color photograph of a snake in action (guarding its eggs, swallowing a rat, etc.). A young student knowing nothing about snakes certainly will gain much from reading this interesting book. Unfortunately, it takes only a reading session of 10 or 15 minutes to complete it. Its greatest value may be in stimulating young readers to seek additional books that provide more complete coverage on this fascinating group of animals!

Hazel Rochman

SOURCE: A review of *Snakes,* in *Booklist,* Vol. 88, No. 16, April 15, 1992, p. 1528.

Even more than sharks, snakes hold a fearful fascination. However many books you have on the subject, it's hard to turn down one as informative and visually stunning as this one. Simon (a veteran science writer for children who has written on the wonders of space as well as biology) intensifies our interest with careful facts on everything from where various snakes live and how they reproduce to their role in keeping down rodents. Opposite each page of clear, spacious type is a close-up photo reproduced in gorgeous color. Simon's style is informal ("Young snakes are on their own. No snakes take care of their babies"). His tone is calm—the only exclamation point is on the jacket flap— he indulges in no melodrama; in fact, he's careful to point out that you're more likely to be hit by lightning than bitten by a snake. But the facts are mesmerizing. What does cold-blooded mean? How does a snake shed its skin? How does it move and coil? And that's before you get to how various species catch and digest their prey. There's a photo of a king snake swallowing a young rattlesnake. The cover shows a python, its muscular coils golden against a glossy black background, its strange, terrible head facing you. Display that cover in classroom or library, or use the double-spread photo of Florida king snakes hatching out of their great white eggs. What a story!

Margaret A. Bush

SOURCE: A review of *Snakes,* in *The Horn Book Magazine,* Vol. LXVIII, No. 3, May-June, 1992, p. 357.

Once again Simon demonstrates his skill in molding a lucid discussion and striking photographs into a compelling, informative overview. In this case he begins by mentioning the varied habitats snakes occupy and goes on to their reptilian aspects, growth patterns, eating habits, senses, skin, egg laying, and defensive behavior. Simon's short, simple sentences occasionally develop a monotonous rhythm, but there are also many succinct observations which effectively distill important information. "Young snakes are on their own; no snakes take care of their babies." The author's viewpoint is one of respect for these animals and concern for their future. Many species are featured in the full-page pictures, each of which illustrate a particular point in the text. There are no captions or labels, but each animal is specifically identified in the facing narrative. A green tree viper coiled around her hatching eggs, a sidewinder moving across waves of sand, the forked tongue of a copperhead, the unusual scales of an eyelash viper, and the view of a yellow rat snake swallowing its prey are among the memorable portraits in a fine presentation.

Karey Wehner

SOURCE: A review of *Snakes,* in *School Library Journal,* Vol. 38, No. 6, June, 1992, p. 135.

Snakes are at their most beguiling in this beautifully photographed, well-organized introduction. The text succinctly describes their general physical and behavioral characteristics, and identifies the four major snake families. Fifteen species are depicted in the large, sharp, full-color photographs that appear on approximately every other page; most close-ups are so finely detailed that individual scales are visible. . . . What distinguishes the Simon title, however, is its superb photography. Browsers will be attracted to the large portraits of the reptiles offered, particularly the photo of a king snake ingesting a rattlesnake and the shot of a yellow rat snake feeding on a rat.

WOLVES (1993)

Kirkus Reviews

SOURCE: A review of *Wolves,* in *Kirkus Reviews,* Vol. LXI, No. 7, September 1, 1993, p. 1152.

Varieties, life cycle, pack and hunting behavior, and the current status of this endangered predator—although with what may seem too many transparently rhetorical questions ("Are wolves savage and destructive hunters of people and livestock?") and fillers ("After wolves kill a large animal, they may rest for a brief time or eat right away"). Without attribution, Simon states that " . . . there is no record of a healthy wolf ever trying to kill a human in North America." . . . Still, though his text isn't up to his usual high standard, Simon again selects outstanding photos-this book's strongest and most appealing feature.

Hazel Rochman

SOURCE: A review of *Wolves,* in *Booklist,* Vol. 90, No. 3, October 1, 1993, pp. 348-49.

As in *Snakes* and his other photo-essays about animals, Simon includes dramatic action pictures by several wildlife photographers. Each full-page photo, splendidly reproduced in full color, faces a page of plain text that gives basic information about how wolves live in the natural world, what they look like, how they hunt, how they rear their young, etc. The facts and the glorious photographs support Simon's plea for the animals' conservation. They debunk the big-bad-wolf horror stories without in any way detracting from the fierce beauty of the wolves' wild nature.

Susan Oliver

SOURCE: A review of *Wolves,* in *School Library Journal,* Vol. 39, No. 11, November, 1993, p. 20.

Simon dispels the traditionally negative images of the wolf in this photo essay. Through the appealing full-color photographs and succinct, conversational text, these dynamic, affectionate, and highly intelligent animals are shown to possess many positive traits, such as loyalty, cooperation, and adaptability. A broad range of information is touched upon lightly, including physical characteristics, habitat, hunting and diet, breeding and raising pups, and some unique facts about pack hierarchy and howling. An introduction uses imagery to conjure up the spirit of the wolf; the conclusion touches on the animal's past and questionable future. An attractive and simple introduction. . . .

WEATHER (1993)

Roger Sutton

SOURCE: A review of *Weather,* in *The Bulletin of the Center for Children's Books,* Vol. 47, No. 2, October, 1993, pp. 57-8.

Gorgeous full-page color photos, helped by a few cogent diagrams, illustrate Simon's outline of how weather works. He explains why the poles are colder than the equator, why that temperature difference causes weather changes, and how clouds and precipitation form, ending with a warning about the dangers of smog and global warming. He does not go into exciting phenomena such as thunder, lightning and tornadoes; for that, readers should turn to the author's *Storms.* The organization is clear and logical, and while the information is available in any number of other books and encyclopedias, the photos, such as a Skylab view of cloud formations, add a dramatic dimension.

Meryl Silverstein

SOURCE: A review of *Weather,* in *School Library Journal,* Vol. 39, No. 11, November, 1993, p. 120.

As with Simon's previous titles on the individual planets, this book is a perfect marriage of words and pictures.

Each high-quality, full-color photograph or diagram is truly a work of art, suitable for framing. The large-print text, sometimes superimposed on the illustrations, is easy to read. Beginning with the general effects of the sun and the Earth's rotation, continuing with wind patterns, temperature, clouds, and precipitation, and concluding with smog and the greenhouse effect, the author lucidly discusses all of the terms and elements that constitute tropospheric weather. Instruments and the possible affects of human activity on the atmosphere are touched upon. Unfortunately, the full-page diagrams that demonstrate the way the sun warms the Earth and the speed of its rotation do not clearly explain those phenomena.

Margaret A. Bush

SOURCE: A review of *Weather,* in *The Horn Book Magazine,* Vol. LXIX, No. 6, November-December, 1993, p. 756.

"Earth's weather is driven by the intense heat of the sun. . . . Our changing weather is the result of a continuous battle between large bodies of air called air masses." This crystalline discussion of the major components of weather—solar energy, atmospheric motion, wind belts, air masses, clouds, human activities—distills the interrelationships of these events into clear, simple explanations linking large ideas with ease. Seymour Simon demonstrates again his mastery in joining handsome photographs and essay text into a lucid and striking presentation. The visual material; selected and prepared with a judicious eye, includes panoramic vistas of sky and earth, magnified views of ice crystals and snowflakes, bold graphics depicting patterns of flow of air masses, an eerie shot of a weather balloon before launching, and a spectacular Skylab photograph of an astronaut poised in outer space against the cloud-covered atmosphere of Earth. Many of the photographs have a dark beauty in portraying the important activity of clouds; the darkness becomes foreboding in the concluding segment on smog. Simon's concluding message is understated. "We can be sure of only two things about the weather: We're going to have it and it's going to change." Depending on industrial activity and automobile use, the change may not be for the better. Readers of all ages should be intrigued by this boldly crafted lesson, which is a fine companion book to Simon's earlier *Storms.*

AUTUMN ACROSS AMERICA (1993)

Kathryn Broderick

SOURCE: A review of *Autumn Across America,* in *Booklist,* Vol. 90, No. 6, November 15, 1993, p. 622.

Simon's first book in a series about the changing seasons introduces autumn as a "season of memory and change." By the book's end, readers will grasp the significance of that phrase. Throughout this tribute, each double-page spread contains at least one, sometimes two, four-color photographs of a typical fall scene opposite two or three paragraphs of Simon's information-packed text, all appearing on a brilliant background color. This makes each turn of the page a delightful shock, not unlike the astonishment of seeing the first orange tree of fall. In his text, Simon discusses the signs of autumn as he covers the tilt of the earth, chlorophyll production, migratory patterns, animal life-cycles, pollination, and harvesting. He also goes beyond that to include special details, such as information about which trees turn what colors and which pigments produce what colors. As usual, Simon presents his subject with flair.

Kirkus Reviews

SOURCE: A review of *Autumn Across America,* in *Kirkus Reviews,* Vol. LXI, No. 23, December 1, 1993, p. 1529.

The noted science writer covers familiar territory with his characteristic flair, offering real specifics on: why leaves turn; the earth's rotation and angle with respect to the sun; the calendar vs. other measures of the season; a sampling of seasonal animal behavior (bison clustering around Yellowstone's hot springs; monarch butterfly migrations); sights across the nation (milkweed, pumpkins, brilliant yellow aspens in the Rockies, heavy rains in the Olympic rain forest). A lucid introduction, presented thoughtfully and with enough scientific detail to convey real understanding. The handsome color photos—by the author himself, among others—are mounted on pages in vivid autumnal colors embellished with delicate traceries of leaves: sometimes dazzling when it comes to reading, but right in the spirit of a perfect October day.

Louise L. Sherman

SOURCE: A review of *Autumn Across America,* in *School Library Journal,* Vol. 40, No. 2, February, 1994, p. 98.

This exploration of seasonal change takes a slightly different tack from most books on the subject. The usual leaf coloration, harvest, and animal adaptation are included here as Simon follows autumn from east to west across North America. A great deal of information is packed into the dense text. It is clearly stated, but often requires conceptualization beyond the reach of the intended audience. For example, many young readers will not understand the Earth's axis tilting at a 23.5 degree angle. Others may not have the geographical background to know what is meant by "Midwest" and other regional names without a map for reference. Simon does not adhere strictly to the trans-American path. While telling of autumn in the Midwest, he describes insect changes, seed scattering, and harvests that occur all across the country. Since there is no index and no table of contents, children looking for specific information will be frustrated. The book's main attraction is its design—beautiful photographs set in pages of glowing fall colors. Close-up pictures of a praying mantis forming an egg case and a milkweed pod's seeds floating away are exquisite. Unfortunately, the last photograph is obscured by an inset of text. Seasonal materials are always in demand; this one is a good choice for browsers.

MOUNTAINS (1994)

Stephanie Zvirin

SOURCE: A review of *Mountains,* in *Booklist,* Vol. 90, No. 13, March 1, 1994, p. 1266.

A fine companion to Simon's books on oceans, volcanoes, and deserts, this features spectacular photographs, including a few extraordinary double-page spreads that make faraway mountain ranges look like they're right in your own backyard. The accompanying text, nicely spaced and in slightly oversize, dark, clear type, concentrates predominantly on different types of mountains—folded, fault-block, volcanic, dome—and how they're formed, with a word or two about erosion and a mountain's effect on climate. There's nothing stuffy about Simon's word descriptions, which are accompanied by maps and cutaway drawings to make concepts even clearer. (Unfortunately, the map and text don't agree in one instance.) The attractive endpapers are a bonus; the world's tallest peaks, in colored sketches, are juxtaposed to show how heights compare.

Kirkus Reviews

SOURCE: A review of *Mountains,* in *Kirkus Reviews,* Vol. LXII, No. 5, March 1, 1994, p. 310.

In the trademark Simon style, carefully selected color photos (including some by the author and five by the noted Galen Rowell), drawings, and a clear and informative text tell the story of Earth's mountains: their formation, relative sizes, ecology, and influence on weather. A particularly striking NASA photo shows the stark contrast between the snow-covered Himalayas and India's fertile plains, which they help to water. Other photos depict a particular type of mountain or simply arrest the reader with their splendor and scope. Simon may have done more than any other living author to help us understand and appreciate the beauty of our planet and our universe; this is a fine addition to his collection.

Carolyn Angus

SOURCE: A review of *Mountains,* in *School Library Journal,* Vol. 40, No. 6, June, 1994, p. 142.

This book's spectacular full-color photographs will capture readers' attention and the text and well-designed diagrams will hold it. The endpapers profile the world's major peaks, allowing for a visual comparison of heights. More information about the major ranges is provided as the different types of mountain formations are considered. Simon also covers their shaping by the forces of erosion, their effect on weather and climate, and their impact on vegetation and animals, including humans. Like the author's other "Earth Science" books, this one will be used by both report writers and browsers.

COMETS, METEORS, AND ASTEROIDS (1994)

Elaine Fort Weischedel

SOURCE: A review of *Comets, Meteors, and Asteroids,* in *School Library Journal,* Vol. 40, No. 8, August, 1994, p. 166.

Simon revisits the territory he covered in **The Long Journey from Space,** this time for a younger audience. Full-color photographs have replaced the black-and-white ones, although there's really not a lot of difference between a black-and-white and a color shot of a meteor. While this new volume does include the basic information necessary to understand what these astronomical objects are and where they come from (including the distinctions between meteoroids, meteors, and meteorites), that's about all it does provide.

Carolyn Phelan

SOURCE: A review of *Comets, Meteors, and Asteroids,* in *Booklist,* Vol. 91, No. 2, September 15, 1994, p. 135.

Simon presents basic information about comets, meteors, and asteroids in an attractive oversize book that follows the format of his series on the planets. Blocks of text appear in fairly large type, usually facing a full-page illustration. Describing these three kinds of space objects individually in terms of their makeup and where they are found, Simon writes in plain language, without talking down to his audience. The intriguing photographs include shots of comets and meteor showers in the sky, a meteorite in Antarctica, and an enormous impact crater in Arizona. A visually appealing introductory volume.

Daniel Brabander

SOURCE: A review of *Comets, Meteors, and Asteroids,* in *The Horn Book Magazine,* Vol. LXXI, No. 1, January-February, 1995, p. 76.

A concise text characterizing comets, meteors, and asteroids accurately portrays the movement of these bodies though our solar system and provides up-to-date theories about their origins. The striking array of photographs includes Earth-based observatory images, computer-enhanced false-color pictures, and a *Galileo* spacecraft image. Unfortunately, the discovery of periodic comet Shoemaker-Levy 9 and its subsequent spectacular collision with Jupiter occurred too recently to have been included.

WINTER ACROSS AMERICA (1994)

Carolyn Phelan

SOURCE: A review of *Winter Across America,* in *Booklist,* Vol. 91, No. 6, November 15, 1994, p. 598.

Winter is not so much the subject here as the unifying theme tying together facts about animals and plants in various North American habitats. The book's focus moves from the Arctic Circle to Alaska to the Baja California coastal waters, then eastward across the continent. Along the way, Simon comments on types of winter storms, animal migration, and the characteristics of particular species. Excellent color photographs, often breathtaking scenes of landscapes and animals, appear throughout the book. A handsome offering in the tradition of the author's **Autumn Across America.**

Kirkus Reviews

SOURCE: A review of *Winter Across America,* in *Kirkus Reviews,* Vol. LXIII, No. 24, December 15, 1994, p. 1577.

Simon has written a lively and informative text as a companion to his **Autumn Across America.** But the stars of this effort are his own and other photographers' memorable pictures of our darkest season. The muted colors of winter might render the book too subtle for the younger reader, a problem ameliorated by the many scenes of animals in their habitats. A whooping crane perfectly framed by a patch of light in a gloomy sky; a herd of huddled deer, curious but not startled by the photographer; a chickadee stared down by a gray owl on the opposing page—these images stand out amid equally remarkable, if more static, photos of snow-encrusted cacti and an icy Grand Canyon. The lone human pictured seems dwarfed by an urban blizzard, a fitting encapsulation of our sometimes uneasy relationship with nature.

A book smart enough to be kept on the reference shelf, but with photos that tempt you to tear them out and frame them.

SCIENCE DICTIONARY (1994)

Hillary Jan Donitz-Goldstein

SOURCE: A review of *Science Dictionary,* in *School Library Journal,* Vol. 41, No. 2, February, 1995, p. 132.

This volume explicates over 2,000 terms culled from various fields of science. Succinct, accurate definitions, which usually provide the origins of the words under discussion, have been masterfully prepared. Brief biographical sketches of renowned scientists emphasize their contributions. The writing style is easy to read, informative, and geared toward the layperson. Unfortunately, the bland format is not an effective vehicle to convey the text. The illustrations do not appear with their corresponding definitions, and the dull drawings add little instructive value to the work. Supplementary maps of constellations, lists of physics equations, and weather map symbols are appended; many of these extras are superfluous and irrelevant to the presentation.

Booklist

SOURCE: A review of *Science Dictionary,* in *Booklist,* Vol. 91, No. 13, March 1, 1995, p. 1276.

The author, an award-winning writer of science books for children, states in his brief introduction that "like any foreign language, science can be translated into ideas and concepts that use simple English words," and that is what he does here.

More than 2,000 up-to-date entries cover all branches of science, from astronomy to zoology. For words that have both a scientific and an everyday meaning, only the scientific meaning is included. In many instances the origin of the word is provided: for example, marble comes from a Greek word meaning "to sparkle", placer from the Spanish American word meaning "sandbank." Definitions are clear and adequate for intended use, ranging from two to about twenty lines. The author indicates that every definition in the book was checked by Sheldon Aronson, professor of biology, Queens College, CUNY, or Alfred B. Bartz, physicist at the College of Education, Duquesne University. There are no pronunciation guides. Also included are brief biographies of about 85 important scientists.

The 250 simple line drawings that illustrate the volume are either in black and white or highlighted with blue. A final section includes classification of living things, maps of constellations, common weights and measures, weather-map symbols, a geological time scale, the periodic table, and eight other charts and tables. . . .

Science Dictionary is a useful, accurate, comparatively inexpensive science wordbook for upper-elementary and middle-school grades. Even older students will find it helpful.

Marilyn Brien

SOURCE: A review of *Science Dictionary,* in *Voice of Youth Advocates,* Vol. 18, No. 3, August, 1995, p. 193.

A science dictionary for young people? My first thought was, "Why not just use a junior dictionary?" Then I browsed through the science dictionary and surprisingly found some charts at the end of the book that are frequently frustrating to locate for children or teachers: the Periodic Table of Elements, a weather map with symbols, facts on the planets and stars, measurement tables, classification of living organisms, and a geological time table. Moving into the alphabetical entries, I compared

several entries with those of a popular junior dictionary and found this dictionary a much more user-friendly resource with a simple definition given first, then expanded explanations and connections. Some entries conclude with Latin or Greek derivatives. The large print, clear illustrations, and simple terminology all make this a dictionary a young person will want to reuse. The greatest value for this book is for the elementary classroom or library, but it is also usable in the middle school.

STAR WALK (1995)

Elaine Fort Weischedel

SOURCE: A review of *Star Walk,* in *School Library Journal,* Vol. 41, No. 4, April, 1985, p. 146.

Simon's latest offering combines stunning full-and double-page photographs with powerful poetry. Each photo is briefly captioned to identify the astronomical feature it depicts, but as Simon notes in his introduction, the pictures " . . . are not intended to illustrate the poems, nor are the poems intended to explain the photographs. Each is a different way of looking at the same thing." Verse by Archibald MacLeish, Sara Teasdale, Stanley Kunitz, May Swenson, and others, along with three anonymous Native American poems (identified by tribal origin), provide a thought-provoking view of the universe. Some quotations from Thoreau set as poetry work well with a fish-eye lens view of the Milky Way. Whitman's "When I Heard the Learn'd Astronomer" has appeared in a few other collections, but most of the selections have not previously been anthologized for children. While older readers will be able to read the poems for themselves, younger audiences might also enjoy listening to some of them. Youngsters drawn by the author's familiar series format will find a very different—and valuable—space experience waiting for them in the pages of this book.

Lauren Peterson

SOURCE: A review of *Star Walk,* in *Booklist,* Vol. 91, No. 13, March 1, 1995, p. 1239.

This unusual picture-book effort from an outstanding children's science book author is a dazzling combination of stunning photography and glorious poetry about stars and space. Simon emphasizes that the photographs should not be thought of as illustrations for the poems, nor the poems looked to for explanation of the photos. Instead, he suggests readers "allow the words of the poem and the shapes and colors of the photograph to swirl together in your mind." This is unquestionably a beautiful book that libraries could easily justify purchasing on the basis of the photographs alone. However, the poetry, by such writers as Whitman, Teasdale, and Wordsworth, is too abstract for even the most astute young picture-book reader, and even fewer youngsters will understand how to take Simon's suggestion to heart. Nevertheless, in this age of whole-language curricula, teachers will find the book useful for integrating science and language arts in the middle grades, and some may find it of value with even older students.

SPRING ACROSS AMERICA (1996)

Kirkus Reviews

SOURCE: A review of *Spring Across America,* in *Kirkus Reviews,* Vol. LXIV, No. 3, February 1, 1996, p. 232.

On the heels of **Autumn Across America** and **Winter Across America** in a series reminiscent of Edwin Way Teale's classic adult collection, The American Seasons, comes this lavishly illustrated book by a veteran science writer for children. On colorful text pages that harmonize with handsome full-color photographs (many taken by Simon himself), the spreads feature the characteristic animals or plant phenomena of the season: the spring peeper, robins, bear cubs, spawning grunion, migrating sandhill cranes, fiddleheads emerging from the forest floor. The clear text presents some fundamental concepts (the progression of spring as related to both latitude and elevation, treeline in the mountains determined not only by temperature but also by rainfall) as well as particulars about the various species mentioned. Beautiful and informative.

Carolyn Jenks

SOURCE: A review of *Spring Across America,* in *School Library Journal,* Vol. 42, No. 4, April, 1996, p. 130.

Simon's book is for slightly older readers, and its arrangement follows spring's journey (April through June) as it " . . . flows one hundred miles northward each week." Full-color photographs appear opposite pages of text that describe 14 plants and animals associated with the season, from skunk cabbage, pussy willows, and fiddleheads to grunion, garter snakes, and mayflies. This unique title is a scientific mood piece that provides bits of information about various parts of our vast country and an awareness of its beauty, reinforced by fine pictures.

EARTH WORDS: A DICTIONARY OF THE ENVIRONMENT (1995)

Carolyn Phelan

SOURCE: A review of *Earth Words: A Dictionary of the Environment,* in *Booklist,* Vol. 91, No. 16, April 15, 1995, p. 1496.

Similar to Simon's **Space Words,** this environmental dictionary features definitions (up to a paragraph long) of terms such as *biodegradable, biome, europhication, food web, oil spill, PCBs,* and *wetland.* Sometimes Simon talks about a word rather than defining it. For example, the entry for sun describes it as "the center of the solar system" and discusses how it affects the earth's climate and ecology, but the paragraph doesn't describe the sun itself or identify it as a star. Less space is devoted to text than to the unusual and sometimes striking illustrations, which vary from the diagrammatic to the impressionistic to the hyperrealistic. In some cases, captions would have been helpful to explain what's happening in the pictures. Although children old enough to read the book could handle more information than is given for each topic, consider the book anyway as supplemental material for classroom units on ecology.

The New Advocate

SOURCE: A review of *Earth Words: A Dictionary of the Environment,* in *The New Advocate,* Vol. 9, No. 1, Winter, 1996, p. 70.

In **Earth Words,** veteran children's science author Seymour Simon has written a most unusual book. Subtitled *A Dictionary of the Environment,* it is a highly specialized picture dictionary containing definitions of "66 essential environmental terms." This is a picture dictionary with a difference; Mark Kaplan's illustrations are equal partners with the words. For instance the word *recycling* is accompanied by a diagram which illustrates the life cycle of a can, from its use through collection, compression, meltdown, rolling into a metal sheet, and rebirth as a new can.

WILDFIRES (1996)

Carolyn Phelan

SOURCE: A review of *Wildfires,* in *Booklist,* Vol. 92, No. 15, April 1, 1996, p. 1360.

Exploring the place of fire in nature, Simon explains that despite Smokey the Bears warning, forest fires have important functions in the ecosystem. With a brilliantly clear and colorful photograph facing each page of text, the book describes the causes and the progression of the wildfires that burned areas of Yellowstone National Park in 1988, explains how the fires were beneficial in many ways, and shows the regeneration of the forests. Lucid writing and excellent book design contribute to the overall effectiveness of the book.

Kathleen McCabe

SOURCE: A review of *Wildfires,* in *School Library Journal,* Vol. 42, No. 5, May, 1996, p. 126.

Clear text and full-page, full-color photographs dramatize the overpowering fires that raged in Yellowstone National Park in the summer of 1988. Simon explains the chemical reactions that cause fire and the conditions necessary for a cataclysm of that magnitude. Using descriptive comparisons such as " . . . 165,000 acres of forest, an area more than twice the size of the entire city of Chicago," the author evokes the frantic effort to save the area from total destruction. But he goes on to explain why wildfires are helpful—that they are nature's method of renewing the ecosystem. Stating that the movie *Bambi* was incorrect in depicting forest animals fleeing in panic, Simon describes how creatures naturally adjust to the momentous change in temperature and atmosphere. Brief mention is made of fires in the Florida Everglades. . . . Simon's outstanding photos and readable text make this a worthy purchase.

Margaret A. Bush

SOURCE: A review of *Wildfires,* in *The Horn Book Magazine,* Vol. LXXII, No. 3, May-June, 1996, pp. 351-52.

Seymour Simon moves beyond the rash of children's books inspired by the 1988 fires in Yellowstone National Park to explain the phenomenon of fire as a cyclical event in nature's scheme. Bold, full-page photographs depict the raging fires at Yellowstone, controlled burning of saw grass in Everglades National Park, and examples of the black-and-green mosaic as new growth is generated after aged plant life burns. Simon explains natural combustion, the effects and benefits of fire for plants and animals, and the larger cycles of fire occurring in different plant regions over long periods of history. Human responsibility and decision-making are viewed in the context of the power of natural fire. Which fires should be fought? Which allowed to burn? Often the balance between human interests and the requirements of nature is precarious. As in his many other beautifully constructed photo essays, Simon provides an illuminating and thought-provoking view of nature.

THE HEART: OUR CIRCULATORY SYSTEM (1996)

Kirkus Reviews

SOURCE: A review of *The Heart: Our Circulatory System,* in *Kirkus Reviews,* Vol. LXIV, No. 12, June 15, 1996, p. 904.

"Make a fist. This is about the size of your heart," Simon begins, and with this simple, concrete image he introduces the wonders of the human heart, circulatory system, and blood to a picture-book audience. Elsewhere, even abstract ideas become comprehensible, e.g., the average human body contains about twenty-five trillion red blood cells, or "hundreds of times more blood cells than there are stars in the Milky Way galaxy." Stunning full-color photos appear on every page, many taken inside the human body with scanners, X rays, and other devices, and then computer-enhanced. The same science savvy and enthusiasm that has made Simon's titles on the universe so popular has been turned inward to uncover extraordinary facts about the human body.

Christine A. Moesch

SOURCE: A review of *The Heart: Our Circulatory System,* in *School Library Journal,* Vol. 42, No. 8, August, 1996, p. 160.

Simon approaches the human heart as he approached outer space and oceans: as an adventure to be explored. As always, the full-page, full-color photographs are spectacular, and the text is crisp and full of detail. In a conversational yet instructive style, the author presents young readers with fascinating information that will almost certainly spur them on to read more. Topics include types of blood vessels, coronary bypass surgery, strokes, and anatomy of the heart. There is no index, but since each two-page spread clearly addresses a specific topic, one isn't necessary.

Susan S. Verner

SOURCE: A review of *The Heart: Our Circulatory System,* in *The Bulletin of the Center for Children's Books,* Vol. 50, No. 2, October, 1996, pp. 75-6.

The hard-working engine of the circulatory system—the heart—gets no relief. It pumps the blood through sixty thousand miles of blood vessels in each and every human. Simon walks us through the circulatory blueprint in his usual informative and accessible style, but it is the startling photographs which command attention. Seen through a scanning electron microscope (SEM) and colored by computer, many of the images are magnified millions of times over—what looks like a shower of molten meteorites, for instance, is actually red blood cells hurtling at the viewer. In addition to the photos, there are cross-section diagrams of the heart, veins, and arteries (kids may find confusing the medical convention of showing the right side of something—atrium, ventricle—on the left side of the page). Especially useful in this day of frequent cardiac treatments is a brief explanation of what can go wrong with a heart and what can be done to fix it. Flap copy indicates that this initiates a series Simon will do on the human body; this first one has heart.

WILD BABIES (1997)

Carolyn Phelan

SOURCE: A review of *Wild Babies,* in *Booklist,* Vol. 93, No. 9-10, January 1, 1997, p. 864.

Simon approaches the general topic of baby animals by focusing on specifics, introducing various little ones from birth until they are grown and/or ready to leave their families: the young kangaroo, opossum, raccoon, polar bear, emperor penguin, giraffe, elephant, baboon, dolphin, frog, alligator, and lynx. He describes the physical characteristics, growth, and care of each youngster in a few paragraphs of cogent text facing a full-page, full-color photograph of parent and offspring. Similar in format to the author's books on sharks, wolves, and whales, this volume combines appealing photos with intriguing details of animal life.

Kirkus Reviews

SOURCE: A review of *Wild Babies,* in *Kirkus Reviews,* Vol. LXV, No. 1, January 1, 1997, p. 64.

Simon introduces 13 wild animal babies—alligator, baboon, dolphin, elephant, emperor penguin, frog, giraffe, kangaroo, koala, opossum, polar bear, raccoon, and lynx— so familiar that they hardly justify the statement, "We'll talk about some wild baby animals you may not have seen." Still, full-page, full-color photographs make for an appealing presentation, accompanied by the intriguing science facts and pithy comparisons for which Simon is known. For instance, opossums give birth to as many as 50 thumb-sized babies that must pull through the mother's fur to reach her pouch. The first 13 attach themselves to her 13 teats, so latecomers do not survive. He describes animal "baby-sitting" and penguin "kindergartens," almost always alerting readers to such anthropomorphisms by placing the term in quotes. Not essential, this is still a pleasing book, facing competition from other, similar titles.

Susan Oliver

SOURCE: A review of *Wild Babies,* in *School Library Journal,* Vol. 43, No. 2, February, 1997, p. 98.

Simon spotlights 13 animal babies from a few different continents and both poles. While the focus is on mammals, a bird, a reptile, and an amphibian are included. The full-color photographs are striking and generous, and most often portray the youngster with its mother. The accompanying page of information is written in a simple but lively manner to pique the interest of young readers. The book has a logical flow as animals from similar environments follow one another, and both the text and the photographs provide some glimpses of the diverse habitats in which these creatures live. This is a beautiful browsing book, but it does not include maps, a glossary, or even all the basic facts about each animal.

THE ON-LINE SPACEMAN AND OTHER CASES (1997)

Christina Dorr

SOURCE: A review of *The On-Line Spaceman and Other Cases,* in *School Library Journal,* Vol. 43, No. 4, April, 1997, pp. 140, 142.

This newest addition to the popular series is reminiscent of Donald Sobol's *Encyclopedia Brown* books, but with a decidedly computer-age slant. This title consists of 10 short stories, each with a scientific inaccuracy that stumps everyone except sixth-grade whiz, Einstein. His real name is

Adam, but he earned his nickname from his kindergarten teacher who recognized his extensive scientific knowledge. The episodes are rather tough tests of scientific phenomena from crying rocks to bovine behavior to extraterrestrials on-line. The spare ink sketches add interest, but no clues. *Einstein* will satisfy middle schoolers with a knack for science and who also like a touch of mystery.

Kay Weisman

SOURCE: A review of *The On-Line Spaceman and Other Cases,* in *Booklist,* Vol. 93, No. 17, May 1, 1997, p. 1498.

Twelve-year-old science sleuth Einstein Anderson (last seen in *Einstein Anderson Sees through the Invisible Man,* returns to solve 10 more short mysteries. Using the deductive reasoning of Sherlock Holmes and an advanced knowledge of science and technology, Einstein is able to unravel brainteasers that boggle everyone else. Clues are presented in short chapters, and readers are given a chance to solve the puzzle before turning the page for Einstein's solution. S. D. Schindler's black-line drawings provide an inviting format for younger readers. The loosely linked chapters span an entire school year, and the fact that several characters are involved in more than one case should please readers looking for a cohesive story. Give this to graduates of Sobol's Encyclopedia Brown series as well as science and mystery fans.

LIGHTNING (1997)

Blair Christolon

SOURCE: A review of *Lightning,* in *School Library Journal,* Vol. 43, No. 5, May, 1997, p. 126.

A purple-hued cover photo attracts readers to this fascinating topic. The stunning, vibrantly colored photographs help to explain the text, illustrating points such as the differences between the three kinds of lightning. Short, simple sentences make this topic accessible to younger readers but do not talk down to older report writers. Simon emphasizes precautions about lightning (for example, "If you are in water, get out as soon as possible"). He also lists safe places to be if you are caught out in the open during a lightning storm. . . . [T]he outstanding photos make Simon's book a striking selection

RIDE THE WIND: AIRBORNE JOURNEYS OF ANIMALS AND PLANTS (1997)

Susan Oliver

SOURCE: A review of *Ride the Wind: Airborne Journeys of Animals and Plants,* in *School Library Journal,* Vol. 43, No. 5, May, 1997, p. 150.

More ethereal than one of Simon's familiar photo-essays, this book, illustrated [by Elsa Warnick] with muted watercolors, looks at animals and plants that "ride the wind." Simon concentrates on the travels of birds in these brief, factual nature stories, but also includes the migration of several insects, spiders, bats, and seeds. Their journeys through the atmosphere serve as a vehicle for a glimpse into the life cycle of these animals and plants, but the strength of this book is in the lovely paintings, which range from fairly detailed to suggestive, using shapes and colors to impart information. Several pages at the end of the book give insight into scientific investigation—how scientists have determined this information and how much they still don't understand. These pages of full text and smaller type are supported by a background of an evocative, blue-and-white sky. A good choice for reading aloud to older children, this is a classy collaboration and an exciting introduction to a new children's book illustrator.

THE BRAIN: OUR NERVOUS SYSTEM (1997)

Carolyn Phelan

SOURCE: A review of *The Brain: Our Nervous System,* in *Booklist,* Vol. 93, No. 22, August, 1997, p. 1896.

The second book in the series that began with *The Heart: Our Circulatory System,* this book features images of the human brain and nervous system accompanied by lucid text explaining their anatomy and functions. Pictures include computer-generated scans, a diagrammatic painting, and many photographs, some greatly enlarged and color enhanced. The vivid illustrations catch the eye, but the clearly written text provides a fuller understanding of what happens in various parts of the brain and nervous system. The relatively large print and generous use of white space make the text look easy, though the occasional use of white print on black pages is a bit harder to focus on. Simon's way of explaining what's happening in everyday terms enhances the book's readability. Attentive readers will be rewarded with a dramatic portrait of what Simon calls "the control center for everything you do."

Christine A. Moesch

SOURCE: A review of *The Brain: Our Nervous System,* in *School Library Journal,* Vol. 43, No. 8, August, 1997, p. 152.

In this most recent effort, Simon brings his deft touch to an explanation of the brain and the nervous system. His clear, concise writing style is complemented by stunning color images taken with radiological scanners, such as CAT scans, MRIs, and SEMs (scanning electron microscopes.) Included in his explanation are descriptions of the anatomy and function of the parts of the brain, long and short term memory, neurons, dendrites, and more. The layout is familiar—a page of text facing a full-page photo. There is no glossary or index, but, as usual, the book is so well organized that they won't be missed.

Margaret A. Bush

SOURCE: A review of *The Brain: Our Nervous System,* in *The Horn Book Magazine,* Vol. LXXIII, No. 5, September-October, 1997, p. 594.

Electronic scans boldly magnify the minute cells of the brain and nervous system as Seymour Simon explains each major component of the human body's electrical system. Beginning with the role of nerves in signaling between the brain and senses or muscles and moving on to the structure of nerve cells, the carefully plotted explanations cover each region of the brain and the spinal cord. As in Simon's many handsome photo essays exploring the universe and planet earth, the text appears on black or white pages, each facing a vivid full-page photograph. The magnified photographs here include very delicate views of nerves as well as surrealistic blobs and tangles; there are realistic pictures of brains and models. In the brief captions or text, Simon occasionally refers to some of the photographic techniques employed, and at one point he names several of the scans used by neurologists to study the brain or diagnose problems, but these methods of creating pictures are not actually explained. The variety of views and the lucid presentation provide an absorbing introduction to this amazing control system that "can do more jobs than the most powerful computer ever made."

Deborah Stevenson

SOURCE: A review of *The Brain: Our Nervous System,* in *The Bulletin of the Center for Children's Books,* Vol. 51, No. 3, November, 1997, p. 101.

Following in the path of *The Heart,* as it were, this book tackles the complicated subject of the brain. Simon explains the work of the nerve cells and the different functions of the various parts of the brain, using specific examples to illustrate. There are some complicated concepts and terms, but they're defined with relative clarity considering their density, and there are some interesting tidbits included ("Synapses always pass signals in the same direction; they cannot work in reverse"). The art includes diagrams, magnified images, CAT scans, and some nifty cross-sections that will appeal to the clinical. The book provokes some questions that remain unanswered (Which end of the brain is which in the pictures showing brain activity when someone's eyes are open? Are the photographed cross-sections real brains, or are they, like the spinal cord image, models?), but overall this is about as entry-level as a treatment of that complicated organ is going to get. Junior MDs will appreciate the look inside.

THE UNIVERSE (1998)

John Peters

SOURCE: A review of *The Universe,* in *School Library Journal,* Vol. 44, No. 5, May, 1998, p. 137.

Simon offers what amounts to an introduction to his long running, literally and figuratively stellar series of photo-essays on matters astronomical. Matching full-color, full- and double-page-spread-sized light and radio photographs of nebulas, galaxies, and sundry deep-space phenomena with two or three paragraphs of explanatory text, he covers a wide range of topics, from the Big Bang to quasars, from star formation to extra-solar planets. Care has been taken to keep the pictures and related text close together, and the choice of detail is guaranteed to whet youngster's appetites for a more thorough, narrowly focused treatment. Asking some of the Big Questions—"Does life exist on earth-like planets in distant solar systems? Will the universe expand forever or finally stop and then collapse into a gigantic black hole?"—Simon writes that "we are just at the beginning of a golden age of discovery." This book, along with the others that it leads to, will give children the solid background they will need to understand—and perhaps even participate in—those discoveries.

THEY SWIM THE SEAS: THE MYSTERY OF ANIMAL MIGRATION (1998)

Kirkus Reviews

SOURCE: A review of *They Swim the Seas: The Mystery of Animal Migration,* in *Kirkus Reviews,* July 15, 1998, p. 1042.

In a companion book to **Ride the Wind,** Simon turns his attention to the migratory habits of marine plankton, plants, fish, and mammals. From alga called spirogyra, spread by moving currents, to the nesting patterns of sea turtles to the great gray whale's legendary 4,000-mile trek from Baja to the Bering Sea, Simon astounds readers with the marvels of migration. The author poses questions to which the answers can't be known, but curious readers may find themselves frustrated, wanting to know how scientists manage to study tuna traveling thre e times faster than the boat from which they're observed. Lilting, liquid watercolors in all the gray-greens of the sea majestically portray barnacle-dappled whales, rushing salmon, or marching spiny lobster. A rougher fit with the picture-book format is the book's continuous narrative, without organizational headings and with additional information about each migrator appearing in a five-page addendum titled, "More About Ocean Journeys." Still, Simon and [Elsa] Warnick beautifully succeed in capturing the wonder of the migratory process.

Chris Sherman

SOURCE: A review of *They Swim the Seas: The Mystery of Animal Migration,* in *Booklist,* Vol. 95, No. 2, September 15, 1998, p. 226.

In spare, elegant language, Simon describes the migrations of marine plants and animals from the elevatorlike movements of microscopic plankton to the 4,000-mile journeys of gray whales. He has selected particularly intriguing creatures whose mysterious habits are certain to fascinate readers: eels who leave their freshwater homes in Europe and the U.S. and disappear in the Sargasso Sea to spawn, spiny lobsters who march single file from Bimini to deeper Gulf Stream waters, and tuna and salmon who return to the same spawning grounds where they were born after roaming thousands of miles around the oceans. In a concluding section, Simon provides additional information about the habits and physical characteristics of these animals. Warnick's fine watercolor illustrations are a perfect complement to Simon's fluid writing. She has captured the purposeful movement described in the text and rendered it in lively paintings that flow across the pages.

Patricia Manning

SOURCE: A review of *They Swim the Seas: The Mystery of Animal Migration,* in *School Library Journal,* Vol. 44, No. 10, October, 1998, pp. 159-60.

In a companion volume to **Ride the Wind: Airborne Journeys of Animals and Plants,** this second book in a projected trilogy on animal migration focuses on the journeys plants and animals make on the glittering surface and in the mysterious depths of the world's oceans. Simon's readable text opens windows and peepholes into treks as diverse in character as the daily rise and fall of enormous aggregations of plankton, through the unseen hordes of eels swarming to disappear in the Sargasso Sea, to the strange autumnal processions of spiny lobsters off the reefs near Bimini. The author marvels at these fascinating odysseys and muses on the reasons for such lengthy voyages and the possible reasons for their origination. A final segment provides additional details that should lure readers into further investigations. The whole is graced with a multitude of delicately sea-toned watercolors depicting everything from minute plankton to massive gray whales, and a wide range of creatures in between. Though there is much grist here for the determined report writer's mill, the lyrical text and sea-lit watercolors will best suit as recreational reading for nature lovers.

MUSCLES: OUR MUSCULAR SYSTEM AND BONES: OUR SKELETAL SYSTEM (1998)

Deborah Stevenson

SOURCE: A review of *Bones: Our Skeletal System* and *Muscles: Our Muscular System,* in *The Bulletin of the*

Center for Children's Books, Vol. 52, No. 1, September, 1998, p. 31.

Simon is working his way through the human body; in now-familiar form, he describes the functions of physiological systems in simple terms while sharp images from scans and 'scopes (and occasionally pictures of models) illustrate. *Muscles* is generally a smooth and accessible introduction to those movers of our bodies: Simon describes the complementary actions of contraction and relaxation, differentiates between skeletal muscle, smooth muscle, and heart muscle, and explains how muscles can be affected by usage ("A warm muscle contracts more quickly and easily, receives more oxygen, and can perform for a longer time than a cold one"). *Bones,* however, is particularly prone to raise questions it never answers. How do "minerals that we get from food make the bones as hard as rock"? Which bones are hollow, and how does that relate to the "honeycomb of spaces" in spongy bone? *How* are the false ribs "connected to the ribs above"? Pictures (which are also occasionally confusing in *Muscles*) and references thereto can further baffle, since all the ribs in the picture seem to be attached to the breastbone despite text describing other arrangements, it's hard to find the fracture in the X-ray "showing two metal screws that have been placed into a fractured upper arm," and it's never stated what the arresting image on the back cover (which is presumably some flavor of bony closeup) actually depicts. There's still information and entertainment in both books, however, and the drawbacks in *Bones* probably don't necessitate amputation for those contemplating the body literary; just be prepared to answer a few questions as well as listen to Oohs and Aahs.

Susan Dove Lempke

SOURCE: A review of *Bones: Our Skeletal System* and *Muscles: Our Muscular System,* in *Booklist,* Vol. 95, No. 1, September 1, 1998, p. 118.

Simon once again proves his remarkable facility for making complicated science clear and understandable. These two entries in his series on the human body discuss the two systems that keep our bodies upright and moving, the skeleton and muscles. In *Bones* Simon explains that despite their lifeless appearance, bones are made of living cells, and he describes each major group of bones, such as the spine, and how they connect (joints) and move (muscles). The muscular system gets its own book as well, where we learn about the voluntary, involuntary, and cardiac muscles. These two books continue the series' outstanding book design, with its large pages using computer-enhanced images as well as photographs and drawings to illustrate points of interest. Giving ample information for report writers, these will also give a young reader a sense of wonder about the "marvelous living machine that you are."

CROCODILES AND ALLIGATORS (1999)

Linda Perkins

SOURCE: A review of *Crocodiles and Alligators,* in *Booklist,* Vol. 95, No. 15, April 1, 1999, p. 1410.

Beginning with the origin of the words crocodile, alligator, and gharial, this introduction to crocodilians then discusses their habitat and relationship to dinosaurs, explains the differences between alligators and crocodiles, and supplies the basic information on life expectancy, hunting techniques, food, reproduction, endangered status, land speed, and methods of locomotion. Simon's familiar elongated format is a perfect fit for these long bodies, with each opening featuring a full-page color photograph. The narrative refers to a few of the pictures, but captions would have clarified the others. Starting with the saw-toothed snout on the cover, the striking photos will attract kids visually, and Simon's casual but clear informative approach will invite them verbally. The lack of a table of contents and index makes this book better suited for browsing than for homework assignments, but children of many ages will snap it up.

Lisa Wu Stowe

SOURCE: A review of *Crocodiles and Alligators,* in *School Library Journal,* June, 1999, p. 153.

Simon's lively text presents fascinating facts and ancient lore surrounding these intriguing animals. Readers will discover that crocodiles and alligators use their powerful tails to spin their bodies around in the water in order to rip apart their prey and will marvel at how a Nile crocodile will allow a small bird to walk through its mouth picking food from its teeth. Simon touches upon the crocodilians that lived alongside the dinosaurs and evolved into the reptiles that we know today. He also points out that despite the dangers that threaten their lives and habitats, crocodilians are making a slow comeback. Report writers may be disappointed by the absence of an index or indeed of any sort of subject division. However, the book is filled with interesting information, and the vivid, well-composed, full-color photographs and entertaining text will draw in browsers.

TORNADOES (1999)

Patricia Manning

SOURCE: A review of *Tornadoes,* in *School Library Journal,* June, 1999, pp. 153-54.

An entry in a handsome series that includes *Storms, Weather,* and *Lightning, Tornadoes* focuses on one of nature's most violent and spectacular phenomena. Large, riveting, full-color photos show a threatening sky, meteorologists at work, a variety of tornadoes (from an eerily ethereal waterspout to an appalling monster), and the resultant chaotic shredding of human possessions in the storms' paths. Simon's clear, well-organized text discusses the weather conditions necessary to spawn these violent storms; how they form; where they are most likely to occur; and how scientists predict, rate, and track them. He also describes some of the major tornadoes recorded in the U.S. and includes weather maps and a diagram. . . . [M]ake room on your shelves for Simon's standout view of a cataclysmic manifestation.

Additional coverage of Simon's life and career is contained in the following sources published by The Gale Group: *Children's Literature Review,* **Vol. 9;** *Contemporary Authors,* **Vols. 25-28R;** *Contemporary Authors New Revision Series,* **Vols. 11, 29;** *Major Authors and Illustrators for Children and Young Adults;* **and** *Something about the Author,* **Vols. 4, 73.**

Cora Taylor
1936-

Canadian author of fiction books.

Major works include *Julie* (1985), *The Doll* (1987), *Julie's Secret* (1991), *Ghost Voyages* (1992), *Summer of the Mad Monk* (1994).

INTRODUCTION

Cora Taylor is best known for her character-driven novels for middle graders, often involving supernatural themes. One of Taylor's characters has ESP, two are capable of time travel, and one finds a spell that makes her invisible, but Taylor's works do not become simply action or adventure stories; the author works to make her characters fully-fleshed individuals. As Sarah Ellis wrote of Taylor's characterization of Meg in *The Doll*, "Taylor enters fully into the fresh perception and raw feelings of a child. In plain concrete language she expresses Meg's claustrophobia in a troubled family situation where adults dissemble, the urgency with which the girl needs to escape, and the grief she feels for a family who lived and died generations before her." Critics have praised Taylor's handling of other complex literary creations, such as the title character in *Julie* and Pip from *Summer of the Mad Monk*. She has also been lauded for her strong descriptions, and her believable dialogue: Heather McKend wrote, "Taylor demonstrates a good ear for dialogue between children, capturing typical sibling teasing and rivalry over possessions and territory." Just as Taylor's characters, not action, are the focus of her best books, the themes the author addresses are more involved than the supernatural aspects of the novels would suggest. Her works depict the realities of families, some troubled and some happy. Taylor's characters deal with poverty, isolation, and divorce. In *The Doll*, for example, Meg is able to travel back in time. Taylor's treatment of the situation, though, makes clear that such temporal wandering is an escape for the girl to avoid dealing with parents who may be splitting up. The characters the author creates, and the sensitive, individual ways they respond to sometimes difficult lives, elevate Taylor's works above typical fantasy literature.

Biographical Information

Taylor was born in 1936 in Fort Qu'Appelle, Saskatchewan, Canada. The author's father died when she was only six years old, and her mother spent years in a sanatorium as treatment for tuberculosis. Nevertheless, Taylor told *Something About the Author* that she "had an idyllic farm childhood on [her] grandmother's farm near Carlton, Saskatchewan." Familiarity with farm life and the

landscape of the western prairies is evident in nearly all of Taylor's books. She graduated from the University of Alberta, where she took her first writing courses, in 1973; her first work was published in 1985.

Major Works

Taylor's first novel for young people, *Julie*, is about the isolation experienced due to being different. The protagonist is Julie Morgan, the youngest child of seven. Julie is different from her siblings not only in appearance—she is a small girl with dark coloring, and the rest of her family is tall and blond—but also because she is "sensitive." From a very young age Julie has visions of both the future and the past; she knows things that she has no way of knowing, and she mysteriously communicates with plants and animals. Julie's siblings at first are amused by her flights of imagination, but as they realize that her visions are more than just the product of fancy they become uncomfortable with her, not sure if she is lying or disturbed. Her mother, too, is uneasy with the girl's gift, although her father accepts her. Julie also struggles with her specialness. While she becomes friends with Granny Goderich, a fortune teller, she also longs to be "normal." Only at the end of the novel, when the girl is able to use her gift to save her father from a tractor accident, does Julie realize she can benefit from the ability that also isolates her. *Julie's Secret* picks up the girl's story when she is eleven years old, and more familiar with her special powers. In this sequel, Julie and her oldest sister are caught unsuspecting by a spring blizzard, but Julie is able to sense shelter in the form of an old barn on an abandoned farm not far from their home. While the girls weather the storm there, Julie becomes aware of evil in the barn; when the Royal Canadian Mounted Police investigate, they discover the body of a teenager and evidence of cult activity, and traces of a much older double murder. Julie is also able to help save her brother from his kidnappers when she receives a vision of the place where they are holding him.

Time travel links two of Taylor's other books, *The Doll* and *Ghostly Voyages*. In *The Doll*, 10-year-old Meg spends time on her grandmother's farm recovering from rheumatic fever. The girl is also aware that her parents are going through a difficult time, and she waits for them to tell her that they will divorce. While Meg recuperates, her grandmother lets her play with the "invalid doll," a china doll that comforted generations of Shearer girls when they were ill. This doll is also the mysterious key that allows Meg to travel back in time, to the period when her great-grandmother's family traveled by wagon out to the western prairie as homesteaders. Whenever Meg falls asleep with the doll, she awakes as Morag, the little pioneer girl convalescing from fever in the back of her family's Red River wagon. To return to the present, Morag also must fall asleep with the doll. As Morag, Meg is able to feel like a vital part of a family in a way that she is unable to in her real life: Morag's family cannot survive unless they all work together to make it across the prairies and build their new home; Meg can't even talk to her parents about her worries. More and more, the girl escapes into the past until her grandmother worries because she is sleeping so much, and shows no signs of getting well, since she is exhausted from living her double life. Finally, though, Morag saves her little sister Lizzie from a prairie fire but cannot herself recover from illness and fatigue. When she dies, Meg is released back into the present and finds that she has the strength to deal with her current situation, after all. In *Ghost Voyages*, Jeremy also finds a talisman that allows him to visit the past. The nine-year-old finds his grandfather's boyhood stamp collection and when he examines the stamps of historic ships with his grandfather's magnifying glass, Jeremy is magically transported back in time to the ship depicted on the stamp. The first ship is one transporting troops to put down the Riel Rebellion, the next is ferrying fur traders north to Hudson Bay. The historical events and setting are described in detail, and Jeremy is changed by the adventures that take him out of his everyday existence.

Summer of the Mad Monk contains no supernatural elements, but the protagonist is not without an abundance of

imagination. Pip is twelve years old in 1932, living in rural Alberta during the Great Depression and the fierce wind and dust storms that plagued the area during that time. The poverty and desperation of Pip's daily life is lightened by his fantasy of a mystery surrounding the town's new blacksmith. Pip decides that the Russian man, named Raspinsky, must actually be the monk Rasputin in disguise. The boy is further convinced when he discovers that the blacksmith is concealing another Russian man, this one injured. Pip imagines that this must be Tsar Alexei somehow escaped from the execution of the rest of his family. These daydreams and fantasies provide Pip with an escape from the dreary subsistence-farming reality of his life, and allow him to hope for something better around the next corner.

Awards

Taylor received several awards for *Julie*, including the Canada Council Award, the Canadian Library Association Book of the Year Award, and the Alberta Writers Guild R. Ross Annett Award, all in 1985. She also received the Ruth Schwartz Children's Book Award in 1988 for *The Doll*, and *Summer of the Mad Monk* received the Canadian Library Association Book of the Year Award in 1995.

GENERAL COMMENTARY

Bonnie Ryan-Fisher

SOURCE: "The Accidental but Fortuitous Career: Cora Taylor, Children's Writer," in *Canadian Children's Literature,* Vol. 23:4, No. 88, Winter, 1997, pp. 31-5.

"It was the luckiest thing that could be," Cora Taylor says of her accidental entry into the field of children's literature. Her first book, ***Julie,*** had its beginnings in a dream and, like most of her books, in a character. The fragment of dream, of a child standing on a hill watching ships coming across the prairie, was jotted down in a bedside notebook and left to rest. But the feeling lingered: "The feeling of the beauty of these ships coming across the fields and also the incredible sadness because she couldn't tell anyone . . . What would happen if she told people?"

A couple of years later, the fragment was resurrected when Taylor took a course with Rudy Wiebeand began searching for short story material. Two surprising things happened then. Taylor, who says she always had difficulty getting short stories long enough, found that she had a story that wouldn't stop. "This one went on to thirty pages, "she says," and I was arbitrarily having to end it." And Julie was taking over. "This character and her point of view was so much more interesting and the others were being pushed into bit parts . . . I was worried, and I think I even said to Rudy at one point 'This is starting to sound like a children's book. . . .'"

Taylor had not begun with the idea of writing for children. In fact, she had the idea that no one takes children's literature seriously. She had no background in the field beyond her introductory course in children's literature at university which covered no Canadian authors and only one living author, E. B. White (who has since died).

Yet *Julie* exploded on the Canadian children's literature scene in 1985, beginning its incredible journey to fame when it was a finalist in the Alberta Writing for Youth Competition, later published by Prairie Books, taking numerous awards including the Canada Council Award for Children's Literature. It has been published in Britain, Australia, New Zealand, and the USA, and translated into Swedish and Dutch. Taylor says that *Julie* and her second book, *The Doll,* are still the ones most familiar to the school audiences she often visits.

Yet, that *Julie* was published as a children's book at all was a surprise to the author. Begun as her master's thesis and intended as an adult novel, the manuscript was put on hold when Taylor's husband was diagnosed with a serious heart condition. The arbitrary deadline of December 30, for the Writing for Youth Competition in 1984, allowed her to finally focus, seven years after the novel's beginning, and bring it to a close. At that time Alberta Culture sponsored two writing competitions and alternated the years. Taylor sent the manuscript off half expecting to have it returned as unsuitable for the youth category. Instead, it was a finalist.

Taylor feels that part of the secret of *Julie*'s success can be traced to the rules she broke in writing it, including not using "pablum words" for her young readers. Julie was written as an adult novel that just happened to have a young protagonist. Taylor says that she was suddenly called upon to speak to a variety of groups across the country on children's literature, while she was still trying to understand just what children's literature was herself.

She began *The Doll,* her second novel, believing that she was writing a book about reincarnation. In a conversation at the Children's Book Centre, she recalls being told "You're writing a time travel, you know. It's a genre." Suddenly she stopped and read dozens of time travel books in the middle of the writing process. Taylor says she is glad that she did this because it helped her to solidify her own ideas. Time travel is not just adventure to her. The experiences of the past must impact upon the present, must change the way the character lives her life in the present. Once again, character is the impetus.

With five novels to her credit now, Taylor has not changed her mind about the importance of character. Her 1994 book, *Summer of the Mad Monk,* is built around the character of Pip, a young boy growing up in a prairie town. Pip's character began in the stories her late husband

would tell her of his own prairie childhood. In fact the story began before her husband's death. It was to be her next novel after *The Doll.* "[T]hat one was based on his life and his childhood and I knew I couldn't work on it right away." Taylor's personal favourite among her books to date, *Summer of the Mad Monk* was voted Book of the Year for Children by the Canadian Library Association.

Asked about the relationship between biography or autobiography and her writing, Taylor smiles. "I remember reading C. S. Lewis talking about his writing, that he saw it and wrote what he saw. Whereas, I just have a character and then move from body to body so each of them is going to contain a lot of bits of me": bits of Taylor and other significant people in her life. Her grandmother, who was the model for the grandmother in *The Doll,* was a very important person in her life. The grandmother in the book Taylor is currently writing is a cross between "Mrs. Polifax and Auntie Mame," she says, but is also the kind of grandmother Taylor would like to be. The relationship between truth and fiction is an interesting one for her. She recalls her own difficulty making adjustments to the truth when she first began writing about the family of her own great grandparents. They had five children and so she used five children in her story. One turned out to be totally superfluous. "When you're teaching creative writing, this is a major thing for people to be able to jump from the truth into playing with the idea of fiction. . . . You start with something based on something and it takes awhile to want to make adjustments." Yet, "things that work best are things based on truth you didn't realize. They sort of drift in and then you think, oh yeah that was based on such and such."

This subconscious work is something Taylor is particularly good at. Her characters live. Their lives are real and their experiences touch readers. However, she admits to some surprise at what touches her readers sometimes. In two separate instances, school children reading *The Doll* were given the assignment of creating a play, a scene from the book. Both groups chose the scene where Meg talks to her parents about their divorce. Taylor had never considered *The Doll* as being a book about divorce and yet she concedes that she had been both parent and grandparent in these situations, worrying about the impact on the child. Perhaps it is her own warmth and intensity when it comes to feelings about family and home that underlies Taylor's success in recreating both in her novels—her laughter is fond when she speaks of writing tales around all seventeen of her grandchildren; she feels regret at missing the opportunity to hold onto some of the "Shearer family" land in Saskatchewan, which was recently sold back to the government. She admits to feeling sorrow even now about giving up "the farm" two years ago and moving into the city.

More and more, she "camps" now, living part of the time in Edmonton where she also maintains a separate, homey office, a space she has come to love. She grabs one of several prepacked suitcases as necessity dictates, travelling to do readings, writer-in-residencies, workshops, speaking engagements and the like. For two precious months each year she forgets the cold north and the bustle of her life and takes respite in California, where a diary substitutes for conversation, and she writes. *Julie's Secret* was written there, as were *Ghost Voyages* and *Summer of the Mad Monk.*

Cora Taylor takes her commitment to writing for children quite seriously now and remembering that she had once thought a book published for kids was a book no one would read, she exudes enthusiasm talking about the wonderful support network children's writers have through libraries and schools. She was once asked to do twelve readings in a Moose Jaw library and remembers thinking "Margaret Atwood couldn't get twelve readings in Moose Jaw."

She has a great deal of respect for her readers. Having learned from the success of *Julie,* she does not consciously write for a young audience, she writes for a "me" audience. And she hopes that "I'm giving in a non-preachy, teachy way some guidelines and some kind of ideals." Books also allow young people an alternative too to the extremely visual orientation of television and film. "[Those] don't bring the smells and the touch and the taste," Taylor says. "And I read somewhere that children's strongest sense is not vision. It is taste and smell. Smell particularly . . . I've always really used that in my books." Perhaps it is because of this that she has mixed feelings about an upcoming film version of *The Doll.* The screen play is being done by Connie Massing and Kicking Horse is doing the movie. Taylor is certain both will do a good job. Still, she says she is dreading the first time she goes into a schoolroom and hears "We've seen the movie but we haven't read the book."

Most of all it seems that Taylor revels in the freedom that writing for youth allows her, freedom to indulge her imagination. "You know," she says," if you wrote a novel like *Julie* for adults, about someone with ESP, it would be in the funny section in the bookstore." In her new book, *Vanishing Act,* one of the young protagonists has discovered a spell for invisibility and Taylor says, "I'm having a ball with it. When I was a kid I desperately wanted to be invisible."

She sets herself new challenges with each book, trying to do something different. *Vanishing Act* was originally conceived as a mystery. She now calls it a spy thriller. It is written from three characters' points of view. In the future she hopes to write a pure fantasy, to bring *Julie* back in a third book and perhaps to write a sequel to *Ghost Voyages.* And yes, she still plans to someday write an adult novel. "But not for awhile yet. I'd like to get ten books out before I would feel I could take the time off to do something. You know, I'm starting in a different field if I do that."

Finding home again is also one of her goals. In the whirlwind of activity, she has a dream of unpacking the boxes that still remain packed since she left the farm, unpacking them in a place on the prairies, on top of a hill with a view. "You can't lose the sky, you know."

TITLE COMMENTARY

JULIE (1985)

Janet Lunn

SOURCE: "Psychic Tale Foretells Happy Future for Taylor," in *Quill and Quire*, Vol. 51, No. 10, October, 1985, p. 16.

Julie is a seer. The youngest of seven children in an Alberta farm family, she is a quiet child who keeps to herself because of this trait the others can't understand. From the time she becomes aware of the world, Julie sees into the past and future, into the spirits of trees, of butterflies, and of small animals, and she is able by force of will to control objects.

Her family thinks of Julie as over-imaginative, and although they love the stories she tells them, they are uneasy about what she describes: herds of buffalo, tiny dancing people. When she realizes that no one believes what she is describing, Julie withdraws more and more into herself.

Only her father, Will Morgan, remembering his Welsh grandmother's powers, is prepared to believe Julie's visions. Her mother, Alice, is not so open-minded. After a visit to old Granny Goderich, a tea-cup reader with whom the child feels an immediate rapport, Alice decides to inhibit the oddness in Julie. It is only when Julie's gift enables her to rescue her father from certain death that her mother can accept Julie as she is—clairvoyance and all.

Cora Taylor has done a good job of bringing the Morgan family and their rural Alberta setting to life. The brothers and sisters bicker and banter their way through the tale; Father and Mother are convincing parents. Through Julie's intense concentration and vision, we watch a butterfly emerge from its cocoon, comfort ourselves in the seat formed by a balm-of-Gilead tree, and watch a long-ago buffalo stampede.

The book's greatest flaw is that it is more chronicle than story. Julie's struggle to be accepted is told as a series of incidents and events strung together in sequence—although the first 59 pages are told in flashback, formidably confusing even for an adult reader. While each event has its own beginning, middle, and end, there is no real build-up, no climax for the whole. As well, the events deal repeatedly and exclusively with incidents of Julie's clairvoyance, giving the book the sense of being one long anecdote. The only excitement comes in the final episode in which Julie races to rescue her father, who is pinned under a fallen tractor.

Julie is Taylor's first book. She writes clearly, with a gentle, somewhat old-fashioned approach. It is a fine first book, a promise of good stories to come. Julie and her family are likeable people, and children will be fascinated by the subject.

Mary Ainslie Smith

SOURCE: "Seeing Things," in *Books in Canada,* Vol. 14, No. 8, November, 1985, p. 36.

Julie, by Cora Taylor, is about a young girl's supernatural powers. But it is grounded firmly in the realistic context of a family farm in Saskatchewan. Julie Morgan, the youngest in her family, is the seventh child of a seventh child, the great-granddaughter of a Welsh woman believed to have had second sight. She is small and dark in a family of tall, practical blonds. But the differences are deeper than that. Julie sees things, hears voices that no one else can. These extra powers, which her family at first puts down to an active imagination, isolate Julie, who realizes that no one else can share or understand them.

The story follows Julie from babyhood to age 10 as she adjusts to being alone with her special gift. Throughout the years various events bring into focus her uncanny ability to know things that should be impossible for her to know. Her father is concerned, her mother broods over what she feels is an unhealthy difference in her youngest child, and her brothers and sisters—although they love her—are half afraid of her and half convinced that she is either lying or crazy. Then Julie summons all her special powers to help her father after a terrible accident and realizes that she is strong enough to use her unique ability as a positive force. *Julie* is Taylor's first novel, and she writes with a clear, strong style, making everything in the story, even the supernatural, very believable.

Heather McKend

SOURCE: A review of *Julie,* in *Canadian Children's Literature,* No. 44, 1986, pp. 75-6.

For those entering adolescence, acceptance of oneself and acceptance from others are pertinent concerns. Cora Taylor's first novel, *Julie,* depicts a young girl's struggle to confront and understand abilities that mark her as "different" from others. Ten-year-old Julie Morgan is a "Celtic throwback" whose psychic abilities, inherited from Great-Grandmother Morgan, set her apart from her siblings on the family farm. Visions, smells and voices provide Julie with knowledge of both past and future events, knowledge which can be at once a helpful gift and an isolating burden. Fellow psychic Granny Goderich and Julie's father demonstrate loving acceptance of the girl, but Julie's mother's fear and rejection contribute to the girl's attempts to hide and deny her abilities. A family crisis motivates Julie to reconsider her special powers, recognizing what she must accept and what she can change because of her abilities. Ultimately, the young adult reader is put in the position of choosing whether or not to "accept" the role of psychic powers in determining the novel's conclusion.

Taylor's evocative and beautifully crafted descriptions draw the reader into sharing Julie's premonitions. When sheets on a clothesline become "ships with rows and rows of full, fat sails tossed as though the black summer fallow field were ridged with waves and not furrows", the rhythmic, poetic prose brings the sea-tossed boats to life. Similarly, Taylor demonstrates a good ear for dialogue between children, capturing typical sibling teasing and rivalry over possessions and territory.

Yet an overall unevenness is evident, and may possibly be attributed to the novel's growth from its original form as a short story. The beginning and conclusion of the novel are clear and dramatic, but the middle is muddled, and this affects reader identification with Julie and her concerns. At five years of age, just as at ten, Julie can outsmart her parents with her carefully worded replies; in this sense she is static. The third person narration allows for different characters' reactions to Julie's psychic experiences, but this can also create a distance between the reader and Julie. For example, when Julie and her mother, Alice, first visit Granny Goderich, Julie's actions are described, but the scene's emotional impact arises from a concentration on Alice's thoughts and feelings. Because of the resulting imbalance, Alice seems more fully realized; Julie seems slightly wooden. Problems like these are frustrating because one wishes to have had the chance to get to know Julie better—her story is haunting.

Julie is the winner of the Canadian Library Association Book of the Year Award for Children, the Canada Council Children's Literature Prize and the Alberta Writers Guild Best Children's Book Award. This thorough acclaim is questionable, and invites comparison between *Julie* and other award-winners. Yet *Julie* is a promising first novel; Cora Taylor's next work is eagerly awaited.

Sarah Ellis

SOURCE: A review of *Julie,* in *Horn Book Magazine,* Vol. LXII, No. 5, September, 1986, p. 628.

The theme of the isolated child is used very starkly and effectively in Cora Taylor's *Julie.* Julie is a ten-year-old child with psychic powers, the ability to predict the future, to sense disaster at a distance, to communicate with animals and plants. The book begins with a description of one of her inexplicable visions. "She could see them. The sails ballooning, coming across the field with a smooth silent motion, rising and falling like a giant horse galloping. Only slowly. Tall ships with rows and rows of full, fat sails tossed as though the black summer fallow field were ridged with waves and not furrows." This recurring picture punctuates the story, culminating in a vision of the Egyptian Ship of the Dead that propels Julie on a headlong horseback ride to rescue her father who has been pinned beneath his tractor. Julie's routes to "knowing" are varied, the smell of geraniums, the sight of a burning granary. But it is the juxtaposition of the things of the sea onto the prairie that is particularly poignant.

Poignant, too, is the description of Julie's interaction with the world of adults. As a preschooler she is humored, dismissed as having an active imagination or as being a precocious storyteller. But inevitably comes the moment when the adult rational world forces her to make distinctions between reality and fantasy. As her older brothers and sisters grow up one by one and cease to believe in her visions, Julie is finally left alone.

The sadness of this process is twofold. First, we feel the poignancy of simply growing up, of leaving behind the integrated world of a child where all time is one, where buffalo still roam the prairies. *Julie* is by no means a florid novel, but it is a deeply romantic one. Second, we sympathize with the more particular plight of a child who has a secret, a gift, a difference, a hidden disability that society cannot accept. We see with regret the creation of a cocoon of secretiveness and reserve, the growing conviction of essential solitude. Taylor uses a fantasy conceit—that of the existence of a psychic world—to tell a very down-to-earth, character-rich story.

Marcus Crouch

SOURCE: A review of *Julie,* in *The Junior Bookshelf,* Vol. 52, No. 4, August, 1988, pp. 191-2.

Granny Goderich, who is "nobody's granny really", sees that Julie is a 'sensitive' child. Mother really knows it too but prefers not to examine her knowledge too closely, feeling that there is danger in the little girl's powers. Julie sees more than other people, including the buffalo which were exterminated long ago and the ashes of George Goderich, hidden away in their jar. She sees Granny dying in her lonely cottage, and the granary burning a day before the real fire. When her vision identifies a threat to her father's life, she learns for the first time how to direct her powers and save him. It is no coincidence that the old tree which has received all the secrets Julie could not share with her family dies in the moment of her success.

There have been other stories about esoteric powers, but *Julie* has a strange persuasiveness of its own. The story is told quietly. Although it offers a picture of an attractive family circle, Julie remains always at the centre in her sadness, her isolation. Julie's visions are managed with much skill and carry complete conviction.

This is Cora Taylor's first book. It is a most impressive debut, and it gives strength to the impression that Canada—Ms Taylor's home and the scene of this story—is becoming an increasingly important part of the children's book world. The book deserves more sensitive handling than it receives from this publisher. The layout is crowded, and the story cries out for the collaboration of a good illustrator.

THE DOLL (1987)

Mary Ainslie Smith

SOURCE: "Ways of Escape," in *Books in Canada,* Vol. 16, No. 9, December, 1987, pp. 11-3.

Taylor's first children's story, *Julie,* was about a little girl with extrasensory abilities becoming aware of the mixed blessings that these gifts brought with them. Meg, the 10-year-old heroine of *The Doll,* is also extremely sensitive, especially to all the little signs that point to the disruption in the world of the adults around her.

Convalescing at her grandmother's home from a serious bout of rheumatic fever, Meg becomes aware of the problems between her parents and waits in suspense for the inevitable news of her family's break-up. Her grandmother lets her have an old china-head "invalid" doll that for several generations girls in the family had been allowed to play with only when they were sick. Meg feels that she is too old for dolls, but finds this one strangely appealing. When she falls asleep holding the doll, she wakes up in another time where she is no longer Meg but Morag, a 10-year-old also convalescing from fever, but travelling with her parents, brothers, and little sister by Red River wagon across the prairies.

Although the work is hard and the journey arduous, Meg enjoys her trips to the past, mainly because of the love and warmth of Morag's family and their feeling of striving toward a common goal. Still, she is glad to know that if she falls asleep as Morag holding the doll, she will wake up safely in the present, back in her room at her grandmother's. Thus the climax is desperate and exciting when the doll becomes lost in a prairie fire and Meg might be trapped forever in a dangerous past. . . .

[As a time travel book] *The Doll* . . . [does] a good job of re-creating the past . . . [it conveys] the challenge and isolation facing people alone in the wilderness. However, . . . [the] book . . . [has] even more value for [its] sensitive and realistic treatment of the problems and tensions facing modern families.

Elizabeth Montgomery

SOURCE: A review of *The Doll,* in *Canadian Children's Literature,* No. 52, 1988, pp. 76-7.

Through a lively and convincing treatment of time travel that calls to mind some of C. S. Lewis' Narnia books, *The Doll* explores how a ten-year-old comes to terms with illness, divorce, and mortality.

Meg Thompson has been ill with rheumatic fever and is convalescing in her grandmother's home on the Saskatchewan prairie. She has more than her sickness on her mind: she has guessed that her parents' marriage is collapsing and she is waiting for them to tell her. She is upset, anxious, and emotionally isolated.

Enter Jessie, also known as the Invalid Doll. Jessie has been in the family since they settled in Saskatchewan. Holding her is a ritual treat for young invalids.

But there's something weird about Jessie. Old Possum, Grandma Cameron's portly and placid cat, goes wild in

Jessie's presence. Grandma herself recalls that Jessie used to make her feel odd. Meg is fascinated by the doll, but finds her eyes cold and disturbing.

No wonder. Each time Meg falls asleep holding Jessie, she wakes up more than a hundred years earlier as Morag, the daughter of a family of her ancestors bound for a prairie homestead. As Morag she is part of a warm, supportive family, and she has exciting days with them that leave her so weary that she can scarcely lift her head in her "other" life. Grandma Cameron and her parents grow more and more worried about her failure to convalesce. This situation has its comic side, but the comedy is sharply edged: it points up the stress of a double life.

The time travel is made plausible by Meg's illness, which distorts her sense of what is real and what is dream. Behind this lurks the larger issue of how we identify our own reality: "What if Meg was only part of a dream? A dream Morag was dreaming. . . . The thought was too big to hold in her mind. She couldn't bear it."

It is not an unusual train of thought for a sensitive child; still less so for one made hypersensitive by illness and worry. This important theme of identity is focused in a single scene that turns on a beautifully integrated structural parallel. Meg is weary from her repeated journeys back and forth in time; she resents the mysterious hold Jessie has on her. Crossing a river on a raft, she almost drops the doll into the water. At once she panics: she realizes that she *needs* Jessie and the double life Jessie symbolizes. She articulates the pain of her impossible situation this way: "I can't keep moving back and forth, being two people all my life!"

How to live two lives authentically: this is the dilemma of the child of divorce, and indeed Meg soon makes it plain to her parents. Her dream-adventure has shown her how emotionally and physically exhausting such a life will be. Yet she is loved dearly by both her parents, just as she is loved by both families in her two lives. Choice is intolerable, for she loves them all in return.

Jessie, the enigmatic catalyst of the novel, brings her to this awareness and beyond it through the convention of the ordeal. Meg's experiences as Morag help her to confront and deal with the conflicts she suffers as Meg. The journey into the past is creative. Meg discovers that she *will* be able to live one life—her own. The journeys back in time cease. Jessie's mysterious powers subside. Old Possum relaxes. Meg grows well and strong.

The serenity is bought by a sacrifice, however, and like any quester after knowledge Meg is irrevocably changed by what she experiences. The supernatural mechanics of how Meg became Morag and got back to being Meg are wisely left to our imagination, throwing the profound implications of how the past lives on in us all into sharper relief.

What finally makes this novel so satisfying is its firm assertion of the love, security, and stability that warm Meg's life even as she faces a series of crises. There is nothing cloying about *The Doll*. Like the Narnia stories, it establishes that courageous living creates love. This is a worthy theme.

A. L. Florence

SOURCE: A review of *The Doll,* in *CM: A Reviewing Journal of Canadian Materials for Young People,* Vol. XVI, No. 2, March, 1988, p. 48.

Recovering from rheumatic fever at her grandmother's while her parents are preparing to separate and divorce, ten-year-old Meg becomes attached to a special doll, Jessie, which has been an heirloom in the Shearer family. Jessie becomes the open sesame for Meg to an ancient pioneer family travelling west from Ontario along the Carlton Trail. Meg transforms into Morag in her pioneer world and, holding the doll, moves back and forth across time, becoming increasingly involved in past adventures and exerting great efforts to "help out" in the pioneer struggle. Only when a prairie fire exhausts Morag and her death frees Meg to live entirely in modern times with her separating parents does Meg finally realize she can learn to cope with these problems, as well.

Cora Taylor creates two very credible worlds with two sets of problems; each world has its own strains and solutions. Young readers will identify with both worlds and will experience Meg's growth pangs as she resolves concrete problems and learns to cope with the more difficult ones of attitude and understanding.

The publisher should give serious reconsideration to the cover. It really doesn't do justice to the content, and won't encourage casual readers.

Sarah Ellis

SOURCE: A review of *The Doll,* in *Horn Book Magazine,* Vol. LXIV, No. 3, May-June, 1988, p. 391.

In Cora Taylor's *The Doll* ten-year-old Meg travels back four generations to join a homesteading family as they journey across from Ontario to the prairies to start a new life. For her the experience of the past lies not in the cold weight of greave and helmet but in thick, itchy woolen stockings; in the jolting ride of a Red River cart; and in the taste of porridge and molasses.

In the present Meg is staying with her grandmother while recuperating from rheumatic fever. To comfort her the grandmother lets Meg play with the "Invalid Doll," a family heirloom that has accompanied several generations of children through various illnesses. When she falls asleep with the doll, Meg is transported to the past where she becomes Morag, a similarly rheumatic child journeying with her family—her own ancestors as she later discovers. Meg/Morag travels back and forth through time gaining perspective on her present misery. In the past she tames a cow, saves a child from a badger, and does real work. In the present she feels, in her own phrase, like a piece of furniture; in the past she is an autonomous contributing member of a pioneer society. She even has an opportunity for true heroism as she rescues her toddler sister from a prairie fire.

As in her first novel, *Julie,* Cora Taylor enters fully into the fresh perception and raw feelings of a child. In plain concrete language she expresses Meg's claustrophobia in a troubled family situation where adults dissemble, the urgency with which the girl needs to escape, and the grief she feels for a family who lived and died generations before her. And the dual drama is enacted against the backdrop of the prairie, described in Taylor's unsurpassed landscape descriptions where Meg sees, "a bluebird flash along the road like a piece of stolen sky." Family and the land connect Meg to the past and give her comfort in the present.

Karen Day

SOURCE: "Connections in Prairie Fiction: Paradigms of Female Adolescent Development," in *Canadian Children's Literature,* No. 67, 1992, pp. 35-47.

The Doll combines three genres. It is a problem novel in that it is the story of Meg's coming to grips with her parents' still unannounced separation. It is also a time-travel fantasy. By holding Jessie, a family doll, when she goes to sleep, Meg is able to travel from the present to the past and to move into the time of her great-great-grandmother. The third genre is historical fiction. The reader travels with Meg into the past and witnesses the settling of Western Canada by pioneer families, specifically the Shearer family who made their way across the prairies to a homestead near Fort Carlton, Saskatchewan, in the 1880s. The author enables the emergence of both the protagonist's sense of identity and her sense of home by substituting a more ordered past in which family members are supportive and the land provides spiritual nourishment for her present problem world.

Meg is a ten-year-old whose relationships with the people closest to her are jeopardized in three significant ways: by her parent's impending divorce, her illness, and her relocation. Janet and Mark, Meg's mother and father, are unable to talk with their daughter about their separation, thus "By protecting Meg they were isolating her." But Meg knows by her mother's tired and sad face that her parents would have more time to argue when she goes to stay with her grandmother. She also perceives that there are problems when her father hugs her a little too long. Janet and Mark both work, so when the sickly Meg does not get well, it is necessary for her to stay with Grandma Grace. Although Meg likes Grandma Grace and the old Cameron home in the country, it is not her own home, filled with the school relationships and connections that were important to her.

Taylor uses Meg's rheumatic fever as an external symptom of the distress that Meg feels inside. Of course, the illness separates her from friends at school. As a result of the separation caused by her illness and the separation caused by her parents' excluding her from their marital problems, Meg requires sleep and escape and comes to appreciate the nurturing care of her grandmother. How Meg ultimately gathers strength to face her problems is the focus of *The Doll.*

In a society in which mothers have careers that leave little time for nurturing their children, this lucky protagonist has a grandmother who can provide not only "hot nourishing broth" but the wisdom to give Meg time to herself. Most importantly, Grandma Grace gives her Jessie, the invalid doll that has had the power to restore the health to generations of sick Shearer girls.

The doll is presented by Taylor as Meg's connection to the past. Its power lies in the fact that it represents family, security and tradition. When she goes to sleep with the doll in her arms, Meg is transported to the time of her great-great-grandmother where she becomes Morag. As Morag, she is a member of what is known today as a traditional family. The Shearers, who are struggling together to establish a homestead in the Carlton District of present-day Saskatchewan, depend upon the co-operation of every member. Morag's relationships are clear and firm. She knows immediately that she belongs to the family by the clothes she is wearing; the fabric is the same as her mother's and the same as Papa's shirt, and even matches Jessie's clothes. Morag builds strong, supportive relationships by taking responsibility for the care of her younger sister, Lizzie. Learning to care for others is important in Meg's development. Her role in the Shearer family is clear and helps to establish her place within the family. She has no such opportunity in the present, as she is an only child.

Meg learns that Morag was good with animals, as well as all generations of Shearer women had been. She gains the respect of family members and a knowledge of her own strengths when she successfully herds the troublesome Evangeline with her newborn calf. Geordie's respect for Morag's ability to handle the difficult cow convinces him to give her the honour of naming the heifer, further strengthening her sense of belonging. It includes her as another member of this family who has kept the tradition of naming cows.

Learning to deal with sibling rivalry is part of her family experience. Initially, Morag calls Geordie a "jerk" for his teasing, not understanding that it is often evidence of his caring. She grows to love and appreciate being called "Midget." Taylor follows Morag's development from being annoyed with Geordie's teasing to being able to tease Geordie in return. Her ability to stand up to Geordie and declare herself "just the right size" foreshadows her ability to stand up to her twentieth-century parents.

Meg does not gain a sense of identity quickly. In the present her legs are still wobbly, indicating that her inner self is still unsure. She depends heavily upon Jessie, the doll, for escape, and she continues to depend on the bed as a way to hide from her problems.

In the present, Meg receives a letter from a school friend, Allison, from whom she has been separated because of Allison's parents' divorce. A summer visit to her father allows Allison to visit Meg. But re-establishing the connection between friends is not easy for either Meg or Allison:

> 'Allison!' There was no doubt that Meg was surprised . . . and delighted. But then she didn't know what to say. She climbed onto the bed and sat crosslegged facing her friend.
>
> There was an awkward silence for a moment as they sat smiling at each other, waiting to see who'd speak first. Meg was afraid she's say something stupid. She did.

By saying "something stupid", the girls are able to mend severed connections with shared giggles. Meg learns that Allison is not unhappy about her recent move away from her father because it keeps her from being passed constantly back and forth between her parents. For her own future benefit, Meg heeds Allison's lesson of objecting to being passed back and forth between parents.

Meg's two worlds begin to merge as she begins to think that the present is a dream and that the past is real. She is confused and hopes that the present is happening to someone else. The confusion leads her to ask questions about the past in order to gain a perspective for coping with the present. She feels a need to establish a connection between her two worlds. She establishes connections for herself by asking her Grandmother about family tradition for naming cows and discovers that many of the names have been used over and over, one being Evangeline. After seeing her reflection in the water, Meg asks her Grandmother who in the family she looks like. When the two look through the family album, they find a picture of the Shearer family where Meg recognizes each member. She discovers that she is most like Morag which helps her make the connection between her nineteenth- and twentieth-century families.

Taylor then builds up the tension between living in the past and living in the present by putting her protagonist in a crisis. Meg can't find the doll and so can't return to the past, a past in which she wishes to find permanent escape. Her feelings of isolation and loneliness increase as she searches in vain for the lost doll. Finally, it is the sensitive cat, Poss, who helps her find it and retreat to what has previously been the safe past. But problems brew there as well. There is a dangerous river crossing and even more dangerous prairie fires. When Jessie is thrown from the wagon and Lizzie jumps out to retrieve the doll, Morag takes the responsibility of retrieving the child and doll which causes them to be caught in a prairie fire. They do their best to survive in a ditch which contains very little water. The girls survive, but the experience weakens the already fragile Morag and she dies just as the family reaches Fort Carlton. The death of Morag forces Meg to live in the present. Her grandmother alerts

the girl's mother and father of Meg's weakened condition when she finds her granddaughter in a coma. The author uses Morag's death to force Meg to realize that she cannot continue to be both Morag and Meg. Meg finds this an exhausting experience, but as she recovers, she is ready to "stand on her own two feet" and get out of bed.

Fortified by the support of her pioneer family, the relationships she has built and the connections she has established, Meg is able to face her twentieth-century problems. She is able to talk with her parents and tell them what she feels is best for her. At first, "Meg hardly recognized her own voice." She screams, fearing that she will not be heard. Then, gaining control, she recognizes that using her voice helps her parents who are having equal difficulty finding their voices. She demands that she be accepted as a person. And then Meg comes to a new awareness of her parents:

> They don't know what to do any more than I do, Meg thought, amazed. Maybe even less than I do. They had to make the decision; I just have to do the best I can, like with the cow, or the badger. She was surprised at how calm she felt.

Her new strength leads Meg to realize that it is herself whom she must know before she is able to help others. Through this strength, and as a result of her established relationships, Meg is able to know her own voice and know that she belongs to a family in a meaningful way. Perhaps her family is not as perfect as she would like, but she knows she will find her place within it. Finding her voice, thus, represents forming the needed relationships and an awareness of her identity.

JULIE'S SECRET (1991)

Phyllis Simon

SOURCE: A review of *Julie's Secret*, in *Quill and Quire*, Vol. 57, No. 4, April, 1991, pp. 18-9.

Julie's Secret, Cora Taylor's sequel to her award-winning *Julie,* continues the story of the Morgan family, who live in a small prairie community. This book should once again bring Taylor critical acclaim for her fine writing.

Julie, the youngest of seven children in a loving family, keeps apart from the general gregariousness and good family feeling because she alone is "special"—she is able to sense events that will occur or tragedies that have happened in the past. This ESP helps her locate a barn buried in a blizzard and allows her and her sister to find shelter in a sudden storm. Later, her heightened senses help locate her brother's kidnappers, who are involved in Satanism.

Taylor's very controlled writing style makes for fine reading—the story moves along with tension building as events unfold. Taylor also has a fine descriptive talent. Depictions of prairie weather are especially powerful. The sudden

Easter blizzard that sends Julie and her oldest sister desperately searching for shelter is so vividly described that its unremitting strength even awed this ex-Montrealer, no stranger to winter snowstorms.

If there is any weakness in the story, it is Taylor's use of coincidence to advance the plot. Relying on this device makes some of the events feel contrived. The sensationalism of the Satanic kidnappers' plot as well as some stock characterization detract slightly from the excellence of the story, but there is no doubt *Julie's Secret* will enjoy a strong following among readers between the ages of 11 and 14 (and will impress many adults too!).

Constance Hall

SOURCE: A review of *Julie's Secret,* in *CM: A Reviewing Journal of Canadian Materials for Young People,* Vol. XIX, No. 4, September, 1991, p. 240.

Set in rural Alberta, *Julie's Secret* is an exciting sequel to Cora Taylor's first book entitled *Julie,* about a girl who experiences ESP. Julie is the youngest child in a family of seven. In fact, according to the town historian, Gil Gordon, she is the seventh child of a seventh child, which may explain her ability to sense things. Although she does not understand her ability very well, Julie believes no one else really knows either, so she tries to act as "normal" as her closest brother, Billy. Circumstances, however, make it necessary for her to use her ESP in a dramatic rescue.

While seeking shelter from an unexpected spring blizzard with her older sister Mary in the barn on the abandoned Tyler farm, Julie senses some horrible things have taken place there. After her father Will and her older brother, Charlie, rescue them from the barn, the family asks the RCMP to investigate evidence of a fire, an upside down cross and the remains of a dead calf. Julie unintentionally arouses the suspicion of the police by having her father tell them where to dig up the floor in the old barn. An unearthed body turns out to be a young teenager from Vancouver. But Julie senses more mysterious happenings connected with the old barn and an old double murder is uncovered, as well.

In the climax of the story Julie must use her ability to help find Billy, who is kidnapped after he accepts a ride from a stranger. Her father asks her to try to sense where he has been taken, and she can see many symbols carved into a wooden door (this image is used for the cover of the book). An exciting chase begins as the police, Julie's mother Alice, driving the family car, and Will, in a small airplane, converge on an abandoned cook shack in which Billy is held prisoner. In the last chapter, Julie begins to realize that several people know about her ability to sense things and she wonders if that means it is no longer a secret. It is still a mystery to me who Billy's kidnappers are or whether or not they were brought to justice, but perhaps that will be explained in the next book.

After reading this book, I was intrigued to learn more about Julie's "pet tree" and to find out how she was able to rescue her father after his tractor accident. Since the first book covers Julie's early childhood, it helps to have read it before reading *Julie's Secret,* which takes place in the months between Christmas and early summer when she is eleven years old. I would make sure I had both books in my library, because if you read one, you'll want to read the other, too.

Sarah Ellis

SOURCE: A review of *Julie's Secret,* in *Canadian Children's Literature,* No. 66, 1992, pp. 91-2.

One of the things that sets me apart from child readers is that I don't usually like sequels. Whereas the kids I know want sequels to every book they've read and liked, I have been too often disappointed by book number two. *Julie's Secret* is certainly one of the exceptions. It is quite different from Taylor's 1985 award-winning novel *Julie,* but just as satisfying.

We learned in the first book of young Julie's unusual and, to her, disturbing psychic abilities. That book ended with a dramatic scene in which Julie rescues her father from a near-fatal accident. As *Julie's Secret* opens, the now ten-year old girl has fallen into a kind of numbness following this event. She is wrenched from this protective state when a spring blizzard maroons her and her sister in a neighbour's barn and Julie senses evil all around them. So begins a plot involving murder, torture, and child abduction. This sounds like powerful material, and it is. In the hands of a writer less grounded and in control than Cora Taylor it could be melodramatic. But she takes the stuff of horror fiction and makes it as real and tangible as prairie gumbo.

The supernatural is given high relief against Taylor's fresh and convincing descriptions of ordinary life. Like Susan Cooper, in *The Dark Is Rising,* she creates a large and ebullient family in which one member, the seventh child of a seventh child, participates fully in family events while bearing the heavy responsibility of his or her particular gift. One of the most winning scenes in *Julie's Secret,* a scene steeped in the details of prairie life, involves the children going "horse skiing."

Julie's Secret is much more plot-driven than *Julie.* We are concerned not so much with Julie's internal struggles as with the unravelling of the stories that lie behind her unease. And Taylor handles the technical challenges of a suspense story admirably, flicking from scene to scene, seeding the plot with hints of revelations to come. She does a lot with a few words: "It was Death and it was at the north side of the barn."

In the course of the plot various people are forced to more or less openly acknowledge Julie's gift. How this new openness will affect the girl is left up in the air. Book number three would be a good way of answering this question. I'm with the kids: let's have another.

GHOST VOYAGES (1992)

Margaret Mackey

SOURCE: A review of *Ghost Voyages,* in *CM: A Reviewing Journal of Canadian Materials for Young People,* Vol. XX, No. 3, May, 1992, p. 153.

When Jeremy's great-grandmother moves, her belongings come to his house. The boxes include a set of albums, one of them devoted to a collection of stamps portraying historic ships. His grandfather collected them as a boy, and when Jeremy looks at one of the stamps through grandad's magnifying glass, he suddenly finds himself on board the ship, an old river boat on the North Saskatchewan River.

Jeremy's adventures on this old boat are resolved satisfactorily and he tries again with another stamp. He finds himself on board a sailing ship travelling into Hudson Bay in 1668.

Normal daily life also continues and Jeremy researches the facts about the ships he "visits" through his magnifying glass. When the magic disappears on his tenth birthday, he has grown as a result of his adventures.

The vivid details of life on the old ships contrasted with Jeremy's ordinary contemporary life are the best part of this book. Limiting the time travel to just two ships is less satisfactory and feels artificially constrained. A single adventure would be satisfying; a group of adventures would add scope and depth; two feels awkward. As a way of bringing Canadian history to life, however, it has considerable merit.

Gisela Sherman

SOURCE: A review of *Ghost Voyages,* in *Canadian Children's Literature,* Vol. 20:4, No. 76, Winter, 1994, pp. 66-9.

Ghost Voyages is a good ghost story with a twist. The main character, Jeremy, becomes a ghost whenever he uses his grandfather's magnifying glass to inspect his stamps of Canadian historical ships. Cora Taylor drops Jeremy into the action and gunfire of exciting historical events, and describes details to interest modern young readers. The historical scenes are vivid, fast-paced, interesting. The story propping them up is weaker. Jeremy suffers through the drip of all mothers and her family complications. We don't learn that he's nine until page 94, even though his age is crucial to the ending, which comes too suddenly. Some foreshadowing of the magic cut-off age would have added suspense and fair warning. My main worry is that the topic, and the 135 pages of small print, make this a book suitable for older readers. If Jeremy were eleven, the right audience would discover this interesting adventure.

SUMMER OF THE MAD MONK (1994)

Patty Lawlor

SOURCE: A review of *Summer of the Mad Monk,* in *Quill and Quire,* Vol. 61, No. 1, January, 1995, pp. 41-2.

Wide open spaces and wide open skies can breed wide open imaginings. In this latest book from Cora Taylor, they do exactly that. The summer is 1932. The Mad Monk is Russia's Rasputin. The imaginings are 12-year-old Pip Tyler's.

Pip is a bright boy, the eldest of three children in a family contending with more than its fair share of disaster and despair during the Depression. Due more to circumstances than to his nature, Pip is a loner and a dreamer. He spends a great deal of time reading books supplied by a friend of his father's.

Spurred on by his reading, Pip learns something about life and people in faraway places. He imagines wonderful changes in his family's fortunes. He wishes for larger-scale adventure than small-town life in southern Alberta normally provides. It's no surprise, then, that, when a Russian blacksmith arrives in town, Pip is primed for romantic interpretation. For various reasons, Pip decides that Raspinsky is actually Rasputin. When he discovers Russian thugs are pursuing a mysterious man Raspinsky is hiding, Pip is even more convinced that royalty is involved. There is no doubt in his mind that he has an important role to play in righting historical wrongs.

Summer of the Mad Monk is a solidly crafted story that breaks new ground for Cora Taylor. Her use of a male voice and emphasis on imagination are successful departures from the female protagonists and supernatural themes that characterized *Julie, Julie's Secret,* and *The Doll.*

Taylor's previous books have featured well-developed characters, evocative atmospheres, distinctive turns of phrase, and effective meshing of the everyday and the extraordinary. It's good news that these elements are all present in *Summer of the Mad Monk.* Ten- to 14-year-old readers will find it easy to relate to Pip and his peers. At the start of the story, they'll taste and feel the grit of a violent prairie dust storm. By story's end, they'll be satisfied that the conclusion is a good fit for what has gone before. We couldn't ask Cora Taylor for much more.

VANISHING ACT (1997)

Elsie Jacobs

SOURCE: A review of *Vanishing Act,* in *Kliatt,* Vol. 32, No. 3, May, 1998, p. 24.

Fantastic! Finally a mystery for YAs which refrains from the usual trite plot and characterizations. 13-year-old twin sisters Maggie and Jennifer unwillingly get pulled into a tale of intrigue, suspicion, and discovery. Jennifer, the adventurous twin, discovers a spell for making herself invisible and uses it gleefully. The only problem is: she doesn't know how to get back! And then she starts disappearing without even trying. But she has some innocent fun with the school snob while she learns how to control the disappearances. Maggie, the dutiful twin, feels obligated to cover Jennifer's disappearances. The natural tension between the sisters is very well done. Add to this mix a trip to Greece with their grandmother, a mysterious ticket to a Greek sightseeing tour, CIA and Libyan agents, a liberal dose of danger, and you've got a great read for J students, or for S readers with low reading abilities and high interest.

This book would make a great addition to a library or classroom reading section. Readers could pinpoint the location of the Greek trip, study the wealth of information about Greek myths, which is used well, and study the Arab countries where the twins' father is being held captive. The spell portion of the book is handled thoughtfully. At first it seems fun, but Jennifer quickly learns she needs to use this sparingly and only for the most necessary of circumstances. Disappearing is not as much fun as she thought it would be.

Janet Gillen

SOURCE: A review of *Vanishing Act,* in *School Library Journal,* Vol. 44, No. 7, July, 1998, p. 100.

When Jennifer, 13, stumbles upon a magic spell that renders her invisible, she enlists the help of her twin sister, Maggie, and best friend, Samuel, in a quest to solve the mystery surrounding their father's disappearance. The young detectives join the girls' grandmother on a cruise to Greece where the girls hope to find their father, a pilot who vanished two years earlier, and whom they believe is being held captive. This riveting mystery is a definite page-turner, complete with engaging, interesting three-dimensional characters and some life-threatening moments created by very real villains. Maggie's methodical and cautious approach to situations is cleverly juxtaposed with Jennifer's carefree, adventurous behavior. Samuel is a conscientious, thoughtful friend whose own lack of familial unity makes his relationship with the two girls a very special one. Chapters blend nicely with one another, never faltering or losing momentum. Jennifer's invisibility acts as a catalyst, propelling the plot along. Dangling subplots may leave readers searching for a connection linking them to the ultimate story line, but young people will overlook these shortcomings, finding delight in the characters and the high suspense.

Margaret Springer

SOURCE: A review of *Vanishing Act,* in *Canadian Children's Literature,* Vol. 25:1, No. 93, Spring, 1999, pp. 88-9.

Cora Taylor's **Vanishing Act** aims at an older audience, and is, therefore, much longer and more densely plotted. Set in smaller print and divided into two parts with a total of forty-four chapters, it will appeal to young teens and fluent readers. The plot follows twin sisters Jennifer and Maggie and their friend Sam on a mystery which eventually takes them from Canada (Part One) to a Greek cruise (Part Two). The style is fluent and often leisurely, with plenty of background material woven in. Dialogue is believable, and the interactions between the young characters ring true.

The mystery elements in Part One—wondering about the father, and looking for the mother's lost watch, which has sentimental value—do not have the heart-thumping importance of the conflicts later in the book. The focus here is on discovering and perfecting Jennifer's ability to disappear and reappear at will, and achieving the kids' goal of going on a Greek cruise with "Grand," the mother of their missing father (another variation on the "vanishing" theme). The way in which the boy, Sam, is able to join the girls on their cruise—a convenient invitation to England, another to Italy, inherited money, etc.—seems contrived and awkward, but for the most part Taylor handles the intricacies of a complicated plot well. Part Two has a much faster pace, with the constant drama of mysterious strangers and hints of spies, plots, kidnapping, counterintelligence, and a beloved father in danger. Taylor writes deftly, letting these courageous kids stay in control: the twins switch for each other when needed; Jennifer disappears and reappears at will; Grand is always on the scene, helpful and understanding. Along the way, readers experience daily life on a cruise ship; though, as with real travellers, they may sometimes feel overloaded by information about those ancient sites and places visited. Each chapter in **Vanishing Act** is told from a different viewpoint. This allows the reader to enter into the head of all three main characters in turn, and to revisit some scenes. Mostly this works well, though sometimes it can be confusing. The situation with regard to the missing father is also sometimes hard to keep track of, with a plethora of murky characters whose relationships and motives are unclear. But there is no doubt of the tension and drama as the young trio escape kidnapping and worse, and Taylor does well at keeping the story unpredictable.

Additional coverage of Taylor's life and career is contained in the following sources published by The Gale Group: *Contemporary Authors,* Vol. 124; and *Something about the Author,* Vols. 64, 103.

William Taylor
1938-

New Zealand author of fiction books.

Major works include *Possum Perkins* (1986, U.S. edition published as *Paradise Lane*, 1987), *Agnes the Sheep* (1991), *Knitwits* (1992), *Numbskulls* (1995), *Jerome* (1998).

INTRODUCTION

William Taylor is known for his novels for middle graders and young adults, both comic and serious. His books, which are set in contemporary New Zealand, deal with family situations and peer friendships in realistic ways. That realism has been praised by critics, who note Taylor's sensitive treatment of the difficulties facing modern young people. His characters are fully-fleshed, with believable strengths and flaws. Nancy P. Reeder wrote of the main character in Taylor's *Possum Perkins*: "Rosie is a particularly complex and well drawn character, filled with uncertainty, anger, frustration, and hurt"; Bill Nagelkerke found the teens in *Jerome* similarly genuine: "Marco and Kate berate, plead, conceal and reveal. Their voices are utterly convincing." Critics have also praised Taylor's facility with dialogue: Tom Fitzgibbon wrote in *Twentieth Century Children's Writers*, "Taylor's novels skim along, the narrative carried by the speed and vigour of the dialogue which is idiomatic and individualised." While Taylor deals honestly with such issues as teen suicide, abusive parents, and homosexuality, he simultaneously conveys the warmth and support some families provide. His works are also leavened with humor; especially in novels for the middle grades, Taylor's works are filled with high jinks and comic adventure. He writes about the world as today's young people experience it, encompassing both joy and sorrow, comedy and drama.

Biographical Information

Raised in rural communities in New Zealand, Taylor was born in 1938 in Lower Hutt, Wellington, to parents with diverse interests and a love of literature. The author attended Christchurch Teachers' College and served as a teacher and principal in elementary schools for twenty-five years. He retired in 1985 to write full time. Taylor was also the mayor of the Borough of Ohakune from 1981 to 1988.

Major Works

Taylor's first book to receive recognition in the United States was *Paradise Lane*, published in New Zealand as *Possum Perkins*. Noted for its sensitive and complex

portrayal of teenagers, the book concerns Rosie Perkins and her unexpected friendship with Michael Geraghty, a member of the only other family on Paradise Lane. Rosie is a smart but isolated girl; she is harassed by classmates (including and most especially Michael) and struggles to deal with an alcoholic mother and a too-attentive—even obsessive—father. One day Rosie finds a baby possum next to its dead mother and decides to raise the helpless creature, naming it Plum. Michael teases her relentlessly about the project, even encouraging classmates to pelt the girl with dead possums. But as he realizes how hurt by this Rosie is, he begins to sympathize with her and even admire the care she takes with the animal. Slowly the teens begin a friendship, Michael and his family providing Rosie with warmth and a feeling of security, and Rosie encouraging Michael in his intellectual stirrings. The budding romance is strengthened when little Plum dies and Michael comforts Rosie. Because of the growth she's achieved through raising the possum and her friendship with Michael, Rosie is finally able to confront her own family and seek change. Another book about teens and the problems they face is *Jerome*, about the complicated friendship of Marco, Kate, and Jerome. The novel is told through mostly through e-mails, faxes, and phone calls between Marco and Kate after Jerome's suicide, which the two work together to decipher. Marco at first cannot believe that Jerome has killed himself; he has further trouble accepting that Kate is gay, and that Jerome was as well. Marco eventually comes to understand his friend's revelations, and himself in the process. Nagelkerke commented that in this novel Taylor "captured with integrity the intense sorrows and joys of being different, and accepting one's identity, in a world that values sameness and stereotypes."

Taylor has also written a number of books for middle-graders that are lighter-hearted, though not saccharin. *Agnes the Sheep* depicts the adventures of Belinda, Joe, and the very contrary sheep of the title. Proper Belinda and rough Joe are classmates sharing an assignment to interview an elderly person about the old days of their town. Their subject is Mrs. Carpenter, a bad-tempered and not altogether innocent old woman who tells the pair wild stories about her younger days, including her stint as a nude model for an artist. Upon Mrs. Carpenter's death, the two inherit Agnes, a mean-spirited aging sheep. Several adventures follow, focusing on keeping Agnes from becoming either dog food or a rug; the comic high point of the novel is a mad chase through a grocery store. The characters in *Knitwits* and *Numbskulls* have their share of fun, as well. In *Knitwits*, Chas Kenny experiences the worst day of his young life: his cat dies, he gets kicked off the hockey team, and his mother announces that she is pregnant. He hides his displeasure at being a brother, though, and even tells his troublemaking neighbor Alice Pepper that he is so pleased about the baby, he will knit a sweater before the birth. Alice bets him to do just that; if he loses, he will have to pay her $5 every week for the rest of his life, and if he wins, he will acquire her impressive skull collection. Chas then takes secret knitting lessons and surreptitiously works on his project. He is humorously discovered by some male friends, who surprisingly reveal that they, too, enjoy knitting. The story also portrays Chas's loving, laid-back family as they prepare for the arrival of his new sibling. *Numbskulls* is a continuation of the Kennys' story, with a baby sister contributing to the plot. Alice Pepper is again making mischief, this time extorting allowance money from Chas and his friends Spikey and Jacko. In return, the bullying Alice attempts to teach Chas how to spell, Spikey the secrets of love, and Jacko how to make lots of cash; her educational plan involves strapping the boys to a dentist's chair and slapping them with a hose as she verbally abuses them. Whether in response to this dubious method or some other cause, Chas does learn to spell. In this book, as well, Chas's family provides warm counterpoint to the crazy antics of Alice Pepper: Chas also learns about caring for his baby sister by reading the child-care manual *Before Babe's First Steps*.

Awards

In 1984 Taylor received the Choysa Bursary for Children's Writers; he was also awarded the Inaugural Children's Writing Fellowship of Palmerston North College of Education, New Zealand, in 1992. Taylor won the Esther Glen Medal of the New Zealand Library Association in 1991 for *Agnes the Sheep*; that book and *Knitwits* were cited by the New York Public Library and the American Library Association.

AUTHOR'S COMMENTARY

Tessa Duder with William Taylor

SOURCE: In an interview, in *Magpies*, Vol. 14, No. 2, May, 1999, pp. 1-4.

I remember, when the Oxford History of New Zealand Literature was published in 1991, you were surprised and gratified to find your six adult novels from the 1970s being taken seriously. Is it true that you wrote those as a deliberate apprenticeship to your writing for children?

No. It was never in my mind that those novels were anything other than middle-of-the-road adult fiction; neither very good nor very bad! Only in retrospect, do I see that stage of my writing career as an 'apprenticeship' for what came later. Incidentally, I have never entirely ruled out writing for adults again, in whatever may be my writing future.

Children's literature is the only genre not actually written by one of the audience for whom it is intended. You are yourself the far side (just) of sixty. Does this matter? What are the secrets to producing work that is fresh and interesting to today's young people?

I am fortunate that my friendships, relationships and associations encompass all age groups from eight to eighty! I am frequently surrounded by the young, particularly when I am touring schools, libraries, etc. I make the most of such opportunities. I know I am now old but, most certainly, there is still a 'youthful' core to me. I look out of the same eyes these days as I did when I was sixteen, thirty, forty, etc.

You categorise your books as 'comic' or 'serious'. Was it with one of the adult novels that you realised you had a gift for comic writing, or was it those first comic books for children, **The Worst Soccer Team Ever** *series published in an astonishing burst in 1987?*

I think I have always been able to write humorous stuff. My serious books, all of them, have streaks of humour. Similarly, my funny books often have serious undertones. I realise that I do write two broad sorts of fiction but often, to me, the lines are blurred. I think the saddest novel I have ever written is my soon-to-be-published ***Jerome***. For all that, there are, I think, some hilariously funny bits in it. I have written a few scenes that are funnier than Marco in ***Jerome*** trying to persuade Katie that she can't possibly be lesbian because she looks like a Barbie doll! *The Worst Soccer Team Ever* wasn't originally intended to be comic; it just happened that way.

1985 was the year of your first award, the Choysa Bursary, and also the year (yes?) you left teaching for full-time writing. Was it this award which opened the creative floodgates? Or was it equally the risk of joining the self-employed in a country with a miniscule buying public?

It was the realisation that given time, and no other work obligations, I was able to write a helluva lot. I took a nine-month leave of absence from teaching when I won the Choysa Bursary and in that time I wrote *Possum Perkins, My Summer of the Lions* and *Shooting Through.* All were quickly accepted for publishing. I had every reason to believe that I could be equally productive in the years to come. I knew I would never make a fortune, but I had enough sense to know that providing I had the mortgage paid off, I could probably make a reasonable living from writing. I appear to have achieved this. Don't get me wrong; nothing is ever quite so clear-cut—I was shit-scared I would fall flat on my face!

Your 1976 **Burnt Carrots Don't Have Legs** *is a short, sharp and very funny 'take' on a teachers' experiences. I think it's your only nonfiction book so far. Apart from classroom teacher and principal, you've been a solo parent, banker, long-serving mayor, restaurant owner and actor. Your writing life has taken you all over New Zealand, to Australia and Iowa. Have you ever thought that there's a book of memoirs just waiting to be written?*

I have only ever thought so when others have mentioned this to me as a reasonable idea. I don't really believe that my life has been interesting enough to write about—much less grab the attention of an audience. When I get old and pompous (like next year!) maybe I'll think about it. I have often been a little derisive of people who write about themselves in an autobiographic sense. I do, of course, write about myself in every book I write. As I say to kids, there's got to be a bit of me in everything I write, in every character I write about.

In 1994, after about ten months of increasing ill health, you had triple-bypass heart surgery. Yet, after what seemed to your friends to be far too short a time convalescing, the books have continued to appear and your visits to schools and festivals maintained. What effect has that 1994 experience had on you?

The actual experience had a devastating effect on me—mentally, rather than physically. I got better very quickly. I made sure I could walk up and down the hills that surround my home—within ten days of getting out of hospital. To some extent I have simply tried to ignore what happened and have just got on with life and living, work and working. My output didn't falter very much. I have held two residencies and written about ten books since the drear event. Friends and family certainly helped me through a bad patch.

Until recently, your books were drafted on large A4 pads with black ballpoints, and then laboriously typed out. How do you work now that you've got a computer? What difference, if any, has it made to your writing?

To the massive, major astonishment of friends and family, I took to my computer like a duck to water. I am no better or worse as a writer, I write neither more nor less than I wrote previously. I got a computer for reasons such as wanting access to the Internet and email (I am devoted to email) and because all of my publishers were beginning to sound very plaintive asking when they could expect to receive my work on disk. I took pity on them, dear souls that they are. My older son, Robin, said he was not only going to be out of the house but out of the country when I bought my computer. However, as a dutiful son, he helped me set everything up—then he ran away and left me to it. I consider it has made no difference to my writing other than I am now obliged to work where the computer resides in my home. I suppose I could get a laptop . . .

Do you consider yourself a disciplined writer? How much time and energy goes into planning? Is this planning on paper or in your head? How long does the actual writing take?

Yes, I am very disciplined. You have to be if you write a lot. Enormous amounts of time go into planning; 99% of which is in my head. I have always held the belief that if I forget anything it wasn't worth remembering. I recently heard of a writer for kids who carries a notebook around in order to note down 'interesting things that children say'. The day I have to do that is the day I give up. What nonsense! Most of my novels take four to six weeks to write the first draft and a similar amount of time to polish up, craft, self-edit and so forth. It is, quite simply, work. I am not, I am so sorry to say, a 'tortured' or 'tormented' artist, I do not suffer from 'writer's block' (whatever that means; I think it's a euphemism for laziness). I never anguish—but I certainly spend a lot of time thinking things through.

How much, thinking of the Graham Capills and others of the moral right peering over your shoulder, do you self-edit?

I pray, with absolute sincerity, that everything I write will offend the moral right—and then I will know I'm okay and got things on the right track and kids will enjoy my work for them! While this answer is tongue-in-cheek, there is an element of truth in it!

What about the 'bad words?' Do you regret or applaud the increasing usage of bad words in young adult literature?

I neither regret nor applaud the increasing use of 'bad words'. I often think that the more we use most of these words the less currency they will have, the less power they will to 'offend'. I MUST be true to my characters. Apropos *Jerome* again, in order to be true to my two central characters I was absolutely obliged to use the words they would use. If I offend their 'elders and betters' well, so be it! Most young adults of my acquaintance, male and female, have the ability and inclination to use foul and profane language. Most particularly (but not exclusively) this is true of young men. Very recently I played 'parent' for a year to a seventeen-year-old Swiss exchange student. The house seemed forever full of noise and young people, the young of our country and of many other countries—it was amazing just how universal and frequent is the use of 'very bad' words!

Jerome, due for publication in the US in August, and by Longacre in New Zealand, has the potential for stirring up a controversy similar to that of **Dear Miffy** *in Australia. Its themes include teenage suicide and homosexuality, and the language is undoubtedly more robust than any I've read in a NZ young adult book. What prompted you to write what is possible your darkest book yet?*

I hope this work does receive attention, and if it does so by stirring up some controversy, that's okay. I hope that it does lead young people to think on those aspects I'm writing about—sexual identity, youth suicide, friendship etc. I hope it also earns an adult readership. I remember a review of my earlier work *The Blue Lawn* where the reviewer was of the opinion that the book should be required reading for parents! The same applies with *Jerome.* The level of youth suicide in this country is an indictment of our society—as simple as that. We must address the issues that give rise to such a tragedy. We must think about it, and, more than that, do something about it. As for the homosexual elements in the story, I really do think that regardless of gains we have made (e.g. the Hero Parade, the 'Queer Nation' programme on TV etc.) we are still a largely homophobic society and the acceptance of 'difference' in our culture is shallowly rooted. A tiny minority of those kids who realise they are gay are growing up happily, openly and with support from their nearest and dearest. For most, life is one helluva battle. Self-acceptance, acknowledgment and so forth are well and truly tinged with feelings of apprehension, confusion and, sadly, elements of self-loathing and, even more sadly, fear.

And down the track, there's a work-in-progress about extreme child abuse in a farming setting that some will find as convincing and upsetting as **The Bone People.** *Do you think your writing is getting bleaker darker?*

No, I don't. It is quite by chance that I have written three of my more bleak novels in a row. I haven't forgotten about funny books and, I hope, there will be a few more of them in the offing.

Do you agree with John Marsden's thesis that in books— if not in the electronic media—today's teens are being short-changed, and that few authors for young adults are writing with honesty and understanding?

Yes I do agree. I often have the feeling that within our own society that much of what gets published has been written with the thought of what our pundits of children's lit will think of it than what the actual intended audience will. If you couple this with our national obsession with political correctness . . . well, of course teens will be short-changed! Most particularly boys! Even with my publishing record it would be very hard (if not downright impossible) for me to get a book published that centred on a couple of sixteen-year-old heterosexual guys who drank large quantities of beer, smoked, used profane language, enjoyed shooting defenceless animals, played rugby quite brilliantly but also violently, enjoyed sex and indulged in petty larceny of some sort, held racist/sexist views . . . no matter how good and honest the story was! No such impediment would exist if the boy were pale and interesting, introspective and sensitive, a pianist about to launch his first CD recording of Chopin Études—a miracle indeed because he has had to overcome the disability of a club foot!

Why do you think award-winning Paula Boock's Dare, Truth or Promise *created such a stir last year, when your own* **The Blue Lawn,** *senior fiction winner in 1995, was in fact the first to deal with teenage homosexuality?*

Quite simple. Paula's very fine novel was the overall winner of our book awards and mine wasn't. *The Blue Lawn* did attract a fair amount of negative attention from the 'moral right' and there was talk of questions being asked in parliament as to its suitability in schools etc. etc. It was damned on radio talkback—an accolade indeed! School principals in one redneck area of our fair country did ban if from their libraries.

What do you consider your finest book?

I don't often rank my own work. I think *Circles* may be my best to date. Of my comic novels, I guess *Agnes the Sheep* and *Knitwits.* The one that appeals to me most has always been *Supermum & Spike the Dog.* I doubt that it is my best. It is the second book in a series of three. There is just something about that particular story of that simple, loving mother of three dreadful hooligans trying to do her best for her boys and their dog!

Paul Jennings and others have commented that writers of comic books generally fare badly in awards. Yet surely everyone knows by now that writing successful comedy is the great, if not greater, achievement. Why do you think this blinkered attitude still persists in the minds of the public and award judges?

I wish I knew—because generally those with 'the blinkered attitude' will always say that writing comedy is a lesser achievement! Then they turn their prestigious backs on it. Jennings is quite right of course. Our New Zealand children's writing community is very small and I feel disinclined to get into comparisons but . . . there have been at least two occasions on which a couple of my comic novels have been overlooked awards-wise when I have known with absolute certainty that they were better novels, in literary terms, than the serious works that won.

Although *Agnes the Sheep* won the Esther Glen medal, it wasn't even shortlisted for the AIM awards in the same year, and it has been overseas that it has achieved its major award and critical acclaim. I am relatively certain that this is tied up with our insecurity as a small, isolated post-colonial society. I've said elsewhere that we are, as a people, a bit lugubrious and have a great inability to laugh at ourselves.

Would you agree with those who say that there's more than a streak of cruelty in the best comic writing? Do you think this applies to your own work?

Yes, definitely. I am sure it applies to my own work. I never think very much about it—any more than I ever think of myself as a 'comic' writer.

Do you think it's this aspect of your work that has led to some (notable female) reviewers commenting unfavourably on books like the **Porter Brothers** *series?*

Couldn't agree more. I can't remember which of my funny books it was but, on one occasion, almost all the main female reviewers panned the work. The one male reviewer who gave it significant space saw the book entirely differently. Of course this is not always true. I do remember when **Annie & Co & Marilyn Monroe** (in my opinion one of my funniest) was published, one reviewer in one of our major daily newspapers took me seriously to task for my 'ill treatment of animals'—and this was the major thrust of the review. I have always found this excruciatingly funny in itself—and so does my cat!

How do you cope with offshore publishers who demand that New Zealand slang and place names be removed or reduced? Is there evidence that this is diminishing?

A small American publisher, Alyson Books, is publishing both **The Blue Lawn** and **Jerome** this year. They have made no demands that I de-New Zealand-ise my work. This has been the most pleasant of surprises. I have also had a fairly good run with Scholastic in the US and although minor changes may have been required, the works have still retained their NZ flavour—nappies have stayed as nappies, Mum has stayed Mum. I was surprised when our own New Zealand firm, Learning Media, saw fit to change Mum to Mom for the US edition of my little wee book **Harry Houdini Wonderdog.**

Tell me about the recognition your work has received overseas through sales and reviews? For instance, **Agnes the Sheep, Possum Perkins** *(as* **Paradise Lane***) and* **Knitwits** *in the US?*

My favourite listing ever has been for **Possum Perkins** which was included on an American list of 'Notable Books Never to Have Won a Major Award'. I think this is delightful. I've had good critical success in the US with reviews in major literary publications. The three you mention have all sold in highly respectable numbers in the States. Less so in the UK.

What is the major Italian award that arrived out of the blue during 1998?

Premio Andersen, 1998 Award—best novel for nine- to twelve-year-olds *'O che beela erudita'* (Salani) which is **Agnes the Sheep** as 'Oh What a Wise Baa-lamb'. I believe it's one of the two major Italian awards.

Who are the writers for children working in NZ today you particularly admire? Do you think there are some who have not figured in award short-lists yet who've nonetheless made a major impact?

Generally I admire the writing of other NZ writers who work in the same field, and most particularly the novels of Margaret Mahy, Jack Lasenby, Paula Boock, Janice Marriott, Tessa Duder (He insisted—T.D.) and Fleur Beale. I always admired the work of the late Gaelyn Gordon for its sheer vitality and enormous range. I particularly enjoy Marriott's humorous work—after all, she and I are the only NZ writers who write funny books for older kids.

Your passion for keeping the lawns immaculately mowed around your remote homestead (near Mt Ruapehu) is well known. But you must get equal pleasure from the gardening and long walks which are regular features of your daily life?

Yes, I like mowing my lawns. So what? I certainly enjoy my garden, particularly the rhododendrons and camellias. Maybe I should write a gardening book? I go on long walks because I have to. It's a sacrifice I make in order to stay alive.

What about non-literary recreations? For Example, listening to opera (especially women's voices), a Mastermind knowledge of Queen Victoria's family, hunting and shooting?

Yes, I love listening to music and have a great love of opera—but I also listen to a wide range of other stuff. My Swiss 'son' introduced me to 'Euro techno' and told me that I would enjoy it! Two sons, a grandson and other close younger friends have ensured that I have a working knowledge of almost all forms of modern music! Should there ever be any more snow on Mt Ruapehu, I shall resume my career as the world's worst skier. Since I acquired my first rifle at age fourteen, I have enjoyed small-game hunting and also duck shooting. I realise that this is absolutely politically incorrect but at this stage in my life I am disinclined to make any apology.

New Zealand children's writers have been crying out for at least a decade for more serious critical scrutiny. Yet, despite the explosion of publishing during the 80s and despite the best efforts of some passionate individuals, this generally hasn't happened. No-one is publicly commentating much in the mainstream media on the big picture—on the decline in submissions to the NZ Post awards, or the drift of a few top authors to overseas publishers.

What effect is this lack of informed commentary having on writers and publishers?

I think this is a universal plea. Writers for children have always been considered an inferior literary species. This is, I guess, the ultimate form of literary snobbery. I believe it is crucial that we make every effort possible, both individually and within our organisations such as the NZ Children's Book Foundation to fight for better, greater and more informed critical attention of and for children's writing. It is not so much that we, as a sub-species, deserve it—but that the young of our country do!

I think you'd agree that writers appreciate the recognition and sales that awards bring them. On the other hand, in your Margaret Mahy Medal lecture last year, you were critical of the way the present awards single out only a few and ignore the broad range of publishing that is going on. A year down the track, do you still think that the awards have their downside for writers?

The main thrust of any comment I make here is that we are such a small country / society. There are so few of us writing for young people it would seem to me to be better to celebrate our total output rather than singling a few as being 'better' than all the rest. However, in this day and age of winners and losers and overtly competitive bullshit, such an argument is pissing against the wind.

How would you like to see them changed?

Sensibly, awards are with us to stay. I think the present structure would work more satisfactorily if we could revert to the system that previously pertained—four sectional winners, no overall winner.

Some ten or so years ago, you lamented that there were too few books for children being published that were set in the here and now, reflecting contemporary lives and concerns. Too much history and fantasy, you said. Is this still true?

I think, happily, this is less true these days. My only concern here is that our fiction for young people is allowed to emerge from the cocoon of political correctness and truly reflect what life is like for the youth of today. Fantasy is marvellous—it just seemed to me that a few years back there was, shall we say, an imbalance.

After thirty-seven novels, thirty-one for children, your range continues to grow—there's a first fantasy called **Scarface and the Angel** *accepted for publication in 2000. Do you feel you still have perhaps some of your finest writing to come? Do you think a time will come when you say—forty-odd books—enough!?*

I don't know when that time will come. I guess it will. It would be chance as much as anything that what is still to be written may be finer than what has already been written!

TITLE COMMENTARY

POSSUM PERKINS
(1986; U.S. edition as *Paradise Lane*, 1987)

Publishers Weekly

SOURCE: A review of *Paradise Lane,* in *Publishers Weekly,* Vol. 232, No. 11, September 11, 1987, p. 96.

An impressive American debut for New Zealand author Taylor, *Paradise Lane* is the simple but moving story of a teenage girl's struggle to understand her parents' apparently destructive relationship and to learn to love. For ages it seems Rosie Perkins has been alone in her world. Her mother is an alcoholic, spending her days in her darkened bedroom, leaving at times to be "cured" at a local hospital, only to begin the cycle anew on her return. Rosie's father ignores his wife, apart from supplying her with booze and pills. He adores Rosie, his "Princess," but his attentions only frighten the girl. In school, Rosie is tormented by her classmates for her intelligence, but she has learned to ignore them, even Michael Geraghty, who usually leads the taunts.

Her family and Michael's are the only ones who live on Paradise Lane. When Rosie discovers an orphaned newborn possum, Michael goads her into keeping it—she names it Plum. Her success raising Plum inspires Michael to humiliate her in grand fashion, but Rosie's reaction leads the two first to friendship and eventually to love. In this tender story, Rosie discovers that her capacity for love includes not only Plum and Michael, but her mother as well. But Taylor has more in mind than an ordinary coming-of-age story—and the tension builds to a shattering, breathless climax as Rosie's independence begins to threaten her parents' status quo. The resolution is both honest and moving; with its gritty, realistic portrayal of the give-and-take of family links and the sometimes blurred lines that define those relationships, *Paradise Lane* transcends its modest theme to become truly memorable.

Kirkus Reviews

SOURCE: A review of *Possum Perkins,* in *Kirkus Reviews,* Vol. VI, No. 21, November 1, 1987, pp. 1580-81.

The day that Rosie Perkins finds a motherless baby possum by the side of the road is the beginning of a change in her relationship with Michael Geraghty—and the beginning of a change in the course of her life.

Michael, previously just one of the many students who has taunted the outcast Rosie, takes an interest in her that mystifies even himself. No one likes her. She lives isolated, with her alcoholic mother and strangely possessive father. And Rosie is surely distrustful of Michael. But as their friendship grows, and as Rosie nurtures the possum, she begins to wonder whether she couldn't change other things, too—such as her relationship with her mother. Rosie begins to question her life and herself, even as she is drawn into the bewildering comfort of Michael's boisterous family. Finally, the many forces in Rosie's tumultuous life clash painfully; only then can she and those who care about her begin to set things to rights.

Taylor's newest is a stunning portrait of a determined, intelligent girl daring to try to effect change in her bruised family. The lyrical account of Rosie's growth and Michael's dawning realization of his own potential is riveting—and unforgettable.

Nancy P. Reeder

SOURCE: A review of *Paradise Lane*, in *School Library Journal*, Vol. 34, No. 4, December, 1987, pp. 105-06.

Rosie just wants to be left alone—by the jeering kids at school, the lauditory teachers, and especially by her overly attentive father. The one person who's attention she craves—her mother—has retreated to her darkened bedroom with her pills and sherry. Considered different, Rosie is mercilessly tormented by the other teenagers. During one especially brutal attack, she is bombarded with dead possums after she decides to raise an orphaned baby possum as a pet. One of the teenagers returns to the scene to find her in tears and realizes the result of his groups' actions. Slowly the two form a friendship which, to their amazement, becomes a romance. The New Zealand setting provides some interesting aspects to the story. All of the characters are well developed and believable, as is the entire story. Taylor describes the events from the viewpoints of several of the main characters, which enables readers to understand better their thoughts and actions. Rosie is a particularly complex and well drawn character, filled with uncertainty, anger, frustration, and hurt. This is an engrossing, well-structured story about the differences in families, about romance and caring, and about growing up.

Margery Fisher

SOURCE: A review of *Paradise Lane*, in *Growing Point*, Vol. 26, No. 5, January, 1988, pp. 4904-05.

Michael Geraghty augments his mother's small income by trapping 'possums for their skins: the aloof, clever Rosie Perkins, his schoolfellow, is determined to rear a baby 'possum found beside a dead mother. The unpromising moment when the two of them first really notice one another is gradually forgotten as they become friends—and friends the girl badly needs, for there is little comfort for her in her family, with a mother whose 'illness' comes from a bottle and leads to frequent disappearances for a cure, and a father whose physical contact with his 'princess' have to be tactfully discouraged. Rosie's only weapons against misery are words—careful

expressions of sympathy for her mother, slangy chat and, later, gentler discussions with Michael about his family, about 'possum behaviour, about themselves; terse, matter of fact excuses for the father whose own hypocritical words provoke scorn and distaste; confessions of her own unhappiness in words ostensibly addressed to Plum, her thriving animal protégé; finally, practical advice from Michael's sensible mother. By way of conversation and soliloquy the author leads us into the intricacies of Rosie's approach to the circumstances and shows how she found a way to end the abuse from her father, emotional and physical, whose cause lay in a marriage distorted by events as much as by temperament. *Paradise Lane* is set in a New Zealand country town and against a background of domestic customs and seasonal changes the author approaches the sensitive subject of child abuse in a subtle way, suggesting through words— tentative, crude, insinuating or openly friendly—the way people hurt and help one another.

R. Baines

SOURCE: A review of *Paradise Lane*, in *The Junior Bookshelf*, Vol. 52, No. 1, February, 1988, p. 55.

Rosie Perkins is beset with major difficulties: she is bullied at school, her mother is an alcoholic, and her father represents the worst problem of all. . . .

One solution to Rosie's loneliness comes when she adopts and manages to rear an orphaned young possum she finds by the roadside, then a little later the apparently obnoxious leader of a gang of bullies finds himself changed by the attraction he begins to feel towards the girl. This is an absorbing and memorable book, establishing great sympathy for its realistic heroine whilst at the same time showing how Rosie might seem to be a superior prig. It deals clearly, interestingly and sympathetically not only with a story of a developing young love but also with the infinitely more difficult topic of incestuous desire.

Elaine R. Twitchell

SOURCE: A review of *Paradise Lane*, in *The Horn Book Magazine*, Vol. LXIV, No. 2, March-April, 1988, p. 212.

A jealous father and a silent, alcoholic mother aren't the only reasons for Rosie's isolation in her school and small-town New Zealand community. Her own aloofness and superior intelligence lead to envy and retaliation on the part of her classmates. But through Plum, the tiny possum orphan she finds and raises, she discovers an outlet for her need to love and permits herself a friendship with Michael, her boisterous young neighbor. Michael and his family are the complete antithesis of her own withdrawn parents and in their noisy and gregarious household provide her with spontaneous warmth and affection. Rosie, in turn, offers Michael the intellectual stimulation he is capable of but has chosen to ignore. The strained human relationships are carefully drawn as tensions between Rosie and her obsessive father reach a dramatic climax, paralleling the fate of Plum, whose captivity and death symbolize Rosie's own bondage and the violent rupture needed to end it. The mystery of Rosie's strange, repressed father and her pathetic mother hovers like a shadow over the book's action, making a complicated mesh of loyalty, fear, and loneliness. While the New Zealand background offers the opportunity to describe a snowstorm in July, the setting is not as vivid a component of the book as are the strong characters, their psychological interaction, and the gentle flowering of Rosie and Michael's love. Well paced and skillfully written, the absorbing novel challenges the reader to sympathize with and understand Rosie's difficult parents.

THE WORST SOCCER TEAM EVER (1987)

Ann Wright

SOURCE: A review of *The Worst Soccer Team Ever,* in *The School Librarian,* Vol. 38, No. 2, May, 1990, p. 68.

The Worst Soccer Team Ever is totally non-sexist and the intentions of its narrator, Tom Colman, are of the highest regarding accuracy of recall. The story reflects a secondary school world similar in tone to Grange Hill but with an American flavour. The general idiom is racy and down-to-earth. In no way a literary challenge, this could appeal to reluctant readers unwilling to 'get hooked' on any kind of book. The characters are adolescents with pronounced and definitive characteristics. Bogdan, for instance, is in training to become a concert pianist while Lavender Gibson (known as Lav to her friends) is already a feminist and intends to become a plumber (hence her nickname). So Ms Hennessey, the team's somewhat reluctant coach, finds herself working with very different team members. As well as portraying the world of soccer and glimpses into school life, this book hints at an adult world of changing relationships and general toughness. The reader does not have to tolerate any condescension on the writer's part, but there is a heightening and exaggeration in the telling which is not totally the result of the narrator's viewpoint.

I HATE MY BROTHER MAXWELL POTTER (1990)

Scott Johnston

SOURCE: A review of *I Hate My Brother Maxwell Potter,* in *Magpies,* Vol. 6, No. 1, March, 1991, p. 31.

This book is an amusing tale of sibling rivalry. After reading only a few pages, I didn't like Maxwell Potter much either!

Frederick Lewis Potter, commonly known as Freddo, is in the last year of primary school, and is definitely the ugly duckling in comparison to his older, handsome, sophisticated, streetwise brother Maxwell. Maxwell utilizes every ounce (gram?) of cunning he possesses to convince all around him that he is a wonderful, caring, responsible person. Only Freddo really knows him for what he is—vain, lazy, self-seeking, and cruel. Freddo knows because he shares a room with him and is the target of Maxwell's sadism.

Their grandmother, who dotes on Maxwell, decides he has a bright future acting in television commercials, and takes him to an audition. Freddo insists on being allowed to go also. The advertising company select Freddo to head a major new campaign.

Maxwell's jealousy takes many forms and the rest of the story is about his attempts at revenge.

Readers will identify strongly with Freddo. I kept issuing mental warnings to him not to fall prey to Maxwell's duplicity as I read. It is a funny story which makes worthwhile comment about the effects of appearances, and flattery, upon family and peer relationships.

AGNES THE SHEEP (1991)

Kirkus Reviews

SOURCE: A review of *Agnes the Sheep,* in *Kirkus Reviews,* Vol. LIX, No. 3, February 1, 1991, pp. 177-78.

From "a country of over fifty million sheep and only three million people" (New Zealand), a farce about an oversized, feisty creature whose personality belies her name.

Agnes is no "lamb of God"; indeed, most of the characters here exhibit behavior at odds with their reputations. Elderly Mrs. Carpenter, who charges two youngsters, Belinda and Joe, with caring for Agnes after her death, is more a former *femme fatale* than a nice old lady; Joe, famous for "nicking" whatever he needs, is actually more upright than properly brought-up Belinda. Meanwhile, Agnes is an unpredictable terror who provides plenty of slapstick as the two kids try to save her from Mrs. Carpenter's grasping heir, from his obnoxious little son, and from a butcher's assistant who hopes to make his mother a rug from Agnes's extraordinary fleece.

Taylor, whose notable skills were more seriously employed in *Paradise Lane* (1987), neatly exploits the inherent comedy in the sheep's unruly behavior and the resulting interaction of his satirically limned human characters. In the end, the story simply stops—dramatically cornered at last, Agnes drops dead of old age. An entertaining romp.

Betsy Hearne

SOURCE: A review of *Agnes the Sheep,* in *The Bulletin of the Center for Children's Books,* Vol. 44, No. 7, March, 1991, p. 179.

A catastrophic comedy, set in Australia but uproarious anywhere, finds two antithetical schoolmates, Belinda and Joe, the heirs to a bad-tempered sheep left them by an equally bad-tempered old woman whom they have interviewed on a school assignment. Agnes butts all comers, especially the greedy relatives (bad-tempered, of course) planning to sell Agnes for dog meat and turn Mrs. Carpenter's estate into a parking lot. The recipe for disaster would boil away to slapstick were it not for Taylor's witty style, which instead turns the whole cast on a satirical spit. No one is spared, and the climactic scene of chaos, reported in the local papers under the headline "Wild Sheep Runs Amok in Supermarket," serves up parody as well as pace. This laugh-out-loud read-aloud will also serve as a springboard to studying satirical literature.

Connie Tyrrell Burns

SOURCE: A review of *Agnes the Sheep,* in *School Library Journal,* Vol. 37, No. 3, March, 1991, p. 196.

What begins for Belinda and Joe as a simple school project of interviewing an older person to learn about their town's past becomes a wild and woolly sheep chase. The eccentric Mrs. Carpenter whom they choose is far from a sweet little old lady, and her large, nasty, holy terror of a sheep, Agnes, is misnamed as the "lamb of God." Taylor, a New Zealander, has written a genuinely funny, fast-paced story of the students' attempts to save Agnes from becoming mutton or a rug when they inherit her at Mrs. Carpenter's death. The humor is found at many levels, from subtle irony, puns, and satire, to coincidence, exaggeration, and slapstick. Taylor pokes fun at teachers, education, priests, and the church in this zany and merry romp. While young readers will find the New Zealand setting and slang accessible, the book's uninspired title may not invite students to select this laugh-aloud story. And that's too bad.

Publishers Weekly

SOURCE: A review of *Agnes the Sheep,* in *Publishers Weekly,* Vol. 238, No. 15, March 29, 1991, pp. 93-4.

In this story set in New Zealand, a school project pairs goody-goody Belinda and roughneck Joe in a research project about the elderly. Mrs. Carpenter, however, is not at all what their teacher had in mind—she's no sweet old lady reminiscing about frontier times, but a spitfire with a wickedly misbehaving sheep named Agnes. Joe and Belinda become friends with Mrs. Carpenter and are entrusted with Agnes when the woman passes away. With a liberal sprinkling of tongue-in-cheek humor, Taylor transforms a fairly thin story into an appealing read that calls to mind the lighter moments of his compatriot Margaret Mahy. His observations about the human condition may pass over the heads of incautious readers, but the slapstick action and foreign flavor should make his novel a favorite with the middle-grade crowd.

Ilene Cooper

SOURCE: A review of *Agnes the Sheep,* in *Booklist,* Vol. 87, No. 18, May 15, 1991, p. 1794.

It's hard to find a good middle-grade novel about sheep. Sheep don't usually lend themselves to high adventure and off-the-wall humor. Especially real sheep, not the talking variety. But Agnes is quite different. True, she's ornery, ill-kempt, and constipated, but that's why her owner, Mrs. Carpenter, likes her. Belinda and Joe, enemies at school, meet Mrs. Carpenter when they are forced to work together on a project about the elderly of the community and record their reminiscences of the "good old days." In Mrs. Carpenter's case, these are remembrances of her time as a nude model for a French artist and the brief occasion she spent with another painter, a Mr. Hitler. When Mrs. Carpenter dies, she leaves the care and feeding of Agnes to Belinda and Joe, but they have a rough time keeping the sheep away from various friends and relations who want to make sausages and blankets out of her. This is a wild and woolly story seared with dry wit. That the story takes place in New Zealand matters not a jot; the odd characters have the same appeal as those found in the Bagthorpe saga—and the same zaniness. There is rather a sad end, however; Agnes dies, and Joe and Belinda drift apart. "After all, it's not as if they were ever close friends, and, sadly, it takes more than a sheep to bring people together and keep them there. Doesn't it?"

Donna Houser

SOURCE: A review of *Agnes the Sheep,* in *Voice of Youth Advocates,* Vol. 14, No. 2, June, 1991, p. 104.

Getting paired with the orneriest boy in school is not Belinda's idea of a fair assignment. Besides, she knows that her mother, who is always writing complaints to everyone about everything, will write a letter to her teacher Mrs. Robinson. As Belinda's mother would say, Joe should not be Belinda's partner, mainly because he steals and belongs to the lower economic class. However, Mrs. Robinson is determined, so Belinda and Joe decide to make the most of their assignment to interview an elderly person to see what it had been like to live in the "olden" times. Little does Mrs. Robinson realize that the kindly looking 87 year old Mrs. Carpenter has had quite a past, which she shares in vivid detail with the students. In fact, because Joe is lazy about writing, he has the whole interview on tape; so once his classmates start hearing Mrs. Carpenter's past, they don't want the tape shut off.

In exchange for the interview, Mrs. Carpenter has Belinda and Joe do odd jobs around her home since it really hasn't had proper care in years. Her pet sheep Agnes is added to the list of chores because she's Mrs. Carpenter's house pet and is treated like one of the family. Mrs. Carpenter later dies, and the sheep is willed to Belinda and Joe although they and the lawyer are the only ones who know about this arrangement. For final payment, upon the sheep's demise, Mrs. Carpenter wills some priceless porcelain china. Mrs. Carpenter's only surviving relative is unaware of this arrangement, and because he hates Agnes so much, he gives her away for dog feed. Belinda and Joe steal the sheep in order to save her life and to fulfill their promise to take care of her. They try to hide the sheep in several places, but each time Agnes causes enough trouble that she is discovered. The final chase scene brings all of the major and minor characters together in a very lively scene in a grocery store.

Agnes dies of a heart attack. The nephew who thought he would be rich from all of Mrs. Carpenter's belongings is a poor judge of what to keep and what to throw away, discarding some priceless carpets because of Agnes's droppings. These carpets are found by an eccentric drama teacher for use as future play props and sets, but she recognizes their value, cleans them up, and sells them, getting enough money to travel around the world. The underdogs—Joe, Agnes, and the drama teacher—win their just reward, and the greedy nephew and family get theirs, nothing. A fun read and good for reading aloud. The characters are funny because they are so typical, and the assignment given to Joe and Belinda is one commonly given to students. The New Zealand dialect may bother some, but it is so far into the story that readers will surely continue. Unimaginative title and book cover.

Pam Harwood

SOURCE: A review of *Agnes the Sheep*, in *Books for Keeps*, No. 93, July, 1995, p. 11.

Mrs Robinson's class have a topic to do, so she puts her two naughtiest children together—clever that! The story unfolds around Agnes, a mean and bad-tempered goat with amazingly filthy habits, and Mrs Carpenter, a sad and lonely old lady who has the most unsuitable but fascinating stories to tell. A gorgeous story of someone's else's topic going all wrong and taking on a life of its own. I loved it!

KNITWITS (1992)

Kirkus Reviews

SOURCE: A review of *Knitwits*, in *Kirkus Reviews*, Vol. LX, No. 17, September 1, 1992, p. 1135.

Taylor's comedies **Agnes the Sheep** and this latest have in common not only references to wool culture, but a zany point-of-view and some fairly unravelled scenes of domestic life in New Zealand. Charles is alarmed by the news of his mother's pregnancy, but makes a bet with precocious next-door neighbor Alice Pepper that he will knit a sweater for the little nipper by the time it is born. At stake: either he will pay her five dollars a week for the rest of her life, or she will bequeath to him

all her notorious collections, including her assembly of skulls. Charles takes knitting lessons from a curmugeonly teacher, the very one to have unjustly suspended him from the hockey team for using bad language (Alice is the guilty party). He is able to keep his project a secret from nearly everyone; his two best chums "catch" him at it and sit down to revel in their own feats of knitting prowess. This is but one of many unexpected twists that will needle the funny bones of most middle graders; regular references to Charles's mother's expanding "boobs" will nail down the peculiar interests of the rest. With unpredictably comical depictions that never lapse into caricature, and descriptions of the sweater's progress that are a study in gleeful boyish pride, this blithe look at an expectant family has no dropped stitches.

Publishers Weekly

SOURCE: A review of *Knitwits*, in *Publishers Weekly*, Vol. 239, No. 45, October 12, 1992, p. 79.

Welcome back to the zany world Down Under, as presented by Taylor. Charlie's mum, a fashion model, is pregnant, and nothing will do but Charlie wants to knit the little tot a sweater. The question is, how? After some secret knitting lessons, the burial of Mr. Magoo the cat, and more than the usual trouble with Alice Pepper next door, Charlie's on his way. "The second sleeve is lovely," remarks the boy about his creation. "I know I shouldn't say so myself, but any knitter would be proud of it." Middle-school hilarity, with an accent on deadpan silliness, characterizes this zestful novel. (The opening sentence sets the tone nicely: "Our cat croaked this morning.") A read-aloud introduction may help reluctant readers get the hang of Taylor's Australian English.

Maggie McEwen

SOURCE: A review of *Knitwits*, in *School Library Journal*, Vol. 38, No. 11, November, 1992, pp. 98-9.

On the worst day of nine-year-old Chas Kenny's life, his cat dies, he is kicked off the hockey team, and his mother announces that she is pregnant. Although unhappy about being a brother, Chas reacts defensively when Alice Pepper, his next-door neighbor and best friend, bluntly voices his negativity. In response, Chas brags that he is so excited he intends to knit a sweater for the baby. Crafty Alice bets him $5 a day for life against her skull collection that he will not be able to produce such a gift in time. As events unfold during the following months, the boy grows truly excited about the new arrival while he struggles to win his bet and prove to Alice that he is not a "knitwit." Taylor tells a humorous, fast-paced story with a pleasant lilt to the language. He paints a refreshing picture of the family's warm relationship and relaxed approach to life. Satisfying role reversals abound without didacticism. Although the female characters are so strong that they border on caricature, they add to the humor of the story rather than detract from its believability. Middle-grade readers will appreciate Chas's frank and amusing telling of his story.

Stephanie Zvirin

SOURCE: A review of *Knitwits*, in *Booklist*, Vol. 89, No. 5, November 1, 1992, p. 511.

Readers who appreciated the pungent Down Under wit of *Agnes the Sheep* will probably like this book even more—despite the fact that there isn't a single sheep in the cast. New Zealand author Taylor has invested all his human characters with great zest and personality—but Alice Pepper is one of his best. A snot, a busybody, and an outrageous liar who says rude words, she gets her way because she's big enough to bully everybody in her class. That includes her next-door neighbor Charlie Kenny, narrator and focus of this funny tale, who isn't above a few high jinks himself. When Alice wagers all her collections that Charlie won't be able to knit a sweater for the baby his parents are expecting, Charlie takes the bet—visions of Alice's marvelous skull collection clouding his brain and Alice's taunts ringing in his ears. That he hasn't the foggiest notion of how to knit is a detail he's sure he can deal with. It's keeping his endeavors a secret—from his parents, from his buddies, and, especially, from snoopy Alice P.—that will be trickier.

Charlie's nonchalance is grand—we know his knitting is frightful, but he's so certain that his colorful creation will perk up the small gray baby he observes in his mother's ultrasound video, we cheer him on. (Imagine Charlie's surprise when he sees his baby sister "pop out," a bit "gooey and messy" but a healthy shade of pink.) Taylor makes Charlie's home a wonderfully comfortable clutter and gives him parents who obviously care about each other and about him. Spiced with comic twists (e.g., his buddies *know* how to knit) and some sterling encounters with Ms. Mason-Dixon, a tough old teacher even Alice Pepper can't strong-arm, Charlie's "adventures in knitting" are touching and hilarious. Sophisticated middle-grade readers will love 'em.

Betsy Hearne

SOURCE: A review of *Knitwits*, in *The Bulletin of the Center for Children's Books*, Vol. 46, No. 5, January, 1993, p. 158.

Having sharpened our wits with *Agnes the Sheep,* Taylor has taken on a slightly less quirky project, putting the twist on a classic new-sibling yarn. Nine-year-old hockey player Charlie gets suckered into a bet with tough-talking Alice next door: if he finishes a sweater he says he's knitting for the baby his mother is expecting, he gets Alice's skull collection; if he doesn't knit the sweater, he pays her five dollars a week for the rest of his life. It's Charlie's efforts to knit the sweater against a fast-approaching deadline that score the most humor. The peer insults get repetitive, albeit always authentic, but the surprising warmth attendant to the baby's birth introduces a moving quality that deepens the book. In fact, under the rough surface, these are loving characters. It's nice to see a happy—but not sappy—family story.

NUMBSKULLS (1995)

John Sigwald

SOURCE: A review of *Numbskulls*, in *School Library Journal*, Vol. 41, No. 10, October, 1995, p. 140.

In this farcical sequel to *Knitwits*, 10-year-old Charlie Kenney's "girl next door," Alice Pepper, is convinced that she can teach him to spell; instruct his mate Spikey in the art of love; and show his other mate Jacko how to make lots of money. Alice is a proponent of the learning-through-intimidation method. Her approach involves strapping these bona fide numbskulls to an old dentist's chair in her garage while indoctrinating them and often employing the additional motivation of a lead-filled hose. Duped into signing contracts giving her their allowances, the three boys fear and hate Alice—even though Charlie actually becomes a proficient speller—and together they plot their revenge. A humorous subplot revolves around Charlie's child-care responsibilities for his baby sister. In fact, most chapters begin with a platitude from *Before Babe's First Steps*, which Charlie is reading, although his observations of the family poppet seldom agree with the professional's detached advice. Charlie is a likable fellow and Taylor has an ear for children's banter that is forthright, funny, and just offbeat enough to show a real empathy with adolescents. The New Zealander vernacular shouldn't prove too much of a problem in context.

Kay Weisman

SOURCE: A review of *Numbskulls*, in *Booklist*, Vol. 92, No. 4, October, 15, 1995, p. 405.

In this sequel to *Knitwits* Chas is concerned about his new baby sister. Since no one in his family has an easy time learning, he fears the worst for poor Jo-Munro. In an effort to become the best big brother ever he consults the book *Before Babe's First Steps* and submits to evil next door neighbor Alice Pepper's learning machine. The baby guide offers generally sound advice, but Alice's instructional device borders on the Machiavellian. After conning Chas out of his allowance and strapping him into an old dentist chair, Alice physically threatens and verbally abuses her student in a attempt to teach him to spell. Although some may be concerned about Chas's self-esteem, readers can rest assured that Alice eventually gets her comeuppance and that Chas benefits from the whole experience in some unexpected ways. A raucous look at educational methods that should find many middle-grade fans.

Deborah Stevenson

SOURCE: A review of *Numbskulls,* in *The Bulletin of the Center for Children's Books,* Vol. 49, No. 4, December, 1995, p. 141.

Chas, who acquired a new baby sister in **Knitwits,** has returned, this time to deal not only with his happy-go-lucky family but also with the maniacal yet powerful neighbor girl, Alice Pepper. Alice tricks Chas and his friends Jacko and Spikey into signing exceedingly binding contracts in which she receives money from them in exchange for teaching them the secrets of, respectively, spelling, riches, and sex. Alice's teaching methods (strapping the boys to a dentist's chair, swatting them with a garden hose, and assigning them bizarre homework) are dramatic but ineffectual—except on Chas, who becomes a good enough speller to challenge Alice for top honors in the school spelling bee. The story is sillier and more frenetic than it was in the first book, and it relies too much on the mental denseness of Chas and his friends. Taylor is still a funny writer, however, and this relentlessly goofy story will appeal to slapstick-inclined aficionados of Gordon Korman and of other practitioners of broad middle-school comedy.

HARK (1998)

Vasanti Sima

SOURCE: A review of *Hark,* in *Magpies,* Vol. 13, No. 1, March, 1998, p. 7.

Chas—(Charlie Kenny)—is challenged again by his formidable opponent Alice Pepper, classmate and neighbour, a girl who holds no punches as she is promoted to producing and directing Ms. Mason-Dixons's end-of-year Nativity play.

As you flip through the pages you become aware as to why Alice ends up with the cast that she does, and the job.

With 'producers' license she makes a few changes—a shift from tradition to modernisation, involving generations of Chas's family, Jo Munro—Mum and Dad—Grandma.

An entertaining trail of humour and wit, as seen and told through the eyes of Chas.

YOU ARE NOT GAY KATY (1999)

Bill Nagelkerke

SOURCE: A review of *You Are Not Gay Katy,* in *Magpies, New Zealand Supplement,* Vol. 14, No. 5, November, 1999, p. 7.

At less than ninety pages, this novel's brevity doesn't detract from its impact on the reader. Jerome is dead and his friends Marco and Kate, in assembling the jigsaw of his death, reveal just how very complex were the pieces of their three-way relationship. The story is told largely through phone calls, faxes and emails, with a face-to-face encounter towards the end of the book. Marco, in New Zealand, is hurting badly at the loss of his close friend, knowing yet denying that Jerome has killed himself. Kate, in the United States, responds with a series of revelations that enable Marco to finally understand the truth. The most important thing writes Kate, is that we are honest to ourselves . . . I think if we are honest we give ourselves a better chance of, well, not perhaps getting over it, but at least coming to terms with it. For Kate this means coming out to Marco, dealing with his initial YOU ARE NOT GAY, KATIE. There is no way someone who looks like you could be gay response. It's Kate's honesty that allows Marco, initially portrayed as the archetypal macho male who uses 'fuck' and its variants with great frequency, to acknowledge that Jerome was gay too (Jerome and me covered for each other Kate tells Marco) and that he Marco, might be as well. If this makes **Jerome** sound somewhat melodramatic and agenda-specific it is Taylor's characters and the painful precision of their interwoven narratives, not the plot, which drive this story. Marco and Kate berate, plead, conceal and reveal. Their voices are utterly convincing. William Taylor has captured with integrity the intense sorrows and joys of being different, and accepting one's identity, in a world that values sameness and stereotypes. In Taylor's long and distinguished writing career, **Jerome** is a major achievement; a landmark in New Zealand literature for young adults.

Additional coverage of Taylor's life and career is contained in the following sources published by The Gale Group: *Contemporary Authors,* Vol. 146; and *Something about the Author*, Vols. 78, 113.

Cumulative Indexes

How to Use This Index

Children's Literature Review
Cumulative Nationality Index

Nationality Index

CHILDREN'S LITERATURE REVIEW
Cumulative Title Index

Title Index

Title Index

Title Index

Title Index

Title Index

Title Index

Title Index

ISBN 0-7876-3228-7

90000